FROM
HELL ISLAND
TO HAY FEVER

The Life of Dr Bill Frankland

FROM
HELL ISLAND
TO HAY FEVER

The Life of Dr Bill Frankland

PAUL WATKINS

Foreword by HRH The Countess of Wessex GCVO

BROWN
DOG
BOOKS

Published under licence by Brown Dog Books and
The Self-Publishing Partnership, 7 Green Park Station, Bath BA1 1JB

www.selfpublishingpartnership.co.uk

ISBN printed book: 978-1-78545-265-9
ISBN e-book: 978-1-78545-266-6

Printed and bound by CPI Group (UK) Ltd, Croydon, CR0 4YY

Dedication

*This book is dedicated to all who served
with the medical services in the Far East War,
1941-1945.*

The Prayer of Kohima

'When You Go Home, Tell Them Of Us And Say,
For Your Tomorrow, We Gave Our Today.'

Attrib: John Maxwell Edmonds

CONTENTS

FOREWORD

BAGSHOT PARK

It is nearly 80 years since the outbreak of the Second World War, and yet many stories of those who served are only now being told. Nowhere is this more apparent than in 'Hell Island to Hay Fever, The Life of Dr Bill Frankland' which details the most remarkable life of a doctor, who was born before the outbreak of the First World War. I am proud to be Patron of The Java FEPOW Club, who support our remaining Far Eastern Prisoner of War Veterans, wives and widows, of which Dr Bill Frankland is currently the oldest surviving member at 106 years of age.

After studying medicine at Oxford and St Mary's Hospital, Bill Frankland qualified in 1938. Barely a year he later volunteered to serve his King and Country. Posted overseas with the Royal Army Medical Corps, he arrived in Singapore just seven days before the epic events of Pearl Harbour. Whilst treating those injured during the fighting, he was also responsible for ensuring many of the military nursing staff secured a safe passage onto a rescue ship moored in Singapore Harbour. Taken prisoner on 15 February 1942, he endured and witnessed dreadful suffering over the following three-and-a-half years. During this time he cared for his fellow prisoners despite a lack of medical supplies. Not only did he witness cruelty and torture, but on several occasions came extremely close to death himself.

Returning home in the winter of 1945, he made a conscious decision not to talk about his experiences, mindful of how fortunate he was to be alive. Returning to St Mary's, he pursued his medical career and for two years worked as Clinical Assistant to Sir Alexander Fleming. He established the medical specialty of clinical allergy, developed the Pollen Count, and became a renowned international expert in his field. His work has benefited tens of thousands, if not hundreds of thousands, of patients the world over.

This book, based on Bill Frankland's personal recollections, describes the remarkable life of an outstanding doctor, who has continually worked to improve the lives of his fellow men, both during war and peace.

HRH The Countess of Wessex GCVO
The Java FEPOW Club 1942

9

PREFACE

In early May 2017, Britain was heading towards its second general election in little more than two years, and the pace of political campaigning was quickening. In the midst of this, news was released from Buckingham Palace that HRH Prince Philip, aged 95, was to retire from royal duties over the coming months. He had served as consort to the monarch for over 65 years. This became headline news, and the following morning the BBC flagship news programme, *Today,* wished to consider the issue of 'late retirement' and sought the opinion of Britain's oldest doctor who, some six weeks earlier, had celebrated his 105th birthday, and was still working.

Dr Alfred William 'Bill' Frankland was living independently, but admitted to the interviewer, Justin Webb, that 'he normally did not get up until 9am, before starting a busy day's schedule'. He was asked why he had lived to such a great age. His reply was quite clear, and given in his typical 'no nonsense manner'. 'Because during my life I have been so near to death so many times,' he replied. He went on to explain just one of those occasions. As a prisoner of war in Singapore in July 1945 he witnessed Japanese troops preparing to kill all their prisoners, on the orders of Emperor Hirohito. This massacre was only prevented by the dropping of two atomic bombs, on the cities of Hiroshima and Nagasaki, in August 1945. During the interview, it was suggested that Bill should have written a book about his life, to which he replied, 'Someone is writing my life history, they think it is interesting,' causing Justin Webb to reply, 'We look forward to that coming out.'

The seeds for this book were sown in August 2014 when Piers Storie-Pugh, the Chief Executive of the Not Forgotten Association, a charity founded in 1919 by Marta Cunningham, invited me to lunch with Bill. We met at the Royal Society of Medicine where Bill kindly hosted the meal; this was the start of his remarkable generosity towards me. I still have the notes from that meeting, in which Bill talked about his incredible life, touching on working for Sir Alexander Fleming through to treating Saddam Hussein, as well as describing his time as a prisoner of war. In March 2015 it was a real pleasure for Piers and myself to entertain Bill to lunch to celebrate his 103rd birthday.

Bill and Piers Storie-Pugh celebrating Bill's 103rd birthday. March 2015.

In April 2016, Bill was invited to speak about his career in medicine by Tim Mitchell, Chairman of the Court of Examiners of the Royal College of Surgeons of England. Tim asked if I would host the session, and I was honoured to do so. Over 45 minutes Bill did all the talking, and enthralled and entertained the audience as he gave a wonderfully erudite and lucid account of his life in medicine, from his decision to train as a doctor through to publishing four scientific papers since his 100th birthday. Having qualified 10 years before the foundation of the National Health Service, he was able to talk with personal authority on aspects of medicine which members of the audience had only read about in the history books. After the session there were many questions for Bill, including my own: 'Who is going to write your life story?' There and then Bill asked if I would and we have worked closely together on this project ever since.

Bill with Tim Mitchell, standing by the statue of John Hunter.
Royal College of Surgeons of England. April 2016.

Over the last two years Bill has continued to show me outstanding generosity, providing me with first-hand detailed accounts of his life, and giving me unfettered access to a remarkable collection of material, especially his extensive collection of photographs, many of which are reproduced in this book. He has entertained me in his home, where at lunch I have always admired the napkin rings, which themselves have their own special story. His generosity has extended to invitations to Drapers' Hall and to The Queen's College Oxford, both very special places to Bill.

The result is a biography of a most remarkable and caring man; a truly outstanding individual. Wherever possible it makes use of Bill's own words and recollections, although written in the third person. I make no apologies that the main thrust of the book is about Bill's life up to 1946. It describes for the first time in great detail his painful experiences as a prisoner of war. At the same time it describes the experiences of others serving with him in the Far East, some of whom managed to escape at the Fall of Singapore (many with the help of Bill) and of others who paid the ultimate price for serving their country. Those of us fortunate to be born after World War 2 find it difficult to imagine such suffering endured by so many. The later chapters describe aspects of Bill's life following the war. I make no attempts to provide an academic account of allergy, the area of medicine which Bill has worked in for over 70 years. There are plenty of well-researched articles and books, written by much better-informed authors than myself, which can provide the reader with this information. Along these lines I would draw the reader's attention to Bill's own biographical paper in 1996, entitled 'Aerobiology and allergy – an autobiography'.[1] Instead, these chapters cover some of the other aspects of Bill's life, including working with a Nobel Laureate, developing a field of clinical medicine, and some of his more challenging and adventurous trips abroad.

I trust that this book will appeal to those wishing to know more about the life of an outstanding individual who, during his own lifetime, has encountered so many changes, challenges, opportunities and upheavals, both in his own country and abroad. Following the Fall of Singapore he was imprisoned by the Japanese under the most dreadful conditions for three and a half years, spending two of these on 'Hell Island'. I hope that the detailed accounts of these years will be of interest to those wishing to learn more about the war in Far East, but perhaps more importantly shed light on how Bill coped with such suffering, both during imprisonment and in the years after. There is undoubtedly a lesson for us all.

In this day and age it is very easy to overlook the contributions made by earlier generations which have allowed us freedom from oppression and tyranny, a freedom that we now take for granted. I hope that this book may provide an insight into the life of one man who has given so much for so long, in both war and peace, and whose contributions will, I trust, never be forgotten.

Paul Watkins
Somerset
7 June 2018

---

1 *Aerobiologia* 12. 55-61 (1996).

ACKNOWLEDGEMENTS

In writing this book I have been helped by many people and organisations over the years and without their assistance, then I am certain that this biography would not have been completed.

Without a doubt my greatest thanks have to go to Bill Frankland who has spent so much of his time helping this project. Not only has Bill told me about his whole life, but he has also shared with me so many of his own experiences, many of which are described in the book. He has welcomed me into his home and his generosity has known no bounds. Added to that, Bill has been the primary reviewer of the drafts which I have produced. Despite, or perhaps because of, his age his attention to detail has been remarkable and he has corrected any faults which I had written. I still remember very clearly how in Chapter 4, when describing the Christmas meal at Tanglin in 1941, I had written, 'Bill talked with the Chinese cooks and two of Bill's own laying chickens were rapidly dispatched, and cooked'. This was incorrect. There was only one chef. I immediately corrected the text.

I am fortunate that I have had the help of another reviewer in developing this book. My great friend Hamish Batten has again given freely of his time to review the drafts. He so kindly helped me on a previous biography, written 7 years ago, and despite having now celebrated his 94th birthday, Hamish's attention to detail remains as sharp as ever. As I write this section of the book I can proudly state that the combined age of my two reviewers is 200 years…. I can think of no other author in such a privileged position.

I must also thank Suzanne Browne of the London Allergy Clinic who has acted as Bill's secretary for many years. She has kindly helped in sourcing and providing material for this book, and for printing out numerous drafts and other papers for Bill to review. She has guided me towards a number of people who have helped in providing details which have enhanced this book. And she has also provided a number of photographs of Bill taken at parties and other celebrations. Thank you.

A number of individuals have provided information about Bill, and about events in Singapore during World War 2. Wherever possible I have included the information in the book, and I am most grateful to: Jonathan Moffatt, Meg Parkes, Malcolm Ferguson-Smith, Andrew Rice, Roger Green, David Ralphs, Louise Reynolds, Fiona Wright, Colin Ince, Sian Ludman, Claire Evans, Peter Dazely, Verity Fitzgerald, Barbara Altounyan, Di Harford, and Liz Higgins.

I have been most fortunate to be able to make use of a number of archives and libraries and would like to record the help received from: the Wellcome Trust, Imperial War Museum, the National Archives, the British Library, the Library of the Royal College of Surgeons of England, the Library of Emmanuel College Cambridge, and the Cumbria County Archives at Carlisle.

Dr Tony Reeves, the archivist at St Bees School, kindly showed me around the school and has allowed me to reproduce a number of pictures from the school's archive.

Sally Munton kindly told me the story of her late father, a man whose life Bill saved twice whilst in Singapore. She has allowed me access to his papers, including many of the drawings that he made in the design of the lych-gate erected at Changi cemetery.

Jackie Sutherland gave me copies of her father's (Dr Jack Ennis) detailed diaries made during his time of imprisonment. These have been a remarkable source of information and I hope that she might be able to publish the full diaries in the not too distant future.

Members of The Queen's College Oxford have generously provided a great number of pictures of Bill taken when he was an undergraduate. I am also very grateful for the interest in this biography shown by the Provost and Mrs Madden.

Lesley Clark of the Java FEPOW Club has not only shown a great interest in this book, but also worked hard to ensure that it has reached completion in the form it has.

Many friends have helped over the last few years whilst I have been researching and writing, and these have, in one way or another, helped me to focus on the task in hand. My thanks go to Ian Fraser, Mike Hinton, Mike Hansen, Tim Mitchell and Piers Storie-Pugh.

Finally I must thank Frances Hughes who, having endured trials and tribulations whilst I wrote an earlier biography, has once again shown her unwavering support, guidance and care to ensure that this book is published: Thank you.

CHAPTER 1

EARLY YEARS

A First Encounter

Bill's first encounter with death was on Tuesday 19 March 1912 when, barely three months after Roald Amundsen reached the South Pole, and three weeks before the loss of the *Titanic*, his mother, Alice Rose Frankland (always known as Rose), went into premature labour. As was typical of obstetric care at that time, Rose knew little more about her condition except she was pregnant. She gave birth to a baby boy; it was her third child. Some 15 minutes later, after a breech presentation, an identical twin brother arrived. Their combined weights were barely 6lb, and in 1912 the prospects for such premature twins were slender, but both survived. The elder, by some 15 minutes, was christened John Ashlin 'Jack' Frankland, and the younger (and smaller) was christened Alfred William 'Bill' Frankland.

Jack and Bill were born in Little Common, near Bexhill-on-Sea, Sussex, where their parents and older siblings were residing, the family having recently returned from Canada. Both their father, the Rev Henry Frankland, a man whom Bill 'very much looked up to', and their mother hailed from Yorkshire where the Franklands can trace their roots back to farming stock in North Yorkshire. When about 9 years old, Bill and Jack were taken by their grandfather, William Frankland, to the ruins of a castle just outside Whitby in North Yorkshire. Here they were given a potted family history, being told that their forebears had been very successful farmers in the region, had built the castle but then had run into trouble, gambling and drinking their money away. The young boys were told that they must avoid such vices. Bill recalled how he and Jack discussed their grandfather's tale and felt that 'if we do not drink we will get very thirsty', so both agreed that they should not gamble.

Henry Frankland was the eldest of four children born to William James and Clara (née Challenger) Frankland. William had been born in 1853 in Guisborough, North Yorkshire, and by 1881 was a 'certificated teacher' working in Huddersfield, but soon after moved to Barnsley, West Yorkshire. Here he was headmaster of St Mary's Boys' School for 44 years, as well as serving as the Secretary of the Barnsley Teachers' Association. Henry was born in Barnsley on 18 November 1878, followed by his siblings, Edward (21 December, 1880) Alfred (1886) and Ella (1896). Henry obtained a scholarship to Barnsley Grammar School, and from there obtained a classical scholarship to Wadham College, Oxford, in 1897. At Oxford he was a keen sportsman, bowling for the college 1st XI, and graduated with a BA in Theology in 1900. Henry immediately sought entrance to Holy Orders at Bishop's Hostel, Newcastle. He was ordained in the spring of 1902, and his first position was Curate of St. Paul the Apostle, Choppington, in Northumberland.

Choppington, lying midway between Morpeth and Blyth, was a grim mining village towered over by the workings and winding towers of Choppington Colliery. After two years Henry moved to West Yorkshire, and the curacy of St. Jude's Church in Manningham, Bradford. He had exchanged life in a colliery village for that of an industrial city, the area being dominated by woollen mills. In 1906 he moved again, to be Curate of St Mary's Church, Boston Spa, and on 25 March 1908, aged 28, he married Miss Alice Rose West at St Mary's Church, Barnsley.

Rose was born on 24 July 1882 in Barnsley, the daughter of Henry West, a successful ironmonger in the town. Her mother died when she was about 21 and Rose inherited considerable wealth from her. Being a very talented musician, Rose used some of her inheritance to fund a year-long trip to Switzerland, during which she studied both singing and the piano. However, as Bill was to later describe, 'she gave up most of these talents when she married an impecunious curate'. Their honeymoon was spent in New York, after a memorably rough voyage across the Atlantic Ocean, after which Rose vowed never to cross the ocean again.

Henry and Rose's honeymoon fitted in well with Henry's next

appointment, a missionary to Marksville,[2] on St. Joseph Island, Ontario, Canada. Situated at the north-west of Lake Huron, the island was an important focus for the lumber trade and Henry was the only priest on the island, serving a population of about 1800 people. On 25 September 1909, Rose gave birth to their first child, Henry Basil Frankland, in the town of Sault Ste. Marie, some 50 miles away. Bill was later to learn that his mother had had a passion for someone called Basil, and hence the name of her first son. Bill never found out exactly whom she had so admired. During his early months, Basil failed to grow as expected and his father was so concerned that he opted to move away. In retrospect this was a shrewd move, as it later transpired that the local milk was of poor quality, being diluted by the farmer and riddled with tuberculosis. Later that year, Henry was appointed Rector of St. Luke's, Fort William, Thunder Bay, in Ontario. Thunder Bay lies at the western end of Lake Superior and was a thriving centre for the fur trade. Henry was also offered an academic post but, on learning that Rose was pregnant again, decided to focus solely on his living at St. Luke's. Just prior to Christmas, on 9 December, 1910 Rose gave birth to her second child, a daughter, Ella Rose Frankland. Events at this time, however, had a serious effect on Rose. Once Ella was born Rose effectively became an invalid, taking to her bed, often for long periods, with what would now be described as postnatal depression. Her situation was made even more painful when she learnt that most of her money had been lost to a 'conman' in Canada and, despite knowing the man responsible, Rose and Henry decided not to press charges. There appears to have been a desire to leave Canada, and despite Rose's earlier announcement 'never to cross the Atlantic again', she did, and this time in the company of her husband and two very young children.

The family returned to Britain in the spring of 1911, and the Census of 2 April that year records Henry serving as assistant curate in Barnsley. Soon after he moved south to be Curate of St. Mark's, Little Common, near Bexhill-on-Sea, Sussex, residing at a house called Fairholme. Rose became pregnant, for the third time. By now, Henry, through his contacts

---

2 Renamed Hilton Beach in 1923.

with Canon Hasell of Dalemain near Penrith, had been informed of a likely future vacancy at St. Andrew's, Dacre, in Cumberland. Rose, however, made it quite clear that she had no intention of moving to the 'cold north' whilst pregnant, and would remain in Sussex. She gave birth on Tuesday 19 March 1912.

Jack was the first to be born, and weighed 3lb 1 1/2oz, fifteen minutes later, Bill arrived. He was smaller, weighing just 3lb 1 oz. He was later told that he had been wrapped in a blanket and placed in a chest of drawers which served as his cot. Little is known about Bill's earliest years, but the next major event came in February 1914 when it was announced that Henry Frankland would be leaving Little Common. On 14 February, the *Bexhill-on-Sea Observer* reported that the Vicar, the Rev M.B. Stuart-Fox, 'bade farewell to the Rev Henry and Mrs Frankland, as he was soon to take up duties as Vicar of Dacre'.

Growing Up

Dacre is a small, isolated Cumbrian village on the northern edge of the Lake District. It lies about five miles west of Penrith, and about two miles from the northern reaches of Ullswater. In early 1914 Henry Frankland took up his new position as Vicar of St. Andrew's, a living that included the neighbouring settlements of Newbiggin and Stainton, a total population of about 900. Despite its isolated position, Dacre has a rich history: St. Andrew's lies on the site of a Saxon monastery, mentioned by the Venerable Bede in AD 731. The monastery is believed to have hosted a meeting of the Kings of England, Scotland and Strathclyde and Cumberland in AD 937, when the 'Peace of Dacre' was signed. More recently, William Wordsworth in his 'Guide to the Lakes' referred to Dacre several times, and his sister, Dorothy, is known to have visited the village. St. Andrew's is a Norman church, built in the 10th century, with additions in the 12th, 13th and 19th centuries. Inside the church are two fragments of Viking stone crosses, discovered in 1900 close to the church. The church also holds a chained Bible, which dates back to 1617. However, for any new arrival to the church perhaps the most striking features are to be found in the churchyard where there are four stone effigies resembling bears. Despite their prominence, little is known about their origin, or even their age. Some have proposed that they are effigies of Roman commanders, others that they are not bears, but pre-Saxon lions, marking the edges of a pagan, sacred site.

St Andrew's Church Dacre

Bear at St Andrew's, Dacre. The bear has a small animal on its back, and is turning its head to the right.

The Franklands arrived in Dacre in February 1914, and Henry preached for the first time on Sunday 1 March. On Friday 6 March a service led by Henry, the Lord Bishop of Carlisle, allowed for the 'Institution and Induction of the Rev Henry Frankland, MA'. It was a busy living, since typically there were three services each Sunday: Holy Communion at 8.00am, Matins at 10.30am, and Evensong at 6.30pm. Services were also held every second Sunday at nearby Stainton and Newbiggin. At the latter, services were held in the local school, but Bill remembered how, prior to the service, people met at a fine house, Ennim,[3] belonging to two rich ladies. The vacancy at Dacre had arisen following the death of the incumbent, the Rev F.N. Hasell, in the autumn of 1913. He had served as vicar since 1896, and prior to that (1887-1895) as the curate. In the interregnum, services were led by the Rev A. H. 'Arthur' Ransome, Curate of St. Andrew's, along with Canon G.E. 'George' Hasell.[4] The latter, aged 61, was a local man born in the nearby country house of Dalemain in 1847. This grand Georgian-fronted manor house, with several 14th-century rooms, and extensive oak woods, was acquired by Sir Edward Hasell in 1679, and has remained in the family for several centuries. George was the youngest of 10 children born to Edward and Dorothea Hasell (great-grandson of Sir Edward). He later read classics (as *Literae Humaniores*) at The Queen's College Oxford, graduating in 1870. He immediately read for Holy Orders, being ordained in 1872. The same year he was appointed as Rector of St. Andrew's, Aikton, a village 10 miles west of Carlisle. The church (built in the 12th century) and vicarage lie in an isolated and exposed position, over a mile from the village. With commanding views over the rugged and beautiful landscape of the Northern Fells, this was undoubtedly a challenging place to live in the 19th century. The Rev Hasell served the parish for 39 years as well as taking on other responsibilities including being Rural Dean for Wigton. From 1897 he was non-residentiary Canon of Carlisle Cathedral. He was also Chaplain to the Westmorland and Cumberland Yeomanry, a position he held for over 60 years.

---

3 Ennim was later owned by The Rt. Hon. Viscount Whitelaw.
4 The Rev F.N. Hasell and Canon G.E. Hasell appear not to have been related.

Canon George Hasell. A memorial plaque to him in St Andrew's, Dacre, reads:
'A valiant heart, A faithful steward, A humble follower'.

Canon Hasell was a strict teetotaller and did all he could to try to warn parishioners of the 'evil' of drink. With his wife, Helen, he established 'The Stingless Cup' in Aikton, described as a 'village institute without intoxicants'. In 1910, his elder brother, Major John Hasell, Lord of the Manor of Dalemain, died. The following year Canon Hasell retired from Aikton, and moved with his wife and sons (Edward and George) to take over the running of the family seat. Canon Hasell was not a man to remain idle, and wished to continue his Christian ministry, assisting with many of the services at Dacre over the next 20 years. He described his 'great pleasure to assist in God's work in the church' and hoped to continue 'so long as he retained his strength'. He brought with him his teetotal views and on arrival at Dalemain immediately closed the brewery in the house. His views extended further, and in his position as a magistrate he tried his best to close Dacre's public house, the Horse and Farrier, when the licensee was declared bankrupt. He declared that 'the inn had done immense harm in the past. We do not want a public house in Dacre, it is disgusting'. Fortunately for most of Dacre's residents, his was a lone voice on the licensing panel. By contrast, the Rev Ransome was a rather diffident character, who had entered Holy Orders three years before Henry Frankland. His career was marked by a lack of progress; he had served as curate in a number of parishes, including Dacre (1895-8), and then spent three years in Canada. On his return to Britain in 1914, he moved back to Dacre, and to his previous position. Bill remembered him appearing to be quite stupid, even 'a fool'. When the Franklands played card games they adopted the term 'a Ransome' to describe a mistake made by other players.

Henry and his family moved into Dacre Vicarage, a well-proportioned house, situated on Vicarage Hill, over a mile and a half from both the centre of the village and the church. Vicarage Hill was steep, and full of potholes, and Bill recalled how it was 'a long walk to church, so we were often late for morning services'. Typical of Victorian houses of the time, lighting was by Aladdin lamps, and there were open fires in the main rooms. In the basement was a large coke boiler for heating water; despite this, the house was bitterly cold in the winter, and all family members appreciated the comfort of hot-water bottles in their beds. The Franklands shared their house with a number of staff including a Cook, a parlour maid and a general 'skivvy', as well as a nanny who looked after the children until they were 6 years old. In what Bill described as 'very much a Victorian childhood', Nanny organised the children's lives, determining where and when they went, even in the house. The boys loved to go to the kitchen to see Cook, but Nanny felt otherwise. Bill clearly remembered a large picture of a 'Stag-at-Bay' in the hall, and told his father that he did not like it. Henry pointed out that it was there for a good reason, namely to hide the damp and mould on the wall behind. Surrounded by generous grounds, the house had its own tennis court. However, this did not drain well, and despite Henry putting in a system of drains, there was always a wet corner which detracted from its full enjoyment.

Dacre Vicarage in the 1950s

One of Bill's first memories from Dacre was his third birthday, in March 1915. He and Jack, with their nanny, were invited to Dalemain by Canon Hasell's wife, Helen, for a birthday party. Having walked the two miles to Dalemain, they were very excited to learn that Cook had baked a special cake, one which was very rich indeed. Bill ate too much, and was sick on the carpet. On arriving home his mother was far from impressed to learn of his behaviour at the party. Nearly 100 years later he returned to Dalemain and was able to identify exactly where he had committed such a *faux pas*.

Bill and Jack did not meet many people in the small village of Dacre but visited the town of Penrith about once a month with their parents or Nanny, travelling in a pony and trap, drawn by their horse, Blackie. They would park near to Penrith Railway Station before venturing to the shops. Slightly nearer to home was Pooley Bridge, a village with just one shop, but fortunately one that sold sweets. One penny bought a good number of 'gobstoppers', although the round trip from Dacre to Pooley Bridge was close on 7 miles. Still, it was a big treat to visit the sweetshop. In early spring as they made their way to Pooley Bridge, they passed a special field covered by small, short wild daffodils, sometimes called 'Wordsworth's daffodils', a site believed to have inspired Wordsworth's famous poem. The landowner, Captain Broadhurst, would never let his cattle graze the field until the wild daffodils had finished flowering. Bill and his brother would often accompany their father on his visits to local farms, taking part in what were long country walks to reach the numerous farmhouses spread out across the parish. It was about this time that Bill had his first encounter with a disease which he, in later life, would make significant contributions to an understanding of its aetiology and treatment. He started to develop hay fever whilst working in the fields of the local farm. Interestingly Jack, despite being an identical twin, did not develop the disease, and when symptoms prevented Bill from working, Jack described his brother as 'feeble'. Bill also remembered the rules or etiquette of visiting houses in the parish; if he called with his mother, then she would leave two cards, her own and one on behalf of her husband. Some 100 years later Bill felt that the whole system appeared somewhat archaic, even then.

At around this time Henry acquired a motor car, a Model T Ford, which would have been a most rare sight in Cumberland; the Franklands would, perhaps, see one other car a week in Dacre. Bill recalled how to start the car: the spark plugs were removed, taken into the house, warmed and then refitted. Next the car would be started using a cranking handle inserted into the engine. Cars such as his father's, if low on fuel, had to go up hills backwards to ensure petrol continued to flow into the engine.

Bill and Jack aged two and a half, with Nanny, Penrith September 1914

By the summer of 1916, World War 1 was entering its third year, and the earlier predictions of 'the fighting being over by Christmas of 1914' were completely wide of the mark. Henry Frankland, aged 37 years, entered military service and joined the Royal Army Chaplains' Department. He presented for medical examination in early June 1916, at which he was deemed fit for active service, the only remarks being 'eyesight, good distant, fairly good near'. At the end of June 1916 Henry was appointed to the Chaplain Force (C.F.) 4th Class (equivalent in rank to captain, although like all chaplains he would be addressed as 'Padre'), and received 10 shillings a day pay along with free rations. His initial posting was to Park Hall Camp, Oswestry, one of the largest training camps in Britain, and where large numbers of conscripts had been sent since May 1916. Henry took his last services at Dacre on 25 June, and then left for Oswestry where he was attached to the 4th Battalion, South Lancashire Regiment, a territorial unit whose men primarily came from the Warrington area. In September 1916, Henry received instructions that he was to be posted overseas, to Egypt, and was to be prepared to embark by 10 October. However, after leaving Britain he served in France, at a hospital, during the later weeks of the Battle of the Somme. He then returned home briefly, and during this time received a number of vaccinations. Bill remembered his father having an injection, possibly T.A.B.,[5] which left him with a high temperature, a very sore arm and confined to his bed. As a small boy Bill thought that his father had been wounded.[6] Next, Henry was sent to Salonika, and this was followed by about a year's service in Egypt, at Cairo and Alexandria, the latter on-board a hospital ship. He maintained contact with his family as best he could, and Bill recalled receiving lovely postcards of the Pyramids and the Sphinx. On his return, Henry said nothing about his time in Salonika, but did tell his family about his time in Cairo, where he had lived on eggs, so much so that 'he never wanted to eat eggs again'.

World War 1 had started when Bill was two and a half years old, and many years later he recalled a number of aspects of the conflict. He heard that France was 'a nasty place', but never heard about such encounters as the Battle of Jutland. In 1917 he saw his first aeroplane flying overhead, spewing out black smoke. Nanny commented to the children that 'the aeroplane was using too much coke', an observation which prompted his father to conclude that she was 'stupid, and should be dismissed' and before long, she was. Henry had his own views on aeroplanes, having encountered them in France, seeing them used in a reconnaissance role, and describing how they were 'very slow and were shot to pieces'. He told his sons that they should 'think carefully before going in one'.

Closer to home, although Cumberland was not directly affected by the

---

5 T.A.B., a vaccine against typhoid and paratyphoid infection. It had been developed by Sir Almroth Wright, who would be one of Bill's teachers at St Mary's Hospital.

6 Bill would encounter similar side effects of the vaccine in 1940 when serving as Medical Officer to the Royal Warwickshire Regiment.

war, Bill remembered hearing of an incident when a German submarine attacked the nearby coastal town of Maryport. The family, like many others, were conscious of the war, not least because of rationing. At the evening meal, the Franklands ate bread, Cook having baked bread twice a week. The first slice was plain, the second had butter on it, and the third, butter and jam. On two days a week, Tuesday and Thursday, the family ate cake. There were occasional luxuries, such as venison, but usually only once a year. They kept their own animals, mostly chickens, but Bill remembered also keeping rabbits as pets. At times these were somewhat neglected, and the children were told to look after them properly, or else the rabbits would 'end up in the pot'. With such a threat hanging over them, the children turned their attention to their pets, but unfortunately barely a week later a fox broke into the enclosure and killed the rabbits. With Henry away serving his country, Rose became very lonely. She could not bear the thought of another cold winter in Dacre, so moved the family to Southport for six months in the autumn of 1916. Bill and Jack celebrated their fifth birthday (March 1917) in the seaside town. It was an experience for them both, seeing crowds of people, cars by the dozen, as well as the sea, the railway and a range of shops; all rather different from the country life in Dacre. Rose did not drive, and decided that there was little use for Henry's car, which she sold for the princely sum of £100.

After their winter in Southport, Rose and her children returned to Dace in the spring of 1917. With Henry away on military service, worship continued at St Andrew's, and Canon Hasell took on much of Henry's work. He was assisted by the Rev J.P. Wilkinson, who had been appointed as Curate to St. Andrew's in December 1915. Canon Hasell, perhaps typical of a Victorian clergyman, became very animated during his sermons, thumping his fist or hand down onto the pulpit. Bill remembered Easter services when he and Jack had helped prepare the floral decorations. These contained primroses and daffodils placed on moss on the top of 1lb jam jars which were full of water. These were arranged on the pulpit and as they sat and listened to Canon Hasell they hoped that the jars would come crashing down as his fists thumped the pulpit.

In December 1917 Henry returned home, having been away from

his family for nearly 18 months. Rose was very pleased and relieved for his safe return. One of his last acts as he left the Army was to return his Field Communion Set to the Chaplain General's Department, a Communion Set that had been with him since July 1916. Events some 25 years later involving a Field Communion Set used, not for religious purposes, but for treachery of the highest order, would impact on Bill and many other Allied servicemen. The Franklands were able to enjoy Christmas of 1917 together, with Henry taking his first service in Dacre on 16 December. It was a busy time for him, officiating at services every second day for the following two weeks, including Christmas Day. On 11 November 1918, the war ended and that day Henry led a service of thanksgiving at St. Andrew's. With the cessation of hostilities, Bill remembered how a fireworks display was held in the grounds of Dacre Vicarage annually to commemorate the end of fighting. In August 1919, Henry Frankland and his churchwardens sought permission from the diocese to erect a war memorial in the church dedicated to the one officer and eleven men of the parish who lost their lives. The officer was Lieutenant Gerald Broadhurst, who was killed in May 1915 in the Second Battle of Ypres. His father, Captain Arthur Broadhurst, lived at Waterfoot and was a good friend of Henry Frankland's. In 1911 he had been responsible for securing the return of the chained Bible to St. Andrew's, having discovered it in the village of Coniston. Broadhurst was a retired regular Army officer (14th Hussars) and Bill recalled how his parents stressed that on visiting Waterfoot they were told explicitly 'not to mention the loss of the son'. Captain Broadhurst drove a Rolls-Royce car, and did so for many years, often giving Henry Frankland a lift. Broadhurst was reluctant to part with his car, believing it would merely end up as a hearse. In fact, after his death, it was sold and Bill recalled that it was purchased by a funeral director in Penrith, who converted it into a hearse.[7]

---

7 Captain Broadhurst died in 1930, and Henry Frankland returned to Dacre to officiate at his funeral.

War Memorial Tablet, St Andrew's, Dacre

Despite her musical training Rose rarely played an instrument. However, there was one exception which stood out for Bill. Weddings normally took place at St Andrew's on a Saturday, but one was scheduled for a Wednesday. Rose played the organ for that ceremony and her children came to help by pumping the organ bellows. This was a memorable occasion for Bill, aged seven, since it was the first time he was ever paid, receiving 6d for his efforts. Bill later described how this was the only time he heard his mother play the organ and the first time that he heard a piece of music which he enjoyed, namely Wagner's Bridal Chorus from the opera *Lohengrin.*

Around this time Bill was given advice by his father which has stayed with him throughout his life. When having a disagreement with Jack, possibly over some strawberries, Bill informed his father that he hated his brother. This was picked on immediately by Henry who explained that, 'You must not go on hating people; it does you harm, but it does not do them any harm.' He continued with advice to Bill: 'No. Christians love, love, love and that is what you must do: love.' This profound and yet simple observation would stay with Bill and fortify him and influence his thoughts and actions during many 'black' periods when a prisoner of war. Nearly 100 years later, Bill recalled that his family were very Christian and that he and his brother had attended church regularly from the age of six, and reflected that, perhaps, he had learnt from his father's sermons. However, Bill did not accept everything at face value, and had discussions with his brother about many of the aspects of the Christian faith. One revolved around the traditional wording of the Lord's Prayer, which reads, 'Our Father, Which art in Heaven'. Bill took exception to these, saying that God was not a 'witch' and could not understand what 'art' had to do with the prayer or God.

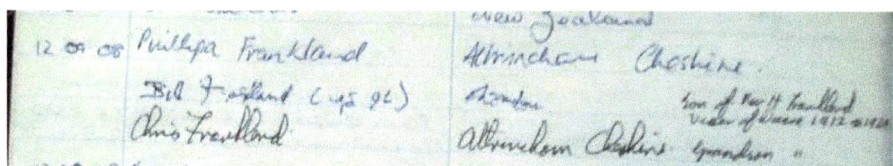

Entry by Bill Frankland in visitors' book, St Andrew's, Dacre, September 2008

Henry Frankland was a serious man, and Bill remembers that his father was not a great joker. However, one amusing incident stuck with Bill. Henry described an incident at Wadham College Chapel, when he was an undergraduate. A worshipper came up to the lectern to read the lesson but read completely the wrong lesson for that day. He closed by saying, 'and here endeth the wrong lesson' which Henry found most amusing. Bill recalled another occasion when his father made an inadvertent comment, seen by some as funny, at a service in Dacre. In January 1919, Canon Hasell's wife died. Bill was keen to see the hearse pass by the vicarage on its way to the church at Dacre, but was told 'no', all the blinds in the house were to be drawn as a mark of respect. Bill attended the funeral and heard his father say that it 'was so nice to see the church full'.

Henry's influence spread much farther than just to his family, and most noticeably he appears to have had an important influence on one parishioner, Miss F.H.E. 'Eva' Hasell. The daughter of the late Major John Hasell, she was a committed member of St. Andrew's congregation. With a desire to undertake missionary work, she travelled to Canada, where she founded the Caravan Missionary Society. Leading this organisation she drove her caravan across the vast plains of Manitoba and Saskatchewan, telling local inhabitants about Christianity. For many years she worked in Canada in the summer and autumn before returning to Britain around Christmas when she undertook fundraising tours. Her life's work was recognised by the award of an honorary doctorate by the University of Manitoba, as well as the OBE. It appears highly likely that her choice to move to Canada was influenced by Henry Frankland, who himself had spent several years there as a missionary.

TO THE DEAR MEMORY OF

FRANCES HATTON EVA HASELL
YOUNGER DAUGHTER OF
JOHN AND MAUD HASELL OF DALEMAIN
MEMBER OF
THE ORDER OF THE BRITISH EMPIRE
DOCTOR OF DIVINITY
OFFICER OF
THE ORDER OF SERVICE OF CANADA
WHO FOR OVER 50 YEARS
WAS THE LIFE SPRING OF
THE WESTERN CANADA CARAVAN MISSION
TO WHICH SHE DEVOTED HER ENTIRE LIFE
BORN: 13TH DECEMBER 1886
DIED: 3RD MAY 1974

Memorial Tablet to Eva Hasell, St Andrew's, Dacre

When aged about 7, Bill and Jack, along with Ella (aged 9), all became ill, having contracted bovine tuberculosis, although at the time it was not diagnosed. Later their father would blame a local farmer, Mr Wilkinson, believing his cows were the source of the infection. The children ran a fever, and the local doctor from Penrith, Dr J. Edward Bowser, was called. A long-established practitioner, who had served with the Westmorland and Cumberland Yeomanry, he pronounced that all three should be 'confined to their beds'. This introduction to the medical profession had a profound impression on Bill. The children did not like Dr Bowser. Noticing his big red nose and soon forming the opinion that he drank too much, they christened him 'Dr Boozer'. Bill considered the man to be stupid, and asked himself, 'Why should this silly old man be a doctor? He doesn't know how to deal with children.' Moreover, Bill decided that if he were a doctor he would deal with patients as people. 'Dr Boozer' visited the children once a month, for four months. Diagnosing that they all had enlarged tonsils, he advised that surgery was required and they were referred to a private nursing home in Cavendish Terrace in Carlisle. The operation was performed under general anaesthesia, induced by anaesthetic dripped onto a mask held over the patient's mouth and nose. Bill found this most upsetting, and developed a phobia to any fluid on his face: even washing his face caused claustrophobia.

It was at this time that Bill learnt of the influenza pandemic that affected millions of people around the world, following World War 1. His Uncle Edward (Henry's younger brother) was a teacher in Barnsley. He had not joined up for war service because of his position as a head teacher. Despite this, Bill heard, through his father and mother, that Uncle Edward had received white feathers, a symbol of cowardice, on at least three occasions during the war. Edward was at pains to point out that he was not a conscientious objector, but still received more white feathers, actions which Bill remembered as causing 'terrible disgrace' to the Frankland family. After the war he contracted influenza and Bill remembered learning that his uncle had taken to his bed, but within four days was dead. Bill's grandfather (Henry West) died about the same time, following a prostatectomy. The telephone at the vicarage rang and Bill answered it. This was the first time he had answered this new acquisition in the house and nearly 100 years later he remembered that the caller 'asked who he was speaking to.' Bill replied quite calmly that 'it is me'. Once the caller had made themselves known and clarified who they wanted to speak to, news was received of the death of Rose's father.

Bill spent many holidays in Barnsley, staying with his grandfather at 5 Cavendish Road, Barnsley, close to the main road from Barnsley to Huddersfield. In the garden a large pear tree hung over one of the garden walls. As such it was an easy target for local children to steal pears. Bill, along with his brothers Basil and Jack, felt that those who were stealing the fruit should be punished and one day they apprehended a young boy as he climbed up to the tree. The brothers locked him away in the coalhouse, but after about 30 minutes began to feel sorry for the lad. They unlocked the door and released him. He was covered from head to toe in coal dust and ran off. A lesson seemed to be learnt and pears no longer went missing. Next door, at Number 3, lived Bill's great-aunts, the Cummacks, who, rumour had it, had never been out of the house. They were exceptionally strict and on Sundays the only book that could be read was the Bible. Rose's uncle was the Mayor of Barnsley, and Bill remembered him as being very well off, and a man who ran a number of factories manufacturing shirts. Another relative who stood out was Miss Crossley who lived in a large house outside Barnsley. Bill, along with his mother and brother, would be picked up in a chauffeur-driven car and taken out to visit Miss Crossley. He and Jack enjoyed the visit since there was a full-sized billiard table and they were allowed to play on it, something Bill later described as 'wonderful'. The purpose of the visits was, however, to have high tea and Bill remembers being told by his mother that he and his brother were not to comment or laugh when Miss Crossley took her teeth out at the table before eating. Holidays to Barnsley were also times when Bill encountered a number of political issues which appeared not to affect his family in the Lake District. Most noticeable was the miners' strike of 1919, in which Barnsley was one of the main areas of unrest. In several northern cities tanks were ordered onto the streets, the government fearing a revolution. Closer to home Bill's uncle made it very clear to his nephews that he had no time at all for the strikers, pointing out that they wanted to live off other people's wealth.

An Early Education

In 1922, aged 10, Bill and Jack started their formal education, enrolling at Rossall Preparatory School. The school is situated in Lancashire, to the north of Blackpool, and south of Fleetwood, adjacent to Rossall Beach. A Church of England school, it was founded in 1844 at a time of significant expansion of Victorian public schools, and was a sister school to the recently opened Marlborough College. It was proposed that it would provide 'the advantages of a Public School for the Clergy and Gentry of the Rural Districts'. It set out its aim 'to provide, at moderate cost, for the sons of Clergymen, and others, a classical, mathematical and general education of the highest class'. The site of the school was often a subject of ridicule, but it was noted by the first school captain that 'to us who could bear the wind and brunt the storm, it gave us a hardening strength which has braced us up for life'.

Aerial View of Rossall School

As Bill and Jack travelled by train to their new school it dawned that this was their first time away from home on their own. This was their first formal schooling, and on arrival they were shocked to find that they were placed in the bottom class. Yet worse was to unfold when they discovered that they were the eldest boys in the class. Soon a competition started between them as to which one would finish bottom of the class. Bill and Jack were the first Franklands to attend Rossall as their elder brother, Basil, had attended Lime House School, Wetheral, near Carlisle. Lime House was described as 'very conservative in all senses of the word', and was owned by Mrs Crosthwaite, who advertised that she 'prepared boys 6-14 years for public schools'. All the staff were ladies, and included Mrs Crosthwaite's daughters. In 1921 Basil gained a scholarship to St Bees School, and Bill and Jack knew that their parents wished them to follow him there.

Rossall had a strict regime; boys were given little, if any, freedom and there were roll-calls three times a day. Boys were not allowed into the nearby town of Cleveleys, where there was a sweetshop, although Bill knew that some boys had managed to 'make the break'. This compared poorly with the relaxed and happier regime which Basil told them about at St Bees, where boys were even allowed the freedom of a bicycle. The twins made their allegiances very clear when a team from St Bees visited Rossall for a rugby match; both boys cheered for the visitors. The headmaster of Rossall Preparatory was the Rev E.B.H. 'Bertie' Berwick MA, described as being 'generous in dealing with one's shortcomings, but a man of monumental efficiency and a great good humour'. He was a fine cricketer, and Bill remembered seeing him score a century. Bill's phobia of water on his face caused him immense stress at Rossall since all the boys had to learn to swim in the open-air swimming pool and the school did not allow any dispensations. On one occasion, soon after starting at the school, Bill found himself at the swimming pool, but without his costume. He was told to swim regardless. The distress of being nude was quite minor compared to that of entering the cold water. Other sports which the boys encountered included a strange variant of hockey played on the beach at low tide.

The archway at Rossall School

As a member of the Preparatory School, Bill remembered going to the main or 'big' school to watch rugby matches. He also remembered one occasion when all the pupils attended an athletics meeting at which the guest was Harold Abrahams. He was a Cambridge graduate and a sprinter who had competed in the 1920 Olympics and would go on to win the 100 metres gold medal at the Paris Olympics of 1924. Abrahams challenged the boys to a race, and gave them all a generous head start. Despite this, Bill saw him win by a fair margin. It was also whilst at Rossall that Bill encountered the radio for the first time, later describing how it was 'marvellous that noise could travel through the air'.

A New Living

On Sunday 22 July 1923 Henry Frankland led his last service at St Andrew's, Dacre. In that summer he and his family moved from Dacre to a new living at St. Michael's, Burgh-by-Sands, in Cumberland, one that included acting as an inspector of primary schools in the county. The village lies north-west of Carlisle, and was a farming community, extending north to the Solway Firth. Compared with Dacre, the terrain is far flatter, but is exposed to the weather from the nearby sea. St. Michael's is a Norman church, built on the site of the former Roman fort of *Aballava* which lay on Hadrian's Wall. The earliest parts of the church were built in the 12th century, using stones from Hadrian's Wall, some of which still bear the masons' initials. This region of England has a long history of conflict with its neighbours, and St. Michael's links with border conflicts date back to the summer of 1307. At that time King Edward I, despite being unwell, rode with his army from Carlisle to do battle with Robert the Bruce (King of Scotland). After two days he reached Burgh-by-Sands where, on 7 July, he died from dysentery. His body lay in state for 10 days in St. Michael's Church, where his court and heir came to pay homage, before the body was moved to London. Over the centuries the ongoing unrest in the region led to many protective towers being built, and at Burgh-by-Sands a fortified tower was added to the west end of the church. It served three functions: as a belfry, in which bells would sound out warning of invaders, as a place of refuge, and as a fortress. The tower has a number of openings in its walls: most are slits to allow arrows to be fired, but one is round, designed for a cannon.

St Michael's Church, Burgh-by-Sands.

In 1921 the Vicar of St Michael's, the Rev J.A. Baker, died after 30 years of service to the parish. Later that year it was agreed that the Rev A.P. Symes of St Mary's Church, Pillerton Hersey, Warwickshire, should be appointed as his replacement, but soon after the invitation had been made, Symes withdrew. In February 1922 the Rev W.H.M. Lonsdale was invited to the parish. He had recently returned from working for several years in India at the SPG[8] College in Trichinopoly, Madras, and he commenced his living in April. However, his time at Burgh-by-Sands was brief, and by May 1923 he had moved to Nottingham. In June 1923, the rural dean noted how 'there was great difficulty attached to the patronage of a living (especially as in the case of Burgh-by-Sands) when the patrons resided at a distance'. However, he noted that a churchwarden, Mr Bertram Carr, 'had acquired the patronage of the parish and had offered the living to the Rev Henry Frankland, Vicar of Dacre, who had accepted'. Bertram Carr was the grandson of Mr J.D. Carr, the founder of the local firm, Carr's Bakeries, the largest biscuit manufacturer in the country. Bertram Carr had carried on the family tradition, working for the company, where he specialised in overseas sales. Recently he had held office as Mayor of Carlisle. Every year the factory held an open day, and Bill remembered visiting on several occasions; each time they were allowed to help themselves to whatever they wanted. Henry Frankland was introduced to the churchwardens at St. Michael's on 22 June 1923, and on Sunday 5 August led his first service there.

By the autumn of 1923, the Franklands were residing in the vicarage, Burgh-by-Sands, immediately adjoining the churchyard of St. Michael's. It was built in 1685, prior to when vicars were reported to have lived in the tower of the church. Their new home was of a different standard to that of Dacre. Even before the Franklands arrived, the churchwardens had recorded the 'dilapidated state of the vicarage and grounds', and recommended that these should be put in order before the new incumbent arrived. Some work was carried out in the summer 'in order to make the place habitable' and Mr Carr offered a new cooking range for the vicarage, the one installed having worn out. The following year

---

8 Society for the Propagation of the Gospel.

a garden fete was held in order to try to clear the debts incurred from work on the vicarage. The house, like the one in Dacre, had a tennis court and both Bill and Jack helped their father to extend it. In the process they uncovered a number of stones from a Roman votive altar which they offered to the County Archivist. He politely refused, saying that he had 'more than enough' of these in the collection, so they were placed in the churchyard, where they remain to this day. Amongst those who played tennis at the vicarage were the daughters of the Rev Day, from Aikton. As Bill pointed out, his name was most apt, since he had seven daughters, 'one for every day of the week'.

Henry Frankland was not the only priest living in Burgh-by-Sands, since its residents included Canon Ernest Danson, the former Bishop of Labuan and Sarawak, whose own visitors included the Bishop of Jerusalem, the Rt Rev Rennie MacInnes. Henry found it somewhat awkward having to preach to a congregation containing two bishops. On other occasions, Bill recalled how one of the visiting preachers brought his dog with him to the service and it joined him in the pulpit when he delivered his sermon. There were a number of other occasions when Henry Frankland was perturbed by activities in his parish, not least the marriage of one of Mr Carr's daughters. Despite the bride's father's high profile, the wedding was a very quiet affair. The reason became apparent a few months later when Henry learnt that the bride was in fact a divorcee; at that time the thought of a divorced person being married in church would be dismissed immediately without any consideration.

In the spring of 1924, Bill and Jack left Rossall and entered Carlisle Grammar School, as day scholars, probably the consequences of a downturn in family finances. The history of Carlisle Grammar School can be traced back to 1570, but the most recent school buildings date to 1880. The headmaster was Mr C.F.C. Padel MA, who had read Classics at Sidney Sussex College, Cambridge. A German by birth, his grasp of English was not very good. However, he was a talented musician whom Rose had met through her musical interests. Bill was unimpressed by the education he received at the school and felt that neither he, nor Jack, made the progress they should have. However, there was at least one consolation. They travelled each day, first-class, on the Port Carlisle

Railway, to and from Carlisle, in the company of 'three very nice girls', daughters of a local solicitor. By contrast, when at home Bill would often hear the sound of people walking out onto the shores of the Solway Firth to pick mushrooms; these were the unemployed from Carlisle who made the whole journey on foot.

Bill and Jack followed their brother to St Bees School in the autumn of 1926. St Bees was a somewhat isolated community on the coast, just south of St Bees Head, the most westerly point of Cumberland. St Bees is named after an Irish princess, St. Bega, who, legend has it, escaped from Ireland to avoid a forced marriage. There has been a community there for many years, with a Benedictine monastery and priory opening in 1120. St Bees School was founded in 1583, by a local man, Edmund Grindal who, at the time, was Archbishop of Canterbury. On his deathbed he set out the statutes and vision for the school which was to be a 'free grammar school for local boys'. The earliest building, Foundation House, dates back to 1587, and engraved in a lintel over the front door is the motto, 'Enter so that you may make progress'.

St Bees underwent significant expansion in the middle of the 19th century as a result of recompense from Lord Lonsdale, a local landowner. At the turn of the century he had illegally gained the mining rights of the school's land near Whitehaven, and had profited considerably. However, a court ruling ordered him to compensate the school. Significant funds were paid to the school, allowing it to prosper, reaching its zenith in 1921, with just over 300 pupils. It was the only public school in Cumberland, and all pupils were boarders.

The school has been described as 'aloof from the neighbourhood and the world', although many have commented on the beauty of the school buildings and playing fields in the summer months. Built in red sandstone, nearly all the original school buildings faced south, over extensive playing fields – The Crease – extending all the way to the railway line. The school offered a range of sporting activities, including what were described as the most northerly 'Eton Fives Courts' in the country. There was a swimming pool, heated all the year round, although in the summer boys swam from the beach. All boys had to be able to swim by the end of their first year.

St Bees School Clock Tower and Foundation North (to the left)

Bill's arrival at the school coincided with that of a new headmaster, Mr E.A. Bell MA, who had previously taught history at Eton and Giggleswick. He replaced Mr C.W. Kaye who had been headmaster for nine years. Kaye was described as 'a large commanding figure with rosy cheeks' who had retired to Bassenthwaite, to a fine house. Henry Frankland had a poor opinion of the man, believing he had been overpaid whilst headmaster, allowing him to acquire the property. Bell was a somewhat complex man, described as 'a forceful and stimulating teacher, whose focus was always the boys of the school'; he would go on to raise the standard of academic work at St Bees. He encouraged boys to follow their own inclinations in both their hobbies and sports. But, it was noted, he could be impetuous and, at times, 'act without discretion and, on occasion, take an active dislike to some members of staff'. Bell would make his mark on St Bees in a number of areas; not least he ensured that 'feeding of the school was of such a quality that it is not likely to be excelled throughout the country'. The prospectus described how 'butter, milk, bread and jam are supplied in unlimited quantities'. Bill recalled that in School House only, unlimited fruit was available for pupils. This undoubtedly influenced observations by visitors who, in 1930, made firm recommendations regarding the school shop, which sold 'tuck'. In no uncertain terms it was suggested that, in light of the high quality of food provided, 'resort to "tuck" seems entirely unnecessary and merely encourages habits of self-indulgence at a time when economy and self-denial are being inculcated on all hands'.

St Bees Masters 1926/7
Back row, On right H.O.Roberts (no cap)
Middle row: left E.A.Bell, right A.B.Cowburn.

To gain entry, boys had to pass the Common Entrance Examination and provide a 'certificate of good moral character' from a previous headmaster or tutor. Fees were £120 per year and there were four boarding houses: Foundation (itself split into North and South), School, Grindal, and Eaglesfield. Bill and Jack were both assigned to Foundation North. St Bees welcomed 50 new pupils in the autumn of 1926, the total number of pupils in the school being 190. On their arrival, Both Bill and Jack were shocked to realise that they were the only pupils in shorts, especially since Basil had started at the school some years earlier and Rose would have been fully aware of the uniform requirements.

Fortunately it was only for a term, and after they returned from holiday they were wearing long trousers. The following year, Mr Bell introduced a new uniform comprising a blazer, cricket shirt (open at the neck) and grey flannel trousers; a uniform that had been shown to 'reduce the liability to sore throats'. However, on Sundays a more formal attire was required for chapel, with boys wearing a hard collar, black tie, black coat and waistcoat. Services were not always held in the school chapel, which is somewhat restricted in size. Bill remembered how the boys would often attend services at nearby St Bees Priory, a church which Bill admired and appreciated throughout his life. There were other changes during Bell's tenure as headmaster, including replacing acetylene lights with electric ones and developing the school's own golf course.

With Bill and Jack entering St Bees there were now three Frankland boys at the school, and they needed to be distinguished: Basil was Frankland major; Jack, Frankland minor; and Bill, Frankland tertius. An apparently straightforward and clear scheme was thrown into chaos after one year when Basil left to pursue a career in Canada in the fur trade: Jack became Frankland major and Bill, Frankland minor.

Bill enjoyed his years at St Bees, and looked back with many fond memories of his time there. The schoolday fell into three main periods. In the morning there were five periods of lessons, and sport was played in the afternoon. Boys then returned to the classrooms for three further periods. Bill remembered many of the staff at St Bees, including Major A.B. Cowburn, who had been awarded the MC in 1917, and was a very strict teacher of rugger. Rugger was also taught by the geography master, Mr H.V.G. Kinvig, himself a fine athlete, who played for Gloucester. Kinvig continued to play for Gloucester, being allowed Saturdays off from school duties to fulfil his club commitments. Bill's housemaster in Foundation North was initially Mr H.O. Roberts, described as 'a very friendly man, who sang and played the piano, although not one of the best teachers'. He retired in 1927, and was replaced by Mr R.G. Ikin, a recent recruit who had previously taught at Trent School and brought with him many modern ideas on teaching. Bill maintained contact with Mr Roberts, and together they later organised a meeting of the St Beghian Society in Oxford. Mr T.A. Brown was noted for his 'very broad Cumberland accent', causing many to believe he was uneducated. Mr P.G. Gow was the senior science master and taught chemistry. Bill judged him to be a very good teacher, a sentiment echoed by school inspectors in 1931.

St Bees: The Crease with the Chapel and War Memorial behind.

One teacher who stood out at this time was Mr C. Collison, who taught Italian, Spanish and typing. A single man, he had never married, and many boys did not look upon him as a 'real master'. He was a seasoned traveller, and every year would take three boys with him on a trip to Europe. Bill recalled going to Mr Collison's house for tea on Sundays and being shown pictures from his earlier tours. Aged 16, Bill, along with Jack and one other boy were invited to travel with Collison on the Orient Express during the Easter holidays. They travelled to London and boarded the train at Victoria, travelling to Dover where they caught the ferry to France. Back on the train they headed via Paris to Venice. Bill described this as a marvellous trip, made all the more memorable by travelling first-class. During the overnight journey to Italy, Bill awoke and looked out of the sleeper compartment to see a wonderful view of Lake Como in the early morning. They arrived to snow in Venice and made their way to a 5-star hotel situated on the Grand Canal. Bill remembered that he was not at all hungry, since the food on the train had been so good. In St Mark's Square, Collison decided to use his Italian to order three ice creams. Unfortunately the order was 'lost in translation' and Bill and colleagues were disappointed to be served three iced coffees. From Venice, the group moved on to Florence, Rome, Naples and then back to Paris where they spent two days. Finally the holiday was over, and they made their way home from France, through London to Carlisle. The final part of the journey made a big impression with Bill, since they travelled from London to Carlisle second-class!

There were also numerous excursions nearer to home. One winter, the playing fields remained frozen throughout February, and could not be used. One master, Mr Boulter, took a party of four boys, including Bill, to Bassenthwaite Lake which was frozen, and here they were able to skate. In the summer Bill would take part in hikes up a number of the fells in the Lake District. On one occasion, a group of six boys had just made it to the peak of Robinson, a fell above Buttermere, when the clouds came down. They were lost, but fortunately Bill had a compass with him, and was able to guide the party to the north, and pick up the correct path which took them back down.

In June 1927, The Prince of Wales embarked on a four-day tour of the north-west, to Lancashire, Westmorland and Cumberland. On Wednesday 29 June the prince spent the morning at the Vickers' shipyards at Barrow-in-Furness before heading north. He arrived at St Bees at 5pm, where he was welcomed at The Crease by the Lord-Lieutenant of Cumberland, Lord Lowther, Mr Bell and all the boys. Bill well remembered the afternoon, noting that the prince was 'very good-looking' and that Lord Lowther (also called the 'Yellow Earl') arrived in a splendid yellow Rolls-Royce. The Prince of Wales toured the school, during which he viewed a pageant on The Crease and then visited the chapel, war memorial, library and swimming baths, finally having tea with a number of senior boys. He then proceeded to open the newly constructed squash court, situated close to St. Bees Priory. It was built using the balance of monies subscribed for the war memorial, itself unveiled in 1921. At the official opening, Bill found himself very close to the prince, and saw him turn to Lord Lowther and ask, 'What do I say when I open a squash court?' The prince appears to have said very little, deciding not to give an address but instead spoke to the school and announced that the boys should have an extra week of summer holiday as a 'memento of his visit'.

Prince of Wales at The Crease, on his visit to St Bees, 1927

Prince of Wales opening the squash court at St Bees. 1927

Bill had not learnt to swim whilst at Rossall, and at St Bees, every boy had to be able to swim by the end of their first summer term. Bill had failed and, aged 16, was classed as a non-swimmer. He was ordered to attend classes on The Crease, twice a week in the evenings, and found himself alongside boys up to three years his junior. Bill felt these classes, designed to show boys the moves to make when in the water, were 'ridiculous' and merely embarrassed all involved. Despite, or perhaps because of, these classes Bill finally swam a length of the pool. However, since he did not complete the required four lengths, he did not have permission to swim in the sea, but had no desire to.

Bill made good academic progress and he was top of the fifth form in a number of subjects, including physics, geography and mathematics. He was told that he would receive five prizes and that he could choose his own. He put forward his request, but soon heard back from Mr Bell who asked if 'he could, perhaps, choose something cheaper?' However, Bill was not successful in all subjects; certainly he found French and Latin taxing. His teacher told him, 'Frankland minor, you are making progress....but backwards!'

St Bees May 2012. Bill Frankland aged 100 at school speech day

Bill's commitment to the school was not only academic, and he took part in many sporting activities. He developed a talent for shooting and represented the school, through the Army Cadet Force, in a number of competitions. In December 1929, Lance Corporals A.W. and J.A. Frankland both competed for St Bees in a match against Taunton

School (undertaken by post) but unfortunately lost. Bill remembers the parades with the cadets, and how they were advised to move their toes in their boots, in order to prevent them from fainting. Bill was aware that a shooting cup was awarded at St Bees, and had hoped to win it. Unfortunately, during his years at the school it was not offered. There was sibling rivalry in many sports, and in cricket both boys represented their house (Foundation North), although it was Jack who was selected in their final year for the school 1st Eleven. Two years earlier, they had both played for Foundation North who defeated School House in the final of the Senior House Cricket Cup. In the first round (against Grindal) Bill scored 11, whilst Jack was out for a duck. In the final, Bill opened the batting, but was out for a duck, caught by G.A. 'Gus' Walker,[9] and Jack made 10, before hitting his own wicket. School House had two most notable athletes in their team, Gus Walker, who would later play rugby for Cambridge and England, as well as captaining the RAF rugby team, and G.W.C. Meikle, who also played rugby for Cambridge and England, as well as representing his school at athletics, swimming and cricket. It was whilst watching Meikle that Bill first saw a player hit a six. In athletics, where Bill was to become a fine miler and steeplechaser, he had opposition not only from Meikle, but also from W.G. Bannister, described as 'an exceptional all round athlete', who won quarter-, half- and one-mile races as well as the steeplechase in the Public Schools Championships, and subsequently earned a Blue at Cambridge. Bill also took part in school productions, and each year the school put on a Gilbert and Sullivan production which he enjoyed greatly, singing in the shows. Bill also sang as chief treble in a choral foursome for the school in several contests, and was pleased that in one competition the judge noted that the 'treble carried the whole show'.

Bill's sporting activities were not solely confined to his time at St Bees. During the school holidays Bill and Jack became involved in a number of sporting clubs near home at Burgh-by-Sands. One was the Gretna Green Cricket Club, which played its matches on a small patch of grass on the Solway Firth, grass that they had to share at times with

---

9 Later Air Chief Marshal G. Augustus Walker.

grazing cattle. The club, and the pitch, were owned by the self-appointed captain of the club. Bill remembered one match when the captain of Gretna Green came in to bat, he took his wicket and was bowled on the first ball. 'Out!' cried the umpire, but the batsman did not move. Instead he informed the umpire of a club rule: 'If you are the captain and are out on your first ball it does not count'. The brothers also took part in tournaments at Carlisle Tennis Club, where invariably they were knocked out of the competition at an early stage. At this point they were appointed as umpires: not only did this allow them to see the matches, but they also received a cup in recognition of their services. However, it was not all plain sailing, and Bill recalled how they had to introduce players with a 'mouthful of names'; one especially made an impression, an Army officer with a double-barrelled surname who played in the mixed doubles.

The library, St Bees

The library at St Bees was described as 'a spacious and dignified room – such not even many of the larger Public Schools possess'. It was noted to serve a valuable function in the life of the school, and here Bill, aged

16, read the recently published *The Story of St Michele*, by Axel Munthe. Munthe, a Swedish doctor, had trained in Sweden and Paris and later practised in a number of European cities, including London. He was physician to the Swedish Royal Family, and wrote his book describing how he treated people all over Europe, including many royalty of the time. Bill recalled that the stories described were full of 'medical curiosities', although as he was to point out, 'some were not quite true, but that did not matter'. Bill found the whole book so intriguing that, combined with his earlier experiences as a patient of Dr Bowser's, he thought, 'I would like to be a doctor, like Munthe.' Many years later, in 1946, Dr Bill Frankland caught a glimpse of Dr Munthe at St Mary's Hospital, when Munthe, wearing a bowler hat and carrying a walking stick, arrived to visit Sir Almroth Wright.

Axel Munthe

CHAPTER 2

DREAMING SPIRES: A STUDENT'S LIFE

The Queen's College Oxford

As the next step on his path to becoming a doctor, Bill needed to gain entrance to a suitable institution for medical training. He applied to The Queen's College, Oxford in 1930. The college was founded by Robert de Eglesfield in 1341 as an establishment of 'fellows, chaplains, poor boys and officials and servants, to be headed by a provost'. Preference was given to applicants from Cumberland and Westmorland, such that by the early 15th century, there was an effective monopoly by men from North-West England. There was significant rebuilding of the college in the mid-18th century, with the erection of new buildings of Baroque design, leading many to comment that the quadrangle was 'the greatest piece of classical architecture in Oxford'. The architect responsible, Nicholas Hawksmoor, was the former deputy surveyor to Sir Christopher Wren. Links between St Bees and Queen's date back to the school's founder, Archbishop Grindal, a significant benefactor to Queen's, and more recently, through Canon Hasell,[10] a governor of St Bees in 1930, who had studied at Queen's almost half a century earlier.

St Bees did not offer biology in its curriculum so Bill planned to sit the entrance examination for Queen's in physics and chemistry. He travelled to Oxford, knowing that he would have to stay overnight. He found his first dinner in hall most exciting, seeing the fellows wearing black tie as they entered the hall. As a prelude to dinner, the Latin grace

---

10 Canon Hasell would not see Bill graduate, as he died in 1932.

was read taking what seemed to Bill to be 'a very long time indeed'.[11] The following morning he found that there was just one invigilator for all the subjects to be examined, a small, short-sighted mathematician who appeared to be a very learned man. Bill was told they could not offer papers in physics and chemistry that day, and instead was asked if he would sit the mathematics paper. In fact mathematics had been his best subject at school, but his masters had not been willing to recognise this. Having agreed to the suggestion, Bill was handed a pile of papers, comprising the papers from the last five years, along with the answers! The invigilator advised Bill to work his way through the papers, and attempt as many questions as he could. He told Bill, 'I want to know what you know, not what you do not.' His other piece of advice was: 'do not write too much'. Bill set about answering the questions, having the luxury of help from the answer sheets. Afterwards, he estimated that his score was at least 99%, but told no one of the assistance he had received. His success was rewarded not only with a place at Queen's, but also the award of a Thomas Exhibition for Natural Sciences. This prize was established in 1794 following the death of a former member of Queen's, John Thomas, Bishop of Rochester, who entered the college in 1730. It was awarded to 'the son or orphan of a clergyman of the diocese of Carlisle'. Interestingly, both Bishop Thomas and Bill were sons of clergymen in Cumberland and both had attended Carlisle Grammar School; in the case of Bill this was prior to joining St Bees.

Bill went up to Queen's in the autumn of 1930, where he found that there had been a change of Provost since his earlier visit. After 52 years as Provost, John Magrath had left the college. Bill was told that Magrath had effectively taken over the whole of one wing on the front quadrangle. No one had seen him for 10 years, except the man who took him his meals. The college were determined to get rid of him as he was taking no part in college functions. They bought him a house

---

11 Over 80 years later, when Bill was elected an Honorary Fellow, he commented that Latin grace still appeared to be very long. He was surprised to be elected to an Honorary Fellowship in 2012, having believed that one had to be 'A Bishop or a Baron to achieve such a position'.

in Boars Hill, south-west of Oxford, and arranged for him to be moved there in an open, horse-drawn carriage on a cold February day. Perhaps not surprisingly, he developed pneumonia, and died three days later. Henry Frankland had encountered Magrath whilst an undergraduate at Oxford, and had told Bill how Magrath's sermons at St Mary's, the University church, had been keenly attended. However, he advised Bill of two facts about the man. Firstly, that Magrath was of the opinion that 'all undergraduates should know both Greek and Latin', although the university only demanded Latin. Secondly, he was adamant that neighbouring St Edmund Hall, established in 1317, should not be part of Oxford University.[12]

Front Quad, The Queen's College Oxford

Before Bill left home to go up to Oxford, he was given some advice by his father about undergraduate life at Oxford. He told Bill to join any society he might wish, to enjoy his time at university, but not to join the Oxford Union. No reason was given for this last piece of advice, but Bill heeded it. Bill received advice not only from his father when going up to Oxford, but also from an uncle, who told him that he should get

---

12 St Edmund Hall was incorporated into the university in 1957.

drunk whilst a student. Bill did, and over 85 years later still remembered how very sick he felt the next morning, vomiting after a heavy night's drinking. This influenced Bill's approach to alcohol throughout the rest of his life, drinking only in moderation, and was later to advise that 'champagne should not be taken on an empty stomach'.

Bill Frankland 1930, The Queen's College Oxford

On 10 October 1930 Bill officially joined The Queen's College, Oxford. It was his first step in becoming a doctor, and also marked his first time away from his twin brother, Jack, who had entered Hatfield College, Durham. This was a theological establishment, part of the University of Durham, described as 'a popular choice for intending clerics.'[13] Meanwhile at Oxford, Bill settled in, living in college for his first year, being assigned Room 7 in Front Quad. He soon encountered other occupants of the quad, large tortoises. There were said to be four, but as Bill recalled, 'However hard you looked you could find three, but never the fourth.' By this time the Provost was the Rev E.M. 'Edward' Walker. Bill talked to him only

---

13 Jack obtained a BA in Theology in 1937. The same year he entered Edinburgh Theological College and was ordained in 1938.

once, when Walker joined four 'freshers' for breakfast. The student living next door to Bill hailed from Watford and had gained a scholarship to Queen's, and appeared financially 'well off' to Bill, who noted how his neighbour could afford 'beer at lunch.' Interestingly the boy's father was a train driver. During the following two years, Bill, along with two fellow medical students, Marcus Slee and Alan Norton, lived in university-approved lodgings in North Oxford. Their landlord suffered from heart disease, but Bill remembered this did not prevent him carrying barrels of cider up from his basement. Being in digs, Bill found a bicycle very useful indeed in the city. In Bill's fourth year he lived at 1 Mansfield House, just a short walk from the college. During his time at Queen's, Bill's academic tutor was Dr Cyril Carter, a Fellow of the College, and Reader in Biochemistry. In college, Bill remembered how he and other exhibitioners had their own table at hall and wore commoners' gowns as opposed to scholars' gowns. Despite being awarded an exhibition, Bill had to budget carefully during his time at Oxford, and kept a small ledger in which he recorded everything he spent.

One feature of Queen's at this time was their own brewery, sited near to the Provost's garden, which produced both ale and a beer liquor called The Chancellor (with a 12% alcohol content). Queen's also supplied a neighbouring college, beer being passed through a hole in the wall of the brewery to New College. At Queen's, beer was served in hall, at both lunch and dinner, where it was also part of a forfeiture process. Bill remembered how at dinner, if the head of the table felt that a member's conversation was inappropriate, he could seek an askance, or punishment. To do so, he had to write, in Latin, to the head of High Table, usually the Provost. If he agreed with the request, he would stand and say, 'Yes.' At which point the steward would be summoned and beer was ordered for all at the table, to be paid for by the guilty party. This was a quite expensive undertaking.[14]

During his years at Oxford Bill developed not only academically, but also physically. He was still quite short when he entered Queen's and

---

14 Beer production at Queen's ceased in 1939 with the outbreak of war. In 2018 plans are afoot to recommence beer production; the beer is to be called 'Frankland Ale'.

grew two and a half inches in the subsequent four years. It was not until his second year that he began to shave.

Introduction to Medicine

As Bill had not studied biology he had entered the premedical year of study and it was not until 1931 that he commenced the true medical course. The staff at Oxford included some of the most illustrious names in medicine. But, as Bill pointed out, students rarely saw these people, and it was even rarer to be taught by them. In 1934, Wilfrid Le Gros Clark was appointed as Dr Lee's Professor of Anatomy following Arthur Thomson's retirement. Le Gros Clark had an international reputation as an anatomist and an anthropologist, and is known by medical students worldwide for his book *Tissues of the Body*. Le Gros Clark never spoke to Bill, whose lasting memory was of a professor spending his time talking to the four female medical students in the year.

The Waynflete Professor of Physiology, Sir Charles Sherrington OM, FRS, was an internationally renowned neurophysiologist. When Bill entered Oxford, Sherrington was over 70 years of age, and in 1932 was awarded the Nobel Prize in Physiology or Medicine jointly with Professor Edgar Adrian of Cambridge. The prize recognised Sherrington's prolific studies of the nervous system, especially his description of nervous reflexes. Sherrington had arrived in Oxford in 1913, having previously served as Holt Professor of Physiology at Liverpool University. To medical students he was somewhat distant, and Bill encountered him only once, in a physiology practical. Sherrington was a strong believer in the individual experience, and argued that 'paradoxical though it may sound, the more skilfully a demonstration experiment is performed the less from it do some students learn.' He devised an extensive series of experiments on decerebrate animals for students to perform. This way of teaching was approved by the Board of Education, whose chairman noted that the course 'was an illustration of the kind of Applied Physiology which should, in my view, be taught in all schools of physiology.' In a class studying decerebrate cats, Bill had difficulty in locating the renal artery. Sherrington came over to Bill; it was the first and only time that Bill had seen the great man. Bill was asked, 'What is wrong, young man?' to which he replied, 'I cannot find the renal artery.' 'Give me your scalpel,' was the request from the professor. 'It is blunt!' he exclaimed and threw it over his shoulder. Sherrington then said, 'Scissors are nearly as good as a scalpel.' Bill passed his scissors to Sherrington. He tried to use them, but saw that the ends of the blades did not meet. This prompted Sherrington to say, 'You shouldn't insult this cat with these scissors,' and proceeded to throw those over his shoulder. Bill never saw Sherrington again. Another physiology teacher, but one far more approachable, was an Australian Rhodes Scholar, Dr J.C. Eccles. He had competed his PhD under Sherrington in 1929, and remained on the staff at Oxford for several years, before returning to Australia. In 1963 Eccles was joint recipient of the Nobel Prize in Physiology or Medicine with Andrew Huxley and Alan Hodgkin for their work on ionic mechanisms involved in the control of nerve function.

During his time in Oxford, Bill was involved in a number of sporting events, at both college and university level. He played hockey for Queen's and was awarded college colours. He also ran, his preferred distance being the mile, although he also competed in the steeplechase. He came across stiff competition in the mile from a Rhodes Scholar, also studying medicine. J.E. 'Jack' Lovelock was a New Zealander, who had commenced studying medicine at the University of Otago. After two years he gained a Rhodes Scholarship and in 1931 entered Exeter College, Oxford, to continue his studies. Bill became friends with Jack Lovelock, who soon made an impact on British athletics. In 1932 he set a British and Empire record in the mile and in the same year competed for New Zealand at the summer Olympics in Los Angeles. In 1933 he set a world record time for the mile. Bill could not beat Lovelock on the track and was later to describe him as 'The Roger Bannister of his time.'[15]

---

15 Sir Roger Bannister CBE (1929-2018) read medicine at Oxford before undertaking clinical studies at St Mary's Hospital, where he was taught by Bill Frankland. On 6 May 1954, Bannister became the first athlete to run a sub-four-minute mile, the race taking place at Iffley Road, Oxford.

Professor Sir Charles Sherrington

Jack Lovelock, representing New Zealand in 1936

Whilst at Queen's, Bill had his first introduction to rowing. One February, the boat club were looking to form a second and possibly third eight and asked if those interested would come to the river. Bill made his way through Christ Church Meadow on a cold afternoon, with sleet falling. Arriving at the boat club he was introduced to 'tubbing': practising rowing in a small, square boat, firmly attached to the bank, and using an oar with holes in it. This made a big impression on Bill who concluded that this 'was not sport, and it will not interest me.' Although he took no further part in rowing, many years later he was asked to advise one of the most successful Oxford rowing coaches, on a medical issue.

The Queen's College Oxford Athletics team 1933
Bill Frankland, standing far left

Despite being told not to join the Oxford Union Bill did listen to a number of guest speakers at the university. One still stood out over 80 years later. In November 1931 Mahatma Gandhi visited Oxford for just one day and spoke to a student audience which Bill felt numbered no more than 40, a remarkably small number considering the increasing prominence of Gandhi in India and the world. Bill, and several of his friends, also joined the Oxford Repertory Company, based in Woodstock Road. They would attend performances every Monday evening, since this was the first night of the new production. Part of the fun of the evening was to watch a permanent member of the company, who would always struggle with his lines, causing great amusement. There were also opportunities to see more accomplished performers and Bill remembered paying one shilling for a seat in 'the gods' to watch Noël

Coward and Gertrude Lawrence in *Private Lives*, which Bill recalled was 'wonderful'. Although able to visit a range of venues in the city, students were subject to strict rules for returning to college. At Queen's the front door would be shut at 9.05pm, corresponding to the end of the 100 chimes by 'Big Tom', the bell at Christ Church. However, if students were late all was not lost, since they could still gain entry to the college up until 10pm if they knocked on the front door.

Members of The Queen's College Oxford 1934
Bill is just behind the Provost

Back Quad, The Queen's College Oxford, December 2016
Bill Frankland, Honorary Fellow of The Queen's College Oxford, attending
the annual Boar's Head Gaudy

A Family Tragedy

In his last year at Oxford Bill was faced with a tragic family situation which almost caused him to give up his studies. In the summer of 1933 his sister Ella[16] was taken ill. She had suffered from scarlet fever when young and had developed renal complications. Her condition had deteriorated and she developed hypertension and pericarditis, and became bedbound. She also lost her sight. Bill returned home and took responsibility for her nursing care, staying with her at night as she slept. It was a difficult time for the family and Bill provided comfort

16 Ella had been educated at Casterton Girls' School, near Kirkby Lonsdale.

and reassurance for the last four months of Ella's life. She died in Bill's arms on 3 October 1933 and her funeral was held two days later at St Michael's, conducted by the Rev Ernest Danson. Ella is buried in the graveyard at Burgh-by-Sands, just opposite the Vicarage. Bill returned to Oxford a few days after her death, having done no academic work or even looked at a book for six months. On arrival he was summoned by his moral tutor and asked where he had been and what he had been doing. Bill felt that perhaps he should give up his studies, but then thought, 'I can't, not after all the help my parents have given.' He continued, and had to make up for his lost period of study. In the summer of 1934, A.W. Frankland graduated with a BA in Physiology, the degree being conferred in November of that year.

Grave of Ella Frankland, Burgh-by-Sands

From Bench to Bedside: First Impressions

After four years at Oxford, the time had come to move to a medical school for his clinical training. Although he had thoroughly enjoyed his time at Oxford, Bill summarised his education there as 'spending lots of time with parts of dead people and some live animals.' Not unsurprisingly he longed to work with patients and hoped to learn how to diagnose and treat their illnesses. He later described how 'solving the causes of people's illnesses would be like solving a detective story.' All Oxford medical students had to move on to another institution, since the university did not offer a clinical course.[17] Bill's earliest memory of St Mary's was attending his first teaching ward round led by Sir William Willcox, who was giving his last teaching round. Willcox was a physician and a Home Office pathologist and analyst who had had a far-reaching career. He had given evidence at numerous high-profile murder trials, including that of Dr Crippen in 1910, and had taught a number of forensic pathologists, including Bernard Spilsbury. Willcox was very much of the old school, and visited the hospital wearing a morning coat and top hat in his chauffeur-driven Rolls-Royce. Arriving at the Norfolk Place entrance of the hospital he was met by a porter who took his umbrella and hat and escorted him through the central doorway. This was normally never opened, but Willcox would not enter via the side entrance. Inside he met his registrar and at the top of the stairs was his houseman, whose duty was to see that the lift was already waiting. Moving up one floor to Princes Ward, the teaching round started. Bill noted that as soon as Willcox stopped by a bed, then a chair, carried by the most junior nurse in the ward, was made available for the rather portly gentleman. That morning, Bill witnessed Willcox teach on patients with a range of conditions including asthma, peptic ulcer and diabetes. He later wrote that this was 'a marvellous and very memorable beginning of clinical medicine for a junior student.'

---

17 The Oxford School of Clinical Medicine was established in 1936.

Bill Frankland 1934

A New Home

St Mary's Hospital, 1902

St Mary's Hospital Paddington was established in 1851, and was the last of the great voluntary hospitals to be opened in London. However, unlike other voluntary hospitals, St Mary's was the first to open with its own medical school attached. In the years prior to Bill's arrival in 1934 both the medical school and hospital had undergone major modernisation programmes, due mainly to the efforts of two very influential men. The first was Dr Charles Wilson, a physician and Dean of the Medical School. Wilson was a Yorkshireman who had studied medicine at St Mary's and qualified in 1908. It was noted that he spent a lot of time on the sports field, especially playing rugby, and failed to demonstrate 'a promising academic side.' He had little, if any, time for women in the profession. Like many of his generation, he had served with RAMC in World War 1 and was awarded the MC at the Battle of the Somme in 1916. He was appointed Dean in 1920, a position he held for 25 years.

Charles Wilson, later Lord Moran

The other highly influential member was the Professor of Bacteriology, Sir Almroth Wright FRS. Born in Yorkshire, the son of an Anglican priest, he grew up in Belfast and then studied medicine and modern literature at Trinity College Dublin, graduating in both subjects in 1883. He held a number of posts before being appointed as Professor of Pathology at the Army Medical School at Netley in 1892, where he started a lifelong interest in vaccination. In 1903 he was appointed Professor of Bacteriology at St Mary's Hospital and soon established a research institute, called the Inoculation Department. Here he developed vaccines against typhoid and paratyphoid (A and B), the vaccine usually referred to as T.A.B. During World War 1 he served with the RAMC at a research laboratory attached to 13 General Hospital in France, and recommended that his vaccine be used on members of the British Army. It was highly effective, and over 10 million doses were administered. The Inoculation Department continued to be involved in vaccine production, often in association with Parke-Davis and Company, for the next forty years. Noted for his intellect and arrogance, he was undoubtedly a polymath. Wright was fluent in a number of languages including Greek and he learnt Russian in order to read a number of important scientific papers. He was knighted in 1906, although was always referred to by staff and students alike as 'the old man.' Despite his many outstanding contributions to medicine, Wright's studies lacked a critical evaluation of data, and he was averse to using statistics. In many cases it was left to others to demonstrate the scientific basis (or perhaps lack) of his treatments. His relationship with medical education and the medical school was not an easy one, one student describing how he was 'a fierce, hoary lion of a man who never spoke to women, who hated students, and who refused to teach except for the few statutory lectures he had to give.'

At the end of World War 1 St Mary's was in a parlous state, with both its buildings and finances needing substantial investment. In 1918 plans were proposed for a new wing to the medical school but despite a campaign by staff and students, money was not forthcoming. When Wilson took over as Dean, the medical school was close to bankruptcy. He brought about many changes, not least in attitude, both in the classroom and on the rugby field. He was an enthusiastic supporter of rugby and due to him St Mary's reputation in rugby grew rapidly during his tenure. He was a strong believer in the need to study and understand people in order to get the best from them, and realised that attitudes were paramount to success.[18] Wilson proposed that the attributes of

---

18 Wilson would later describe his observations of men in battle in his book, *The Anatomy of Courage*, in 1945.

'unselfishness, fortitude and courage' were as applicable to medicine as they were to rugby. Under his leadership, student enthusiasm was noted to abound, both in academic and sporting pursuits, and staff themselves showed that they could embrace student antics. At the same time he had an unceasing quest for efficiency to make a good medical school.

Sir Almroth Wright

As Wilson attempted to obtain funds for the medical school the governors of the hospital were also seeking money for its rebuilding. This led to significant friction with Sir Almroth Wright, especially when Wilson tried to identify research that had emanated from St Mary's as a focus for the medical school campaign. Wright stated quite clearly that he did not wish to be associated with Wilson's plans. In a meeting he said, 'I want to warn you off making use of any of my work for propaganda purposes.' Despite this obvious tension Wilson pushed on regardless, with what colleagues described as 'the drive of the Devil', and one member of staff added, 'He will not let us alone to do our work. It's all committees and appeals.' The task before Wilson was epitomised by observations in 1928 by a medical student arriving at St Mary's who described the medical school as 'simply a house near Paddington Canal where students' rooms were in the hospital cellars and were disgracefully furnished'.

Despite the setbacks and even opposition from within parts of St Mary's, Wilson's determination paid off and he managed to gain funding from a number of sources. The first large bequest came in 1929 from the 2nd Baron Revelstoke, a senior partner at Barings Bank. This was followed by a significant contribution from the politician and newspaper proprietor, Lord Beaverbrook, who was a patient and personal friend of Wilson's. In 1928 land to the east of the hospital was purchased from the Grand Junction Canal Company, and three years later work began on the new medical school. Not only did the funds obtained by Wilson support the rebuilding programme, but they also allowed him to establish scholarships to enable students to study at St Mary's. There is no doubt that the entrance requirements for these involved both academic and sporting prowess, and because of Wilson's great interest in rugby, the awards soon became known as 'rugby scholarships.' However, they allowed the medical school to recruit a number of men who not only played (or in some cases, rapidly learnt to play) rugby, but also went on to make significant contributions to medicine, especially at St Mary's. These included George Bonney (orthopaedics) Jack Suchet (obstetrics) and Harry 'Felix' Eastcott (vascular surgery). The results were also apparent on the rugby field, where St Mary's was triumphant in the Inter-Hospital Cup every year from 1934 to 1939, having won it only once before in the history of the competition. Wilson remained a huge supporter of rugby at St Mary's, even after his retirement. Bill remembered one occasion many years later, attending the Inter-Hospital Cup final to watch St Mary's play. Wilson, now Lord Moran,[19] arrived with Lady Moran in his Rolls-Royce, parked up and watched the match being played under a blanket of sleet and snow. At the end of the match three very merry St Mary's students passed nearby and in loud voices wondered why 'old people came to the match'. Bill was near Moran and

---

19 Wilson was appointed as Physician to Winston Churchill in May 1940, and subsequently ennobled as the 1st Baron Moran on 8 March 1943.

was minded to draw the students to one side and tell them that without Lord Moran and his efforts and contributions, they would not have had any rugby at St Mary's.

While Wilson had been campaigning for the medical school, the governors of St Mary's Hospital had been progressing with their own appeal, advertising in 1930 how 'gifts of £7500 per annum' were needed to maintain their buildings. They exploited Sir Almroth Wright's connections, including Lord Iveagh (Rupert Guinness, the 2nd Earl of Iveagh) who donated £40,000 to allow redevelopment of the Inoculation Department. The governors also created a fund to allow building of wards for 'paying' beds, a fund which was augmented by the donation of £100,000 from one governor, Mr F.C. Lindo, and led to the building of the Lindo Wing. The efforts by all concerned were rewarded by the visit of The Duchess of York (the future Queen Elizabeth) in June 1931 to lay the foundation stone for the new medical school building. Barely two years later, in December 1933, King George V officially opened the new medical school and the extension to the hospital. On 15 November 1937, the now Queen Elizabeth returned to the hospital and officially opened the Lindo Wing.

St Mary's Hospital, 1930. Site for new Medical School

In 1934 St Mary's Medical School advertised that it was in 'a unique position, adjacent to a large district of over 500,000 poor people, and yet within a few minutes' walk of the delights of Kensington Gardens'.

It reported that over £250,000 had recently been spent on the medical school, with the provision of a library, restaurant, billiard room and a full-sized swimming pool, along with squash courts, a boxing ring and an underground garage for cars. In the same year Bill Frankland arrived to commence his clinical medical training. His choice of St Mary's can be traced back to connections at Dacre. Canon Hasell's elder sister, Henrietta, had married Henry Verey in 1876, and the following year she gave birth to a son, Henry Edward Verey. He served with the Army in World War 1 and was awarded the DSO. Retiring with the rank of colonel, he became Chairman of the Board of Management of St Mary's Hospital, and had paid for the construction of a swimming pool in the new medical school building. St Mary's was not the only hospital to have offered Bill a place, the Westminster Hospital Medical School wrote and offered him a scholarship. A year later, in 1935, when they had not seen him, they wrote again and asked if he was still intending to join them.

Teachers and Future Colleagues

Amongst the staff of St Mary's who taught Bill, several later became his colleagues when he joined the staff. One very influential member was Dr John Freeman, a lecturer in Bacteriology. He was described as a 'fine type of man, active and vigorous who was full of charm, and generous in his nature.' Educated at Charterhouse, he read medicine at Oxford, where his studies were interrupted when he served with the Oxfordshire Light Infantry in the Boer War. He undertook clinical studies at St Mary's, graduating in 1905. Like many of his era, he came under the influence of Sir Almroth Wright and pursued an interest in bacteriology. In 1906 Freeman persuaded Wright that he should appoint a newly qualified doctor to the Inoculation Department, for the sake of St Mary's Rifle Club, which they both belonged to; the young man in question was Dr Alexander Fleming. Freeman developed an interest in allergy early in his career, focussing on hay fever. He persuaded his old school friend, Dr Leonard Noon, a man whom Bill would later describe as 'a brilliant man', to join the staff at St Mary's and pursue an interest in allergic conditions. Both had been at Charterhouse together, where

Noon's father, James, taught mathematics. As pupils they were two of the few who studied science and were both excellent shots with a rifle. Noon entered Trinity College Cambridge where he excelled in Natural Sciences, gaining a double first, before moving to St Bartholomew's Medical School, qualifying in 1903. After positions at the Lister Institute and at Cambridge University, he returned to St Bartholomew's. In 1909 Freeman persuaded Sir Almroth Wright to offer Noon a position in the Inoculation Department, allowing Noon and Freeman to work together. Freeman later described him as 'probably the best brain that ever entered our famous laboratory.' They found work engrossing, usually not finishing until midnight and in some cases not leaving the laboratory until three in the morning.

Leonard Noon

John Freeman

Charles Blackley in 1873 had shown that the essential factor in causing hay fever was grass pollen. Noon explored the possibility that hay fever might be treated by immunising against grass pollen. He suggested that 'the form of recurrent catarrh was caused by a soluble toxin found in the pollen of grasses.' Noon went on to suggest that treatment might be achieved by administering very small doses of pollen in increasing amounts by subcutaneous injection and that this would provide 'active immunity against the pollen.' He undertook a study in which people suffering from hay fever received weekly and increasing doses of pollen prior to the summer period when hay fever was most symptomatic. The results were published in June 1911. This was the first paper to show successful immunotherapy in a cohort of patients, although, as Bill was later to point out, it was published just at the start of the pollen season. However, this was to be Noon's last paper, since, by the time of its publication, he was suffering from tuberculosis and died in December 1913. Freeman followed up Noon's patients in 1911 and recorded that the treatment had given benefit after the pollen season was over. In 1914 Freeman was appointed Lecturer in Bacteriology at St Mary's.

Not only was Freeman closely involved in developments in the field of clinical allergy, he was also a keen and talented marksman, whom Bill described as 'the marvellous benefactor of the rifle club'. St Mary's Rifle Club was very successful and Bill noted how it had won many cups and trophies. As a student Bill got on well with John Freeman, who he described as 'very kind' and who would lend him his 'vast car' (a Lanchester) at weekends. This allowed Bill to take other students down to Bisley for shooting competitions. Here Bill again found himself competing against his own university, shooting for St Mary's against Oxford, and on one occasion scoring 101 out of a maximum of 105. Bill was also able to use the car when working at weekends, being required to visit patients in their homes. When assigned to the community midwifery service Bill had to attend 12 births. He had to visit the mothers and their babies every day for the first week, and then every second day for the following week. On one occasion Bill drove Freeman's car to the Harrow Road, to see a mother and baby. This was a far from salubrious area and it was believed that in neighbouring Cirencester Street 'all the male residents had been in prison.' After completing his visit, Bill was offered a cup of strong tea which he accepted. He went back to the car only to find a number of 'rather grimy' children from the local area playing all over it, and leaving their mark. He returned the car to Freeman's home in Devonshire Place, and told Freeman's technician, Fred (who worked at the house) about the incident and asked him to clean the car. Fred replied, 'I always clean the car after you have borrowed it.'

For anyone joining the Inoculation Department one of their first tasks was to master the correct method of handling samples. Sir Almroth Wright had written a handbook in 1912 on the subject entitled *The technique of the teat and capillary glass tube and its application*, and it was essential reading for any new member, be they staff or students. Later, when qualified and working in the Inoculation Department, Bill recalled how everyone had to assemble for tea and listen to the great man speaking. Although he had a reputation for his scientific work, he would talk only about women, and 'how stupid they were.' He was a misogynist of the first order who had written widely in opposition to women's suffrage.[20]

Fighting Infection

Although St Mary's Hospital is today known for the discovery of penicillin by Alexander Fleming in 1928, Bill was to witness another pioneering advance in the treatment of infectious diseases. One morning in 1937 Bill was one of a small number of students taken to Queen Charlotte's Hospital in Goldhawk Road, Hammersmith, by Dr Leonard Colebrook. Colebrook, usually referred to by his nickname of 'Coli', was a bacteriologist, who had qualified from St Mary's in 1906, a direct contemporary of Alexander Fleming. He had fallen under the influence of Sir Almroth Wright and pursued a career in pathology and bacteriology. Initially working for the Medical Research Council (MRC) at Hampstead, he moved to the Inoculation Department, working alongside his mentor, Wright, and in 1930 was appointed as Director of the Bernhard Baron Memorial Research Laboratories at Queen Charlotte's Hospital. This maternity hospital, based on the Marylebone Road, underwent a significant rebuilding programme in the 1920s, funded by the MRC and the Rockefeller Foundation. The initial phase involved the erection of isolation wards for the treatment of women with puerperal fever, as well as research laboratories, all on a new site at Goldhawk Road.

Puerperal fever is a potentially lethal complication of childbirth, the result of infection by streptococci. Early studies into its control were made by the Hungarian physician, Ignaz Semmelweis, in 1850 and, although he had identified the mode of transmission, via the hands of doctors and nurses, his recommendations for prevention had been dismissed by the medical community. It would not be the last time that the results of scientific investigations of this condition would be rejected.

---

20 In 1913 Wright published a treatise, *The Unexpurgated Case against Woman Suffrage*, arguing that women had no right to the vote.

Coli had taken an active interest in the control and possible treatment of puerperal fever. He was described as 'primarily a laboratory worker, but one who cared intensely for individual patients, he was also an extraordinary perfectionist.' In the late 1920s the mortality rate from puerperal fever was about 30%. Coli had tried to persuade doctors and midwifes of the need to wear gloves and a mask when examining patients, but his advice appears to have been ahead of the time, and fell on deaf ears. He met huge resistance from senior medical staff, although interestingly gained support from junior doctors. At about this time he trialled the use of a new disinfectant 'Dettol' to reduce the bacterial load on the skin. Although used successfully at Queen Charlotte's, there remained strong resistance to its adoption at other hospitals.

When Bill visited Queen Charlotte's, he entered a hospital where Coli's research on puerperal fever was in full swing. To ensure adequate numbers for his scientific trials, Coli had arranged that half of all patients in Greater London with the condition were sent to Queen Charlotte's. Bill recalled seeing patients who had been treated with a new drug from Germany. A very prominent red line was added to the patients' notes, indicating that they were receiving the drug. Their charts showed clearly a very high temperature, but with the administration of the drug, their temperature fell rapidly, and they recovered. The drug in question was prontosil rubrum.

Prontosil was an azo dye that had been developed at I.G. Farbenindustrie in Germany in the early 1930s. It was noted to have antibacterial action, and a German bacteriologist, Gerhard Domagk,[21] successfully treated patients suffering from bacteraemia with Prontosil in 1935. Coli, on learning of this new agent, started a clinical trial in puerperal fever, the first woman receiving prontosil rubrum in January 1936. He reported that temperatures returned to normal within 1 to 4 days of commencing treatment. The impact on mortality was significant; in 1935 the mortality at Queen Charlotte's was 24%, but in 1937 it had fallen to 5.5%. Bill had witnessed the very first treatment

---

21 Domagk was awarded the Nobel Prize in Physiology or Medicine in 1939, but was prevented by Hitler from receiving it. He finally received the award in 1947.

of patients with what Coli would later describe as 'a new weapon in our hand which is going to prove very valuable.' Bill remembered that Coli, believing the bacteria may have altered as a result of treatment, undertook a small double-blind controlled trial, with some patients receiving the new drug and others placebo. This demonstrated the continuing efficacy of Prontosil, but the results were not published in a 'stand-alone' paper. By 1937, it was apparent that the mechanism of action of prontosil rubrum involved its breakdown in the body to para-amino-benzene-sulphonamide, and it was the sulphonamide (also called sulphanilamide) which had the ability to kill bacteria. It would not be long before Bill encountered another new drug which would have dramatic actions against infections, one discovered by Coli's medical school classmate.[22]

Leonard Colebrook

---

22 Colebrook was elected as a Fellow of the Royal Society in 1945. His nomination
paper recorded '…his outstanding contribution has been the extension
of bacteriological knowledge to clinical conditions. This has always been
characterised by good and well controlled techniques.'

Bill would meet Leonard Colebrook, some 40 years later. In the intervening years Coli had continued to make important contributions in a number of fields. He had served with the RAMC in World War 2 in France in 1940, overseeing the use of sulphonamides in casualties. As France was overrun by German forces he managed to escape from Saint-Nazaire on-board the Polish liner MS *Sobieski* on 16 June 1940. Fortunately he was not on-board the much larger British ship, SS *Lancastria*, which was bombed in the mouth of the harbour and sank with the loss of over 4000 lives the following day. Coli led the MRC Burns Unit at Glasgow in the early years of the war, and then moved to the Birmingham Accident Hospital in 1943. Here he worked with Dr Ethel Florey (wife of Professor, later Lord, Howard Florey of Oxford) on the newly available antibacterial, penicillin. He developed new techniques for controlling cross-infection of burns through air, developing pioneering systems of laminar flow, which would later form the basis for those widely used in orthopaedic surgery. He retired in 1951 but worked tirelessly to help prevent burns, lobbying for the introduction of the Fireguards Act (1952). In the 1960s Coli's wife developed severe respiratory symptoms and she sought Bill's professional opinion at St Mary's. Unfortunately he was unable to help her, since the problem was not one of an allergic nature, but a case of severe emphysema. At the consultation, Bill was accompanied by an attachment of medical students. After the patient and her husband had left, Bill asked if anyone knew who the gentleman was. Not a single student had heard of the man. Bill felt very disappointed that no one was aware of Coil, or of his contributions to medicine.

Student Life

At St Mary's Bill pursued a number of interests which were variously associated with the medical school. He was President of the St Mary's Gazette, a regular production distributed to staff and students. As such he was responsible for producing the gazette and had to ensure the agreement of Dr Mitchell-Heggs, a consultant dermatologist, before going to print. On one occasion a student wrote complaining that Dr Mitchell-Heggs had not given his 12 o'clock lecture, but had sent his registrar instead. The student, who by now was in Boston on a 3-month elective, wrote a three-page letter, describing the disgraceful situation of a consultant sending along their 'minor people' to give the lecture. Mitchell-Heggs was angry about such a blatant criticism, and refused to sanction its publication. With just one day before copy was due to be delivered to the printers, Bill was forced to leave three pages blank. The impact was felt far and wide, not only in the medical school and hospital but the whole saga featured in the *News of the World*.[23]

Bill continued with his sporting interests at St Mary's. By 1936 he was Secretary of the Hockey club, although the season was marred by the poor state of the ground at North Wembley, leading to many matches being abandoned. However, St Mary's had a good run in the Inter-Hospital Cup, reaching the semi-final against the London Hospital. In a tough match Bill scored 3 of the goals, with St Marys winning 4-2, allowing them to proceed to the final. Here, in a closely contested match, St Mary's lost to St Thomas', by a margin of 3-2.

A popular feature of the student calendar was the annual sports day, usually held at North Wembley in May, as it gave them all a good opportunity to meet the nurses socially, and when not on duty. Bill later wrote that there were invariably as many women as men at the event (there were no female medical students at that time) and how 'many St Mary's men met their future wives on those days.' In 1935, Bill went to his first St Mary's sports day and raced against Jack Lovelock in the mile, losing narrowly. Lovelock had entered St Mary's a year before Bill. He continued to excel in athletics, both for his hospital, and for his country. At that meeting, Bill watched his great friend David Foster compete in the quarter mile. With Bill's best distance being the mile, he made a wager with Foster for the prize of 6d. 'I will bet you that I can beat you in the half-mile, next year,' said Bill, with the view

---

23 About 30 years later, Bill was the Chairman of the Gazette, fulfilling the same position as Mitchell-Heggs. He recorded that he only stopped publication of one article, a joke which he considered 'too smutty'.

that this was twice Foster's best distance and half of his own. The following year, 1936, Bill beat Foster in the half-mile and won the bet; he also came second in the high jump, with a height of 5 feet 1 inch. His time in the half-mile, 2 minutes 15 seconds, was so good that he was ordered to the hospital trials. Running over the half-mile Bill won again and next he competed in the University of London trials held at their athletics stadium at Motspur Park. Bill won, and was selected to run for a university (of which he was not a member) against his own university, six years after entering the latter, in a competition held at the Iffley Road track in Oxford.

In 1937, St Mary's sports day moved to a new ground at Teddington. The move was at the behest of the Dean who had realised that many of the sporting activities of the medical school were held back by a lack of satisfactory grounds. Many of the playing grounds around London were waterlogged for much of the winter, since they lay on clay soil. Wilson obtained a geological map of London in order to identify areas where the subsoil was sand. Whilst doing so, land at Teddington came up for sale by Merchant Taylors' School. The soil was sandy and it was known that the ground drained well throughout the winter. The asking price was £2000 per acre. Wilson met significant opposition from his staff but he was able to purchase the grounds following a gift from Lord Beaverbrook. At the official opening of the new ground Wilson had invited a pole-vaulter from Cambridge to give a demonstration. He agreed, with one condition: that he landed in sand. This was agreed, and several lorry loads of sand were ordered to make a landing pit. When they arrived, the ground staff removed turf from the planned site, only to find sand underneath; the requirement of imported sand immediately fell significantly.

At sports day, Bill beat Foster in the half-mile, taking the lead in the last few yards. Later that afternoon, Bill raced in the mile, and won. The prizes were presented by Mrs Wilson, the Dean's wife. It was recorded that the 'afternoon's competition had been marked by the attendance of a representative from the Amateur Athletic Association who had brought with him an official starting gun.' This was a relief to many, since in previous years the official starter had been a surgeon from St

Mary's, Mr A.E. 'Arthur' Porritt.[24] A New Zealander and a Rhodes Scholar, he won a bronze medal at 100m in the 1924 Olympics in Paris and had been captain of his country's team at the 1928 Olympics in Amsterdam. At St Mary's he maintained his keen interest in athletics, acting as race starter, using a shotgun. It was noted that 'spectators kept a healthy distance when he was undertaking his official duties.' That year Bill again represented the University of London in the half-mile. At the trials the official starter was Jack Lovelock who was not racing, since the previous summer he had won the gold medal at 1500m at the Berlin Olympics. Later that season, Bill ran for the University of London against Cambridge University. He was beaten by Arthur Smith (a future international runner) who was about 12 seconds ahead at the finish; Bill had never seen anyone so far ahead at the tape. Following this defeat Bill decided that he was not going to become an Olympic runner!

Bill was to make many media appearances, especially later in his life, when he was able to look back on his exceptional career. However, his first appearance probably occurred in 1936. Students at St Mary's were approached to act as 'extras' for the film *A Yank at Oxford* being filmed at Denham Studios. It was an early start from Marylebone as they caught a train before 7am, allowing them to return the same day on a ticket costing 1 shilling. The star of the film was the American screen idol, Robert Taylor, described as 'tall, handsome and very athletic', supported by Vivien Leigh and Maureen O'Sullivan. During the intervals between filming, Taylor talked to Bill and his colleagues and gave them his potted life history. He was Italian by descent but had changed his name to an American one. His father was a doctor, and his parents wanted Taylor to pursue a medical career, but he had failed his exams. He opted for a career in acting which had, in fact, been his first choice. During filming he undertook all his own sporting scenes, including rowing for Oxford in a mock-up of the Oxford-Cambridge Boat Race; he was a member of the winning team. For Bill, being an 'extra' meant a lot of hanging around, so he, and his friends, passed the

---

24 Later Sir Arthur Porritt, who served as Governor General of New Zealand 1967-72, and was ennobled in 1973 as Baron Porritt of Wanganui and Hampstead.

time by playing bridge. On one occasion, a game was in full swing as the leading actors were waiting nearby for the sun to come out. At the exact moment when the sun emerged, Bill realised he had a good hand and shouted out, just as Robert Taylor was saying to Maureen O'Sullivan, 'I love you.' Courtesy of Bill's interruption they were forced to reshoot the scene. However, Bill saw the day as a great success, especially since they were each paid 20 shillings.

A Doctor in the House

In 1937, with finals not far away, Bill was one of 35 students who wrote to the medical school seeking extra tuition. Noting that 'the standards of medical finals had increased significantly', they asked if extra lectures could be provided to cover specialised subjects in the medical curriculum. Those identified included ENT, neurology, venereal diseases and dermatology. At the completion of medical training, students in the 1930s were able to gain the right to practise through a number of routes. They could sit the final examinations offered by their university, and for Bill this was Oxford (since he was never a member of the University of London), or by obtaining a 'basic medical qualification.' For the latter, two routes were available. The English Conjoint Diploma offered by the Royal College of Physicians of London (RCP) with the Royal College of Surgeons of England (RCS) led to a Licentiate of RCP and Membership of RCS. Bill felt that this was an expensive examination and instead opted for the Licentiate in Medicine and Surgery of the Society of Apothecaries (LMSSA), which was about one-fifth of the price. There was also another advantage to the Apothecaries examination, since Bill found that all the examiners were charming. Students normally took one, or perhaps two, papers at a time. Somewhat unusually, Bill took three papers in January 1938, passing in Medicine, Forensic Medicine, and Midwifery. He sat the final paper, Surgery, in February 1938. The examiners included C.A. Pannett, Professor of Surgery at St Mary's, who had the reputation of being 'the most dreaded examiner for the final part of FRCS.' When Bill entered the room, Pannett was surprised to see him, and asked him what he was doing there. As Pannett knew

Bill, he could not ask him any questions, so passed him over to his co-examiner. Bill was presented with a patient suffering from carpal tunnel syndrome, and he ran through the examination very smoothly, giving all the answers required. The examiner then asked if Bill had more answers, at which Pannett interrupted and said, 'You best repeat the answers, my co-examiner is deaf.' Bill passed.

Although now able to practise medicine, Bill still intended to take the final examinations at Oxford. He returned to the city in June 1938, where the examination took place at a number of venues, including several hospitals. Men sitting the examination did so in *subfusc*, wearing white bow ties. He remembers arriving at one examination hall to be greeted by one of the few female students, a non-medical student, shrieking as she rushed out of the examination room; whether she ever passed remains a mystery. In the ENT examination, he was presented with a patient suffering with nasal polyps and a perforated nasal septum. After examining the patient, he reached the correct diagnosis and was well placed to discuss the case with the examiner, who commented that 'You must have been qualified already.'

Having completed his clinical training at St Mary's, Bill, like other students, sought locum positions. It was an unwritten rule that if a newly qualified doctor took a position at his own hospital, it was viewed as an honour for them, and they received no salary. By contrast, working at another hospital allowed the doctor to earn money. Bill contacted a lady who ran a locum agency to seek a position but made one stipulation: he did not want a surgical post. She asked if a position in Chichester would suit him. Bill replied yes, since his future father-in-law had a cottage nearby at West Wittering, and went sailing from Chichester Harbour. One hour later she rang back, 'Could he start tomorrow?' to which the answer was 'Yes.' Having agreed to the position he was informed it was in psychiatry at Graylingwell Hospital, just outside Chichester. Although initially appointed for a month, Bill spent five months at Graylingwell, and thoroughly enjoyed himself. He had 'his own tennis court, terrific food and his own maid.' Amongst the patients were several women who had been treated over a prolonged period with bromide for their mental health issues, leading to toxicity, itself affecting their behaviour.

Bill recalled treating these patients with sodium chloride, to replace the high levels of bromide, and within a day they were back to normal.

Bill Frankland at West Wittering 1938, with, left to right,
Pauline Jackson, Melody Jackson and Roland Jackson

Bill started his first established post, as House Physician at St Mary's to the Dean, Sir Charles Wilson,[25] in late 1938. As a junior doctor, applying for a post of houseman at your own teaching hospital, it was deemed to be an honour to be selected by the establishment, and was rewarded with neither a contract nor a salary. Only two people had applied for the position, Bill and Henry 'Cocky' Cockburn, the latter a member of the First XV, where he played alongside the English international T.A. Kemp. Cockburn also played for the Barbarians. Everyone thought that it a foregone conclusion that Cockburn would be appointed, in light of Wilson's great interest in rugby, and many were surprised that Bill had even applied. When it came to selection Wilson asked his senior registrar, Dr Taylor, to set a question for both applicants to answer. Taylor was to assess the answers, and advise Wilson who should be appointed. Much to everyone's surprise, Bill was successful, although initially many

---

25 Wilson had been created a Knight Bachelor in the New Year's Honours List, 1938.

thought Wilson (who had a nickname of 'Corkscrew Charlie', as he was always changing his mind) might actually appoint Cockburn. He didn't, and many felt how lucky Bill was. In his position he was entitled to a room with a bed and a telephone, and his keep. He was able to supplement this by earning £64 during the six months from providing legal reports and by attending at inquests. During those six months Bill rarely saw Wilson, the only times being those Saturdays when St Mary's First XV were playing at home. When this happened, Bill would ring up Wilson on the Friday night and tell him what teaching material was available on the wards. Next morning Wilson would teach brilliantly for two hours on patients he had never seen before.

Work for a newly qualified doctor was very hard, and when on 'full duty' Bill was responsible for the Casualty department.[26] He recalled that there were both a surgeon and obstetrician assigned to Casualty, but the rule of thumb was that anyone presenting with abdominal pain was to be treated as a medical condition until proven otherwise, although as he pointed out, 'most were either surgical or obstetrical'. One case he saw during this time remained with him throughout his life. Very early on a Saturday morning, he was rung in his room. This room had previously been a laboratory where Alexander Fleming had identified penicillin, some 10 years earlier. He was asked to see an emergency, a lady with her very sick child. He arrived in Casualty to find a mother with her baby. Bill found the body was cold; the baby had been dead for some time. The mother gave a history that her child had suffered from acute chest trouble for 3 days. Bill was not convinced, having noted signs of bruising around the child's throat. A post-mortem was ordered which was undertaken later that morning by the senior registrar in pathology. He found no obvious pathology in the lungs, or anywhere else, and it was Bill who pointed out the bruising around the neck. Just at this point the Professor of Pathology, Professor W.D. Newcomb, arrived, and strongly suggested that 'the examination need go no further', since the lungs were apparently normal. Bill was quite sure that this was a case of murder: the parents had had seven children and the father had

---

26 Now called Accident and Emergency (A&E).

served at least one prison sentence. Nearly 80 years later he considered that this was his worst medical mistake, having not realised that the mother's history was all lies.

Other cases also stood out. One evening, Bill had finally cleared Casualty when a young lady arrived, just before midnight. Complaining of abdominal pain he took a history and then examined her, only to find an abdominal tumour. To his surprise the tumour started to contract, and about five minutes later he helped deliver a healthy baby. He admitted her to the hospital, and a porter took mother and baby up to Zunz Ward,[27] the obstetric ward. The following morning Bill was keen to know how his patients were. He called into Zunz Ward and asked Sister where they were. He was told in no uncertain terms that the woman was 'an Irish lady and unmarried' and therefore had been moved to Harrow Road Hospital. St Mary's was not an establishment where unmarried mothers should be giving birth. Almost a month later a very similar episode occurred. A woman arrived at Casualty in labour and Bill immediately transferred her to the obstetric ward. The following day Bill went to check on her, only to be greeted by the ward sister who informed him: 'Dr Frankland, you are making a habit of this. She was unmarried and we've got rid of her.'

---

27 The full name was Annie Zunz Ward, named following a gift of £25,000 left to the hospital by her late husband, Mr S.R. Zunz.

CHAPTER 3

TO SERVE HIS KING
AND COUNTRY

Joining Up

As the storm clouds of war gathered over Europe during the summer of 1939, Bill Frankland did not like what was happening in mainland Europe, having previously gained first-hand experience of the situation in Germany. In the summer of 1937 Bill was a member of the Old Cranleighan Hockey Club party which toured Northern Europe. Bill's departure was delayed slightly, as he was hosting a 'thankyou' cocktail party in London, the one and only time he ever hosted such an event. Consequently, he missed the first match in Antwerp, but caught up with the team in Germany. The players stayed with local families in their homes and at breakfast Bill noted there was no butter to put on toast; his hosts were following Hitler's orders of 'guns before butter.' As Bill travelled through Germany he saw the impact of Nazi persecution, with destruction of Jewish shops. He also saw young Germans marching off to work at 6am; there was no unemployment in a country preparing for war. At the hockey matches the touring players were ordered to give the Hitler salute, they refused and at the end of the match they stood to attention and sang 'God Save the King'. They played in Hamburg and Hanover and won all their matches, except the last. In this, the visitors lost to a team from East Prussia and Bill put this result down to the 'good party' they had had the night before the game.

Bill enlisted in the Army as a Civilian Medical Practitioner (CMP) on Friday 1 September 1939. On that day Germany invaded Poland, and two days later Neville Chamberlain, acting for the British people, declared war on Germany. Bill felt it was his duty to serve and knew that the armed forces would need doctors, and he was now in 'the right place at the right time.' He had always been proud of being English, and was proud to fight for his country. He offered to go to the garrison town of Tidworth in Wiltshire, having previously worked there as a locum, and was now to earn £1 a day.

Tidworth Military Hospital was built in 1907, and would be Bill's home for exactly one year. During that time he thoroughly enjoyed being responsible for 150 hospital beds along with the isolation hospital. He had barely unpacked when, on Sunday 3 September, all the regular medical officers left as they were posted to fighting regiments, leaving him in sole charge, having to work 16 hours a day for the next 6 months, before any help arrived.[28]

Early on at Tidworth Bill encountered a number of senior officers. As a CMP he was not constrained by King's Regulations and was able to deal with these as he would wish, regardless of their rank. Perhaps the most notable was Major General A.P. Carton de Wiart VC, often called 'The Unkillable Soldier.' Born in 1880, he had joined the Army in 1899 and served in the Boer War, where he was wounded. At the outbreak of World War 1 he served with the Somaliland Camel Corps where, in action against the dervishes of the Mad Mullah, his elbow was shattered and he lost his left eye. Following hospital treatment he was provided with a glass eye which he immediately threw away, preferring an eyepatch. Next he served in France, and at the Second Battle of Ypres in 1915 was hit by shrapnel, causing significant injury to his left hand. Despite medical care he remained in persistent pain and insisted on amputation of the hand. Returning to France he was in action at La Boisselle on 3 July 1916, in the early days of the Somme Offensive. For his gallantry he was awarded the VC, and the citation read: '…his conspicuous bravery,

---

28 Unknown to Bill, on 3 September at St Mary's Hesket-in-the-Forest, the reading selected by his father was from Ephesians 6:13: *Therefore put on the full armour of God, so that when the day of evil comes, you may be able to stand your ground, and after you have done everything, to stand.* Henry Frankland had moved from Burgh-by-Sands to the living at Hesket-in-the-Forest in 1936.

coolness and determination…. His dauntless courage and inspiring example.' Two years later he was injured again, sustaining a wound to the hip which became septic. By the summer of 1918, he had become such a frequent visitor to his hospital in London that they retained a pair of his pyjamas, in anticipation of his next visit. Following the Armistice, Carton de Wiart lived in Poland but returned to Britain just before the German invasion in September 1939. He was attached to the Royal Artillery at nearby Larkhill where he was reviewed by their medical officer. Carton de Wiart was informed that he would only be deemed 'fit for home service', a decision that displeased him immensely.

Major General Carton de Wiart

Unhappy with the real possibility of his military service being confined to Britain, Carton de Wiart sought Bill's opinion. He told him what categorisation he wanted, namely to serve anywhere in the world, and informed Bill that 'the doctor just signs the form' and so expected it to happen. Bill replied, 'You have been abroad, I know nothing about you and am going to examine you fully. You need to make a special appointment.' This was a new experience to 'The Unkillable Soldier' who was far from impressed with Bill's professional attitude. However, realising that without the completed paperwork his military service would be very dull and boring, Carton de Wiart relented. When Bill undertook his examination he was struck by the number and extent of scars on the man's body, as well as the number of missing bodyparts! Bill was able to sign him as 'fit for service in all theatres of operation.' Barely six months later, Carton de Wiart led the Anglo-French forces to Namsos, just north of Trondheim, part of the brief and unsuccessful Norwegian Campaign of April 1940.

On 10 November 1939, after a few months at Tidworth, Bill was commissioned as a lieutenant, in the Royal Army Medical Corps (RAMC). He travelled to London to a military outfitter to acquire his new officer's uniform, but one part was old: his Sam Browne belt, which Bill inherited from his father. To Bill, wearing the Sam Browne was carrying on a tradition that there were things worth fighting for. He explained: 'We were told to fight for our country, and this is what we were doing. And I was lucky that I was an officer and so it was to me a privilege to wear something that my father had worn in the First World War.'

Henry Frankland had given his son advice on his military service, most noticeably that he should be 'wary of military nurses.' His reasons related to his own service in World War 1 on-board a hospital ship where he had encountered a soldier with a serious leg wound. The man had not been vaccinated against tetanus and the nursing sister told him he would receive anti-tetanus serum. The soldier, aware that the anti-serum was produced in horses, told the nurse that he was allergic to horses, and should not receive the anti-serum. Sister replied that 'it was not for him to decide what treatment he should receive, that was a case for the nursing staff.' The man, now very concerned indeed, talked with the Rev Frankland about his situation. However, Frankland was serving as a padre, not a doctor, and felt powerless. Worse was to come, since the anti-serum was administered and the man was dead within 10 minutes, the result of anaphylaxis.[29]

One of the first military nurses that Bill encountered was a Sister in the regular Army whom, he noted, 'seemed to be more interested in polishing objects in the wards rather than looking after patients.' Her

---

29 Later in his career Bill Frankland was appointed Honorary President of the Anaphylaxis Campaign, a charity which supports those at risk of severe allergic reactions.

attitude became even more obvious when soon after his arrival he, along with Sister, commenced a ward round of all 120 beds in the hospital. They had seen about half the patients by lunchtime, and Bill said he would do the rest of the ward round on Wednesday afternoon. He was quickly informed that 'We never do serious work on a Wednesday afternoon', causing Bill to reply, 'But Sister, there is a war on!'

Just a few days after Bill arrived at Tidworth, men and women in Australia were responding to Prime Minister Robert Menzies' decision to support Britain and France, and declare war on Germany. The ranks of the Australian armed forces swelled, especially after the introduction of conscription in November 1939. The first troops left Australia in January 1940 and were sent to support British forces in the Middle East. On 4 May 1940 RMS *Queen Mary* left Sydney carrying Australian troops. This was her first voyage as a troopship, and she sailed in convoy with six other liners, including RMS *Aquitania*, *Mauretania*, and SS *Empress of Japan*. Heading west, they took 16 days to reach Cape Town, and many on-board expected they would follow earlier convoys and head north to the Middle East. However, whilst crossing the Indian Ocean, important developments occurred in the European war, as Germany invaded France, Holland and Belgium. German forces were now advancing rapidly towards the English Channel and Britain faced the real threat of invasion. The convoy was ordered to sail to Britain to provide much-needed support for Britain's defence. *Queen Mary* anchored at Gourock, to the west of Glasgow, on 16 June 1940. The convoy had brought some 14,000 Australian troops, described as 'of highest quality, but not fully trained or equipped'. They disembarked the following day and by 18 June Australian soldiers had arrived on Salisbury Plain where they were billeted at Tidworth, Amesbury Abbey and Lopcombe Corner. Here they formed 25th (Australian) Infantry Brigade which was deployed as a mobile force behind the beaches of Southern England, sites where there was a real risk of invasion.

In June 1940, Bill was faced with an outbreak of meningococcal meningitis[30] amongst British soldiers of Southern Command. Of 100

---

30 A potentially life-threatening bacterial disease caused by meningococcus *syn Neisseria meningitidis*.

cases, he treated 99 successfully, and the only death occurred in man who also developed a brain abscess, and died from an epileptic fit. Accurate diagnosis required a lumbar puncture followed by treatment with sulphapyridine. Bill became adept at making the diagnosis, and issued instructions that any serving soldier with a temperature over 100 °F was to be referred to him for diagnosis. Just as this outbreak was abating, the contingent of Australian troops arrived in the area, bringing with them their own medical conditions.

In the convoy which sailed from Australia, two liners each carried one man suffering from the viral disease, mumps. Within the confines of each ship, the disease spread rapidly and by day 10 of the journey many hundreds were suffering with classical mumps. Mumps may lead to a range of side effects and complications, perhaps the most well-known being orchitis. A much rarer complication is meningoencephalitis. With the arrival of Australians at Tidworth, Bill was soon faced with a large number of patients suffering from the side effects of mumps; of the 234 presented to him, nearly 30% had meningoencephalitis. He recorded how this could occur in patients with no other obvious side effects. Bill treated the first five cases with sulphapyridine, and in three of these, symptoms actually worsened. He soon found that supportive treatment of aspirin and phenacetin along with copious glucose and fruit drinks was best. When a senior officer visited Tidworth he was impressed by Bill's regimen for treatment and commented that 'he was a most clever doctor.' He asked Bill what tests he used to differentiate between patients with meningococcal meningitis (requiring sulphapyridine), and those with mumps meningoencephalitis needing only supportive therapy. Bill's answer was quite simple: he spoke to the patients, and if they replied with an Australian accent they had mumps meningoencephalitis, and were treated accordingly!

In early summer 1940 Bill received some medical help with the arrival of a consultant physician at the hospital. No sooner had the man arrived than, on a Sunday morning, Bill found himself unwell, suffering from a sore throat, anorexia and vomiting and was confined to his bed. Despite this, his commanding officer ordered him to undertake a ward round. He did so but, halfway through, almost collapsed. The consultant physician was summoned from the golf course, examined Bill and observed a prominent rash on his chest. With the diagnosis of scarlet fever confirmed, Bill was immediately placed in isolation. Not surprisingly, he was very concerned about his prognosis, especially as his sister Ella, and two of his uncles, had died from complications of scarlet fever. Worried about his renal status, he collected a urine sample and approached the Australian doctor who was in charge of the isolation hospital, requesting a urine analysis be performed. The colleague showed no interest at all, so instead Bill asked the nurse who was caring for him, Sister Naomi Davies QAIMNS.[31] Henry Frankland had had a poor opinion of nursing sisters from his service in World War 1 and told Bill not to get 'too friendly with them.' However, Bill found that Sister Davies was very different; she was a friendly person, rather 'bouncy', and did not consider herself to be superior (unlike many QAIMNS nurses). Bill remained in isolation for about a week, and made a slow but steady recovery. His only treatment was careful nursing and Bill remembered that Sister Davies insisted he be given tea in a china cup, rather than a mug, since he 'was an officer', and on the day of his admission she brought him a plate of sandwiches; it was the first food that he had eaten since his illness had started.

Not long after Bill's recovery, Sister Davies moved to a new appointment as matron of a military convalescent hospital at nearby Ludgershall; however, their paths would cross again in the not too distant future. Bill was fortunate to have been nursed by Sister Davies and to have had no input from his Australian colleague. It transpired the latter administered sulphonamide by injection to a number of soldiers with disastrous consequences. Ignoring the manufacturer's clear instructions, he had given twice the maximum injectable dose, on the grounds that this was 'life-saving.' Bill later encountered many of the patients who were suffering from tissue damage at and around the injection site in the buttock; several had damage to the underlying sciatic nerve, leaving them useless for military service.

---

31 Queen Alexandra's Imperial Medical Nursing Service.

In November 1940, Bill wrote a letter to the *British Medical Journal* [32] detailing some of the dangers of sulphapyridine when injected into the gluteal muscles. Subcutaneous injection could lead to sinus formation and ulceration, whereas deep intramuscular injection carried with it the risk of injury to the sciatic nerve. Bill had seen six cases of foot drop following injury to the nerve, and, although some recovered, one patient still had a foot drop after 3 months. He recommended that 3ml was the maximum dose which should be injected at any one site, and suggested that complications were more common following administration by the intramuscular route when given by inexperienced clinicians.

With the Warwickshire Lads

After exactly one year at Tidworth, Bill was posted as Medical Officer to the Royal Warwickshire Regiment's (RWR) depot, and soon after was promoted to the rank of captain. The regimental depot was situated at Budbrooke Barracks, on the outskirts of Warwick. The Royal Warwickshire Regiment dates back to the mid-17th century, and its illustrious history records amongst its commanding officers, Lieutenant Colonel B.L. Montgomery DSO, who was appointed in 1931. In September 1940, men at Budbrooke included members of the 2nd Battalion who had escaped from France in May 1940 in Operation Dynamo. During the campaign, the battalion had lost many men, including soldiers killed at Wormhoudt in May 1940. [33]

---

32 Frankland A.W., Dangers of Sulphapyridine. *British Medical Journal*, January 1941, p33.

33 The Wormhoudt Massacre was an atrocity undertaken by the Waffen SS on 28 May 1940. 100 Allied prisoners, including many injured, were herded into a barn on the outskirts of Wormhoudt. The Germans threw hand grenades into the barn, killing many prisoners. Those still alive were taken outside and shot in groups of five. Only six prisoners survived.

Captain A.W. Frankland RAMC

Bill had his own hospital at the barracks, a facility which was overstaffed so that he found himself free of duties from lunchtime each day. There was plenty of time for sport, and Bill was able to play tennis at Leamington Spa Tennis Club, some 5 miles away. Bill was not the most senior medical officer at the barracks. That distinction fell to a rather old lieutenant colonel, who would arrive at work each morning at 11am. After a glass of sherry and a review of the newspapers, he would sit down for lunch. His interest in the patients was effectively non-existent, and he would undertake a cursory ward round once a week. He was surprised to learn that Bill treated patients suffering from pneumonia at the barracks, since previously these cases had been sent to civilian hospitals at Warwick or Leamington Spa. Amongst his many duties, Bill had to sit on medical boards, assessing the health and fitness of soldiers. At Budbrooke he would often work alongside his colonel, whom he found completely useless. This contrasts with his experiences at Tidworth where he sat on medical boards with Major W.J. O'Donovan OBE RAMC. Donovan was a well-respected dermatologist who practised at the London Hospital and had been the Conservative Member of Parliament for Mile End from 1931 to 1935. Although regarded as very unconventional, both as a consultant and as an officer, Bill found Donovan to be very straightforward and efficient in the medical boards.

Whilst at Budbrooke, Bill found he broke one of the cardinal rules of an RAMC doctor by talking 'shop' in the mess. One lunchtime a newly commissioned young officer came into the mess and sat opposite Bill. Bill learnt that the man had been an undergraduate at Cambridge, and gained a blue in hockey. He also noticed that the man had a 'lazy left eye' and asked him, 'How did you get a hockey blue with such poor eyesight?' Bill stopped himself straightaway, realising he had committed a 'terrible crime of talking shop', and realised that if he had been overheard by a senior officer, the young officer may have been dismissed the service there and then. In an attempt to placate the situation, Bill asked if the man would visit him at his medical inspection room that afternoon.

Later that afternoon the young officer called on Bill, who immediately apologised for 'talking shop', but asked if the man had a visual deficit. Yes, was the reply and he went on to say that Bill was the first doctor to note that he was blind in his left eye. Since joining up he had taken three eye tests and on each occasion he always learnt the letters in the bottom line of the sight test card as he walked into the room. When asked to close one eye, he always shut his left eye; no one had picked up on this. Despite having problems with his left eye, his right was sound and Bill thought this would not affect his ability to use a rifle, since only the right eye was used. After his time at Budbrooke the officer served with the 2nd Bn Royal Warwickshire Regiment, was promoted to the rank of major, and despite his visual defect, had a most successful war, being recommended for a gallantry award, although this was not confirmed.

Bill's responsibilities extended to troops stationed at nearby Warwick Racecourse. Many had severe COPD (chronic obstructive pulmonary disease), having been heavy smokers. Bill observed that in many cases symptoms worsened at the time of a full moon. This was linked to the smokescreen produced to protect Coventry from aerial bombardment and inhalation of the smoke exacerbated their respiratory symptoms.

One patient whom Bill clearly remembered was a colonel who had recently retired from the Army, but rejoined at the outbreak of war. He appeared to be a charming and educated man who, before the war, had lived in Monte Carlo with his German wife, a lady several years his junior. They returned to Warwick at the outbreak of hostilities and he presented to Bill on several occasions complaining of gastric problems which, although long-standing, were very vague. In fact the problem appeared to be linked to the fate of his wife, who being German, had been locked up in a flat in Leamington Spa as an 'undesirable alien.' Bill decided to refer the officer to a psychiatrist, and wrote a letter of referral which he gave to the man; in this he referred to the patient's domestic issues. The colonel arrived at the barracks where transport was waiting to take him to his appointment in Lichfield. Bill handed him the letter of referral, which unfortunately was not sealed, a move which proved a huge mistake. The patient read the referral letter before departing, and was far from pleased with its contents, especially its reference to his wife. He asked Bill how he knew about his wife, since it was meant to be a complete secret. Bill advised him that he had been informed in confidence of the issue and he would not divulge by whom. The patient flew into a tirade, directing abuse towards Bill who was more than a little taken aback by the way he had been addressed. He replied that he thought the colonel 'to have been an officer and a gentleman, but was in fact neither!' The patient was eventually examined by the psychiatrist, and he advised that officer be discharged from the Army on medical grounds, a decision supported by many senior officers.

Bill's encounter with another psychiatric patient at Budbrooke presented him with an opportunity to use some of his 'quasi-medical' skills. Bill had taken an interest in hypnosis several years earlier, having witnessed it as a medical student. Before long, he was able to spot those people who were candidates for hypnosis, and hypnotise them. Whilst at Tidworth several soldiers had been presented to him, unable to use their fingers, so could not pull the trigger of a rifle. Using hypnosis he was able to help them overcome the problem, a feat he later described as 'rather showing off' on his part. Before long his patients found themselves deemed fit for military service, and several were sent to join the British Expeditionary Force in France. At Budbrooke, Bill had one patient in hospital who was suffering from a psychiatric disorder. On the weekly ward round held by his colonel, the latter took no interest at all in the patient, a decision which annoyed Bill immensely. The hospital was overstaffed with nurses and there was not a great pressure on beds, so Bill decided to keep the man in hospital for a further week. During this time Bill hypnotised the man, telling him that when approached by the colonel the man should give a Hitler salute. This appeared to work, and on the morning of the ward round, Bill duly hypnotised his patient. As the colonel approached the bed and asked why the patient was still in hospital, the man gave a Hitler salute. 'This man is mad,' the colonel said to Bill, 'Yes, Sir, and I have been trying to tell you that for some time,' replied Bill. His ploy had worked.

Another patient who challenged all of Bill's investigative powers was a young RWR officer, who repeatedly went sick just before a full moon, and was found to be drunk at this time. When examined by Bill, the man was unable to walk in a straight line. From further investigations Bill learnt that the officer became drunk, fearing the bombing of nearby Coventry. He was not the last patient whom Bill would encounter where drunkenness was used in an attempt to ameliorate the impact of an enemy's actions.

Budbrooke lies about 12 miles south of Coventry, and in 1941 Bill saw the city come under repeated heavy bombing from the Luftwaffe, causing widespread damage. At Warwick Racecourse, men of the RWR were billeted along with a number of conscientious objectors, so-called 'conchies', many of whom later joined up after seeing the result of German bombs falling on Coventry.

In his role as medical officer, Bill had use of two ambulances, one a Ford, the other a Bedford, for collecting and transferring sick men. The drivers were young women, and one in particular made a lasting impression with Bill. She hailed from Blackpool where her father appeared to 'own half of the town', as well as his own aeroplane. Bill recognised that she was a very good driver, although lacking in knowledge on the ways of the Army. On one occasion she returned late and drove right through the quadrangle of the barracks, coming to a halt between the adjutant and a number of officers. This was not the way to return Army equipment, and the next morning Bill was summoned by the commanding officer and berated for 'employing a poor driver, and especially one who had no understanding of Army etiquette.'

Bill and companions

Many of the young men called up to serve with the RWR were from the local area. After their initial three months of training they were granted a long weekend of leave, returning to their families. Many used this as an opportunity to ask their general practitioner to write a letter saying that they could not return on medical grounds. This became increasingly problematic, and if they had not returned by Monday, Bill would venture out in one of the ambulances to try and retrieve them. When finding an absentee he gave them a choice. Either they could return with him in the ambulance and be admitted to his hospital or, if they were fit, they would resume normal duties. One man stood out. Bill found his address near Stratford-upon-Avon, and drove to his home. As he pulled up he thought he glanced a man digging in the garden, but was not sure. Knocking on the door, a lady finally opened it. Bill explained the situation, and the lady replied that her husband had been very ill with a temperature and a doctor had been summoned. Bill asked to see the man, and was taken to the bedroom where the soldier lay in bed, apparently very ill. However, Bill noticed he still had his muddy boots on. With his cover broken, the soldier was ordered to the barracks there and then, where he immediately returned to full duty.

A Married Man

On 27 May 1941, Bill married Miss Pauline Jackson. Pauline was born in 1913, the eldest daughter of Mr and Mrs Rowland and Winifred Jackson. Her father was a stockbroker in the City of London. During World War 1 he served with the Royal Naval Reserve, at Sandringham, manning a unit which was a Rolls-Royce Sedan with an anti-aircraft gun mounted on the back. Pauline and her sister, Melody (born in 1917), grew up in London.

Pauline and Melody Jackson, 1923

Pauline and Melody attended Francis Holland School, near Sloane Square in London, and Saint Felix School in Southwold, Suffolk. In 1934, their mother died suddenly and the sisters took a flat on the Embankment in the newly built Dolphin Square. Pauline studied in Knightsbridge at what was called a 'pre-bride' course, after which she should have been well placed to find a husband. She then joined St Mary's Hospital working as an orthoptist, and it appears likely that she had some help in gaining the position from a relative, Mr Frank Juler, Surgeon-Oculist to the King's Household and Consultant Ophthalmologist at St Mary's.

In 1937, as junior medical students, Bill and his colleagues would each pay two visits to the eye department, and two to the ENT department, in order to be taught the fundamentals of these specialities in preparation for final examinations. He remembered entering the eye department and seeing a blonde girl with beautiful blue eyes, and immediately thought he should get to know her. On his second trip he met her again and was convinced that he needed to know more about her. The opportunity soon arose since the hospital employed two senior medical students to be responsible for outpatient departments attached to the eye and ENT departments. This position could provide a great opportunity for Bill but, as he later commented 'it was risky, this was a very busy job.' He applied, was successful and, despite still being a medical student, was given a long, white coat;[34] soon everyone called him 'doctor.' The appointment was for 6 months, during which time he had to work hard, but as he later reflected, 'there was time to get to know Pauline well.'

Bill and Pauline became engaged in the summer of 1940, in Oxford. Their wedding preparations the following year felt the full force of Hitler's attack on Britain. They had planned to marry in Chelsea Old Church which was just a short walk from Pauline's home in Petyt Place. Plans had to be hastily rearranged when the church was attacked with parachute mines on the night of 16/17 April 1941. These caused significant damage, with the west tower collapsing onto the church. Services would not be held there for many years, and their wedding was rearranged to take place at St Leonard's, Chesham Bois, Buckinghamshire. As Bill later remarked, when it came to marriage he was rather a slow worker!

The weeks leading up to the wedding had been a period of frantic

---

34 Medical students would wear short, white coats.

organisation, responding to the change in circumstances. On 5 May, Bill wrote to Pauline, describing how he had been very busy, added to which his senior officer had gone away for the weekend and left 'a whole pile of work.' Writing 'settled in the sun, but a little disconnected in my thoughts, as Ken Lane has just arrived and is asking me all the gossip,' he wrote that 'Daddy can marry us on Saturday 24th. They also think that Jack can get off, what do you think?'

Bill punting at Oxford, Summer 1940. On the reverse is written 'Engagement Ring Day'.

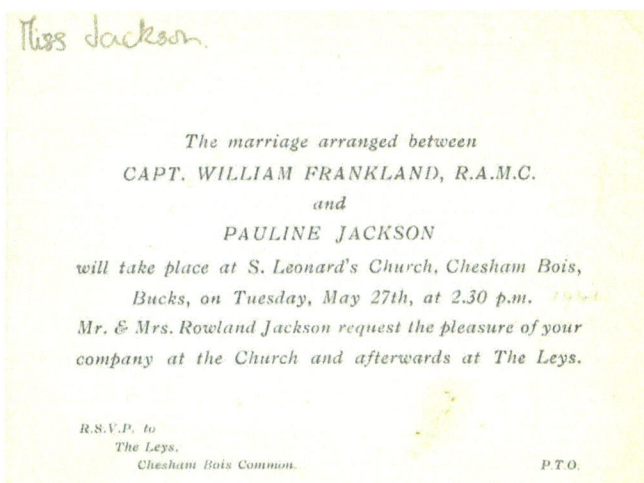

Wedding invitation

Bill arrived at Chesham Bois on Sunday 18 May and wrote in the visitors' book 'Last time single.' After a week of preparation, the wedding took place at 2.30pm on Tuesday 27 May 1941, and the service was conducted by Bill's father, Rev Henry Frankland, who had travelled from his home at Hesket-in-the-Forest. Pauline, who was now serving as a VAD[35] at the Queen Alexandra's Military Hospital (which had been evacuated to Watford) was given away by her father, and she had one bridesmaid, her sister, Melody.[36] Bill's best man was his brother, Jack, who was now ordained and serving as curate at St Mary's Church, Ulverston. Bill insisted on one aspect of the wedding, namely that Pauline wear a sprig of lily of the valley, so that he could smell the scent during the ceremony. After the service, a guard of honour was formed for Captain and Mrs Frankland by the Frobisher Battersea Crew of the Sea Rangers (of which Pauline was skipper), along with members of the 2nd Chesham Bois Brownie Pack. The reception was held nearby at The Leys, Chesham Bois, home of Mr and Mrs Maurice Strode.

Although the newly-weds had been offered a flat for their honeymoon, they were both keen on getting away to Devon. Bill had written how he was going to 'beg, borrow and steal all the petrol I possibly can' in order to do so. In fact, one of their wedding presents was 2 gallons of petrol, which was enough to travel to Devon. They left immediately after the wedding reception and drove to Lynmouth where they stayed at The Bridge Hotel for the week. They spent their time walking on Exmoor but also ventured to sea. Pauline arranged for them to go out with local fishermen checking lobster pots. She was totally at home on the water, loving every minute of the trips, whereas

---

35 Voluntary Aid Detachment, a voluntary unit of civilians providing nursing care for military personnel.

36 In 1943, Melody married Dr John C. Ryle, who was serving with the Royal Naval Medical Services. They made their home at Drapers' Hall in Shrewsbury. Later, Pauline and Bill would visit at Christmas, but there would often be disagreements over attending Christmas activities. The Ryles were opposed to attending church and the Boxing Day Hunt, whereas the Franklands were keen to attend both. John Ryle's brother, Martin (later Sir Martin), was an astronomer who shared the Nobel Prize in Physics in 1974.

Bill found himself without his 'sea legs' and was almost seasick. At the end of the week, they had just enough petrol to motor home.

Captain and Mrs Frankland leaving St Leonard's Church
Bill's twin brother, Jack is standing behind next to Melody Jackson.

Captain and Mrs Frankland passing the guard of honour

FRANKLAND—JACKSON.

The marriage of Capt. William Frankland and Miss Pauline Jackson took place at St. Leonard's Church, Chesham Bois, last week. The ceremony was performed by the Rev. H. Frankland, Vicar of Hesket-in-the-Forest, father of the bridegroom. The bride, who was given away by her father, Mr Rowland Jackson, wore a dress of a delicate eau de nil colour, with hat and short veil to match, and carried white carnations and lilies-of-the valley. She was attended by one bridesmaid, her sister, Miss Melody Jackson, who wore a dress of dusky pink and carried a bouquet of yellow and mauve irises. The Rev. J. Frankland was the best man. The church was prettily decorated with wild apple blossom, tulips and narcissi. The congregation included a detachment of nurses from the Queen Alexandra Military Hospital (now at Watford), where the bride is serving as a V.A.D., and also several Sea Rangers of the Frobisher Battersea crew, of which the bride is Skipper. The Sea Rangers, with the 2nd Chesham Bois Brownie Pack, formed a guard of honour as the bride and bridegroom left the church. The service was choral, the hymns being " Lead us, Heavenly Father, lead us," " O Brother Man" (Songs of Praise), and " Jerusalem." During the signing of the register, Bach's " My heart ever faithful," was sung as a solo. After the ceremony, Mr and Mrs Rowland Jackson held a reception at The Leys, Chesham Bois, lent by Mr and Mrs Maurice Strode, and later the bride and bridegroom left for a short honeymoon in Devonshire.

MCDOUGALL—BELL.

Report of Bill and Pauline's wedding in the local paper

Setting Sail

After one year at Budbrooke, Bill was informed that he would be serving abroad. He sailed from Liverpool on-board QSMV[37] *Dominion Monarch* on 29 September 1941. The 27,000-ton ship, owned by the Shaw, Savill & Albion Line, was launched in July 1938 at Swan Hunter yard on the River Tyne. She was a refrigerated cargo passenger liner which could

---

37 Quadruple-Screw Motor Vessel.

accommodate 525 passengers, all in first-class. Described as 'a ship with a rather unusual appearance, with long, sweeping lines, elegant superstructure and twin funnels', she sailed on her maiden voyage in February 1939 from London to New Zealand. In August 1940 she was converted to a troopship, enabling her to accommodate 1500 troops. At the same time she was armed with two guns, one salvaged from the 1899 frigate, HMS *Venerable*. The second was an anti-aircraft gun whose arc of fire had to be restricted, to avoid its shells hitting her funnels.

Dominion Monarch sailed as part of convoy WS12[38] made up of 19 ships, carrying more than 41,000 troops. The convoy sailed down the River Mersey on a Sunday, through a grey mist and the following morning those on-board saw their last sight of English coast, at Blackpool with its famous tower. For many, including Bill, it would be a long time until they saw the British coast again; for others, it was to be their last glimpse of their own country. As they sailed north they were joined a day or two later by vessels sailing from the River Clyde. Soon the convoy ran into a heavy storm, causing all of the barrage balloons to break their mooring lines and be lost. *Dominion Monarch* had a cruising speed of 22 knots, but was reduced in convoy to 16 knots, this being the speed of the slowest ship in the convoy. The ships sailed west, towards the eastern seaboard of America, with an initial Royal Navy escort of three destroyers and one cruiser; by the time they had crossed the Atlantic they were accompanied by just one destroyer.

Bill was one of a group of 35 RAMC doctors on-board and all were unclear as to their final destination. At the time Bill felt that they may be sent to the Middle East. Also on-board were a number of QAIMNS nurses, including Sister Naomi Davies, who had nursed Bill at Tidworth the previous year. The ship also carried some 1700 men of 137 Field Regiment, Royal Artillery, known as the 'Blackpool Regiment.' This was a territorial unit, raised in Blackpool in the summer of 1939, recruiting local men. They had spent the early part of the war training in North-

---

38 WS series were fast-moving convoys taking both equipment and troops to the Middle East, India and the Far East. They were sometimes also referred to as 'Winston's Specials'.

West England before moving south to the School of Artillery at Larkhill, on Salisbury Plain. There, in mid-August 1941, they were ordered to mobilise, being alerted to the possibility of 'deployment to tropical regions.' One of their officers, Lieutenant Hartley, wrote a series of letters home during the voyage. He described how it was 'pleasant but boring', but noted that the food was 'excellent', and that they were able to swim in the pool every day. On-board *Dominion Monarch* Bill shared a cabin with two other doctors, and had the top bunk. He recalled that on one occasion he had a nightmare, and fell out of his bunk, landing with a heavy thump on the cabin floor.

Dominion Monarch

The ship reached Freetown, Sierra Leone, on 14 October, but no one was allowed ashore. They set sail again on 19 October, and Bill described how their crossing of the Equator coincided with a U-boat alert. Avoiding action was taken rapidly, causing the ship to cross the Equator at least three times in a sinuous track as she eluded the enemy. The convoy headed south to Cape Town, arriving on 29 October, where shore leave was granted. It was at Cape Town that Bill discovered that on docking a telephone line was immediately put in place between the ship and the dock, allowing medical officers on-board to talk with their local counterparts. Bill spoke with a local medical officer and asked about the issue of smallpox; the doctor replied that there was none in Cape Town. However, Bill challenged this, pointing out that there was known to be smallpox in Africa, and that Cape Town was part of Africa; reluctantly the South African doctor had to agree with Bill. As a result, Bill ordered that only men who had been vaccinated against the disease could disembark. Four unvaccinated men were most upset, and soon were reporting to Bill's clinic in order to receive the vaccine.

Those on-board were very excited at the prospect of time ashore, as they had been at sea for over a month. Bill recalled that they were treated marvellously by the city's residents. However, it was not all good news, as one medical officer had to remain on duty, and this was to be Bill. He was very disappointed not to be going ashore, but luckily was approached by a senior, and experienced, officer, Major J.W. Malcolm OBE MC & Bar RAMC. Malcolm had served in the Army since 1915, seeing service in both war and peace, and in a number of countries, from France to China. He was awarded the MC in 1917 and a bar in 1918. Both citations recorded his 'conspicuous gallantry and devotion to duty.' 'You want to go ashore,' asked Malcolm, to which Bill replied, 'Yes,' and Malcolm agreed to assume the role of duty medical officer.

Bill ventured ashore as quickly as possible, taking a tram from the docks to the centre of Cape Town. Whilst on the journey he encountered the system of apartheid for the first time. A pregnant coloured woman boarded and Bill immediately gave up his seat for her. This act of good manners caused mayhem; the tram stopped and the woman was ignominiously ejected. This left a lasting impression on Bill. Arriving in the city centre, Bill quite fortuitously met a fellow St Mary's man, Surgeon Lieutenant I.S. 'Ivan' Jacklin RNVR.[39] Born in South Africa in 1917, his father was a diplomat at the League of Nations. Jacklin initially attended school in Pretoria and then followed his brothers to Cranleigh in England, where he excelled at rugby. In 1935 he entered St Mary's with a Dean's Scholarship, and was remembered for his 'charming manners and shy smile.' His headmaster had written that he was 'a gentleman by birth, breeding and instinct and his influence on all around him has always been for good.' Like so many St Mary's men, he combined his academic studies with a strong commitment to rugby. He captained the 2nd XV which beat the previously unbeaten 1st XV, and then helped St Mary's win the Hospital Cup in his first year. He was selected as a county player, and continued to represent St Mary's up until qualifying

---

39 Royal Naval Volunteer Reserve.

in 1940. Jacklin was noted at St Mary's for being a 'demon for work.' Upon qualifying he had proven to be a very competent house surgeon and subsequently joined the naval reserve in January 1941. Bill and Jacklin went to a Turkish drinking club where drinks flowed freely, and Bill, not being a great drinker, soon found that he had drunk more than enough. Now, somewhat unsteady on his feet, he bade farewell to Jacklin,[40] and returned to his ship where he was immediately informed that he was now back on duty and there was work to be done.

A naval rating had sustained a wound which was in need of treatment. Fortunately Bill had the services of an RAMC orderly who prepared all the instruments and materials, including threading the suture needle (since Bill found this too difficult) and the operation proceeded. Bill awoke the next morning, fearful that he had not tied the sutures. To avoid embarrassment of his surgical shortcomings at a sick parade, Bill requested to review the patient in a separate clinic that morning. He was relieved to find that all the sutures were intact and of an appropriate standard.

Dominion Monarch sailed from Cape Town on 5 November, this time in a small convoy with the troopships RMS *Empress of Canada*, and SS *Duchess of Richmond*. By now it was clear that they were not heading to the Middle East, but instead were destined for the Far East. They sailed to Colombo, Ceylon, arriving on 23 November, escorted by HMS *Glasgow* and, at times, HMS *Repulse*. The following day, *Dominion Monarch* and *Empress of Canada* sailed with *Glasgow* (which was relieved by HMS *Dragon* on 26 November) to Singapore, arriving on 28 November 1941.

---

40 Jacklin served in HMS *Kent*, *Griffin* and *Express*, the latter an escort for HMS *Prince of Wales* and *Repulse* when they sailed to Singapore in December 1941. Bill would never see Jacklin again. In March 1943 Jacklin, who had recently married, travelled to the UK on board RMS *Empress of Canada*. Sailing from Durban to Takoradi, she was carrying some 1800 passengers, mostly Italian prisoners, along with Greek and Polish refugees (the latter having previously been imprisoned in the Soviet Union, and released after the German invasion of Russia). Late on 13 March, after two weeks at sea, she was attacked by the Italian submarine, *Leonardo da Vinci*, and started to sink. The submarine launched a second torpedo whilst passengers scrambled to leave the helpless vessel. At this time Jacklin gallantly went down

As Bill was often to point out, they arrived a week before the critical events of Pearl Harbor.

into the sick bay to help bring up patients, including many terrified members of the Women's Royal Naval Service. The ship sank in 12 minutes. Later Jacklin was seen swimming and helping passengers into lifeboats, as well as tending to the wounded. When he could do no more he got into one of the crowded lifeboats, only to find it so tightly packed that he got out and hung on the back of the boat. In the morning he was gone, perhaps taken by sharks which were seen to attack those in the water. Nearly 400 people were killed in the attack. Survivors later testified to Jacklin's 'wonderful courage.' Arthur Dickson Wright, Consultant Surgeon at St Mary's, was later to write: 'He was the most outstanding man St Mary's had seen for many a long day and it will be long before we see his like again.'

CHAPTER 4

MEETING THE ENEMY

Fortress Singapore

The outbreak of war in the Far East can be traced back to the Japanese invasion of Manchuria in 1931 followed, in 1937, by their invasion of the eastern provinces of China. This was followed by the establishment of their own government in Nanking. However, as the Japanese expanded their sphere of interest, and with that, their military forces, they became increasingly reliant on importing raw materials. Most important of these was oil, 80% of which was bought from the USA. In Japan moves were afoot to circumvent this, to acquire their own sources of raw materials by further expansion, and creation of the 'Greater East Asia Co-Prosperity Sphere.' In a number of calculated steps, the Japanese government prepared for further expansion and in September 1940 Japanese troops entered French Indochina at the invitation of the Vichy government. At the same time Japan signed the Tripartite Pact with Germany and Italy.

Military strategists, responding to the potential Japanese threat, concluded there were two possible routes for an attack on Malaya; either from Thailand across the border, or a landing on the east coast. The Japanese however, were fully aware of the British line of thinking and of their plans for defence, having obtained a copy of the Chiefs of Staffs' secret report on the defence of Malaya in 1940. In what now seems remarkable folly, the report had been sent to the General Officer Commanding Malaya on-board the merchant vessel SS *Autonedan*. The ship had been attacked by a German vessel in the Indian Ocean on 24 September 1940 and, despite a heroic counter-attack by her crew, she was crippled. German boarding parties blew open the strongroom and found a heavily sealed bag of government mail. This contained a range of naval and military intelligence reports, including the plan for the defence of Malaya. This was duly sent from Berlin to Tokyo, where Japanese intelligence officers were delighted to be able to study the British plans.

Britain sent military reinforcements to Singapore in the summer of 1939, dispatching an Indian infantry brigade, and further troops were sent from India towards the end of 1940. The first Australian troops arrived in Malaya in February 1941. Winston Churchill took a keen interest in the Japanese expansion, but his views changed over the year leading up to the invasion. In December 1940, he wrote of his concern that Japan is 'thrusting southward through Indo-China…bringing them within a comparatively short distance of Singapore.' Only a few months earlier, a significant number of Japanese fishery boats were sighted off the coast of Malaya, apparently investigating the mouths of rivers. This had been reported to the Director of Fisheries, who informed the authorities. He was somewhat taken aback to be told to 'mind his own business!' In what appears to have been a confused situation, where political and military strategy was rather disjointed, Churchill voiced his criticism of plans to send reinforcements to the Far East. In August 1941 he opined that Japan would not pursue aggressive action against the combination of Britain, Russia and the USA,[41] whilst still heavily involved in military operations in China. Even as *Dominion Monarch* was sailing towards South Africa in October 1941, Churchill remained doubtful that Japan would launch an attack in the Far East.

Bill arrived in Singapore on 28 November 1941, finding a city that he later described as 'very relaxed in so many ways', and where the prospect of war seemed unbelievable for most of its residents, many knowing little about the war in Europe or the Middle East. The colonial way of life continued unabated, with dances at Raffles and other hotels. The vast majority of residents were of the view that Singapore could not fall, a sentiment echoed at the time by the Governor, Sir Shenton Thomas. The initial plan for the 35 newly arrived doctors, fresh off *Dominion Monarch*, was for them to be posted to Johor Bahru, at the southern tip of Malaya,

---

41 Russia had entered the war in June 1941, following the German invasion. At this time, however, the USA still remained neutral.

where a new General Hospital was to be formed. No sooner had the party arrived than they were informed that the plan had changed. They were to remain in Singapore where Bill was posted to an Indian Field Hospital. By the end of 1941 there were more than 50,000 Indian troops serving in Malaya, making up 3 (Indian) Corps and supporting these were elements of the Indian Medical Service. Posted to his new unit, Bill was given his own batman, an Indian. On the first evening he was informed that they 'dressed for dinner', something he found somewhat strange, having just lived through two years of bombings in England. However, he had seen that the lights were still on in Singapore, and war seemed a long way away. The batman asked if he wished him to 'dress and undress' Bill for dinner, and before an answer could be given, the man was trying to remove Bill's trousers. 'Get away!' Bill called; he was certainly not having anyone remove his trousers.

Four days after arriving in Singapore, Bill and another new arrival, Captain R.L. 'Lance' Parkinson RAMC, were summoned to a meeting with a senior officer. Parkinson was born in 1911 and hailed from Alderley Edge, near Wilmslow in Cheshire, qualifying from the University of Manchester in 1938. In September 1939 he joined the Army and was later posted as Medical Officer to Tŷ Croes Camp on Anglesey. Here he met a young FANY[42] officer, Sheila Kershaw, who had recently returned from working in Kenya and Palestine. They married in the summer of 1941, knowing full well that he was likely to be posted abroad before too long. It was just a few months later that Parkinson sailed in the RAMC party on *Dominion Monarch*, taking with him an engraved gold cigarette case. His wife later recalled how they believed that if all else failed, and they had no money, they could always sell the cigarette case. In November 1941 Sheila Parkinson received news that her brother, Lieutenant J.M. 'Michael' Kershaw, had been killed whilst serving with the Royal Horse Artillery in North Africa, near Tobruk. He had with him an engraved silver cigarette case, a present he received when he was 21. This was returned to Sheila Parkinson a few months after his death.

---

42 First Aid Nursing Yeomanry.

Captain R.L. Parkinson RAMC

Captain Parkinson did not agree with the war and, unlike Bill, who had volunteered to serve his King and Country, Parkinson had been drafted into the Army. In his discussions with Bill he made it quite clear that his sights were set on the end of hostilities, and a career as an obstetrician. Bill did not form a high opinion of the man, feeling that he was very much self-centred in his actions and beliefs. At the meeting, the senior officer informed the men of two postings to be filled, one at the newly opened Alexandra Military Hospital, administering anaesthetics in the minor operations theatre, and the other at Tanglin Military Hospital, where the caseload was dermatology and venereal disease (VD). Bill said he was very bad at giving anaesthetics and was much more interested in dermatology, and would like to go to Tanglin. Parkinson did not want to be assigned to Alexandra Military Hospital. To break the impasse, the officer took a coin from his pocket, spun it and said, 'Frankland, you call.' Bill shouted, 'Heads!' He was right, and was posted to Tanglin.

Tanglin Military Hospital

Tanglin Military Hospital was established in 1912, and had been the main military hospital in Singapore until the opening of Alexandra

Military Hospital in July 1940. From that time Tanglin specialised in the treatment of skin conditions and venereal diseases. When Bill arrived at Tanglin his commanding officer was Lieutenant Colonel W. H. Cornelius RAMC, a doctor who had seen service in World War 1. Just a few months earlier, Cornelius had reached retirement age, although he continued to be employed in the Army. The hospital diary for November 1941 portrays an air of relaxation, with Cornelius departing on leave in the middle of the month. Command of the hospital passed, temporarily, to the second in command, Major L.E.C. Davies RAMC. Aged 32, he was born in North Wales. After attending Rugby School he read medicine at Brasenose College Oxford and then St George's Hospital London, qualifying in 1936. Davies was granted a commission in the RAMC in August 1939, and was appointed Dermatologist to Malaya Command in March 1940. Bill recalled that Davies was a very good golfer, despite a physical handicap; Bill was unsure if this was the loss of an eye or a damaged arm.

Meanwhile, continued expansion of the Japanese sphere of influence in the Far East during 1941 had caused further tension between Tokyo and Washington, with the latter imposing economic sanctions as well as freezing Japanese trading assets. Despite Churchill's reluctance to accept the reality of Japanese intentions, the prospect of war seemed imminent to his military commanders. On 29 November all British and Australian forces in Malaya were ordered to report to their units, and on 2 December the Governor declared a state of emergency, responding to reports of Japanese warships north of Borneo in the South China Sea. At this time Tanglin's state of readiness was raised and Lieutenant Colonel Cornelius returned from leave. On Monday 8 December the unit diary recorded that 'Singapore was attacked by Japanese planes. State of war exists.' The war in the East had begun, with the bombing of Singapore coinciding with the attack by Japanese aircraft on the US Pacific Fleet at Pearl Harbor, Hawaii and the invasion of Hong Kong. The raid on Pearl Harbor occurred on Sunday 7 December, due to Hawaii lying on the 'other side' of the International Date Line. These attacks came without a declaration of war by the Japanese and took many around the world by surprise. For Bill, however, it was a case of having had a premonition, being told in 1940 by a representative from the War Office that the Japanese would 'declare war in a strange way, possibly on a Sunday.' That prediction was not far from the truth.

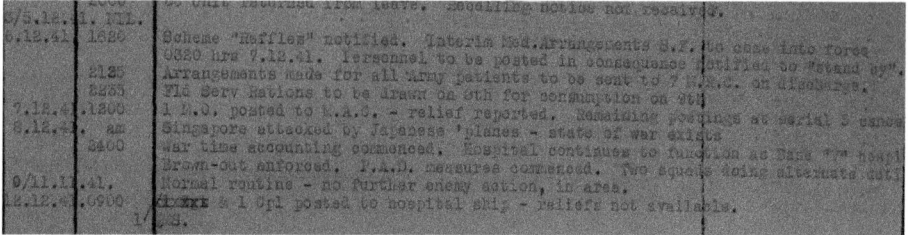

Entry from Tanglin Military Hospital, detailing that 'state of war exists' on 8 December 1941

The first attacks by Japanese aircraft on Singapore took place early in the morning of 8 December when the city's lights were still on, and caused 300-400 casualties. Bill was painfully close to the very first attack as a bomb dropped near to Tanglin. He remembered hearing a bomb fall, and instinctively sought safety under a bed just before the bomb exploded. The main thrust of the Japanese attack on Malaya had taken place in the early hours of 8 December when a seaborne invasion took place at Kota Bharu, on the north-east coast of Malaya, just south of the Thai-Malay border. At the same time troops landed in Thailand, making their way across the border towards North-West Malaya. Tanglin was to come under repeated bombardment in the weeks that followed. On one occasion Bill was about to examine a patient, the wife of a fellow officer, who had sprained her ankle. As she arrived at the clinic, an air raid started. Both Bill and his patient threw themselves into a nearby malaria drain for shelter. They were lying head to feet when the bombs dropped, and shrapnel was sent in all directions. One piece of shrapnel just missed Bill's head and landed very close to the lady. He picked it up to dispose of it, but burnt his finger and thumb; as he was later to remark, 'it was the only war injury I sustained'.

As hostilities intensified, Tanglin Military Hospital increased its capacity to 260 beds by the end of December 1941 and expanding into nearby infantry barracks. The most difficult conditions amongst the patients were tropical ulcers: at any one time the hospital had over 40 cases. Tropical ulcers usually occurred on the legs, most commonly below the knee, and often appeared where the skin had been traumatised by brushing against bamboo or lalang grass in the jungles of Malaya. The incubation period was variable, from a few hours to a few days, and was followed by extensive discolouration of skin and subcutaneous tissues. No specific organism was isolated from these lesions, although most reports indicated a 'mixed staphylococcal infection' and it was suggested this was a result of the ulceration, not the primary cause. As the condition progressed, the central region of the ulcer would slough, allowing a dark, viscid fluid to exude. The disease could spread deep into bone and/or tendons, especially in poorly nourished patients or those with concurrent disease. Swelling of the leg occurred, often preventing the patient from putting on their boots. Ulcers were at first painful, but with time became painless. This condition was extremely difficult to treat. Drugs had apparently little effect, and dressing the wound proved to be the most beneficial treatment. Some ulcers responded to surgical excision, although the scar tissue which formed was often very disabling. Tropical ulcers rarely healed in under 100 days, often taking twice that time. Doctors would be challenged in treating tropical ulcers over the next five years, and were to find that in some patients, amputation was the only option to eradicate the condition.

Gonorrhoea was the commonest venereal disease amongst soldiers, followed by syphilis; for both treatment options were limited. Although sulphonamides were now starting to be used for these conditions, it would be several years before penicillin became available. Before the war, the issue of brothels in Singapore had been highlighted by the DDMS[43] as 'disgraceful', and there had been criticism of the civilian authorities for failing to control the prostitutes. Bill had experience of managing soldiers with venereal disease, whilst serving at Budbrooke Barracks: any soldier who spent time with a prostitute had to wash themselves out thoroughly. If they failed to do so and contracted the disease they were immediately placed on a charge. In Singapore venereal diseases

43 Deputy Director of Medical Services.

were diagnosed almost exclusively in soldiers, most having acquired infection through their visits to ladies plying their trade in Lavender Street in Singapore. However, Bill was faced with at least one officer who had acquired an infection, and recalled how the whole affair was 'hidden' by the medical authorities. Bill had intended to visit the 'street of shame' on 9 December to identify the women responsible for passing on venereal diseases, and treat them. However, as events unfolded, the ever-increasing workload in response to the hostilities prevented Bill from pursuing this line of medical investigation.

Although Lieutenant Colonel Cornelius was listed as the Commanding Officer at Tanglin, Bill remembers another officer who, although not directly attached to the hospital, did a far better job of running it, and one whom Bill greatly admired and described as a 'marvellous man, who was very easy and helpful.' This was Lieutenant Colonel A.R.F. Clarke MC RAMC, who commanded a locally raised unit, No 1 (Malaya) Field Ambulance, at Tanglin. He had qualified from the University of Edinburgh in 1915, and then joined the RAMC, serving in the Middle East, where he was awarded the MC. Following demobilisation, he emigrated to Australia, but re-enlisted at the outbreak of war.

As hostilities continued on the island, civilians started to leave, and tried to sell their belongings. One lady offered Bill her car, 'a rather smart Hillman' for £100, but he replied that he would not even give her £1 for it. He did not need a vehicle since he was able to borrow Clarke's car, allowing him to explore the island and visit the Tanglin Club. Bill described this as 'very posh', whereas one colleague was more forthright, calling it 'the most snobbish place ever.' Every time he visited, Bill remembered seeing one lady member who was always there wearing a 'huge diamond ring.' Bill was able to swim and play bridge at the club, his bridge partner being another medical officer at Tanglin, Captain C.D. Chilton RAMC, a Welshman who would later enter general practice in Lewisham, London. At the end of December 1941, Major E.M. Hennessy RAMC, a regular Army officer, and an Irishman, assumed command of the hospital from Lieutenant Colonel Cornelius.

Mess Secretary

At Tanglin, Bill's duties extended beyond the care of patients. He was appointed as the Mess Secretary, a job for which he admitted he had 'no idea what it involved.' Despite this he was most successful, and by selling cigarettes and alcohol, he made a handsome profit, so much in fact that after two months there was no longer a need to raise mess charges from any officers. With Christmas approaching he was determined to show that Tanglin could host a fine celebration, despite the ongoing hostilities. By Christmas the Japanese advance in Malaya was proceeding at pace. The island of Penang had been evacuated on 16 December and the retreat of Allied forces continued in northern Malaya. On 25 December the first Japanese broadcast was made from Penang and news was received of the fall of Hong Kong. Despite this, many in Singapore still believed that they were not at risk.

Bill's first Christmas meal was actually eaten at Alexandra Military Hospital, where he was a guest of their officers' mess. He felt it was a good occasion, but was determined that the Tanglin event would be better. Bill's Christmas menu commenced with soup, followed by a main course of chicken, and finishing with Christmas pudding. There was one problem; the main course was so well appreciated that many guests asked for a second helping. Not wishing to disappoint, Bill talked with the Chinese chef who had prepared the meal on his own, and two of Bill's own laying chickens were rapidly dispatched, and cooked. None of the guests was aware of the behind-the-scenes action, and all agreed that Bill had surpassed the Alexandra meal. Afterwards, Bill sat down and wrote to his wife, Pauline, telling her that he had probably had a far better Christmas meal than her, despite there being an air raid in Singapore at the time.

Royal Naval Base Sembawang

Following the end of World War 1 the British government took the decision to build a large naval base in the Far East. The site was to be Singapore. Although the decision was made in 1923, construction of the new facility on the north-east of the island at Sembawang was slow, at times in the extreme. Royal Naval Base Sembawang was finally completed in 1939, and hosted the largest dry dock in the world. Military strategists believed that any threat of Japanese hostility would easily be met by dispatching the fleet to Singapore. In August 1941 Churchill, despite his earlier suggestions that Japan would not pursue an aggressive stance in the region, had written to the First Sea Lord, suggesting that a force of modern capital ships be sent to the Far East in order to deter any Japanese aggression. Force Z was dispatched in October 1941. This was to be composed of the battleships HMS *Prince of Wales* and *Repulse*, the aircraft carrier HMS *Indomitable* along with a number of frigates and destroyers. In the first of many setbacks, *Indomitable* ran aground in the Caribbean and had to enter dry dock for repairs. This left the naval contingent effectively lacking air support. Bill remembered Force Z arriving at Singapore on 2 December; many there felt that its presence would be more than enough to deter the risk of a Japanese invasion.

Less than a week after its arrival Force Z went into action. In the early evening of Monday 8 December, with the war having now started, the Force Commander, Admiral Sir Tom Phillips, decided to take the fight to the Japanese. They sailed that evening into the South China Sea, making their way north in the hope of intercepting and destroying elements of the Imperial Japanese Navy. The mission was ill-fated, and the lack of air support would prove critical. On 10 December, the ships came under attack from Japanese aircraft and both were sunk. Nearly 900 men were killed, although some 2000 survived and returned to Singapore on-board the accompanying destroyers. The loss of two capital ships was to reverberate around the world, dispelling in an instant the idea that Singapore could be defended by the Royal Navy. Churchill's plan had been shown to be lacking; he received the news by telephone the same day. After taking the call he put the receiver down, and later wrote: 'I was thankful to be alone, in all the war I never received a more direct shock.'

As a medical officer Bill visited Sembawang on a number of occasions, being responsible for meeting the arriving ships. He took with him six ambulances, prepared to evacuate any sick men. Despite the situation in the region, men arriving on-board ships looked out on the beaches running down to the Straits of Johor, and were struck to find that none were reinforced or defended in any way. This came in stark contrast to what men had left behind in Britain, where all the beaches were secured with barbed wire along with numerous anti-tank placements. Bill recalled attending Sembawang in mid-December, by when the base had been bombed twice, but was still operational. On this visit they came under attack as five ships arrived carrying Indian troops. Bill saw most of the bombs fall into the water, or onto Johor Bahru; it was another lucky escape for him. One of the ships was carrying men of the 19th Hyderabad Regiment. Their medical officer was a St Mary's man, who had qualified ahead of Bill. He informed Bill that one soldier was suffering from 'confluent chickenpox' and had been unwell during the passage, but was now recovering. Bill immediately went to see the soldier. He inspected his medical card, only to find that the man had received no inoculations at all, and on examining him, found he was actually suffering from generalised smallpox. He immediately ordered an ambulance to take the patient to the fever hospital in Singapore. Bill was far from impressed by his colleague's failure to differentiate between chickenpox and smallpox.

On another occasion Bill arrived at main gates at the head of the convoy of six ambulances to find the gates open and unguarded. He was unsure as to what was happening, but was told by a soldier that an air raid was in progress. He looked around to see that the men from all his ambulances had jumped out of their vehicles and were taking cover in the nearby storm drains. Bill followed them, and watched the Japanese aircraft make their attack. He had come to recognise the formations, comprising 27 aircraft, all seeking to drop their bombs on strategic targets on Singapore, and witnessed just how accurate they were. This time it was different, and, although they appeared to be heading for the naval base, all aircraft managed to drop their bombs on the mainland, near Johor Bahru; this was the first and only time Bill saw Japanese aircraft miss their targets.

Reinforcements Arrive

As Japanese forces advanced rapidly south through Malaya, a critical decision was made in London. Further reinforcements of Singapore were identified and 18 Infantry Division was ordered to the increasingly beleaguered island. The division was composed of territorial soldiers, primarily based in East Anglia, who had left Britain a month after Bill, on 28 October 1941. Initially they headed west to Halifax where the men and their equipment transferred to a number of American liners, which had been converted to troopships. Although at the time America had not entered the war, they were providing ever-increasing assistance to the Allies and when the convoy left it sailed with an escort from the US Navy. Their destination had been planned for the Middle East, but as they sailed through South African waters, news was received of the Japanese attacks on Pearl Harbor and Singapore. Immediately 18 Division was diverted to the Far East. The first ships arrived in Singapore on 13 January 1942, and on 23 January the remainder of the division, based temporarily at Bombay, sailed with the last ships, arriving in Singapore in early February.

As the Japanese advanced south, the naval base at Sembawang came under attack, both from Japanese aircraft and, in late-January, from Japanese artillery on the mainland at Johor. By early February 1942 the base was effectively abandoned, the only activity being destruction of vital facilities and equipment, rendering them useless to the enemy. With the loss of the naval base, Bill's duties of meeting the arriving ships involved him travelling to Keppel Harbour, in the south of the island. On 5 February 1942 the last ships carrying elements of 18 Division docked. They included the SS *Félix Roussel*, a French vessel carrying men of the Northumberland Fusiliers. Sailing in convoy with MV *Empire Star*, they had reached Sultan Shoal, just to the west of Singapore, on the morning of 5 February. They were about to embark the harbour pilots when they were attacked by waves of Japanese bombers. Over the next 45 minutes, the *Félix Roussel* was hit twice, and caught fire. Several men were killed and others were injured by flying splinters. The *Empire Star* was more severely damaged and ran aground. When the *Félix Roussel* finally docked at Keppel Harbour later that morning, a telephone line was installed, allowing Bill to speak with the medical officer on-board. This was Captain V.W.J. 'Bill' Hetreed RAMC, attached to 196 Field Ambulance, whom Bill knew. Hetreed had graduated from St Mary's in 1939 and commissioned in the RAMC in October of that year. Bill was informed that the bodies of the men who had been killed had been hastily buried at sea, but Hetreed had a very seriously injured man, who had lost the top of his head. Acting swiftly, Bill contacted Colonel J. 'Julian' Taylor OBE RAMC, who was both an experienced soldier and a neurosurgeon, to seek his advice.

Taylor had qualified in medicine in 1912, obtaining FRCS in 1914. As a student before World War 1, he drove horsed ambulances 'for fun', and in January 1915, the newly commissioned 2nd Lieutenant Taylor served with the 85th Field Ambulance in France. In April 1915 he served at the 2nd Battle of Ypres, where he, with other officers, undertook surgery on casualties some 3-4 miles from the front, much to the consternation of senior officers who expected all cases to be evacuated to base hospitals. In the battle, Taylor and his troops were the last to return from the front, at one point there was nobody between them and the Germans, a period later described as a 'sticky time.' After serving at the Battle of Loos in December 1915, he was posted to Salonika, where he managed to rekindle his interest in horses. He rode a large, 16-hand chestnut horse called 'Ugly' and also took part in polo matches played on mules. Whilst serving in Salonika he developed a serious infection of his hand, which led to the loss of the terminal phalanx of his index finger, although it was noted this 'did not affect his surgical skills.' His next appointment was in charge of a number of general hospitals. Following demobilisation he was appointed Consultant Neurosurgeon at University College Hospital and the National Hospital for Nervous Diseases in Queen Square, London. He was recognised as a highly competent surgeon as well as a superb teacher, willing and able to take on any case 'from the top of the head to the soles of the feet.' Following the outbreak of war he enlisted in the Army in the autumn of 1939, despite being aged over 50, and served in No 1 General Hospital in Egypt. In August 1941 he was appointed Consultant Surgeon, Malaya Command.

Colonel Julian Taylor

Bill remembered seeing the patient from *Félix Roussel* being transferred to an ambulance, and clearly saw the exposed meninges and associated blood vessels over the brain. Bill later learnt that Julian Taylor treated the wound the best he could, covering the bony defect with the patient's scalp, which meant that the pulsating vessels on the brain's surface could still be seen. Despite this, when Bill met the patient about 6 months later, he observed the results of a quite remarkable recovery, the only residual neurological deficits being a limp and weakness of the right arm.

Although Bill's focus of professional activity was towards medical cases, it was whilst at Tanglin he undertook his first, and possibly only, surgical operation. A soldier was sent to Tanglin with a wound to the hand; it was self-inflicted as the man was attempting to be evacuated from the island. The wound required surgical exploration and repair. Bill enlisted the assistance of a private to administer the chloroform anaesthesia. Unfortunately this assistant had no experience in anaesthesia and failed to monitor the patient. After nearly an hour, during which Bill became engrossed in repairing a number of tendons, he noted that the blood coming from the wound was blue, not red. The patient was nearly dead, poisoned from chloroform. Acting quickly, Bill removed the chloroform mask and closed the wound. They took the patient back to his bed; he was now at least breathing more regularly.

The next morning Bill visited his patient, concerned that the man might never recover from the anaesthetic. He found his patient fully awake and grateful that he had had 'a marvellous sleep.'

Prisoners' Friend

Another of Bill's duties at Tanglin was to provide medical care to the inmates of nearby Tanglin Military Prison. By January 1942 all British prisoners had been evacuated and the prison was now home to just a few men, all prisoners of war. As Bill was to point out, he is probably the only person to know about the four Japanese prisoners on Singapore. Three were paratroopers, who experienced problems in their descents and were captured whilst still unconscious. The fourth was a soldier who had been shot in the chest in close combat, so close in fact that his wound had soot marks tattooed around it. A bullet had passed through his chest, but quite remarkably, failed to hit any of the ribs. There was a large wound, with a pneumothorax, a collapsed lung and signs of pericarditis. The internal injuries resolved, although the skin wound became infected and required treatment. For any Japanese soldier, to be taken prisoner was viewed as completely dishonourable, a personal failure and a betrayal of the Emperor. Bill was now faced with trying to keep alive a patient who not only had a significant chest wound, but also wished to die. Despite the patient's best efforts, Bill succeeded with his medical care and looked after the man for nearly two months.

A fifth prisoner was neither Japanese nor in need of medical care, but was a British officer serving in northern Malaya. Captain P.S.V. 'Patrick' Heenan was a spy and one of the most infamous men to have served with British forces in the war.

Heenan was born in New Zealand in 1910, the illegitimate son of Annie Stanley. His early years were spent in Burma, before moving to Britain in 1923. It was noted that he had problems 'fitting in', problems that would stay with him for the rest of his life. He entered Sevenoaks School in 1923, where he was noted to have little academic ability, but was a fine athlete, excelling in many sports and noted to be an outstanding boxer. In 1926 he left Sevenoaks and spent a year with a number of private tutors, subsequently entering Cheltenham College in January 1927. His time with tutors resulted in little, if any, academic advancement and when he arrived at Cheltenham he was placed in a form of boys nearly four years younger than himself. At Cheltenham he again pursued his sporting interests and joined the OTC. He was noted to be 'tall, well-built, with slightly dark skin', but known to 'throw his weight around' at times. Despite his sporting abilities he was not popular, being described as 'graceless and a bore, a strange boy, liked by no one.' He left Cheltenham in 1929 with no qualifications. As one master observed, 'if he arrived with a chip on his shoulder, he was leaving with a plank.'

Next Heenan joined a trading company in London. He had hoped for opportunities to travel but these did not arise, and after four years he rekindled hopes of a military career. Unable to gain a regular commission in the British Army, his only route was to apply to the Supplementary Reserve. This he did, and was attached to the Indian Army. In 1935 he travelled to Poona to begin his military career but, reminiscent of his time at school, he was dogged by issues and, much to his chagrin, was forced to repeat his initial regimental training. Finally, in 1936 he joined 1/16 Punjab Regiment, an infantry regiment based at Fort Sandeman, Balochistan, south of the North West Frontier. On arrival it was noted he had 'a huge grudge against society and was out to get his revenge.' He continued his pursuit of boxing, becoming the Heavyweight Boxing Champion of India, but also used his strength and power to bully other officers. The following year the regiment moved to Waziristan but it became increasingly apparent that Heenan did not fit in, and was transferred to the Royal Indian Army Service Corps (RIASC), often referred to as the 'Rice Corps.' This move must have further alienated Heenan, removing any chance of showing his fighting prowess in combat, and instead being assigned to delivering supplies to fighting units.

In the autumn of 1938 Heenan travelled to Japan where he spent the full six months of his long leave entitlement. It appears likely that he was approached by Japanese intelligence agents at this time. Other Army officers visiting Japan around this period described how they received quite blatant advances from Japanese agents seeking intelligence about the state of British forces. Heenan also struck a relationship with a Japanese woman and learnt Japanese 'at night, in bed.' After the war it was revealed that his mistress was 'very high up' in the Japanese intelligence service. His time in Japan was highly productive and Heenan learnt how to use a radio along with Japanese codes, as well as developing photographic skills. He was proving very useful to the Japanese and after all his setbacks in life, he had now found people who actually valued him and his contribution.

Having returned to India, Heenan rejoined the RIASC in early 1939 but before long was in trouble yet again. Following an issue involving him and several members of the military police, he was posted back to his original unit, 1/16 Punjab. Here, at least one officer recognised that Heenan was very angry and recommended that he should be dismissed from the Army. This warning fell on deaf ears, and it was not long before Heenan was transferred out yet again, this time to 2/16 Punjab Regiment. Quite remarkably in light of his history, Heenan was promoted to the rank of acting captain. By now his reputation as a troublemaker went before him, and had spread through many officers' messes in the Indian Army.

Before long, Heenan was handed yet another stroke of luck. In October 1940 his regiment, part of 11 (Indian) Division, sailed to Malaya, one of many regiments dispatched to shore up the defences of the area. In early 1941 his regiment moved to the north of Malaya, close to the Thai-Malay border, and he crossed the border several times, presumably passing information to his Japanese controller. Following several unauthorised trips he was dismissed from 2/16 Punjab in March 1941. However, next, in what seems a most remarkably stupid move, Heenan was posted to a secret unit responsible for air intelligence liaison; he, and his handlers, could not have been more thrilled.

Heenan was initially posted to RAF Seletar in Singapore, but in June 1941 moved to RAF Alor Star in North Malaya, one of the few operational airfields on the Malay Peninsula and home to 62 Squadron RAF. His role as an air intelligence liaison officer at Alor Star included planning of air defences and liaising with the Army; all very valuable sources of intelligence for the enemy. In June 1941 he was involved in an air defence exercise, acting as 'umpire' between the two sides during which he flew an aerial reconnaissance over the border. His role was not confined to Alor Star, as he travelled to many other airfields in Malaya, lecturing on Army-RAF liaison. This undoubtedly provided further opportunities to gather intelligence. By the autumn of 1941 Heenan had become a rich man, with some £65,000 in his bank account in Penang, a substantial amount at that time. When later challenged, he was unable to account for the money, explaining that it was 'a gambling debt that had been repaid.'

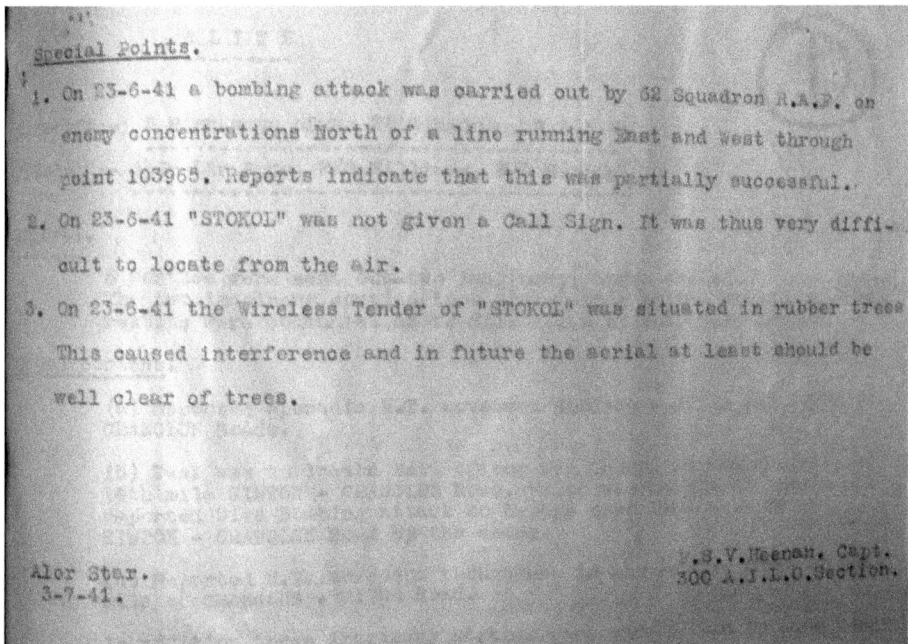

Special Points.

1. On 23-6-41 a bombing attack was carried out by 62 Squadron R.A.F. on enemy concentrations North of a line running East and West through point 103965. Reports indicate that this was partially successful.

2. On 23-6-41 "STOKOL" was not given a Call Sign. It was thus very difficult to locate from the air.

3. On 23-6-41 the Wireless Tender of "STOKOL" was situated in rubber trees This caused interference and in future the aerial at least should be well clear of trees.

V.S.V.Heenan. Capt.
300 A.I.L.O.Section.

Alor Star.
3-7-41.

Record of Heenan's role in air defence exercise, 1941, RAF Alor Star

Heenan's Commanding Officer, Major J.C. France, became suspicious of his activities in the autumn of 1941, hearing that he had photographed the roads and road junctions from Alor Star up to the border. But again, suspicions fell on deaf ears. When Bill later heard of this he described the whole situation as 'criminally stupid.' Heenan continued to gather intelligence, at one point attempting to obtain top secret documents held in the commanding officer's safe. By now the situation was best described as one of 'incompetence on the part of superior officers, combined with exceptionally good luck for Heenan.' Worse was to follow in mid-November 1941 when Heenan became second in command of the liaison unit. By now, tension was increasing in North Malaya, with the question being not will the Japanese attack, but when. Major France was convinced that Heenan was spying and on Sunday 7 December 1941 searched his room. He found substantial evidence of Heenan's activities, with reports detailing aircraft positions along with a code book. Why he was not arrested immediately remains one of many unanswered questions of this saga.

Early next morning the Japanese launched their attack on Malaya, with troops landing at Kota Bharu. Aircraft of 62 Squadron went into action just before dawn. At the same time the Imperial Japanese Air Force launched attacks on airfields in North Malaya, including Sungai Petani, which lies south of Alor Star, and home to 27 Squadron RAF. This was attacked at around 7.30am. By contrast, at Alor Star there were no signs of enemy aircraft, despite the clear skies. Several men serving on the airfield noted how 'Heenan kept disappearing.' Aircraft of 62 Squadron returned at about 10.00am to refuel and by this time people were asking why they had not been attacked. Heenan replied, 'Oh they will do, they will do.' No sooner had he said this than they came under attack, with most of the aircraft on the ground destroyed. As one man later recalled, 'it was as if they knew exactly when to attack.'

Following the devastating attack, RAF Alor Star was evacuated the next day. As Major France loaded up his car he offered to take the padre's Communion Set for him. When they reached Butterworth, some 65 miles to the south, France's attention was drawn to one of his own trucks where he saw a Communion Set. Baffled, he wondered if the padre had two sets. He examined the set in the truck, and found it to be a perfect replica of a field Communion Set on the outside, but inside was a two-way radio receiver and transmitter. Returning it to the truck he watched from a distance, only to find Heenan arrive and pick up the set. At last the game was up for Heenan who, having realised that he had been found out, quickly changed into civilian clothes and attempted to make a run for freedom. This was short-lived and he was soon apprehended. It was found he had a second transmitter, disguised as a typewriter, and had been able to communicate with the Japanese whilst they were attacking airfields and other targets. Heenan was arrested and charged with treason and espionage on Wednesday 10 December 1941.

Following his arrest, Heenan was brought down to Singapore by train at the end of December 1941. His court martial started on Friday 2 January 1942. Although there was considerable security, news had reached Singapore that an officer was coming down under escort. Bill was one of several who had heard this gossip, and that in common parlance 'the officer was a spy.' The court martial lasted several days. Heenan was found guilty of spying, and sentenced to death. However, the sentence had to be confirmed by the War Office in London, a process which took some time.

Heenan, now under sentence of death, was held in Tanglin Military Prison, guarded by a contingent of military police made up of a sergeant and three or four military policemen. The sergeant was described by Bill as 'being in his mid-thirties, with a broad East Anglian accent.' Bill was told very little about Heenan, merely that he 'was Irish and was attached to the Indian Army', but most importantly, Bill was not to discuss the man with any of his fellow officers. On meeting Heenan for the first time he introduced himself by saying:

I am a doctor: if you have any medical problems report them to me, but I will be coming to visit you as a 'prisoner's friend.' If there is anything you cannot get from the military police or others looking after you, I might be able to help.

Heenan complained of having nothing to do, and on a couple of occasions Bill provided light reading material, such as *Reader's Digest*. Bill remembered Heenan as being a fit man, tall, stocky and with a slightly swarthy complexion, but Bill despised him, because of his treachery.

In his role as Mess Secretary at Tanglin, Bill came across numerous fellow officers. One, an RAMC major, possibly attached to the newly arrived 18 Division, stood out. The man described himself as 'the most senior RAMC major east of Suez.' Bill took an alternative view, and summarised his attributes as '...so lazy, so stupid and so inefficient'. In fact he felt that the man should not be wearing the King's uniform as he appeared really quite anti-British. The officer approached Bill and asked about the prisoner, enquiring if Bill knew his name. Bill's reply was quite succinct: 'I'm not allowed to tell you what his name is, I'm not allowed to tell you anything about him.' He then took a different tack, and told Bill that he was worried about a cousin, and asked if Bill could recognise the prisoner on a photograph. Bill agreed to try, and was shown a picture of an 'old boys' gathering'. Bill easily recognised Heenan and said, 'There's the man I'm looking after.' The major was aghast and, as Bill noted, 'I've never seen a man go so white so suddenly.'

During Heenan's imprisonment in Tanglin he did not enter into discussion with Bill, and *vice versa*. Bill remembered Heenan's attitude as the Japanese advanced through Malaya, suggesting that 'my friends will be here soon, and I will be alright.' This was misplaced optimism, as events would show. There was an occasion when Bill remembered Heenan being demonstrably frightened. One evening, the air raid alarm sounded and Bill suggested that they go up onto the prison roof to see what was happening. Up on the roof, Bill wondered if the bombs would be falling on Keppel Harbour, the naval base or perhaps one of the airfields; Bill finished by saying, 'It won't be on us.' This prompted Heenan to reply, 'Well, it might be, it might be, they may not be accurate.' Bill looked up to see the man obviously frightened. A few minutes later, having watched three aircraft being shot down, Heenan was insistent that they left the roof, and go back to the cells. Bill saw the man as an even greater coward in the light of his behaviour, and despised him even more for his actions.

Allied troops retreated from the Malay Peninsula on 31 January 1942, when they blew a hole in the causeway linking Singapore to the mainland. The delay in the Japanese advance was only temporary and their troops landed on Singapore on Sunday 8 February. A day or two later Heenan was taken from Tanglin to Outram Road Gaol for interrogation by a Special Branch Officer. He was detained there until 'Black Friday', 13 February 1942. This was the last day of any real concerted resistance to the Japanese advance, whilst at the same time desperate efforts were made to evacuate as many women and children as possible from the beleaguered island. It was on Black Friday that Heenan met his fate, an event that Bill learnt about some three months later when he met one of the policemen responsible for guarding him. Bill asked about Heenan, and was told that one of them had decided 'something had to be done about him.' By Black Friday, Heenan had changed from his gloomy despondent self into a very cocky individual, telling his captors that 'you'll be in the bag soon, you'll be in prison or you'll be shot.' It was decided that the sentence of the court martial should be carried out. All the policemen were keen to do the deed, so the sergeant pulled out a pack of cards. The men drew cards to determine who would have the 'privilege and pleasure and honour', and the sergeant won. Heenan was taken to Keppel Harbour late in the afternoon, and instructed to stand on the edge of the wharf, facing out to sea, and to look at the setting sun, since 'it would be the last time he would see it.' A shot was fired into Heenan's head, he was given a push and fell into a watery grave.

The story of Heenan, 'The Singapore Traitor', remained untold for many years, not fully surfacing until the book *Odd Man Out* was published in 1988. The authors attempted to identify exactly who had shot Heenan on Black Friday, a question that Bill has been asked several times. His answer remains as diplomatic as always – 'I have a terrible memory for names' – so ensuring that the man's identity remains unknown. Bill saw the actions of Heenan as totally reprehensible and after the war was shocked to see that he was commemorated on war memorials at both his schools. Bill wrote to the headmaster of Cheltenham School and subsequently visited to inform him of the true nature of Heenan's war service. As a result, Heenan's name was removed from the school's war memorial. Heenan is also commemorated by the Commonwealth War Graves Commission (CWGC) at Kranji, Singapore, and the official list describes him having 'died in service' on 15 February 1944. On learning of this, Bill wrote on several occasions to alert the CWGC to the true facts behind Heenan's action and demise. The reply was that the man 'died on active service' and should be commemorated as such. As a consequence, in the 1980s Bill wrote to the editor of *The Daily Telegraph* to highlight the man's actions. The first line read: 'Why should we have the name of a traitor on the Kranji War Cemetery memorial?' He went on to state that 'there is every reason why it should be erased as I made sure it was from the war memorial of his public school.' Bill also sought to correct the failings of the CWGC regarding the date of death: 'he did not die on February 15 1944 but at sundown on Friday 13 February 1942'. He concluded the letter stating that Heenan 'did not die in service'. The letter was not published and to this day Heenan's name remains on the Kranji War Memorial.

Kranji War Memorial, Singapore, where Heenan's name is listed amongst those of 24,000 with no known burial site.

Bill at Kranji Cemetery.

CHAPTER 5

THE FORTRESS FALLS

Last Days at Tanglin

At the end of January 1942, medical staff attached to HQ 18 Division were billeted at Tanglin, causing Major Davies to note how this 'raised hopes amongst those there.' A few days later a party from Tanglin Military Hospital, led by Lieutenant Welch,[44] the Quartermaster, managed to drive to the now deserted naval base where they acquired a significant amount of medical equipment. Tanglin was now coming under regular heavy bombing, which started at about 9.30am each morning. On 6 February many of the patients in the hospital requested to be discharged in order to return and serve with their units, especially men of the Argyll and Sutherland Highlanders. There were even reports of men returning later that day to receive continued treatment for their conditions. At the same time Indian troops, parts of 9 and 11 Brigades, established their positions near to the hospital. Major Davies also recorded how, on 6 February, 'Major France was admitted to the hospital, as his health had broken down'. This may not have been unexpected, since France was Heenan's commanding officer, and over the last six weeks had been faced with having a traitor in his unit.

Japanese troops landed on Singapore Island in a well-planned assault. Later, when a prisoner of war, Bill learnt that troops, dressed as locals, had earlier crossed over from Johor Bahru to reconnoitre the island's defences. They decided that the eastern quadrant, guarded

---

44 Bill recalled that Lieutenant Welch suffered from alcoholic neuropathy, and that later in Changi he was the first patient to develop neuropathy as a result of beriberi.

by men of 18 Division, was too well protected. Instead they found Australian troops, many of whom were drunk, on the western coast, and decided that this was the most favourable site for landing the main force. Once Japanese troops landed on the night of 8/9 February, they rapidly advanced south towards Tanglin. Before long, Indian troops manning guns on the perimeter of Tanglin deserted their positions. By Tuesday 10 February Japanese tanks were moving along the Bukit Timah Road and Bill estimated the enemy were less than 400 metres from his hospital. Under intense mortar fire, which continued through the night, Bill and his colleagues spent much of their time sheltering in the huge slit trenches, named QE (Queen Elizabeth) and QM (Queen Mary). These had been built early in the war, using Chinese labour. The other major protective structure was a reinforced concrete shelter which could accommodate 40 stretcher cases, and up until now had served its purpose well. Wednesday 11 February was to be Bill's last day at Tanglin, and on that day the Dermatology Ward took a direct hit, although no one was hurt. The bombardment continued and Bill witnessed Lieutenant Colonel Clarke being hit by an explosion as he was sitting in his office, an explosion which quite literally blew his head off.[45] Later a padre, a man whom Bill did not much care for, suggested that they should leave and move to the centre of Singapore City; sound advice indeed.[46] Bill arranged for the 100 patients in the hospital, many of whom were very ill, to be transferred to a makeshift facility in Singapore. But, before leaving, Bill gathered together as much mepacrine as he could find from

---

45 Clarke's body was buried in one of the slit trenches to the rear of C block at Tanglin, and Bill later learnt that local people would come and place flowers on the site. At the end of 1945, Bill was living in Dolphin Square, London, when two motorbike riders arrived, almost at the same time, one from the War Office and one from the BMA. They were each carrying letters from Mrs Winifred Clarke, who had written to Bill, his name having appeared in several of her husband's letters sent from Singapore. She wanted any information about her late husband, as she had received none. Bill provided her with significant details, which helped her in gaining an enhanced pension for the loss of her husband. In October 1947, Clarke's body was exhumed and reburied at Kranji War Memorial.

46 An order to evacuate the hospital was made by GHQ in the afternoon.

the pharmacy buildings, knowing that this would be of great value in the weeks and months to come. As he was loading the boxes onto the lorries, Lieutenant Welch told him that he could not take it since he did not have 'the correct paperwork or countersignatures.' Somewhat irate, Bill challenged him by asking if 'he knew that there was a war on'.

Grave of Lieutenant Colonel Clarke, Kranji

Bill was seated in the front of a lorry as they sped down Orchard Road, reaching speeds of 50-60mph, on a journey that was the most frightening he ever made. The driver, a Malay, was wearing neither shoes nor socks, and Bill recalled seeing the man's big toe pushing down hard on the accelerator pedal. The road was under attack from mortars, with shells landing about every 15 seconds, and creating large potholes. The lorry sped off with the driver trying his best to avoid the incoming munitions as well as the potholes. Unable to avoid all the potholes, it was both an extremely bumpy and frightening ride for all on-board.

The Victoria Theatre

Bill made his way to the Victoria Theatre, in the city centre. It is situated just opposite the Singapore Cricket Club, lying next to the Singapore River and just a few hundred yards from the Fullerton Building, which was one of the main administrative centres in Singapore. Built in 1862, it originally served as both the town hall and a theatre. By the turn of the century it was proving to be too small, and in 1902 there was agreement to build a new building on land adjacent to the Victoria Theatre. The two would be joined by an impressive clock tower. The new hall, named the Victoria Memorial Hall[47] opened in 1905 and soon after the Victoria Theatre was refurbished, reopening in 1908. Bill described the facility as a traditional theatre building which he felt 'would not be out of place in Shaftesbury Avenue.' Here they became attached to No 1 Malay General Hospital (1MGH) which had moved to Singapore City the previous day. 1MGH was under the command of Lieutenant Colonel D.S. Middleton RAMC, a territorial officer who was doubly qualified, as a dentist and anaesthetist, and a man who impressed Bill through his continual attention to protocol and detail. A Scot, he had worked in Edinburgh before the war, and had led 155 Field Ambulance in France in 1940, before evacuating through Dunkirk. In 1941 he was posted to the Far East. 1MGH had been established in Johor Bahru in January 1941, and had taken over two floors of the recently completed Johor Bahru General Hospital. With the advance of the Japanese, 1MGH left Johor Bahru on 27 January and moved to Singapore and Selarang Barracks, Changi, where in early February, Middleton assumed command. That facility came under attack from 8 February, causing significant damage to the buildings and interruption of both water and electricity supplies. On 10 February Middleton was ordered to evacuate to Singapore City, and soon identified new locations for his facility at Victoria Memorial Hall where he opened an operating theatre, and set up 400 beds for patients. One of his officers, Captain G.K. Marshall RAMC, described inside Victoria Memorial Hall that evening as 'like a scene from a painting of

---

47 Now called the Victoria Concert Hall.

Nurse Cavell, with patients lying packed closely together on mattresses and stretchers on the floor.'

Victoria Theatre in the foreground (with clock tower). To the right is the Supreme Court, the town hall, and at far right, St Andrew's Cathedral. Smoke rises in the distance from the naval base at Sembawang.

On arrival at the Victoria Theatre, Bill quickly created a makeshift hospital, where the sickest patients were placed in the lower parts of the building (the expensive seats) and the more able, placed in the 'gods.' On Thursday 12 February after further heavy fighting, troops retreated to form a defensive line on the perimeter of Singapore City, causing some to feel that there was 'little hope left.' That day an ambulance carrying a number of severely injured patients arrived at Victoria Theatre since other hospitals were overwhelmed by casualties. The facility was not equipped to manage surgical cases, but under the circumstances Bill attempted to do his best. Perhaps the most severely injured was the adjutant of a Norfolk regiment, part of 18 Division. The man was unconscious and his abdomen lay open, revealing his liver and spleen, both badly damaged by shrapnel, and the remains of his right kidney. He had already received morphine and there was little more that could be done for him. Further morphine was administered and he died about 30 minutes later. After the war, the soldier's father, a doctor, wrote to Bill who was able to tell him about his son's final hours.

In the last few days of the battle for Singapore, many troops effectively gave up fighting, and were resigned to defeat and being taken prisoner. Many, but by no means all, were Australians who felt the best way to capitulate was in a drunken stupor. Amongst the men at the Victoria Theatre was an Australian sailor who had arrived in Singapore on-board a warship (possibly HMAS *Vampire*) but had contracted gonorrhoea following a visit to Lavender Street. As such he was listed as sick and unable to rejoin his ship. Hearing of the behaviour of many of the troops, he ventured out in a lorry, and located as many drunks as possible. After destroying any alcohol they had, he brought them back to the hospital.[48] Here Bill had to deal with them the best he could, and instructed an RAMC non-commissioned officer, Sergeant Smith, to wash out their stomachs using an enema tube. The men were allowed to stay overnight, but were not given any breakfast, before being sent to rejoin their units. Although appearing somewhat harsh, Bill knew that his actions may well have saved many lives since the Japanese, if confronted by drunken troops, would have bayoneted them there and then.

Many of the staff of 1MGH were billeted in the nearby Singapore Cricket Club, although Bill remained at the Victoria Theatre. Those at the cricket club recorded that their first night was spent on the floor 'rudely disturbed by shelling.' Bill clearly remembered shells being fired from the coastal guns, which had been turned to fire north.[49] Shells would shoot over Singapore City, aimed at Johor, making an 'amazing noise.' Bill heard the impact of the shells 4-5 seconds after they had passed overhead. The Allies were faced with two problems regarding their

---

48 After the war, the sailor wrote to Bill. His ship HMAS *Vampire* was sunk in April 1942 off the coast of Ceylon, and all records were lost. He was in danger of being charged with desertion, and wrote to Bill asking for a statement explaining why he had been on Singapore at this time; Bill happily agreed to do so.

49 An ever-recurring myth in the history of Singapore is that the coastal guns could only face to the sea.

coastal armaments. Firstly the vast majority of the ammunition was armour-piercing, designed to attack ships, rather than high-explosive which is far more effective against buildings. Secondly, they were instructed not to attack the Japanese military headquarters situated in the Sultan of Johor's palace, as they wished to stay on 'friendly terms with the Sultan', despite his palace being the temporary headquarters of the Japanese. As a result, one of the major targets for the gunners was the railway station at Johor.

The cricket clubhouse housed not only troops but a number of civilians, including Mrs Mulvaney, wife of Major D.P.C. Mulvaney RAMC attached to 1MGH. She was a nurse and was noted to be doing 'wonderful work, cheering up the patients.' Also staying there was Lieutenant Colonel Hennessy's wife and his young son, 'Tinker.' On 12 February Bill assisted a number of officers at the club to destroy all supplies of spirits and beer, an act which was described as causing 'many a muttered comment.' When visiting Singapore Cricket Club 72 years after the event, Bill described how the fumes of whisky were so strong that he had not had a drink of whisky since.

By Black Friday, 1MGH had hospital facilities running in Victoria Theatre, as well as the adjacent Victoria Memorial Hall, Government Buildings (Law Courts and Municipal Buildings) and the Fullerton Building. Colonel Middleton was planning to requisition the exclusive Singapore Club, which occupied the upper floors of the Fullerton Building, in order to provide a further 250 beds for the sick and wounded. At the same time many people started to pose the question: was anyone still fighting? It was against this background that Bill made contact with old friends working at the nearby Alexandra Military Hospital, itself under attack from the Japanese.

Alexandra Military Hospital

The construction of Alexandra Military Hospital can be traced back to the British government's plans to strengthen Fortress Singapore after World War 1. With increased numbers of troops deployed to the region, more accommodation was provided by major developments to the east of the island, at Changi. New medical facilities were required and construction of Alexandra Military Hospital began in 1938. Housed on a 32-acre site, work was undertaken by Royal Engineers. Described as a 'stately building built on gracious lines of colonial architecture', Bill felt it somewhat akin to Buckingham Palace. It officially opened in July 1940, when 32 Company RAMC transferred from Tanglin Military Hospital. The hospital had 356 beds, and was described as 'the most up to date and one of the largest military hospitals outside Great Britain.' However, its position meant it would be a target in the war, lying as it did just opposite the main ordnance depot for the island, with the main railway running alongside, and two large fuel dumps only a quarter of a mile away.

Alexandra Military Hospital Singapore

The first commanding officer was Lieutenant Colonel J.W. Craven MC RAMC. He had qualified in 1912 from the University of Durham and, after working for a shipping line, joined the Army at the outbreak of World War 1. He served throughout the conflict with 1st Northumbrian Field Ambulance, being awarded both the Military Cross and Cross of Chevalier of the Legion of Honour, the latter for 'exceptional resource, courage and good work, as well as exceptional ability in leading and directing bearers collecting wounded' at Ypres and Menin Road in the summer of 1915. After demobilisation, he emigrated in 1925 and was appointed Superintendent of Auckland Hospital, New Zealand. With the outbreak of hostilities in 1939 he enlisted in the Army and was subsequently posted to Singapore.

When Alexandra Military Hospital opened the Chief Surgical Assistant was a young doctor, Lieutenant T.B. 'Tom' Smiley RAMC. An

Ulsterman, he was born on 9 May 1917 at Castlewellan, Co. Down, and later educated at the Methodist College, Belfast, where he was head of school and excelled at rugby. He entered Queen's University Belfast and studied medicine, qualifying in 1939. After completing a house surgeon position, he joined the RAMC in 1940. Posted to the Far East, he initially travelled through France but before departing he became engaged to Elizabeth Mary Mills, a medical student. Announcing their engagement on 18 April 1940, his fiancée gave him a silver cigarette case with her signature engraved on it. As events would demonstrate, this present would literally save his life. Making his way to Marseilles, he joined his ship in April 1940. Sailing east through the Suez Canal, stopping at Aden and then Bombay, he arrived in Colombo in May 1940. Soon after, he sailed on the final leg to Singapore, arriving later that month; Smiley was one of six lieutenants on-board who were to serve in the new hospital. However, it was not yet complete, so they were posted to Tanglin Military Hospital. Here Smiley's experience in ENT Surgery was much appreciated, although the level of surgical treatment offered was very limited. Surgeons would operate on patients with hernias, although slightly more complex cases, for example, appendicitis, were referred to the civilian hospitals. Smiley recorded in letters to his fiancée that Singapore was 'a beautiful city', one in which there was no black out and how 'all the cinemas and shops remained open and lit up'.

Tom Smiley and his fiancée

Bill and Tom Smiley met on several occasions in late 1941, both professionally and socially. Amongst the subjects they discussed was smoking. Bill did not smoke: he admitted to having smoked a little when a student at Oxford, but gave it up as he neither enjoyed it, nor could afford it. He suggested to Tom Smiley that he should stop smoking, since it was bad for his health. Smiley decided not to take that particular piece of medical advice.

Alexandra Military Hospital expanded in response to the deteriorating military situation in 1941, and by January 1942 had over 500 beds, with an annexe opened in the adjacent nurses' home. Medical care was not just the remit of doctors, and nearly 50 QAIMNS staff were posted to the hospital. Some had arrived with Bill on-board *Dominion Monarch*. As the hospital expanded, there were also contributions from the territorial and emergency medical services. A few civilians also joined, including Edith Stevenson, a missionary nurse in Singapore, who responded to an appeal issued by the hospital just after Christmas 1941. Now aged 29, she had embarked on nurse training at North Staffordshire Royal Infirmary when aged 17. Once qualified, she undertook midwifery in Sheffield and in 1937 entered missionary training at the College of the Ascension, Birmingham. After 2 years she set sail for Singapore, arriving in September 1939. She initially worked at St Andrew's Hospital for Women, but after about a year was appointed Matron of St Andrew's Orthopaedic Hospital at Siglap, on the island's east coast. This hospital was evacuated just before Christmas 1941. Edith started in her new role at Alexandra Military Hospital on 28 December 1941 and noted how many of the regular nurses were 'resentful of outsiders, trying to make them feel uncomfortable.' Fortunately, the Matron, Miss Jones, warmed to the new arrivals and supported them the best she could. Many of Edith's patients were sailors who had survived the sinking of HMS *Prince of Wales* and *Repulse*, and their injuries ranged from loss of limbs to significant burns. Edith noted that many had fractures of their os calcis (of the ankle), sustained when jumping between decks of the stricken ships.

During January 1942 Alexandra Military Hospital came under increasing attack from the air but despite this, Edith recalled how she and the medical staff remained cheerful 'for the sake of the men.' Air raids intensified further in February, and by the end of the first week, Edith's two wards, designed to accommodate 40 patients, housed 140. A red cross was laid out on the lawn of the hospital, but the building continued to come under attack due, in part, to its close vicinity to nearby ordnance and supply depots. Edith described how the now Captain Smiley 'did all he could to send men away to Australia on ships, as soon as they were fit to travel.' She described him as 'a wonderful doctor, who always put patients first, and before capitulation was working day and night.' Once Edith asked him what to do about painkilling, his reply was, 'Sister, do what you can to relieve pain. I don't have time to write on charts, so use your own discretion. The poor souls will have a worse fate if the Japs come.' Smiley's consent in this way allowed Edith to give pain relief to the dying.

Another civilian nurse serving at the hospital was Dorothy Lucy (née Hawkings). She had been a teacher at Tanglin Nursery School, in the Cameron Highlands, working for its owner, the redoubtable Miss Griffith-Jones. With the Japanese advance she had made her way to Singapore, and when the school closed she joined the VAD. Dorothy remained convinced that Singapore would never fall, and on 7 February 1942 married a tin miner from Malaya, Peter Lucy. Theirs was the last wedding to take place in St Andrew's Cathedral for many years. The following day she reported for work at Alexandra Military Hospital, where she found casualties spread all over the floors. One of her first jobs was to cut up red and white material to make red crosses which were hung from the top balcony of the hospital.

By 8 February 1942 plans were afoot for the evacuation of many of the nursing staff, but realising their importance, there was a call for volunteers to stay. Eight volunteers were requested by Miss Jones, who put her own name at the top of the list, and soon after, Edith Stevenson added hers. The situation continued to deteriorate and within three days, the hospital had lost all electricity supply. Outside there were Japanese snipers. A medical officer attempted to raise a Red Cross flag, but as he did so a sniper opened fire, and the officer narrowly missed losing a finger; it was obvious that the Japanese merely saw the Red Cross as a target. On 11 February a number of nurses, including Dorothy Lucy, made their way to Singapore Harbour where, along with women and children, they boarded SS Empire Star. The ship, carrying over 2000 passengers, came under air attack the following day, but Dorothy reported how the captain, a Norwegian, who had experience of dodging bombs in the North Sea earlier in the war, managed to steer through the Japanese assaults. However, their luck eventually ran out on Black Friday when the ship was struck. Many were killed and their funerals were held at sea, straightaway. After two days the *Empire Star* reached Batavia, where Dorothy Lucy disembarked and subsequently made her way to India. The *Empire Star* sailed on, and arrived safely in Fremantle, Australia.

Back at Alexandra Military Hospital, Edith Stevenson had refused to be evacuated and remained on duty. On the following day, Thursday 12 February, a neighbouring oil tank was set on fire, and thick smoke engulfed the hospital. Bill later learnt that the Japanese commanders had given strict instructions to their pilots to avoid targeting oil tanks since, being short of fuel, they had hoped to obtain as much fuel as possible on their advance. In fact, the pilot responsible for the attack was later disciplined for his actions. The situation around the hospital continued to worsen and on Black Friday, 13 February, Edith, along with all the remaining sisters, were summoned to a meeting by Miss Jones. They were instructed to get their cases and be at the front entrance straightaway. Edith was reluctant to desert her patients, and later described how she 'felt like a traitor.' The order to leave had come in the wake of news of the massacre of nurses in Hong Kong following the Japanese invasion just 6 weeks earlier.[50] One of her colleagues, Sister Harley, described 'the faces of the boys watching us leave, saying "it's all up now".' All the sisters had left the hospital by 1.30pm, and made their way to join SS *Kuala* in Singapore Harbour.

Helping Old Friends

Kuala was a small ship, built in 1911 in Scotland, and in peacetime served on the coastal route between Singapore, Port Swettenham and Penang, where her passengers were primarily young civil servants and

---

50 On 25 December 1941, Japanese troops had entered St Stephen's College, Hong Kong, which was being used as a hospital, raped and then killed many of the nurses working there.

their families. Perhaps as an omen of her final fate, when sailing on her maiden voyage, on 13 February 1911, her superstitious owner doubled her insurance. His forebodings were justified as she ran aground on an island in the Red Sea, was looted and had to be towed to India where she was effectively rebuilt. *Kuala* had arrived in Singapore earlier on Black Friday, having come under attack by Japanese aircraft the previous day. Her passage had been organised by Brigadier C.H. Stringer L/RAMC OBE DSO, the DDMS Malaya, with the aim of evacuating women and children, the former including British, Australian and Indian nursing sisters. There were also a few places for men, primarily stretcher cases, including survivors from HMS *Prince of Wales* and *Repulse*. A small number of places were also made available for civil servants. One of the youngest to join the ship was Shirley Natten, aged two and a half. She had been living in Kuala Lumpur with her Dutch mother and Irish father, at her Dutch grandparents' home. They had been evacuated to Singapore where her father arranged for them to have a berth on the *Kuala*. Shirley remembered the scene at the wharf that day, where hundreds of suitcases were laid out, waiting to be loaded. At about 3pm they started to embark on launches taking them out to the *Kuala* as she lay at anchor, and Shirley's father pushed both her, and her mother, on-board.

SS Kuala

Nurses from Alexandra Military Hospital were instructed to assemble at Singapore Cricket Club. As they arrived just after lunch shells hit both ends of the building, but no one was hurt. They were met by Bill

147

who had been detailed to ensure their safe passage to the *Kuala*. Each was given a Red Cross armband, which effectively acted as a passport, although as Edith Stevenson noted, 'many deserters around and about tried to snatch the armbands from us.' The first group to move to the harbour were Indian nurses, each laden with suitcases. Bill informed every one that they were allowed just one case; his party did not move off until each nurse had conformed to his instructions. The next group was made up of British nurses, and amongst them was his friend Sister Naomi Davies. Having worked with her at Tidworth in 1940, they had next met in the autumn of 1941 on-board *Dominion Monarch*. On arrival in Singapore, Sister Davies was appointed to Alexandra Military Hospital. On that Friday afternoon as they made their way to the harbour, Bill gave Sister Davies all his Singapore dollars, along with his wife's address in England, and asked her to give the money to Pauline, if she got home. Bill accompanied her out in a launch to *Kuala* and on reaching the bottom of the gangway, they encountered an Australian soldier armed with a rifle. He allowed Sister Davies to board, but told Bill he could not. The man was a deserter and Bill realised he was in no position to argue, but pointedly said, 'I have no intention of wanting to join you as I have plenty of work to do back on land.'

At about 5.15pm *Kuala* came under attack from Japanese aircraft, and at least one bomb hit the ship, killing several passengers and injuring many more. Edith Stevenson was boarding when the bomb hit. A nurse next to her was struck in the head by shrapnel and died. Amongst the civilians on-board was Mrs Violet Duncan, with her three children, Jean, aged 11, Clare, 10 and Sheila, 4. Violet was British/Eurasian and her Scottish husband, Mr W.W. Duncan, was the newly appointed Director of ARP.[51] He had only decided to send his family on the ship earlier that afternoon. When boarding the ship they saw enemy aircraft overhead, and when bombs fell Jean was injured by flying splinters. Her wounds were dressed by one of the nurses on-board. An hour after the attack the ship, under the command of Lieutenant Franklin Caithness RNR, and laden with nearly 600 passengers, weighed anchor and set sail into

---

51 Air Raid Precautions.

the night in the company of *Tien Kwang*, a ship carrying some 250 RAF personnel. As they sailed, Singapore was ablaze behind them.

On the following morning, Saturday 14 February, both ships anchored in deep water just off the island of Pompong,[52] part of the Riau Archipelago, about 45 miles south-west of Singapore and 30 miles east of Sumatra. In an effort to camouflage the ship, parties were sent ashore in boats to collect branches. Much of this task had been completed by 9.30am. Later that morning, the ship was attacked by Japanese aircraft, with bombs hitting the bridge and engine room. Shirley Natten recalled how the aircraft 'came from nowhere', and suddenly the ship was on fire; people were screaming as panic spread. Her mother's skirt was ripped off by the blast wave. Below decks, Miss Jones had been holding a meeting with six sisters in her cabin; all were killed. All those on-board were told to jump into the water, and Shirley Natten remembered how some started to go crazy, 'calling out for taxis' amidst the panic. Many were killed in the water by bombs dropped from the aircraft, resulting in a scene described as 'too awful to be forgotten.' In the strong currents bodies were quickly swept away from the island.

Arthur Ross, of the PWD,[53] on-board the *Kuala* had to make his way over dead and dying bodies as he carried a 10-year-old girl with her leg in plaster towards the side of the ship. A number of boats were coming towards the stricken vessel, and he managed to pass the girl to two colleagues from the PWD who were in a lifeboat. Ross then jumped into the water and came under further attack from Japanese aircraft, but fortunately was not injured. He drifted towards some cliffs and scrambled onto the rocks where he found two other survivors. Quite fortuitously an empty lifeboat was stuck against the rocks, and he swam to it. He arrived at the same time as two members of the RAF, Corporal Ray Fraser and an officer. They rowed out towards the stricken ship and Fraser dived into the water on several occasions to rescue women and children. Ross saw a woman floating on a mattress and hailed her; she waved back and they said they would return for her.

---

52 Also called Pom Pong or Pom Pom Island.
53 Public Works Department.

Having picked up women and children, they rowed towards the mattress and dragged the woman on-board. Ross noted that she had 'a gaping bleeding wound of her buttock.' He told her it needed treatment, to which she replied that 'she was a doctor and it was alright.' They had rescued Dr Margaret Thomson (née Hunter) who had worked for the Malayan Medical Service, and was married to Daniel Thomson, an agricultural engineer and rubber planter at Port Swettenham. With the retreat from Malaya, Dr Thomson had worked in Singapore General Hospital (a civilian hospital) as an anaesthetist, alongside two Australian doctors, Dr Marjorie Lyon and Dr Elsie Crowe. When the *Kuala* was attacked in Singapore Harbour on Black Friday, Dr Thomson was injured, suffering extensive lacerations to her thigh and buttocks. The wounds had been sutured by Drs Lyon and Crowe that night. Her wound had opened as she swam in the sea and then climbed onto the mattress. Despite her wounds, Margaret Thomson insisted on helping those in the boat, and then assisting Fraser as he rowed.

Sister Naomi Davies was in the water holding onto a wooden box, about to be swept out to sea, when she was pulled into the boat by Arthur Ross. Soon after he pulled a young girl into the boat, it was Jean Duncan.[54] She had become separated from her mother and sisters and was immediately cared for by Sister Davies. More were helped into the boat, including Sister Harley, making a total of 39 on-board. The treacherous currents soon swept the boat away from Pompong. Under the scorching sun the crew made a small sail and along with rowing, they made their way towards an island on the horizon. Three people in the boat died and their bodies were pushed overboard. Later that night they reached the island of Kebat, where Sister Davies and Dr Thomson did their best to care for the sick and injured. Of the 36 who landed, 27 were women, and many of these had little more than their underwear, having lost their clothes when they fell into the sea. Many were suffering from sunburn, having been at sea all day under the equatorial sun.

The next morning, Sunday 15 February, they awoke to find there was no fresh water on the island, and that more survivors had landed,

---

54 Corporal Fraser believed that Jean Duncan was the first to be rescued.

many in a very serious medical condition. Amongst those who died that day was D. H. Kleinman, a former Wimbledon tennis player, who had run the Queens' Sport Shop in Singapore. Sister Davies reclaimed her trousers which she had given him, to replace his own that had been lost in the shipwreck. In fact the trousers had previously been given to a sailor who survived the sinking of HMS *Prince of Wales*, but had died from his wounds on the *Kuala*.[55] After four days, those still alive on Kebat were rescued by a Chinese junk and spent two weeks island-hopping as they made their way to the island of Singkep, which was not occupied by the Japanese at the time. Here they were able to find hospital facilities for the sick and wounded at Dabo. At this point Arthur Ross explained that he would have to part company with the doctors and nurses, since he could not claim immunity which a Red Cross might provide for them; he left that night by sampan. The rest of the survivors made their way in small groups across the sea to Sumatra, where they sailed up the River Indragiri to the town of Tembilahan. From here they made their way to the west coast port of Padang but on arrival found that it was empty of ships, the last having sailed a week before. Sister Davies, along with Sisters Lydia McLean, Louie Harley and K.M. Jenkins, made their way to Padang Salvation Army Hospital where they set to work.

Arthur Ross successfully returned to Britain, where he wrote to Sister Davies' sister:

I last saw Naomi at the Daboh hospital on Sinkep Island attending to the wounded.

I had the honour to be the leader of the party on Kebat Island and it is up to me to tell you of the courage of your sister. We had a terrible four days there with many wounded amongst us and only two gallons of water. Naomi was a tower of strength in the party, always cheerful and courageous. She helped me greatly by clearing away thorn bushes to make a camp on our arrival and when our water supply was almost finished she volunteered to come out into the open with me to wave distress signals to the next passing Japanese plane. For the sake of the children amongst us, she was prepared to run the risk of being

---

55 Sister Davies sold the trousers three years later over the fence of an internment camp in exchange for an egg.

machine-gunned in cold blood, Thank God, the arrival of a Chinese junk saved us from this desperate measure.

Unless you have heard to the contrary, Miss Davies is now a prisoner of war.

Sister Davies was taken prisoner of war and held in Padang until December 1943. Along with other prisoners she was then moved to Bangkinang, a camp in the jungles of Sumatra. Throughout this time she looked after her young charge, Jean Duncan, but became a minder for several other children who followed her around the camp, rather like the 'Pied Piper of Hamelin'. However, Jean was never to see her mother and sisters again. After the attack on *Kuala*, they had landed on Pompong where, on the night of Monday 16 February, they were amongst 180 women and children rescued by the coastal vessel SS *Tanjong Pinang*. They sailed south, and on the evening of 17 February, were attacked by Japanese naval gunfire and aircraft. Forced to abandon ship, the majority of passengers died over the following week. Only 15 adults and two children made it to land; this did not include any of Jean's family.

Both Jean Duncan and Naomi Davies survived internment and in September 1945 were flown back to Singapore. Naomi Davies finally found Jean's father, who had been imprisoned in the civilian gaol at Changi, and was reunited with his daughter. Perhaps as the result of Sister Davies' influence during their years of captivity, Jean entered nursing. She later married, and Naomi was godmother to Jean's first child. Naomi Davies returned to Malaya after the war, and married a local planter, John Hedley. He had been a prisoner of the Japanese and forced to build the Pekanbaru Railway on Sumatra. They later returned to Britain, around 1950, when John worked in the automotive industry. Naomi Hedley died in 1995 in Warwickshire; John died in 2009.

p 10/1

204

10259/45.

Colonial Office,
P.W. and C.I. department,
2, Park Street, W.1.

November, 1945.

Dear ~~Sir~~ Madam,

I understand that you were a passenger on the ss.'Kuala'
which was sunk in February 1942 while carrying evacuees
from Singapore.

Since the Colonial Office is anxious to give to the
relatives all possible information about their people and since,
as you will agree, this is a most important work, I hope that you
will forgive me for writing to you to enquire whether you are
able to supply any information about any passengers. ~~No~~ Complete lists are
not available of the people on this ship at the time of its sinking.

First of all we should like to know who were on board when
the ship sailed, secondly whom you can say for certain to have
lost their lives as a result of the sinking, and thirdly whom
you can say for certain to have reached land safely.

It would be much appreciated if you would supply any informa-
tion on the lines indicated about individuals, or any other
information on this matter which might be of use. I'm understood that
Doreen Dunlop after the 'Kuala' was hit and How believe her to have died and been buried
at sea. I enclose copies of a form which has been produced in order
to minimise trouble and to standardize the information which
people can supply, as well as to define the information which is
required about each individual. Perhaps you would use these forms
in giving any information that you can about individuals, ~~or would~~
at any rate supply, ~~so far as you can,~~ the information about each
individual ~~indicated on this form is being required.~~

Your cooperation will be greatly appreciated.

Yours faithfully,

Miss Naomi Davies Q.A.I.M.N.S.,
Brookfield House,
Rryhgwyn, nr. Raglan, Monmouthshire.

*Letter to Sister Naomi Davies from the Colonial Office, 1946, seeking information about the
sinking of the Kuala*

Others Escape

Having ensured that the nursing sisters had boarded *Kuala*, Bill returned to the Victoria Theatre to continue his work of caring for the sick and injured. A little later that day, and unbeknown to many of those working in the makeshift hospitals in Singapore City, including Bill, a group of doctors were summoned to Medical Command. They included Major Davies who described in some detail the subsequent events. Davies arrived at Medical Command at 8.30pm and met a number of medical officers and some NCOs. He was responsible for commandeering two ambulances to take the party (13 officers and 5 NCOs) to the waterfront. The party was under the command of Brigadier C.D.K. Seaver L/ RAMC, the DDMS of 3 (Indian) Corps, and included Lieutenant Colonel Hennessy. Before they left they noted that two officers on the list were not present, one of whom was Captain Smiley.

At the wharf, the medical party was joined by a number of other military personnel attempting to escape, and together they boarded a Chinese riverboat, the *Shu Kuang*, that night. By the morning of Saturday 14 February Bill was aware that Major Davies was missing, and assumed he had made his escape. Up until that time Bill had had significant respect for Major Davies, but on being aware of the manner of his departure, Bill's respect for the officer plummeted. Bill was left thinking why had he to stay behind whilst others had been able to make an escape? The *Shu Kuang* sailed at dawn that day, but was soon attacked by Japanese aircraft, with about 40 men being killed or injured. A second attack soon followed and they were ordered to abandon ship, with many of the medical officers having to use makeshift rafts to stay afloat. Two hours after the first attack, survivors were picked up by two ships, the *Pinang*, a small coastal launch, and HMS *Malacca*, a minesweeper of the naval reserve. These made their way west, to Sumatra and sailed up the River Indragiri to Tembilahan, arriving on Sunday 15 February. Here they encountered a number of casualties who had been rescued from the *Kuala*. Hearing of the fate of that ship, *Pinang* and HMS *Malacca* sailed east in order to locate survivors from the tragedy at Pompong Island. The medical party at Tembilahan set up a treatment facility, and

154

Major Davies recorded that 15 operations were performed there that day.

The next day, Major Davies led a party of medical staff upriver on-board a commandeered yacht, arriving at Rengat where they established a second treatment facility. Lieutenant Colonel Hennessy remained at Tembilahan with the team treating casualties, whilst he waited anxiously for news of his wife and child who were both on-board the *Kuala*. Major Davies continued west from Rengat, reaching the coastal town of Padang on Saturday 21 February, where he heard rumours that two Royal Naval destroyers would be calling at the nearby port of Emmahaven. However, soon after he arrived at Padang, Davies was sent back to Rengat. He was driven there in a lorry by four Roman Catholic Brothers, and on arrival they helped evacuate casualties from Rengat to the westerly town of Sawahlunto. On 26 February, Davies was working at Sawahlunto and recorded that General Gordon Bennett, the GOC of Australian forces, passed through the town that day. He noted that 'the Dutch cannot understand a general escaping and leaving his men as prisoners of war.' The next day more survivors from the *Kuala* arrived, including Drs Crowe and Lyon, the former suffering from a fractured skull, sustained when the *Kuala* was attacked.

On 1 March, news was received that Padang was virtually deserted after a couple of naval vessels had called into port and taken off escapees. The prospect of evacuating casualties from Sawahlunto was looking increasingly difficult, although by now several nursing sisters who had escaped from Singapore were helping care for the injured. Major Davies received news that Colonel Hennessy had moved east to Ayer Molek in a desperate attempt to locate his family, a search that would prove to be of no avail, since both his wife and son had been lost on-board the *Tanjong Pinang*.[56] News was received that Japanese troops had landed on the island and were moving closer by the day. On 6 March more casualties were moved by train from Sawahlunto to Padang, and on their arrival women were placed in the Salvation Army Hospital and

---

56 Hennessy was taken prisoner of war on 17 March 1942 at Padang, Sumatra, and was imprisoned on the island throughout the war.

men in the Military Hospital. By this time there were some 600-800 men still trying to leave Sumatra, but were unable to do so because of a lack of transport, both on land and on sea. On Sunday 8 March Major Davies met a Royal Marines officer, Lieutenant Colonel A.F. Warren, who was part of the SOE (Special Operations Executive) organisation. He told Davies to meet him at 8.30pm that evening.

Major Davies had been selected to be one of a party of 18 men to make an escape attempt from Padang on the day when the Dutch East Indies capitulated. The party was made up of 16 officers, both civilian and military, along with a Malay and a Chinaman. Many of the party had served with SOE in Singapore and Malaya, being responsible for establishing both escape routes as well as inserting 'stay behind' parties. Warren had purchased a native sailing vessel (a prahau), the *Sederhana Djohanis* (the Lucky John). Having victualled the vessel for a trip which was predicted to take 6 weeks, they departed at 3.03 the next morning. The north-east monsoon was blowing, and it was hoped that this would help them sail the 1300 miles to Colombo, Ceylon. The voyage was far from plain sailing. The sails were thin and in need of almost constant repair and, on several days, they had to negotiate extensive coral reefs. After 10 days thunderstorms arrived and the wind changed direction, blowing them on a south-westerly passage. This was then followed by long periods of calm where little if any real progress was made each day. There remained the constant threat of Japanese aircraft, which flew over them on almost a daily basis. Although on most days they were left alone, on 29 March they came under air attack, but fortunately damage to the vessel was minimal. Davies remained busy throughout the journey treating men who developed severe sunburn. On 12 August they spotted the coast of Ceylon, but were unsure as to whether the island had fallen into enemy hands. Two days later they were sighted by a British freighter, SS *Anglo-Canadian* and taken on-board. They sailed to Bombay, arriving on 19 April where they were transferred to HMS *Formidable* and then HMS *Warspite*, for debriefing by the Royal Navy. They had been at sea for 35 days, and were less than impressed that officials were reluctant for them to land at Bombay as they 'did not have the correct papers.'

For the Toss of a Coin: Massacre of the Innocent

Back in Singapore, Saturday 14 February was a grim day indeed and at Victoria Theatre Bill was faced with a reduced water supply along with news from HQ that, with the continuing Japanese advance, it was likely the water supply would be completely cut off. At other medical facilities nearby, surgical teams were hard at work performing over 200 operations under general anaesthesia. However, an attitude of resignation could be felt by many: was anyone was still fighting? Bill was in no doubt of the likely fate of Singapore, and had been resigned to its fall from as far back as mid-January 1942 when he saw men of 18 Division arriving in a desperate attempt to shore up the beleaguered Fortress Singapore. However, episodes at nearby Alexandra Military Hospital on 14 February would remain with Bill for the rest of his life, as he was to realise just how close to death he might have been, had it not been for the toss of a coin just two months earlier.

Those serving at Alexandra Military Hospital had seen the advance of the Japanese over the past week. Major F.L. Webster RAMC had been a medical officer for the Anglo-Saxon Petroleum Company in Sarawak for nearly 20 years, and joined the RAMC two days after Pearl Harbor. Later described by Bill as 'a charming man', he was posted to Singapore, and wrote how on Sunday 8 February, before the first Japanese landings on the island, he had had lunch with 'Allardyce, Parkinson, Smallwood and Halstead' and that 'Smiley was unable to come.' Within three days casualties were coming to the hospital all day and night. On Black Friday, he recorded that 'Colonel Craven was breaking up all bottles of alcoholic drink.' Telephone contact was lost later that day, and by midnight the electricity supply had totally failed. The hospital was now effectively isolated and very few admissions were received. Early on Saturday 14 February the situation worsened as the water supply was cut off, and mortar attacks increased in intensity. By this time, Japanese troops were literally on the doorstep of the hospital, which was refuge to some 900 patients, many of whom were housed on makeshift beds in the wards or on stretchers in the corridors.

Later that day, at around 1.40pm, the hospital came under attack from about 100 Japanese soldiers. The exact sequence of events remains unclear, undoubtedly clouded in part by 'the fog of war.' The perimeter of the hospital was being guarded by men of the Loyal Regiment and 22 Punjabi Regiment; some sources describe the latter having mounted machine guns on the balconies of the hospital, despite the building displaying several red crosses. Other reports stated that there were no such emplacements, and that the critical development was a number of unarmed sappers and miners from the Punjabi Regiment fleeing from the grounds, passing into the rear entrance of the hospital and being followed by Japanese soldiers. On seeing the situation unfolding, Lieutenant W.F.J. Weston RAMC, walked out of the hospital towards the advancing troops, waving a large sheet as a white flag. He was immediately bayoneted and killed; he was 27 years old. His headstone poignantly reads: 'Greater love hath no man than this.'

Grave of Lieutenant Weston, Kranji

When Japanese soldiers entered the hospital, Captain Smiley was operating on Corporal R. Veitch, a member of the Volunteer Armoured

158

Car Battalion, FMSVF.[57] The anaesthetist was Captain R.M. Allardyce RAMC. An Irishman, born in Dublin in 1902, he had graduated in medicine from Trinity College Dublin in 1925. After a period in general practice in Manchester, he joined the RAMC and spent some time at the International Hospital, Kobe, where he learnt to speak Japanese. Despite the ensuing mayhem, Smiley completed the operation, amputating a foot, and as he did so a bullet was fired into the theatre. Japanese troops ordered the men out, and bayoneted Veitch on the operating table. Nearby was Captain Parkinson, the man who had lost the toss of a coin with Bill just a few weeks before. In the intervening weeks he had initially worked at Alexandra Military Hospital, but on 12 December 1941 had been posted to No 5 Casualty Clearing Station (CCS) in Malaya. Here he had managed to write some letters to his wife, describing the situation and how he had treated casualties not far from the front line. As the CCS moved south, he rejoined Alexandra Military Hospital in early 1942. As Japanese troops entered Parkinson was anaesthetising another patient, Corporal Holden of the Loyal Regiment. Holden was bayoneted whilst on the operating table and died, whilst Parkinson was bayoneted through the abdomen and gravely injured. He managed to escape into a nearby corridor, but collapsed and died less than thirty minutes later.[58]

Captain Smiley, along with several other men, was lined up against a wall by Japanese troops; he pointed towards the Red Cross brassard he was wearing and said that the building was a hospital. The Japanese took no notice of him whatsoever. For no apparent reason, a soldier lunged at Smiley's chest with his bayonet, the blade struck his cigarette case lying in his top pocket and deflected the blade from entering his chest. This undoubtedly saved his life. A second soldier bayoneted him in the groin, and Smiley was later to recall: 'It went straight into my iliac fossa.' A third soldier lunged towards Smiley who raised his hand. 'My thenar eminence was cut open.' He collapsed onto Corporal Sutton

---

57 Federation of Malay States Volunteer Force.
58 His gold cigarette case was somehow recovered and was later returned to his widow Sheila Parkinson.

whom he told to feign death, which they both did. Remarkably the two men survived, and 15 minutes later saw their commanding officer walking along the corridor towards them.

In the hospital wards, Japanese brutality and inhumanity was rife amongst the sick and wounded. Amongst those in the wards was Gunner F.G. 'Fergus' Anckorn, of 118 Field Regiment, Royal Artillery. Anckorn had arrived in Singapore on 29 January 1942, on-board USS *West Point*. Although serving as a gunner, he had an important second string to his bow, namely as a magician. Born in 1918, he had first shown an interest in magic when aged 4, and was the youngest member of The Magic Circle, having joined in 1936.

On Black Friday, Anckorn was driving a lorry through Singapore, towing a 25lb-gun along Thomson Road, to replace one that had been damaged. Soon after 1.00pm he came under attack by a formation of 27 Japanese aircraft which dropped bombs in the area. His lorry was hit, and he was unable to get out of the vehicle. He noticed that his right hand was 'hanging off' his arm and blood was pouring out 'like a bathroom tap.' The lorry was on fire and he kicked the door open, jumped, and was shot in the left leg. He was found in a ditch and pronounced dead by a friend, who removed his dog tags; the friend later escaped to Ceylon. This diagnosis of death was somewhat premature and Anckorn was rushed by lorry to a Casualty Clearing Station at the Fullerton Building. He was told by a surgeon, 'I'm sorry, son, I can't save your hand. It's got to come off.' Placed under anaesthetic, he woke the following day in Alexandra Military Hospital to see his heavily bandaged right arm supported from a hook in the ceiling. Fearing the worst, he asked the man next to him to count his fingers; to his relief, they were all there. There was, however, still significant bleeding, and the bandages were blood-soaked, a feature that caused some panic amongst the neighbouring patients. Drifting in and out of consciousness, Anckorn awoke to the sound of heavy footsteps and saw men, with their hands tied by barbed wire, being led from the ward at bayonet point. He then saw a Japanese soldier for the very first time and heard the cries of men nearby being bayoneted as they lay in their beds. Anckorn pulled his pillow over his face, and was later to write that he 'did not mind dying, but he did not want to see them killing him.' Drifting off to sleep again he woke to complete silence; he looked around the ward, there was no movement. All the other men were dead: he was the sole survivor in the ward from this atrocity. He later suggested that his survival was due to the Japanese seeing his blooded bandages along with his covered face and presuming that he was already dead.[59]

Fergus Anckorn (left) Bill Frankland and Dr Jan Bras. London, Summer 2017

Men who were led from the hospital (the exact numbers are unclear, but reports indicate at least 200) were tied together by barbed wire; many had serious injuries and hobbled as best they could. Many were killed on the lawns outside the hospital, and others were confined in a bungalow in nearby Alexandra Park. Here they were held in appalling conditions, some 50 to 70 men in rooms barely 9ft by 10ft. They were unable to move, and were forced to urinate on each other. Many men

---

59 Fergus Anckorn died on 22 March 2018, aged 99.

died from thirst and exhaustion or as a result of their wounds. They received no water from their captors, despite having been promised it. The bungalow came under attack from artillery, and eight men tried to escape, only one was successful, a man later described by Smiley as a 'rugby-playing infantry officer' who made it back to the hospital. The following morning, men were taken out in groups and killed. Those left in the bungalow probably had little doubt as to their fate, especially when hearing the men's screams, only to be made more obvious when a Japanese soldier returned to the bungalow, wiping blood off his bayonet. Amongst the men taken to the bungalow was Captain Allardyce, along with two corporals. Those remaining were under the impression either that he was being singled out as a hostage, or that he was required to treat Japanese casualties. However, his fate was no different from others who had been held in such appalling and inhumane conditions, and all three were killed.

A senior Japanese officer arrived at the hospital on Sunday 15 February at about 6.00pm and ordered all movement at the hospital to stop. Somewhat pointedly, Smiley, having had his wounds dressed by Corporal Sutton, defied the order and set about tending to the wounded who were still alive. Before long, he was back operating.[60] On Monday 16 February, Lieutenant General Yamashita, the GOC, called at the hospital and met with Lieutenant Colonel Craven. He expressed his regret for the 'hard time that the hospital had endured' and assured those still alive that 'they had nothing further to fear.' Yamashita said that he was a representative of the Emperor and that 'no higher honour could be paid to the hospital.'

---

60 Captain T.B. Smiley was awarded the Military Cross in December 1945. The citation read:

For conspicuous devotion to duty on 14th January (sic) 1942, when, although he had received three serious bayonet wounds, Captain Smiley insisted on carrying out his duties and continued to attend his patients in hospital. The recommendation was made by Lieutenant General A. E. Percival.

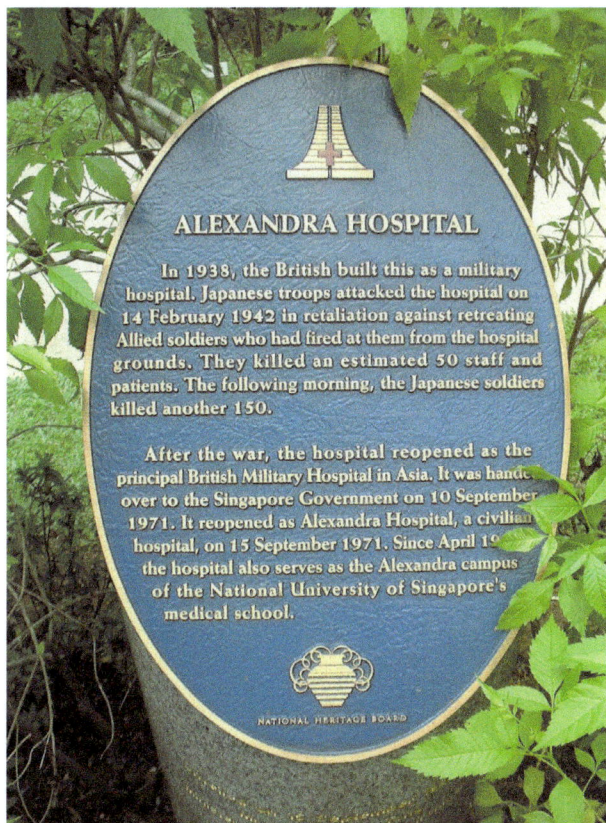

Commemorative plaque erected outside Alexandra Hospital, Singapore

The Final Hours

The final days of the campaign were marked by the ever-growing realisation by senior officers and politicians that, despite their earlier announcements, defeat was a very likely outcome for the Allies. Details of correspondence at the time clearly demonstrate the pressures that commanders were under. Churchill, writing on 10 February 1942 to General Archibald Wavell, Supreme Allied Commander, South West Pacific,[61] pointed out that the Allied troops under his command must

---

61 Wavell was appointed as Supreme Allied Commander on 30 December 1941, and first visited Singapore on 7 January 1942.

outnumber the Japanese and that 'There must at this stage be no thought of saving the troops or sparing the population. The battle must be fought to the bitter end at all costs.'

Wavell received the telegram on the same day that he travelled from his headquarters on Java to the beleaguered island. He met with Lieutenant General A.E. Percival[62] and saw the advancing Japanese forces in the north of the island. Three days later, on Black Friday, the Japanese forces had surrounded Singapore City and were within 5000 yards of the seafront; all of the city was now in range of the Japanese field artillery. Close on 1 million people were trapped in a city where the dead were lying in the streets. Wavell wrote to Percival advising him that 'You must fight it out to the end as you are doing.' Percival's reply showed significant insight when he wrote, 'There must come a time when in the interest of troops and civil population, further bloodshed will serve no useful purpose.' On the following day, 14 February, Churchill appears to have recognised the inevitable fate of Singapore.

General Percival took Holy Communion at his headquarters, Fort Canning, early on Sunday 15 February, before reading the latest reports from his experts. The gravest threat was the complete loss of water which was predicted to be imminent as the Japanese controlled all the main reservoirs on the island. Percival met with his commanders at 11.00am, when he summarised the options: either to counter-attack in order to gain food and water, or capitulate. He received a 'heartening' telegram from Wavell which read: 'I give you discretion to cease resistance. Whatever happens I thank you and all troops for your gallant efforts of the last few days.'

Percival decided to send a delegation to the enemy lines to seek a surrender, with hostilities to cease at 4.00pm. The delegation returned with news that Lieutenant General Yamashita[63] of the Imperial Japanese Army had other plans, and wanted a ceremony of surrender which was to be as degrading as possible to the Allies. He ordered that Percival and his staff, carrying the Union Jack and a White flag, were to go to the Ford

---

62 Percival, General Officer Commanding Malaya.
63 Also known as the Tiger of Malaya.

Automobile Works to surrender. They were also to fly the Japanese flag from the Cathay Building, itself Singapore's tallest. As Percival walked to sign the document of surrender he was accompanied by a number of his staff, including Major Cyril Wild, carrying the white flag. He was one of the few men who spoke Japanese, having previously worked in Japan for the Rising Sun Petroleum Company. The spectacle was captured by Japanese photographers, and provided images which have haunted the British ever since. Only one copy of the surrender document was signed, and this was kept by the Japanese. At 8.30pm on Sunday 15 February 1942 hostilities ceased: the Battle for Singapore was over.

In October 1945, Major Wild interrogated Yamashita who was then on trial for war crimes. He told Wild that if Percival had not capitulated when he did, the Japanese would have launched their final attack on the city at midnight. It can only be assumed that, if the actions of the Japanese in Nanking in 1937 were to have been repeated, many thousands in Singapore would have been raped, murdered and massacred on that day.

Although hostilities had ceased, medical officers of the RAMC were still faced with treating large numbers of sick and injured in truly testing conditions. As news sank in, Lieutenant Colonel Middleton remarked that for the medical services there was mixed emotions, since 'although they had been tried they were not found wanting.' He had, however, been incensed by a press release from the governor, describing 'four or five hundred wounded soldiers in the Fullerton Building receiving little or no attention.' 1MGH had taken the brunt of surgical cases during the last days of fighting, and Middleton later wrote to the governor explaining in no uncertain terms the devotion to duty by all medical staff at the time of capitulation, and how the death rate amongst casualties was, in fact, remarkably low considering the circumstances.

On the last day of hostilities, Lieutenant Colonel Middleton received a short note; it read:[64]

Tanglin hospital officers doing duty at 1MGH on the 15/2/1942

---

64 Some three months later, Middleton asked Bill for a report on the Tanglin Military Hospital, since Bill had, by default, become the commanding officer. His report was very brief, since, as he pointed out, he had only be in command for three days.

Sir

The following officers from Tanglin remained at the capitulation

Captain Hamilton-Gibbs

Captain Frankland

Captain Chilton

Lieutenant (QM) Welch

Signed A.W. Frankland.

Capt RAMC

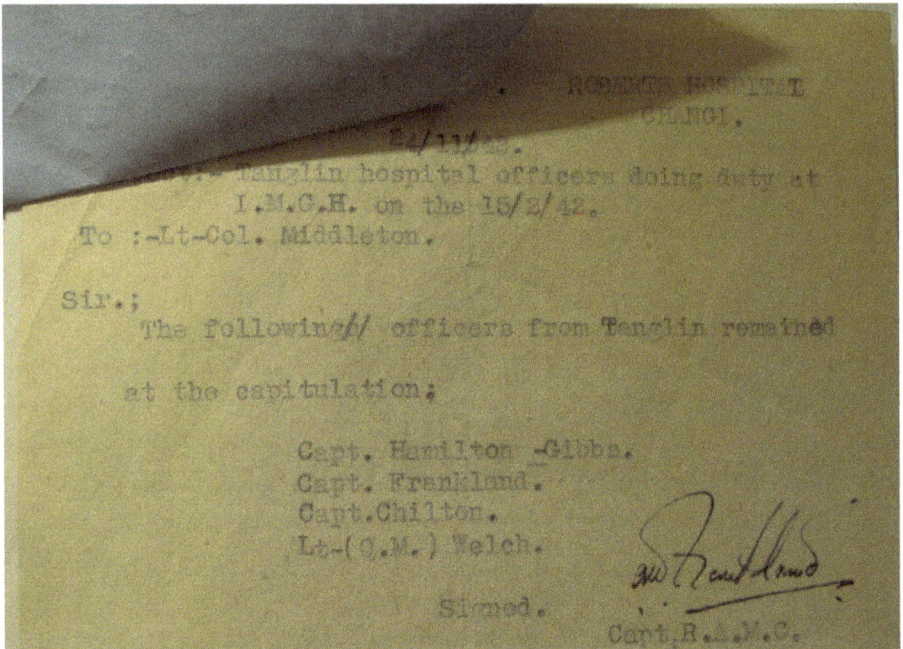

Memorandum signed by Captain A.W. Frankland RAMC, 15 February 1942.

For Bill, and thousands of other men serving their King and Country, the war was about to enter a most dreadful period, where faith and resolve would be challenged to extremes.

CHAPTER 6

CHANGI

In the Bag

Allied troops surrendered on Sunday 15 February 1942, with hostilities officially ceasing at 8.30pm. The Fall of Singapore was undoubtedly the greatest defeat for Britain during the war, sending shock waves back home and throughout the Empire. The figures make stark reading. In 70 days, 35,000 Japanese troops had advanced over 500 miles to effectively defeat a force three times its size, and captured thousands of square miles of territory. As the ink dried on the surrender document over 110,000 British, Australian and Indian troops, including many from the local volunteer forces,[65] became prisoners of war. For the Japanese, surrender was viewed as completely dishonourable and, for them, a betrayal of their Emperor. They were not prepared for such a rapid capitulation, nor for the sheer numbers of prisoners, and had no plans for managing the situation. Not surprisingly, many prisoners did not see a Japanese soldier for days; for some several weeks would pass before glimpsing their new masters.

Japanese troops march through Singapore. 16 February 1942

---

65 An estimated 14,400 members of the volunteer forces were taken prisoner.

Despite the surrender, Bill and many other medical officers still had a great deal of work to do, caring for the sick and injured under very difficult conditions. Water had yet to be restored to the hospitals, and casualties continued to be admitted. As Bill later explained, they felt that they had *become* prisoners, rather than *been taken* prisoners. Few Japanese were seen, although Bill recalled hearing that one soldier had entered the Victoria Theatre soon after the surrender, but left almost as quickly as he arrived; no one had bowed to him. Just a few weeks later such failure to show deference to their captors would provoke instant and savage retribution. Despite having not yet seen a single Japanese, Bill soon saw stark evidence of how the victors intended to rule.

Bill's POW Record Card. Note the incorrect spelling of his name

The Japanese were ill-prepared to control the population of Singapore and maintaining some semblance of law and order amongst the prisoners and the large civilian population (many of whom were considered undesirable by the Japanese) was a challenge. Under the terms of surrender, the Japanese allowed 1000 Allied troops to keep their weapons for 24 hours so as to maintain law and order. However, before long, looting started and three days after surrender Bill witnessed the Japanese response. Looking out from the Victoria Theatre, he saw a gruesome sight on nearby Fullerton Bridge. Placed high on poles were the heads of four looters. The message was very clear: if you were caught stealing you would lose your head. Bill summarised this occurrence as 'gruesome.'

As the fog of war started to lift, Bill and his colleagues at 1MGH were faced with more patients. By Tuesday 17 February there were 1847 patients in the different buildings, although 350 of them did not have a bed. Soon news was received that all prisoners were to move to Changi, a military cantonment 17 miles to the east of the city. Movement of the main bulk of prisoners commenced on 17 February, with men marching through the day and night. Each man was required to carry as much as possible, including rations, since the Japanese only allowed one lorry for every 1000 men. Australian and British troops were kept separate, and because of slow progress many were forced to sleep on the roadside. Men of the Argyll and Sutherland Highlanders were led by a piper, whilst other groups sang 'There'll always be an England' as they marched east. It was during this time that many learnt of the massacre at Alexandra Military Hospital which had taken place just a few days earlier. Along the route they passed many civilians who had turned out to watch; virtually all had put up hastily made Japanese flags in deference to their new masters. Some Indians and Malays jeered, but in contrast the Chinese were stony-faced. One 18-year-old boy, Lee Kuan Yew,[66] described seeing 'an endless stream of bewildered men who did not know what had happened.' A few made surreptitious waves, some even attempted to offer small gifts of food and drink. As soldiers made their way to Changi they saw and smelt the results of a recently finished conflict, with burnt-out vehicles, pitted roads and rotting bodies. Amongst those making the journey was Lieutenant E.S. 'Eric' Lomax[67]

---

66 Later to be the first Prime Minister of Singapore.
67 Lomax would later write of his captivity in the Far East in a book, *The Railway Man*, published 1995. A film of the same name was produced nearly 20 years later; Bill Frankland attended the premiere in London, in December 2013.

of the Royal Corps of Signals. He had been stationed at Percival's headquarters, Fort Canning, during the Battle of Singapore, and later summarised the move to Changi as '…the British Army marching to its humiliation… obeying orders of an enemy which could not be seen.' By the evening of 18 February, 45,000 men had arrived at Changi.

Not all the prisoners were sent to Changi. On 17 February, Indian troops were separated from their British officers, one of the latter remarking, 'I suppose this is the parting of the waves.' They were led to the former racecourse at Farrer Park where about 45,000 men were addressed by Captain Mohan Singh of the Indian Army. He had served with 1/14 Punjab Regiment, but was taken prisoner at the Battle of Jitra, in North-West Malaya, in mid-December 1941. He was responsible for founding the Indian National Army (INA), whose aim was to gain independence for India through military action.[68] He relayed the views of the Imperial Japanese Army, that 'the Japanese Army will treat you not as prisoners of war, but as friends.' The exact numbers who joined the INA is unclear: estimates vary between 20,000 and 40,000, and many who did were sent to Changi. Here they guarded men who, just a few days earlier, had been their comrades. Many of the INA relished their newfound position and the humiliation that they could inflict on the prisoners, their former leaders.

Responsibility for moving the sick and wounded from Singapore City fell to a senior Australian medical officer, Lieutenant Colonel J.G.G. 'Glyn' White AAMC.[69] A small, slim and wiry man with boundless energy, his nickname was 'Splinter White.' Often quick-tempered, he was noted to be shrewd and uncompromising in whatever he did. He had arrived in Malaya in January 1941 to prepare medical services for the main bulk of Australian troops due to arrive in the following months. At the time of surrender in 1942 he was running a hospital facility at St Andrew's Cathedral in Singapore. On Monday 16 February, Brigadier Stringer ordered him to carry out the Japanese instructions to move all prisoners

---

68 Singh was later replaced by Subhas Chandra Bose as leader of the INA in the
    spring of 1943.

69 AAMC: Australian Army Medical Corps.

from the various hospitals in Singapore. British and Australians were to go to Changi and Indians to Nee Soon Camp (to the north of the island). The senior Japanese medical officer, Colonel C.L. Sekiguchi, allowed just seven days, and allocated a mere five ambulances for the task. White protested vehemently stating that it would be impossible to move the patients (numbering at least 9,000) in that time and asked for more vehicles. Sekiguchi agreed telling the Australian that if he could assemble the vehicles, he would consider the matter. Next morning, White lined up twenty 3-ton trucks, fifty-five ambulances, and a car for himself. Quite surprisingly, he was given passes for all of them. Despite clear orders that only 250 hospital beds could be taken, and no medical equipment or supplies at all, White ensured 4,500 beds and 7,000 mattresses were moved, hidden under which was a range of medical stores. Good fortune held. After a few days, Sekiguchi was replaced and White had to deal with his successor. He successfully convinced him that Sekiguchi had actually given a week to move each of the British, Australian and Indian contingents, allowing three weeks in total.

Changi: A New Home

By the end of February 1942 Changi was home to nearly 50,000 British and Australian troops. The name Changi has become synonymous with the events following the fall of Singapore, and an understanding of its history is necessary to appreciate the conditions which many thousands, including Bill, faced over the ensuing months and years.

Following the cessation of World War 1, there was political upheaval throughout the world, not least in the Far East, where Japan emerged as a potential world power. The British response was to enhance Singapore's defences, building the naval base at Sembawang. Fixed defences were also needed along the southern and eastern coasts of the island as military strategists believed any assault on the island would come from the sea. Changi, an area roughly 4 miles square, to the east of the island, was first surveyed by Major General Sir Webb Gillman in 1924, when he found little more than a few atap huts, one Public Works Department building and, perhaps ironically, a Japanese hotel next to the sea, serving as a brothel. The initial plans for development were drawn up in 1926 and the following year Gillman returned to prepare detailed plans for the defences and two main camp areas. The latter, named Kitchener and Roberts Barracks, were to house men of the Royal Artillery responsible for manning the newly installed coastal guns. There were numerous setbacks with the project, many relating to acquisition of land. Once these were overcome, building took place rapidly and the first officers' quarters were completed by early 1928. The following year, as a result of political and economic developments following the Great Depression, the British government enacted wide-ranging economies. By the middle of 1930 all military building on Singapore had stopped. In 1931 Japan invaded Manchuria, an act which prompted the British government to reassess the situation in the Far East. Building works recommenced in 1932, and continued unabated through until 1941. Construction of the Johore Battery, comprising three 15-inch guns, started in 1935, being funded in large part by a gift of £500,000 from the Sultan of Johor. The guns were made in Britain, at the Vickers Yard, Barrow-in-Furness. By a remarkable coincidence, boys from St Bees had visited the yard in 1929. Amongst the party who saw the guns being assembled was Bill Frankland, aged 17. He recalled being told that the guns were to be shipped abroad to form part of coastal defences. Perhaps as part of the security for the operation, he was told that they were to go to Spain.

Both Kitchener and Roberts Barracks were completed by 1936, by which time another barrack block, composed primarily of wooden huts, had been established to the east of Roberts Barracks. This housed men of the Indian Army, mostly Punjabi regiments, serving with anti-aircraft regiments, and was named India Barrack (or India Lines). One further barrack block was built in 1936 at the highest point in the area, about 1 mile south of Roberts Barracks, to house an infantry battalion. Named Selarang Barracks, it was the most modern in design and the only place in Changi with hot baths. By 1941, all the barrack blocks were fully occupied: Kitchener Barracks was home to Royal Engineers; Roberts Barracks to the Royal Artillery; anti-aircraft regiments were in India Barracks; and Selarang Barracks was home to the Gordon Highlanders. Changi also hosted a new civilian gaol, built in 1935, and this would, like the barrack blocks, later serve as a place of imprisonment for Allied soldiers as well as civilian internees following capitulation. Despite all these developments a number of coastal swamps were overlooked; they were liable to flooding, and served as breeding grounds for mosquitoes.

Following the surrender, the organisation of Changi was the responsibility of HQ Malaya Command, which answered to the Imperial Japanese Army. Six administrative areas were established, each with their own command structure, and movement between areas was rigorously controlled. Troops were allocated into four administrative areas, namely: Australian Imperial Force (AIF), Fortress Troops, 18 Division, and 3 (Indian) Corps. The other two areas were Central Hospital of Roberts Barracks Hospital, and the garden area. As Allied prisoners arrived, men of 18 Division were allocated to Roberts and India Barracks, men of 11 Division[70] to Kitchener Barracks and the Australian Imperial Force to Selarang. Now 50,000 men were housed in accommodation which was originally designed for about 3,600.

The New Hospitals

The Australians established a hospital in Selarang Barracks (where 1MGH had been based until 10 February 1942) and the transfer of all their patients was completed by 23 February. They opened 14 sickbays, each holding ten men, but kept dysentery patients in a separate building. They also established an operating theatre and an X-ray facility. British medical services occupied Roberts Barracks, which consisted of seven brick-built, three-storey buildings,[71] a two-storey NAAFI building, a sergeant's mess, a cinema, a gymnasium, and about 20 atap huts. Named Roberts Hospital, it officially opened on 26 February 1942, with the first operation taking place on 2 March. One barrack block was converted to an operating theatre, another to an isolation ward and two blocks

---

70 11 Division was part of 3 (Indian) Corps; however, it contained a number of British regiments including 2nd East Surrey, Leicestershire, and elements of the Royal Artillery.
71 Arranged around the perimeter of the barrack square.

(Numbered 144 and 151) into dysentery wards. Wards were made up of barrack rooms, each designed to hold 40 men, but as more patients arrived each room became increasingly crowded, housing up to 140 men.

Roberts Hospital

On 25 February, 10 days after surrender, the Victoria Theatre closed, with the last of the sick and wounded being moved to Roberts Hospital. Bill made the journey in a vehicle (he remembers it was either an ambulance or a truck), caring for some of his patients. As they passed the Singapore Cricket Club he spotted a Japanese soldier in the middle of the pitch, defaecating in public. It was the very first time he had seen the enemy following the surrender, and the memory of that incident stayed with Bill for the rest of his life. The final elements of 1MGH closed on 2 March, by which time all patients had been transferred to Roberts Hospital, along with a range of equipment and rations.

No sooner had the last of the British prisoners arrived at Roberts Hospital than the Japanese ordered the Australians to move their hospital from Selarang to Roberts Barracks. The move took a week, and was completed by 11 March, by which time 950 patients had been transferred. Roberts Hospital was now a combined facility, although the Australians maintained their independence. Australians, under the command of Colonel D.C. Pidgon OBE AAMC,[72] occupied three barrack blocks, the NAAFI building, the gymnasium, and the sergeants' mess, and they also took over some atap huts.

Hospital staff found Roberts Barracks in a very poor state. Both Roberts Barracks and Alexandra Military Hospital were situated near important military targets, the former supporting the local heavy artillery; both had come under heavy attack by the enemy. Men arriving at Roberts Barracks found there was no electric lighting, no sewage disposal and water supply was extremely limited. These deficiencies combined with shortages of equipment and stores made conditions extremely difficult; many of those arriving summarised the situation as 'perfect chaos.' The skill and determination of Royal Engineers ensured that electrical generators were operating within a few days, and by the time Bill arrived, the electricity supply was working. Restoration of piped water took rather longer, and for the first weeks the supply was very limited. One doctor described how 'teeth were foul, bodies were foul, sheets were foul and there was stench of wounds and dysentery.' Due to the water shortage, Bill could only wash his hands and face during his first 10 days at Changi. As Bill looked out from Changi he could see thunderstorms breaking over Johor, and wished that the rain clouds would venture just a little further south and bring rainfall to the camp. Finally a thunderstorm struck Changi and Bill was able to enjoy his first shower for close on a month. But there were other challenges,

---

72 Colonel Pidgon died whilst a prisoner of war in Manchuria, 6 July 1945.

not least being able to shave, and Bill had one razor blade which was sharpened on a number of occasions and served him well for two years.

At Roberts Hospital there were a range of specialist doctors, with surgeons, led by Colonel Taylor, anaesthetists, radiologists and pathologists, supported by a number of junior medical staff, including Bill. However, as a hospital it was lacking one vital component: nurses. Virtually all had been evacuated in the days leading up to surrender. As a consequence soldiers had to act as nurses, but this soon led to problems, since they had no real nursing experience. Colonel Taylor summarised the situation as:

There was a fraction of the minimum necessary water, and never any possibility of feeding and nursing the wounded as they should have been fed and nursed.

The situation in Roberts Hospital during these early days was noted by one visitor: Captain C.W. 'Charles' Wells, MRCVS, a Government Veterinary Officer, who had worked in Malaya since 1936. By the time hostilities commenced he had an established career along with a wife and two young daughters. Like so many government employees he was a member of the volunteer forces, serving as an officer with the 3rd Battalion FMSVF, where he was responsible for a number of anti-aircraft batteries. As the Japanese advanced south in December 1941, he ensured that his family were evacuated, whilst he continued with both his military and veterinary duties. Taken prisoner on Singapore, he was imprisoned in Changi and on 20 March visited a colleague, Lieutenant J.N. Hughes, 1st Bn Malay Regiment, in hospital. Hughes had been shot in the thigh and his right leg was subsequently amputated. He was one of the first to be admitted to Roberts Hospital, where he spent three and a half months. Wells recorded the situation in his diary which, like him, survived until the end of the war:

...the hospital was an absolutely bloody mess – a lazar house; foul-smelling, dirty and overcrowded. I can't help feeling a few Army nurses about the place would work wonders.

Wells' views regarding nurses were shared by Bill who felt that their presence would have been so valuable in ensuring care for the sick throughout the years of imprisonment.

Captain Charles Wells 1938
In centre of picture, to the right of his wife and daughter

Many of the first to be admitted to Roberts Hospital were suffering from battle injuries sustained during the fighting: Julian Taylor recorded 986 battle casualties, of whom 40 died. Bill recalled seeing men in hospital, including survivors from the sinking of HMS *Prince of Wales* and *Repulse* in December 1941, who still required hospital treatment. The hospital was not equipped to provide the treatment for many of these casualties, who were in need of repatriation to appropriate and specialised facilities. Taylor described how at this early stage:

...medical officers identified men who were in need of repatriation, and despite the acceptance of this by medical members of the IJA, not a single sick or injured man was repatriated over the ensuring three and a half years.

Diet, Disease and Death

Colonel Taylor visited Roberts Barracks soon after the surrender and recorded numerous problems with the infrastructure. Most worryingly, he found that slit trenches, dug very close to the barrack blocks, were used as latrines. He saw fly larvae around the trenches and predicted that with the impending move of prisoners to the site, a 'formidable epidemic of dysentery was to be expected.' Before long, he wrote how 'a plague of flies visited the hospital with biological punctuality, attracted by the pus of the wounds. Maggots were soon seen in wounds, although the beneficial effects of their activities were not.'

DYSENTERY

By 24 March 1942 Roberts Hospital housed 2600 patients, many of whom were suffering from dysentery, with the first cases presenting soon after their arrival at Changi. It appears likely that some may have arrived with symptoms and/or carrying the infective organisms. Soon there was an epidemic of bacillary dysentery, which did not abate until November 1942. Once infected, the disease was acute in onset and associated with abdominal pain and the frequent passage of stools. Invariably patients also developed nausea and were febrile. Bill noted that patients who were about to die invariably developed nystagmus during their last 24 hours. Stools contained mucus, usually with blood, and when samples were examined microscopically in the laboratory, bacteria and a typical bacillary exudate were seen. Interestingly, Bill never sent stool samples to the laboratory since, faced with patients passing blood and mucus, he did not require a microscopic confirmation of his clinical diagnosis of dysentery. To control the disease special dysentery wards were opened at Roberts Hospital. The initial plan was for two wards to be sited next to the kitchen area, which Captain Marshall noted ironically was 'a great start.' Sense prevailed and the isolation wards were placed further away. They opened on 15 March, by which time there was an average of 80 admissions per day for dysentery. Bill was responsible for one of the dysentery wards, where he treated the sick whilst, at the same time, attempting to control the spread of highly infectious and potentially lethal diseases. His other duties at this time included seeing all patients due for discharge from the hospital and return to their units.

Bill felt that the management of the dysentery wards left much to be desired, and he was not impressed by some of his more senior colleagues. The senior officer responsible for the laboratory facilities supporting the wards was Lieutenant Colonel L.R.S. MacFarlane RAMC. He was a regular Army officer, who had been serving in Singapore for at least two years before the outbreak of war, and had been accompanied by his wife, who gave birth to their son in July 1940. His wife and son had been evacuated from Singapore just prior to the surrender when MacFarlane had been Senior Medical Officer (SMO) at Changi. Despite his seniority, Bill was not impressed with MacFarlane's management of patients nor with his attempts to control the spread of disease, both of which left considerable room for improvement. His lack of ability finally led to him being sacked from the dysentery ward and he was placed in a tent on his own. Bill lost contact with him during the war,[73] but many years later, when visiting the Royal Army Medical College at Millbank in London, he was quite shocked to find that MacFarlane had risen to the exalted position of Professor of Pathology (a post once held by Sir Almroth Wright).[74]

Another officer serving in the dysentery wards was a pathologist, Dr J.E. 'Jack' Ennis IMS,[75] a man whom Bill found most efficient in his work, and from whom Bill learnt a great deal. Ennis had qualified in medicine in London and joined the Indian Medical Service in 1938. He trained in pathology and was sent to central Malaya, where he was in charge of a small hospital at Kuala Lipis. Here he met a nurse, Elizabeth Petrie, and after falling in love they were engaged in July 1941. With the outbreak of war and the Japanese advance, Ennis retreated to Singapore where he was attached to 1MGH. Ennis served as an anaesthetist and worked in the hastily configured operating theatres in the Fullerton Building, alongside Colonel Taylor. However, on 11 February 1942 he managed to find time to marry his fiancée. This required a special licence issued by the Governor, Sir Shenton Thomas, and *en route* to the ceremony the bride and groom felt the full force of the Japanese attack, twice coming under machine gun fire. Following the surrender, Captain and Mrs Ennis were able to spend a few days together, but at the beginning of March they were moved to Changi, he to Roberts Hospital, and she to internment in the civilian gaol. Ennis kept a diary throughout this time which records

---

73 MacFarlane was at Nakom-Pathon on the Burma Railway from 1943 to 1945.
    Interestingly he was described as 'particularly useless' by some of those with him.
74 MacFarlane served as Professor of Pathology, 1952-60.
75 Indian Medical Service.

in great detail both his professional activities, and those of other medical officers, including Bill's, as well as his more personal thoughts.

Captain Jack Ennis

Mrs Elizabeth Ennis

As one of the few pathologists in Roberts Hospital, Ennis was responsible for the diagnostic laboratory. He commenced duties there on 2 March, being one of the last medical officers to arrive, and immediately witnessed a victory cavalcade of 11 cars carrying senior Japanese officers driving through the camp. Ennis set up the laboratory the next day, having brought some equipment with him, as well as scrounging other pieces locally. On 4 March he wrote how the epidemic of dysentery was beginning, and noted how his laboratory was 'near to three latrines'; added to this he was suffering from dysentery himself. His work in the laboratory was primarily focussed on the diagnosis of dysentery and malaria, but he was also responsible for undertaking post-mortem examinations, the first being of a man who had died of a pulmonary embolism following a fractured femur. Before long, he was undertaking post-mortems on men who had died of dysentery. During this period, Ennis described how 'we work and sleep to the sound of flies, defaecation, vomiting and the rattle of bedpans all the time.'

Care of the sick was not only the responsibility of medical staff, as there were many ancillary tasks to be undertaken. Doctors found that many of those recovering from dysentery made excellent ancillary staff to help on the wards, and had the 'advantage' of personal experience of the disease, as well as ongoing recovery. A number of soldiers were housed in Roberts Barracks, amongst them Gunner J.B. 'Jack' Chalker, serving with the Royal Artillery. A member of 18 Division, he arrived in Singapore on-board USS *West Point* on 29 January 1942. Chalker was a talented artist and recorded life in captivity, both at Changi and later on the Burma Railway. Many of his paintings and sketches depict the sick and their care by doctors. Chalker described the conditions at Roberts Hospital as '…pitiful, as they were packed together in the heat of the day. Initially there had been a critical shortage of drinking water in the hospital.' Although not formally assigned to the hospital, Chalker and a number of his colleagues routinely tried to wash blankets from the wards. These, soiled with blood and faeces, were taken to a nearby beach where the men would wade in and attempt to clean them as best they could, then dry them in the sun.

The extent of the dysentery epidemic is revealed in the admission records for Roberts Hospital; in March 1942 there were 2739 admissions for dysentery, and in April 1942, 2325. The disease respected neither rank, race nor creed, and in April seven RAMC officers were admitted, including Lieutenant Colonel Middleton and Bill's friend, Captain Hetreed.

The effect of dysentery from a patient's view was vividly described by Charles Wells who was admitted to hospital in late-March 1942. His diary records:

23 March

Brought to hospital 2 days ago, got dysentery, passing blood, awful belly-ache and feeling like death. 3 dysentery deaths last night, one within 3 feet of me; he died in delirium.

25 March

Feeling a bit better. Hospital under-staffed. Still passing blood. It is essential here that one does all one can to help one's self, because individual attention is out of the question. Been put on a light diet – sweet rice pudding, shepherd's pie, porridge, savoury rice and tea. Legs feel wonky. First nightmare for years last night. Haven't had a smoke for 3 days.

27 March

Bored to hell in hospital, destitute of anything to read.

Acutely homesick today.

28 March

Discharged from hospital today, had to walk back a mile and half in boiling sun to my billet.

Weight: 10st 2lb, have lost 3 stones since capture.

Bill also developed dysentery and was off duty for seven days. He was not admitted to hospital, but treated himself the best he could, by drinking as much water as possible. Like so many who had the condition, he described how 'he felt like death.'

Initially the only treatment available for bacillary dysentery was administration of a sea water enema combined with fluid by mouth. Drugs which might help were in varying supply, and included castor oil and magnesium sulphate. Calomel was used in small doses when neither was available, but it was not found to be effective and gave little relief to the pain. More severe cases were treated by the intravenous administration of sterile saline, but this was not without risks, particularly those from the dubious sterility of solutions. Antibacterial agents such as sulphonamide and sulphaguanidine were used for treating some cases, but their supply was exhausted within just a few days. However, it was reported that three days' treatment returned a man who was passing 40-50 stools a day to one with almost normal bowel habits.

Although the majority of cases of dysentery were of the bacillary form, some were the more serious amoebic dysentery, caused by the protozoa *Entamoeba histolytica*. Records show that at Roberts Hospital about 10 cases were admitted each week. The condition often progressed very rapidly, with death occurring in 7-10 days following initial symptoms. Amoebic dysentery was associated with excruciating pain and distension of the bowel, with patients needing to pass up to 40 stools a day. They rapidly became dehydrated, and often passed a dark-coloured stool, described as resembling 'anchovy sauce.' Men often became deranged in the last few hours before death. At post-mortem the appearance was one of ulceration of the bowel, in contrast to the findings in bacillary dysentery of 'plum-coloured' swollen bowel.

Diagnosis of amoebic dysentery involved examination of stool samples, a task that kept Jack Ennis and several others very busy. There was a high incidence of carriers, those in whom the protozoan cysts could be found, but who did not have symptoms. A number of factors appeared to have exacerbated the condition, notably the diet which was deficient in both quantity and quality, with the lack of fats and vitamins believed to be critical factors. Presentation of amoebic dysentery could be unusual and confusing. Bill recalled one such case where, from the history and clinical examination, a diagnosis of carcinoma of the distal colon was made, which was deemed to be inoperable. Colonel Taylor was later very upset to find at post-mortem that the man had, in fact, been suffering from amoebic dysentery.

Treatment of amoebic dysentery involved the administration of either emetine which, although active against protozoa, also induced vomiting, or one of a number of arsenical compounds. Many of those suffering from amoebic dysentery remained carriers for many years, and continued to have intestinal disease, perhaps intermittently, for long periods after the war.

Although the number of admissions from dysentery abated slightly during the middle of 1942, they increased again in the autumn. This coincided with the arrival of a large number of Dutch troops from the Dutch East Indies. Again Bill was faced with treating many sick men, and he noted how the will to survive was an important factor in overcoming disease. The Dutch contingent included a significant number of men native to the islands who, at the time of the Japanese invasion in March 1942, had quite literally been placed in a Dutch military uniform and told they were now soldiers. These men had received little, if any, military training, and the vast majority had never been out of their own villages, let alone left their islands. Bill noted that in Changi when they developed dysentery they appeared to give up the will to live, and soon died.

The scale of the epidemic facing Bill and his colleagues is illustrated in the records from Roberts Hospital. From February 1942 to February 1943, there were 15,379 admissions for dysentery. It is testimony to the professional care provided by the medical services that Colonel Taylor recorded an overall death rate during this period of only 1.5% for bacillary dysentery and 2.2% for amoebic dysentery. These figures do not, however, match Bill's experience as a medical officer responsible for a dysentery ward. He found that bacillary dysentery was exclusively responsible for deaths in his ward, and in his practice he never actually diagnosed a case of amoebic dysentery.

PSYCHIATRIC DISORDERS

Despite his duties in the dysentery wards, one of the first cases Bill was asked to treat at Changi was unrelated to any form of intestinal disease. In late-April 1942, he had to treat Captain Smith, a paranoid schizophrenic. Fortunately Bill had considerable experience in psychiatry, having undertaken a number of psychiatry locums before the war. Bill made his instructions regarding Captain Smith quite clear to those responsible for his care, and stressed that there were to be no sharp objects, such as tools, near the patient. The men responsible for Smith included an Australian medical orderly (Private Jeeps) who had previously worked with psychiatric patients, and was aware of the dangers when nursing these patients. Smith was to be kept under close observation on a chair. For some reason, the chair broke and Jeeps set about repairing it. He found a number of tools, including a small axe. Rather stupidly he placed the tools near the chair before starting the repair. In an instant Smith seized the axe and struck Jeeps on the head, impaling the instrument in his skull. Bill was quickly summoned and saw a man walking towards him with an axe protruding from his head.

Acting rapidly, Bill immediately contacted Julian Taylor and within 10 minutes had taken the patient to theatre for surgery. That evening Bill was sitting next to Julian Taylor as they ate their meal, when a clerk approached Taylor with a copy of a 'Dangerously Ill' (DI) form for signature. Taylor was not impressed and told the clerk in no uncertain terms that none of his patients were on the list. Taylor made it clear that he expected the man to make a full recovery from his head injury. Bill met the man some 4-5 months later, when the only residual neurological deficit was a loss of colour on one side of his visual field.[76]

DIPHTHERIA

At Roberts Hospital, dysentery was just one of several infectious diseases confronting Bill and his colleagues, and he treated over 1000 cases during his years of imprisonment. In August 1942 there was an outbreak of diphtheria, which worsened over the following month, and at its height 846 patients were hospitalised. The very first cases, involving the typical lesions of the pharynx and formation of a faucial diphtheritic membrane, were recorded in March 1942. If untreated, these patients would die in 2-3 days. As the infection spread the presentation of disease changed, with a significant number of cases showing cutaneous signs, either with ulcerative lesions or a diphtheritic membrane forming at the scrotum, the latter being a secondary infection in those already suffering from scrotal dermatitis. The latter was due to a deficiency of B vitamins, a condition which Bill studied in some detail (*vide infra*). Many also developed complications of either myocarditis or neuritis. Bill suffered from a mild bout of diphtheria, affecting his nose and lips, as a secondary infection to cheilitis (inflammation of the lips), itself a consequence of B vitamin deficiency. His reddened and inflamed lips were now covered by white membranes. Similar changes occurred at his nostrils, although the infection at neither site actually caused any

---

76 Captain Smith survived imprisonment and was liberated from Kranji Hospital in August 1945.

clinical problems.[77]

By early July 1942 staff at Roberts Hospital were faced with an epidemic of diphtheria, and one floor of one barrack block was put aside for the hospitalised cases. This soon proved totally inadequate and medical staff took over a whole block as well as some atap huts. The disease spread rapidly and medical staff were not immune; one medical officer and 14 orderlies contracted the disease. The medical officer was Captain H.E. 'Hugh' de Wardener RAMC, who described how he developed cutaneous diphtheria in his foot. When playing football he damaged the skin of his feet, leaving an open sore, and believed that bacteria from the diphtheria wards had entered his body by that route. The condition, he noted, was 'very, very painful.'

The epidemic reached its height in the autumn of 1942, when over 300 cases were admitted in both September and October. Despite repeated requests to the Japanese for diphtheria anti-serum, none was forthcoming despite, as Jack Ennis wrote, 'there being huge stocks at Tanglin a few months earlier.' To try to circumvent the shortage, doctors took blood from patients who had recovered, and made their own anti-serum from this. Captain de Wardener received this anti-serum and described how 'I had one shot and the pain just disappeared, it was marvellous.' However, he noted it was not effective for cases of diphtheria involving the respiratory tract.

Bill found himself in an ethical dilemma as he treated a man with diphtheria. The patient, a private, was also suffering from dysentery and malaria and was extremely sick. Bill felt that even with treatment

---

77 This was not the first time Bill had suffered from diphtheria. In 1937 he had suffered from bilateral diphtheritic conjunctivitis after taking a throat swab from a 12-year-old boy with pharyngeal diphtheria. During the procedure the boy, who was being most uncooperative and had to be restrained by two nurses and three medical students, coughed all over Bill's face and three days later he developed a 'mildly uncomfortable membranous conjunctivitis'. He remained on duty and the infection cleared the following day after Bill received anti-diphtheria serum. However, 10 days later he developed severe serum sickness in response to the anti-serum and was forced to take to his bed. The boy was the only patient Bill ever physically restrained.

he was unlikely to survive, but without anti-serum he was convinced he would die. Bill was aware that the pharmacy had just one dose of anti-serum and asked Captain E.K. Cruickshank RAMC if that last dose might be given to his sick patient. He was told that an hour earlier another patient had been admitted, an officer, suffering from diphtheria and malaria and was relatively well. Before him was the classic case of 'the Doctor's Dilemma', not too dissimilar from that described by George Bernard Shaw in his play of 1906.[78] The officer received the anti-serum and, in hindsight, Bill felt that his patient would have died, regardless of whether he had received treatment or not.

A DEFICIENT DIET

For the thousands of men taken prisoner by the Japanese in the Far East, malnutrition would be the greatest threat to their health throughout the long years of captivity. In February 1942, as the men of the defeated army made their way to Changi, all were advised to take as much food as they could carry; many took tinned food, which lasted about 10 days. This advice was fortuitous. On arrival at Changi it was almost two weeks before the Japanese started to provide what came to be known as 'the basic ration.' Despite its name, this was severely deficient in both quality and quantity of nutrients. In the first months at Changi the daily ration for each prisoner was:

Rice 450g, Sugar 15g, Salt 20g, Tea 4g, Fish 70g, Vegetables 100g and Oil 25g. In addition, 20g of rice polishings (the bran layer of rice, removed with milling) were provided, but at erratic intervals.

The rice-based diet became their staple, but inadequate, diet for over 1250 days. The first effect recorded by the men was constipation, which lasted for about 10 days, one prisoner noted it was similar to being 'egg bound.' One man noted that eating rice three times a day led to pain in the stomach straight after the meal but within 1 hour a feeling of hunger had returned. Men also developed urinary frequency, a symptom due

---

78 The play had been written by Shaw following a conversation with Sir Almroth Wright. In June 1943, rehearsals for a production of *The Doctor's Dilemma* started at Changi, but the play was dropped for a more easily produced play.

to the lack of salt in the diet. The diet was dangerously lacking in fats and proteins and provided barely one-third of the daily requirement of B vitamins. During the first year in captivity, rations were reduced numerous times: for example, in April 1942, as retribution for alleged mistreatment of Japanese prisoners in India. Further starvation followed from reduction in supplies; milk was no longer available by the end of April, and flour was not provided after September 1942. Overall the quantity of rice provided by the Japanese fell by some 20% during the first year. Unsurprisingly, deficiency syndromes occurred in many held in Changi, and these led to specific clinical symptoms and contributed to the impact and effect of infectious diseases.

Probably the first deficiency disease to become clinically apparent was beriberi, due to a lack of vitamin B1 – thiamine – which was recorded within the first month of arrival at Changi. The timing was to be expected, since the body's stores of thiamine are depleted after 4-6 weeks on a deficient diet. Many of the earliest cases were seen in older men, regular soldiers with an established career in the Army. They were already suffering from subclinical liver disease, the result of long-term alcohol consumption which contributed to a reduction in thiamine stores. By June 1942, nearly 1000 cases had been diagnosed, and despite the medical authorities seeking help from the Japanese, little in the way of treatment was forthcoming. The attitude of the Japanese was painfully apparent when an Australian medical officer requested vitamin supplements, and was informed that 'vitamins are luxuries'. The extent of the problem is illustrated in records from Roberts Hospital: between February 1942 and May 1944 over 2000 men were hospitalised because of beriberi.

Several forms of beriberi were recognised, although the most common were the wet and dry forms, the former being more numerous. Wet beriberi was characterised by development of oedema, initially of the legs and feet, later spreading to involve the abdomen and face. Neurological changes were also noted, with the development of painful feet, so-called 'happy' or 'electric' feet, and in some patients there was loss of motor nerve function, leading to a foot drop. The more serious form was dry beriberi, which caused optic nerve damage. Bill had to treat many patients and noted how those with dry beriberi lost their central vision early in the disease. One man who developed this problem was a footballer who played in goal, and reported that this affected his eyesight, causing him to let in goals. Worryingly, Bill also noted that he had lost his own central vision, a sign that he, too, was suffering from beriberi.

The first case of wet beriberi was recorded by Jack Ennis on 14 April 1942, who noted two weeks later that 'beriberi is on the increase, with many cases dying'. Less than a week later, he recorded how six medical officers were showing signs, of the disease, with oedema of the ankles and legs. The impact of beriberi is clearly shown by personal accounts from Charles Wells. Having recovered from a bout of dysentery in March 1942, he suffered a number of blackouts in April 1942. When standing up he had to hold onto a support for 4-5 seconds, to prevent himself from collapsing. Several others in his unit were also affected, and Wells suggested that the cause was a low-protein diet, contributing to a loss of tone of blood vessels throughout the body. Just a few weeks later he found he was suffering from beriberi, and his diary records his experiences:

30 April 1942
I have now almost recovered from hospital. Legs, not so good – knee reflexes are definitely reduced but so far I have not noticed any oedema of the legs or feet or any skin anaesthesia, both of which are becoming increasingly common in camp – early symptoms of beriberi.
1 May
Last night found my ankles and feet were very oedematous, possibly the first stages of beriberi. Overall, feel rather in the dumps today.
2 May
Saw a medical specialist today; I've got beriberi alright, the wet oedematous type. Am to go into hospital tomorrow for a week's treatment.
3 May
In hospital, started on new a diet today; is qualitatively marvellous, quantitatively meagre. Sweet oat meal porridge, tinned herring, a little rice a slice of bread and a cup of tea with milk in it for breakfast.13 army biscuits to eat in the day, 24 vitamin B1 tablets, and Ideal milk. Lunch M&V[79] pie with

---

79 M&V: meat and vegetable.

pastry, rice and spinach, then sweet rice pudding.
It is really shattering to see officers wandering around like scavenging dogs at mealtimes, trying to cadge some extra food.
9 May
Still in hospital and feeling pretty well.
There are some pretty grim beriberi cases in here, one or two absolutely paralysed.
Rations, worse than ever, no milk ration what-so-ever.
11 May
Out of hospital today

Another manifestation of beriberi affected the heart, so-called cardiac beriberi, which caused heart failure and death. A fourth form of beriberi was seen to affect only the central nervous system. This was Wernicke's encephalopathy, a condition first described in 1881, with symptoms which had been previously been attributed to alcoholism. The classic features are double vision, rapid eye-movement and confusion. Bill diagnosed and treated several cases at Changi in 1942 and assisted Jack Ennis with a number of the post-mortems. Here they found evidence of haemorrhages within the fourth ventricle of the brain.

Their initial observations on the condition were later extended by Captain de Wardener and another pathologist, Captain B. 'Bernard' Lennox RAMC, who worked alongside Jack Ennis. Lennox was born in Wallsend, Newcastle, in 1914 and graduated in medicine from Durham in 1936. He trained in pathology at the Royal Victoria Infirmary at Newcastle-upon-Tyne before joining the RAMC in 1941. At Changi, Lennox and Ennis lived and worked alongside each other, although certainly during the middle of 1942 Lennox suffered a number of ailments which kept him off work. There may have been more than a little tension between the two men, as revealed by Ennis who described how Lennox was suffering from lymphangitis and an infected bee sting, commenting that he was 'not surprised at the latter in light of Lennox's failure to wash thoroughly.' Bill remembered Lennox as a rather small man, who had spent several summer holidays in Cumberland, a county that Bill knew well. Lennox, perhaps because of his size, came in for an inordinate amount of bullying from one colleague, Captain J. Ledingham RAMC, an ENT surgeon, 'a tall red-haired Scot', originally from Banffshire, who had qualified from Aberdeen in 1933. To Bill, the bullying seemed almost relentless and came to a head one day, when Lennox had had enough of this victimisation. Unbeknown to Ledingham, Lennox was an accomplished Cumberland wrestler, and having reached the end of his tether, threw Ledingham to the ground; that ended any further bullying. In 1946 de Wardener and Lennox[80] published a seminal paper on Wernicke's encephalopathy, describing the clinical and pathological findings in 52 patients, some of whom had died on the Burma Railway. Many years later, Bill pointed out that this paper, published in *The Lancet*, failed to mention, let alone acknowledge, the contribution made by either Jack Ennis or himself.

Bill shared accommodation with de Wardener at Changi in 1943 and came to learn a lot more about him, and his personal life. De Wardener had been born in 1915 in Paris to American parents and spent many of his early years travelling around Europe, attending schools in a number of towns and cities. He had been in a war zone before when, in 1936, he and his mother were evacuated from the island of Majorca on-board HMS *Repulse* at the start of the Spanish Civil War. After schooling in England he had read medicine at St Thomas' Hospital, qualifying in June 1939. A tall, handsome, athletic and charming man, he had obtained the nickname 'Ginger' because of the colour of his hair. He had married the day before declaration of war in 1939 and, after joining the RAMC, was posted to 198 Field Ambulance, part of 53 Brigade and arrived in Singapore three weeks before the surrender. Whilst sharing mess accommodation with de Wardener, Bill learnt all about de Wardener's many love affairs.

---

80 Both men were later to have illustrious careers in academic medicine. De Wardener was appointed Professor of Medicine at Charing Cross Hospital and made important contributions to the area of nephrology, especially renal dialysis. He died in 2013 and Bill attended a commemoration service, where, after an address given by his brother, the mourners were invited to a champagne reception. Lennox was appointed Professor of Pathology at Glasgow and developed an international reputation as a medical geneticist.

Captain Hugh de Wardener

Another deficiency disease affecting many men was later described in some detail by Bill in the *British Medical Journal*. Termed 'deficiency scrotal dermatitis', the condition first appeared in May 1942. In the six months from 1 July 1942, a total of 1371 cases were admitted to the dermatology ward at Roberts Hospital, of which 501 were deficiency scrotal dermatitis. The presenting symptoms were an irritation of the scrotum, worse at night which often prevented the patient from sleeping. Working during the day tended to exacerbate the condition. There was marked variation in the duration of symptoms; sometimes they would last for just a few days, abate and then relapse, persisting for a much longer period. The main stimuli for relapse appeared to be heavy work, heat or illness. In the most severe cases men had a thickened and cracked scrotum, with a fetid discharge, and the disease spread to the skin of the perineum and inner surfaces of the thigh. The scrotum enlarged, sometimes to the size of a football, making walking almost impossible, often made worse with pus discharging from the area. The worst cases were marked by a spreading gangrene with infection of *Corynebacterium diphtheriae*. In some cases flies laid their eggs in subcutaneous tissue, with maggots later hatching and could be seen under the skin. Maggots would be killed by applying phenol from the head of a match. The irritation was such that some men had to be sedated with morphine to control their pain and in the most severe cases, men died from the condition and its complications. In light of the involvement of the scrotum it is not surprising that a range of colloquial terms were applied to the condition, including 'Changi Balls', 'Rice Balls' or 'Itchy Balls.'

Patients with deficiency scrotal dermatitis often showed other manifestations of B vitamin deficiencies, including angular stomatitis, painful feet and ocular disorders, such as retrobulbar neuritis. Bill reported a favourable response to the daily administration of Marmite,[81] just one teaspoon a day was often sufficient, with the duration of treatment depending upon the severity of the condition. Early cases could respond in about four days. Bill argued that the disease was the result of deficiency of vitamin B2, riboflavin, and demonstrated that both Marmite (and Vegemite) were good sources of the vitamin. This was borne out by his own experiences of the condition in late-June 1942. He approached Captain Cruickshank, the leading physician at Changi. Cruickshank, a Scot and the son of a bacteriologist,[82] had been working at Massachusetts General Hospital at the outbreak of war and sailed home to join up, receiving his commission in June 1940. On the transatlantic passage he shared a cabin with Professor Alexander Fleming from St Mary's, who was a good friend of Cruickshank senior's. He was described as a man with 'sparkling blue eyes, which could charm or chill, comfort or condemn.' Bill had met Cruickshank several times in Singapore and described how he had been very kind to Bill on his arrival in 1941. He had taken Bill to the Tanglin Club in his car and recalled one amusing incident when, on their way, Cruickshank stopped to buy some cigarettes. It was raining very hard and when Cruickshank got out of the car he stepped into a malaria drain, becoming completely drenched. Returning to the car, he apologised to Bill that he was 'rather wet.' [83]

Suffering from deficiency scrotal dermatitis himself, Bill asked Cruickshank if he could spare any Marmite; he could and gave him a teaspoonful which was duly swallowed. Bill described it as 'gold' since it cured his ailment almost overnight, relieving the pain and allowing Bill to sleep peacefully. His colleague Jack Ennis also suffered from the condition at the same time and described how his scrotum was 'awfully itchy' but went on to record that seven days' treatment with Marmite led to a 'definite improvement' in his symptoms. Marmite became a

---

81 The Australian product was called Vegemite.

82 John Cruickshank was the Professor of Bacteriology at Aberdeen University.

83 After the war, Eric Cruickshank served as Dean of the School of Medicine of the University of the West Indies. Bill visited him in Jamaica in his new role and he offered Bill a position at the university, which he declined.

very valuable commodity in the camp, and in October 1942 one medical officer, Captain M.G. Braham RAMC, came under investigation for allegedly having sold Marmite which he had been given for his own treatment. Ennis was perturbed by these allegations and made clear his opinions that Braham should have been court-martialled.[84]

Bill had a great interest in dermatology and saw a range of conditions at Changi. Before long, he was having to deal with many cases of scabies, caused by the burrowing mite, *Sarcoptes scabiei*, resulting in severe irritation and pain at the skin. The treatment at the time involved topical application of sulphur compounds, but these were soon in short supply, and before long, exhausted. Bill, like many others, was suffering from scabies and sought an alternative treatment. In 1941 he had read a report in the *British Medical Journal* by Captain L. Saunders RAMC of the use of Derris root for the treatment of scabies. Saunders reported that the accepted treatment involving topical sulphur was 'greasy and messy and was associated with a terrible smell', men could also develop a sulphur dermatitis on their hands through applying the ointment. Saunders described treating over 500 cases of scabies with a solution of Derris root powder, derived from the dried roots of *Derris elliptica* and *Derris malaccensis*, climbing plants which grew in Malaya and Singapore. He reported satisfactory resolution of infection in about three days, much to the surprise of one commentator who suggested patients with scabies should be hospitalised for four weeks. Bill was aware that both the manager and assistant manager of a company that supplied Derris root from Malaya had been taken prisoner, both having been serving with the volunteer forces, and he located them. He managed to obtain some Derris root, tried it on himself, and found it worked well, eliminating the infection. About a month later he wrote to the ADMS[85] reporting his experiences and suggesting that this botanical preparation should be used throughout the camp. He heard no more until learning that all units in Changi received an advice note from ADMS advising them of how to treat scabies with Bill's preparation. Bill was slightly

---

84 Captain Braham died on 21 September 1944; he is commemorated at CWGC Kranji.
85 Assistant Director of Medical Services.

taken aback that there was reference neither to him, nor to his studies in assessing this new treatment.

BURNING FEET

Another challenging condition facing Bill and his colleagues at Changi was that of 'Painful Feet Syndrome', which has more recently been called 'Burning Feet Syndrome.' This was first seen at Changi in July 1942 and Captain Cruickshank took a special interest in it, later reporting his findings from 500 patients. Bill saw some of these, but also witnessed Cruickshank's approach to both the diagnosis and treatment of the condition. Cruickshank described in some detail the symptoms of the condition, which started as a dull, throbbing ache at the balls of the feet, initially only apparent at night. As the condition progressed, sharp stabbing pains became apparent, shooting up through the feet, ankles and at times the shins. Although primarily affecting the legs, the hands also became involved in some long-standing cases. As the disease progressed the pain was constant, causing men to be kept awake all night. Nearly a quarter of patients demonstrated exaggerated reflexes from about 6 weeks after the onset of symptoms; interestingly, this was observed in both the hands and legs, even if the pain was confined to the legs. With the constant pain, men's appetite fell and they lost even more weight. It was summarised by one doctor as an 'intense burning of the feet, exquisite sensitivity which scarcely enables them to walk, and they cannot get any rest or sleep.'

Nearly all men with the condition had suffered from either dysentery and/or malaria and nearly 80% had a history of vitamin B deficiency, presenting as defective vision, stomatitis, or deficiency scrotal dermatitis. Cruickshank was aware of a paper published in 1935 describing a similar syndrome in malnourished prisoners in a Malayan jail, which concluded that the condition was the result of vitamin B2 deficiency. Despite this, Bill recalled that Cruickshank believed the first three cases to be psychoses, since the pain appeared to disappear when the patients stood up. However, as he examined more cases, it became apparent to Cruickshank that this was not a mental health disorder, but was due to a vitamin deficiency. Cruickshank evaluated a number of treatments for the condition, but in spite of this, a firm conclusion as to the cause was never reached. He pointed out in his own wartime papers that, due to the circumstances and nature of the syndrome, there were no control groups receiving placebo treatment. A number of therapies were tried, including Marmite, rice polishings, vitamin B, boiled green gam (mung beans) and even boiled grass. In some cases, a combination of treatments was given. However, with all treatments there was a variable response and no single therapy could be recommended. Bill saw six cases of painful feet syndrome during his 18 months at Changi, all in men suffering from deficiency scrotal dermatitis. He treated them all with vitamin B2; four responded and two did not.

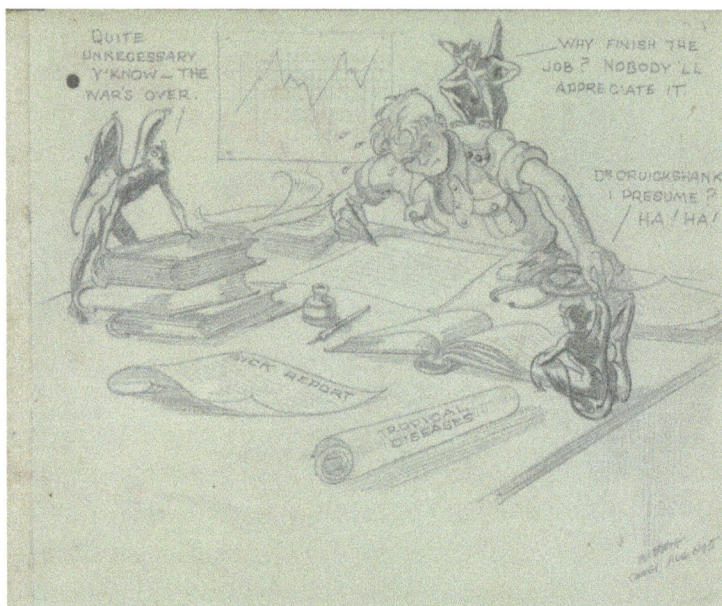

Sketch of Captain Cruickshank at Changi, 1945

Many of those suffering with painful feet syndrome moved on from Changi as members of working parties sent away from Singapore. In some, especially those sent to the Burma Railway, the condition remained. Bill was later sent to the island of Blakang Mati, just to the south of Singapore, and during nearly two years there did not see a single case of the condition. As he was to point out, on Blakang Mati they were able to grow their own vegetables which may have provided sufficient vitamins to prevent the condition.

The issue of painful or burning feet syndrome was the subject of a paper published in early 2017. Reviewing the literature on the condition, the authors also undertook a re-examination of clinical record cards made by Flight Lieutenant A.N.H. 'Nowell' Peach RAFVR, a medical officer who had been taken prisoner in Java during the war. Peach maintained the record cards of 54 cases with the syndrome who presented to him, and detailed his meticulous neurological examinations. Bill Frankland was one of the authors of the paper; it was his fourth scientific paper to be published since celebrating his 100th birthday.

NO WASTE OF RATIONS

Faced with malnutrition at Changi, prisoners soon developed numerous schemes to try to improve their diet. Food could be obtained from local Chinese traders who ran shops at the borders of the camp, supplying fish, eggs and fruit. There was also the black market run by the Chinese. Regardless of route of acquisition, the price of food rose dramatically, doubling every month or two. Working parties assigned to Singapore were able to acquire extra food, either by trading, or in some cases by straightforward theft.

In Changi farming enterprises soon started up, with men attempting to grow vegetables and fruits, as well as rearing animals. Gardening was not helped by the poor soil nor by the movement of men both within Changi, and later away from the island as members of working parties. The common crops grown were sweet potato, tapioca and Ceylon spinach. The Japanese provided manure in the form of peanut meal, but this was used as a source of B vitamins by the prisoners. It was noted that 'taken in the form of biscuits it was not as unpalatable as it sounds'. All food items were used fully: one report described how 'surprisingly tasty a banana skin pie could be'. Others grew yeast extract as a potential source of vitamins, and Captain Marshall described how one and a half ounces of the cocktail was 'rather pleasant and tasted not unlike cider.'

Having grown, reared or obtained food it was imperative to store it securely. Early on at Changi, Holy Communion had to be cancelled as someone had eaten all the Communion wafers the night before. Similarly, one medical officer described bringing 400 cigarettes into the camp, only for 200 to be stolen on the first night. However, one of the other threats was the guards themselves. Sikh guards would intercept fish that was destined for the hospital, and buy it from the prisoners. Several Japanese guards traded on the black market, and one with the nickname 'Nancy Ming' was a frequent visitor to the camp. He came to buy cameras, watches or pens from the prisoners to then sell on. In May 1943 he visited and purchased a Zeiss Ikon camera for 100 dollars, and told them to find a Leica camera which he would buy. He was not seen for several weeks, but returned in June when he came to see Bill and Jack Ennis. He ate 21 of Bill's ripening bananas and then paid him 70 cents for them. Ming told them that he was billeted in Changi village where the food was very poor, 'only rice and rice and three bananas with it', but told them that if they could shoot a monkey it made a good meal.

Despite being next to the coast, fishing was relatively unsuccessful, and the small catches were reserved for the patients in hospital. But the access to sea water was useful for some who, because of the salt deficiency of their diet, were able to satisfy their craving for salt.

Various livestock enterprises were started at Changi. By the end of 1943 there were over 300 pigs in the piggery, allowing a pork issue of 4 ounces per man every 2 months. Chickens were a valuable source of protein, both as eggs and as meat (when egg laying had come to an end). By the end of 1943 there were over 8000 chickens in the camp. Many of the medical officers were involved in rearing chickens, some more successfully than others. Jack Ennis described how 'the front of the mess is a mass of chickens and ducks, nearly everyone has a share in a farm.' Lieutenant Colonel Middleton bought six chickens but lost three and decided to sell on the remainder. However, he trod on one, killing it, so decided to cut his losses and gave away the remaining two. Bill was more successful, working with Jack Ennis and Ledingham on their farming enterprise. He started to raise chickens, obtaining eight hens and a cockerel from a small shop on the edge of the camp. The birds were covered in ants, which soon spread to the chicks which had hatched. Painstakingly he removed the ants by hand, and then set about protecting the chickens' nest. Bill placed the feet of the nest in water, preventing any ants from crawling up. One hen, called Blondie, sat on a clutch of 14 eggs, of which 8 hatched and all grew well. However Jack Ennis noted that they had to be protected as there was a sparrowhawk which visited every day, attempting to snatch young birds. In August 1943, Ennis recorded that 'Frankland, Led and I are having an egg a day from our hens.' There were, however, other issues to contend with, and birds were not resistant to dietary deficiencies: one duck developed a thiamine deficient neuropathy and had to be nursed in a sling for a month before it recovered.

Men explored other food sources, with doves being trapped, killed and cooked. A python was captured in the camp and this was also dispatched to the kitchens. A few monkeys were captured and killed; they were skinned and served whole, causing one medical officer to describe how 'they looked like a child.' Other animals were also eaten, especially as food supplies dwindled. Cats and dogs were sought after, trading on the black market at 1 dollar and 3 dollars, respectively. There were several camp dogs, which had become pets, although Charles Wells noted that, just like the men, dogs did not do well on a rice diet. Using his veterinary skills, he felt it only right to kill them, administering an overdose of magnesium sulphate injection.

Bill recalled one incident involving a dog, a spaniel, owned by Captain E.R.S. Phillips RAMC, which had made its home at Roberts Hospital. On 29 August 1942 Captain Phillips vanished whilst bringing a patient up to Roberts Hospital. It appeared he had made an escape attempt with a few Eurasian prisoners, leaving his dog behind. As men became hungrier, they debated whether to kill the dog for food. Feelings were running high, so much so that an ethical committee was established to consider the situation; it found in favour of killing the dog. However, there was still the issue of how to dispatch the animal. The dog was hit on the head in an attempt to kill him, but this failed miserably. Bill remembered seeing the dog jump up and run away, never to be seen again. By contrast, his former master, Phillips, did not get far and two days after going missing was sent to Changi gaol.

Working Parties

Following their arrival at Changi, working parties were established. Initially these worked in and around the camp where one important task was collecting wood, which often meant venturing into the mangrove swamps. This was not without risks and several incurred wounds from stepping on the sharp underwater roots, whilst others were attacked by leeches. Other parties set to work controlling malaria and dengue, by filling in pools and puddles to control the breeding grounds for mosquitoes. However, in April 1942 the Japanese demanded parties to work in Singapore. For some prisoners this provided an opportunity to get away from Changi, where, as one described, 'there were men everywhere, and no opportunity for privacy.' That month, W.E. 'Lanky' Lancaster, a private in the Straits Settlements Volunteer Force, joined a party of 200 destined for Singapore City. He wrote how 'he was glad to get out of Changi', as it allowed him an opportunity to see what was going on 'in the outside world.' They were sent to a camp at Pasir Panjang, close to Keppel Harbour, where their accommodation was a room originally meant for two Tamil 'coolies' which was now home to eight. Work involved loading and unloading ships. They were struck by the kindness of the Chinese who, whenever possible, and despite the associated risks, tried to help the prisoners as best they could. A friendly smile was always welcome, but Lanky noted how some gave the men small amounts of money, cigarettes or even new pieces of clothing. However, prisoners on these work parties, such as Lanky, witnessed the savage responses of the Japanese, who thought nothing of beheading Chinese they considered a threat, leaving their severed heads in prominent positions for all to see. Working parties of Australians were also sent to the docks where they gained a reputation as 'scroungers par excellence' who would steal tins of food and manage to take them back to Changi. Others became adept at sabotage, in order to delay the Japanese war machine. Sabotage actions included stealing half a barrel of petrol, replacing it with water, and selling the stolen fuel on the black market. However, if they were caught in any of these acts, they would receive brutal treatment from their captors.

A medical officer was assigned to each working party. After a few months Bill met up with a good friend from St Mary's, now a medical officer attached to a Singapore work party. Captain John Diver RAMC had studied medicine at St John's College, Cambridge, where he held a scholarship, before moving to St Mary's for his clinical training, qualifying a year before Bill. He was one of the few St Mary's students who did not play rugby, but instead rowed in the St Mary's eight which beat St Thomas's Medical School in 1935. Bill recalled that Diver was quite a playboy, but a 'wonderful character.' Diver had an Austin 7 car in London and on one occasion told his colleagues that it could go 'anywhere.' To demonstrate this he drove up the steps of St Mary's Hospital, along the corridor to Matron's office, turned around and drove back out. Unfortunately, coming down the steps, the engine's sump struck a hard surface and broke open with oil flooding out. Diver cleared up the mess, but his car was deemed 'unserviceable.' On qualifying in 1937 he worked at the Woolwich Memorial Hospital where he was described as 'a voluble colleague, long-haired and irrepressible.' He returned to St Mary's for further appointments, and Bill next met him in the summer of 1941 when they attended a short course, lasting just two days, in tropical medicine at the Royal Army Medical College, Millbank. Here Bill learnt that Diver had made important contributions at the evacuation from Dunkirk in May 1940. Diver, like Bill, had been taken prisoner with the fall of Singapore, although until they met in Changi, Bill was unaware that his friend was even serving in the Far East.

At Changi, Diver was a reception medical officer, as well as liaison officer between British and Dutch troops. Described as a man with 'a big booming voice', as a student in London he had sung in the London Bach Choir, and in Changi continued to sing in a male voice choir. As medical officer to a working party in the docks he lived in a warehouse close by, which he described as 'a place full of bedbugs…big red juicy ones!' However, his time at the docks presented opportunities to buy luxuries such as bread, jam and fish which he then brought back to Changi, and for which Bill and many others were very grateful. He also bought back news, and on 12 June 1942 Captain Marshall recorded that 'The Japs are tightening their control in Singapore. Anyone opposing the Japs is in for a thin time.' Bill described Diver as 'a superb doctor and a very gallant officer, one who was respected by all.'

In June 1942, the Japanese started to send working parties north to Siam (Thailand) and assigned to the building of the Burma-Siam Railway or, as more popularly known, 'Death Railway.' The railway ran 260 miles from Ban Pong in Siam to Thanbyuzayat in Burma. The idea of a railway had been first been muted in 1885 by the British who, in 1910, put forward a route for the railway. However, this project was abandoned in 1912 because of the difficult terrain, epidemic disease and monsoon rains. The Japanese resurrected the plan, since the railway would allow troops and supplies to be sent to Burma, avoiding the sea routes through the Straits of Malacca where their shipping was vulnerable to attack.

In May 1943 Diver was one of two medical officers attached to H Force, a party of some 3200 Australian and British soldiers sent to the Burma Railway. Here he was noted to be a devoted doctor, and a man of great courage. He demonstrated untiring energy under dreadful conditions and stood up to the Japanese, prompting reprisals: he was imprisoned at least once by the Kempeitai (the Japanese secret police). On one occasion he secretly gave medical assistance to a Japanese soldier who had fallen out of the line-of-march and was lying, totally exhausted, near to death (he subsequently died). The Japanese reacted in the only way they knew, and gave Diver a brutal bashing for his actions. He subsequently returned to Singapore at Christmas 1943, and was asked to go as medical officer to Normanton Camp, Singapore. Here he worked under terrible conditions, with almost no drugs or dressings, whilst surviving on effectively a starvation diet. Again he demonstrated his professional skill as well as his untiring efforts for the men in his care. Despite suffering from severe beriberi and starvation, he refused to be sent to either Changi or the newly established Kranji Hospital until it was too late. He was finally admitted to hospital on 30 April 1945, and died early the following morning, the result of bronchopneumonia and beriberi. This shocked many, not least those of Normanton Camp who described how 'he martyred himself in their cause.'

After the war, monies from his estate were given to St Mary's Hospital and at Bill's suggestion funded many new books in the library. Diver's parents wrote to St Mary's and offered to give money in memory of their son. They were unsure what to do, but were advised it should be given to the Secretary of St Mary's Medical School. Bill was having none of that, knowing full well that the money would then most likely be 'lost' and instead arranged for the money to go directly to the library fund.

Behind Barbed Wire: Security and Escape

As men arrived at Changi the Japanese imposed significant changes to their way of life. Firstly, Singapore was now part of the Greater Eastern Co-Prosperity Zone and so kept Tokyo time, effectively one and a half hours ahead of Singapore time; prisoners now woke up in the dark. Next, all officers had to remove their rank details, and instead were permitted to wear a small star insignia above the left breast pocket.

By the end of March 1942 Changi was home to over 50,000 prisoners but lacked most of the features associated with a conventional prisoner of war camp of that time. There were no large barbed-wire fences or lookout towers, although two sides adjoined shark-infested waters, itself quite a deterrent to escape. Following the surrender of Singapore, the Japanese recruited members of the INA to help guard the prisoners. Many were Sikhs, who Bill remembered were initially issued with clubs, and later World War 1 rifles. The Sikhs have a history of being fighters, and now found themselves responsible for men who, just a few weeks earlier, had commanded them. Many grudges were addressed and the guards soon gained a reputation for brutality, a behaviour which appeared to give great pleasure to the captors. At the end of March, orders were given that all prisoners were to salute their captors, be they Japanese or Indian; failure to do so would lead to swift retribution, and a 'bashing', a fate which few, if any, of the men would escape. Bill experienced this first-hand when part of a group of men returning from the beach, having been swimming. The men were talking, and one claimed that he was 'the first person to be stung where I didn't want to be' to which Bill added that he 'was the second member.' The party included Colonel Taylor who, heavily in thought, failed to notice and salute a Sikh guard as they were walking back to the hospital. The guard immediately punished Taylor, hitting him several times. There were very few Japanese troops in Changi, such that some prisoners reported not seeing a Japanese soldier for nearly 8 months. Bill recalled the vast difference between British prisoner of war camps and Changi. When serving with the Royal Warwickshire Regiment in 1941 he was aware of a prisoner of war camp near to the racecourse at Stratford-upon-Avon. He was led to believe about 30 German submariners were guarded by about 20 men. Looking around ChangI, he sometimes wondered if the Japanese guards did not number many more than 20, despite having at least 50,000 prisoners to guard.

It was only after several weeks of captivity that the first elements of physical security became apparent, when barbed wire was issued, and prisoners were ordered to erect it, effectively creating barriers between the different camp areas. From this point on movement between camp areas required special permission from the Japanese. Despite these measures, or perhaps because of them, it was not long before escape plans were hatched. Although 'hindsight is a wonderful view', an assessment of the situation reveals the difficulties facing any escapee. Singapore was now some 1000 miles from friendly territory, the island was surrounded by dangerous waters, the mainland was mostly unforgiving jungle, well summarised as 'not a health resort', and prisoners would be noticed as foreign by natives. Although some felt they could rely on locals to help, many were to find that the price of 100 dollars on their head would swiftly lead to betrayal.

In late-March 1942 three men from the Royal Artillery escaped to the mainland where they were caught and executed. This was witnessed by their commanding officer who described how, when asked for any last words, all cried out, 'To hell with the Japs!' Later that month, several Australians made an escape attempt but were apprehended by the Japanese and executed. By the end of March 1942, six would-be escapers had been shot.

In mid-July 1942 four or five soldiers from the 2nd Bn Gordon Highlanders made an escape attempt to the Malayan mainland. They reached Johor but here the escape turned sour. At least two men managed to get back to Changi, where their absence had not been noted. However, Malays betrayed two other men, William Turnbull and Hamish Johnson. Following typical Japanese summary justice they were taken to the island of Pulau Ubin, just to the east of Changi. Their belongings were taken from them and their hands tied behind their backs. As they were being led to the site of execution, Johnson managed to free his hands. Made to kneel, Turnbull was decapitated, but as the sword came down on Johnson he freed his hands and made a dash for the water. In the commotion, the executioner's sword struck Johnson's left shoulder, passing deep through the muscles and exposing underlying bone. Quite amazingly, he staggered to the water where he thought he had lost his arm but then realised it was still attached, so tucked his left hand into his belt to support it. Despite his injuries and loss of blood, Johnson made his way across the sea towards Changi. On reaching a beach he managed to crawl out of the water. As he staggered back to the camp he was spotted by a Japanese guard. Rapidly Johnson made up an alibi. He told the guard he had been very hot and had gone swimming to cool down, but had been attacked by sharks. The guard believed him, gave him food and water and took him to Roberts Hospital, being admitted on 18 July. Bill clearly remembered the man and his wound, and how everyone was quite convinced that it was not a shark wound. A surgical opinion was needed, urgently, and Bill sought the expertise of Captain R.W. 'Dickie' Doyle RAMC. Described by Bill as 'not loved by everyone... he was a personality, a very competent surgeon but very self-opinionated', Doyle was of Irish descent, a confirmed Catholic, who had qualified from Liverpool University in 1928, where he had been a student boxing champion. He pursued a surgical career in London, as well as continuing to box. A former flatmate described him:

He was as Irish as they come, full of charm, talent and not a little unpredictability, and a man who never did things by halves. I recall going to the London Hospital to see him box, he gave better than he got and was cheered to the echo. Later we went to a restaurant and chose steaks. When it arrived he remembered it was Friday, and sent it back in favour of fish.

At the outbreak of war Doyle joined the RAMC, initially being posted to a military hospital in Lucknow, India. He subsequently served with an Indian Casualty Clearing Station in Malaya in 1941, and like many others was taken prisoner on Singapore in February 1942. Presented with Johnson's wound, Doyle repaired it as best he could.[86] Johnson recovered but had a stiff left shoulder. Captain Marshall wrote how several months later a Japanese general visited Johnson and said that he knew that Johnson was an escaped prisoner, but that he had not come to take him away, but instead to apologise for the barbarity of Japanese soldiers.

Another man who attempted to escape but returned, having evaded capture, also came under Bill's care. He was suffering from tropical ulcers, dysentery, severe beriberi and malaria, and was admitted to Roberts Hospital. Bill looked after the man for about two months and was very proud that after this time the man was significantly better; Bill advised him that could return to his unit the following week. Just before discharge a member of the Kempeitai came to the ward and seized the man. The Kempeitai were the secret military police (similar to, if not more brutal than, the Gestapo in Europe), who were feared by all. Bill summarised how 'they ensured complete control and fear; if they were around you knew there would be death.' The patient was taken away by a party of 6 or 7 Sikhs, members of the INA, and ordered to dig his own grave. The padre in attendance reported that he was too weak to do so and it fell to the Sikhs to dig the grave. They then formed a firing squad, but were so hopeless that they caused just one minor wound. Finally the man was shot at point-blank range by the Kempeitai officer.

The issue of escaping came to the fore again later that year, in an episode remembered as the 'Selarang Incident.' At the end of August 1942 the Japanese were holding four prisoners, two British and two Australian, who had been recaptured after attempting to escape. The Australians, Corporal R.E. Breavington and Private V.L. Gale, fled Singapore in May

---

86 On another occasion Doyle had to treat a man who had survived a beheading by the Japanese. After the third stroke descended, doctors rushed forward and to their astonishment the man was still alive. The man was rescued surreptitiously and taken to the operating theatre where Doyle repaired the severed muscle and skin, using wire from the camp piano. The patient survived, and was repatriated at the end of the war. Some years later he was introduced to a meeting of the Liverpool Medical Institution, alongside his surgeon, Doyle, now a Consultant at the Royal Liverpool Hospital.

1942. Stealing a boat, they sailed and rowed for some six weeks west towards Ceylon. Having covered nearly 1300 miles they were intercepted by a Japanese warship, recaptured and returned to Singapore in July. Breavington was very ill, suffering from malaria, and was admitted to Roberts Hospital. The two British soldiers, Privates H. Water and E. Fletcher, had both been caught whilst escaping in May, and after being apprehended, were initially returned to their units in Changi.

A new Japanese commanding officer arrived in Singapore August 1942, Major General Shimpei Fukuye. His arrival coincided with the departure of most of the senior Allied officers at Changi (those of the rank of colonel and above, who were sent to Formosa and then to Manchuria) and Fukuye had plans for this to be a 'proper' prison camp, and was determined to use the escapees to his advantage. The new commanding officers of the British and Australian forces, Lieutenant Colonel E.B. Holmes MC and Brigadier F.G. 'Black Jack' Galleghan DSO, respectively, were summoned by General Fukuye and told that all prisoners were to sign the following:

I the undersigned hereby solemnly swear on my honour that I will not under any circumstances attempt escapes.

For a British soldier to sign such an undertaking was a breach of King's Regulations, and, although just a very few (probably three) did, the overwhelming majority refused.

On 1 September the Japanese were informed that prisoners would not sign the declaration. On the same day, as part of the increased control by the Japanese, a roll-call was introduced for all prisoners. On the first morning, men at Roberts Hospital paraded at 8.30am and were not dismissed until 1.45pm. The following day, Wednesday 2 September, the Japanese retaliated further by ordering all the men to move to Selarang Barracks. An appeal by a senior medical officer resulted in one exception: patients and staff in Roberts Hospital did not have to move. Men had to walk some two and a half miles to Selarang, taking solely what they could carry, some even taking their precious livestock of chickens and ducks. Anyone not at Selarang by 6pm would be shot. Jack Ennis described the scene that afternoon as 'like the retreat from Moscow..... baggage dragged along the road, old men sweating to get in by the deadline.' At the same time, Holmes and Galleghan along with Lieutenant Colonel Craven were forced to witness yet a further example of Japanese brutality: the four soldiers who had been caught escaping were to be executed. None had been put on trial. Breavington was taken from Roberts Hospital and, with the others, made to walk to a beach near Changi; two of the condemned men could not stand without walking sticks. Under the command of Lieutenant Okasaki, a firing squad was formed of Sikhs from the INA, themselves under the command of Captain R.A.K. Rana, formerly of the Kapurthala State Infantry. All four prisoners refused blindfolds and Breavington pleaded for the life of his younger colleague, Gale, but to no avail. All four saluted their senior officers before the order to fire was given. As the officers looked on they witnessed a scene of complete horror. The four men fell to the ground, but at least three were still alive. Breavington had been shot through the arm and cried out, 'For God's sake shoot me through the heart and kill me!' The firing squad continued their botched attempts: most prisoners received five shots, one eight.[87] Afterwards, Galleghan described Breavington as 'the bravest man I have ever known'. After the execution Okasaki told the senior officers that 'This is the punishment that will be meted out to any persons in future making escape attempts.'[88]

News of the executions reached the men at Selarang later that afternoon. Here about 17,000 men were being squeezed into what had previously been home for about 600. Each of the seven barrack blocks would normally have housed up to 120 men but were now home to over 1000. Dozens of latrines were dug in the middle of the once 'sacred' Barrack Square and tents placed at either end. Yet, despite the appalling conditions three concert parties were held on the square on the first night, hosted quite literally where the men were living. They

---

87 All four men are commemorated in Kranji War Cemetery.
88 Both Fukuye and Okasaki were tried at the War Crimes Tribunal in 1946. Found guilty, Fukuye was sentenced to death. He was executed by firing squad on 27 April 1946, on the same beach at Changi where Breavington and his colleagues had been executed in 1942.

were guarded by men from the INA, mostly Sikhs, with fixed bayonets, along with Japanese troops manning machine guns positioned at each corner. Anyone stepping outside the marked lines was liable to be shot. Conditions rapidly deteriorated, the stench was appalling, and water was only available for cooking. The site soon resembled the 'Black Hole.'

Grave of Corporal Breavington, Kranji War Memorial, Singapore

Selarang Barracks, September 1942

On 3 September the Japanese made further threats. If the prisoners did not sign, then all water would be turned off, no food would be allowed, and the men would be moved into an even smaller area. By this time diphtheria and dysentery were already present in Selarang, although this did not stop the Japanese issuing a further threat: the patients from Roberts Hospital would be transferred. Negotiations continued and, late on 4 September, Holmes issued an instruction that, since the Japanese had now **ordered** the men to sign the escape declaration, they were to do so. The order read:

The regulation issued by the IJA under their Order No 17, dated 31/8/42, that all ranks of the POW camp, Changi, should be given the opportunity to sign the Certificate of Promise not to escape has now been amended in a revised IJA Order No 17, dated 2/9/42 to a definite order that officers, NCOs and men of the POW camp, shall sign this undertaking.

I therefore now order that these certificates will be signed by all ranks and handed by Area Commanders to Area HQ by 11.00hrs on 5/9/42

The circumstances in which I have been compelled to issue this order will be made the subject of a Special Order No 3, which will be issued later.

Signed B. Holmes. Lt Col.

Men signed under duress, although many used aliases: M. Mouse and Ned Kelly appear to have signed many times. All forms were handed in by late-morning of 5 September, and men were allowed to return to their original billets. Bill was only involved peripherally in this incident, since working on the dysentery wards at Roberts Hospital he was not required to move, instead staying to nurse the many sick men. Had those at Selarang not signed, then he, and his patients, would undoubtedly have moved with the inevitable consequence of compounding the already dire conditions at Selarang.

Surgical Opinions

Throughout his career Bill has worked as a physician, and many years after the war was to recall that he had only ever undertaken one surgical operation, which he did at Tanglin Military Hospital in early 1942. In Changi, although working as a physician, he would often be faced with patients requiring a surgical opinion. The senior surgeon at Roberts Hospital was Colonel Julian Taylor, whose wealth of clinical experience and surgical expertise had been apparent to Bill in the weeks leading up to surrender. If Bill required a surgical opinion he would, wherever possible, seek Taylor's. However, Taylor was often busy operating and in such circumstances Bill would seek the opinion of another surgeon, Major S.G. 'Sydney' Nardell IMS. Described by Bill as 'Jewish and a very pleasant man', Nardell was a precocious and talented doctor who, at the age of 19, had gained a BSc along with the Hallett Prize from the Royal College of Surgeons of England. He qualified from St George's Hospital in 1932 and gained the FRCS in 1938, aged 25. At the outbreak of war he joined the Indian Army and, along with his wife, was posted to Shillong Military Hospital in Assam. From there he was posted to Lucknow and then on to No 5 (Indian) Casualty Clearing Station (5CCS) in Malaya whilst his wife, with their newborn child, returned to Britain. With the retreat of 5 CCS to Singapore, Nardell asked to be posted to Alexandra Military Hospital, where he always wore his steel helmet when operating. When the hospital was attacked on 14 February 1942, Nardell lay in a room feigning death and was one of the few to survive. Bill considered Nardell's opinion as being second-best to that of Julian Taylor.

Major Sydney Nardell

Among the more junior surgeons (in rank) at Roberts Hospital was a Canadian, Lieutenant J. 'Jacob' Markowitz RAMC. Born into a Jewish family in Toronto in 1901, he had studied medicine at the University of Toronto, where he was described as 'a good thinker, good worker and a good sport.' He qualified in 1923 and the editor of his student yearbook wrote 'we shall hear of him again', a prediction which soon came true. Markowitz remained at Toronto, gaining a PhD in 1926. The same year, he travelled to Glasgow, where he spent one year as second assistant to Professor E.P. Cathcart FRS, Professor of Physiological Chemistry, and an international authority on nutrition. It may have been during this period that Markowitz learnt something about military medicine, since Cathcart had served in World War 1, rising to the position of Deputy Director of Anti-Gas Services, as well as undertaking research into the interactions of nutrition and energy expenditure by soldiers. After a productive year under Cathcart's wing, Markowitz returned to Toronto where he worked for Professor Charles Best. In 1921 Best, still a medical student, had assisted Frederick Banting in groundbreaking research which identified the hormone, insulin. Markowitz himself became a pioneer in experimental surgery and physiology, and moved to America, firstly to the Mayo Clinic in Minnesota, and then to Georgetown University. Working with Frank Mann from the Mayo Clinic, he undertook seminal studies into rejection of the transplanted heart. His interests and talents were, however, not confined to medicine, and he could compose poetry in Latin, and was an authority on Keats and Houseman. Following the outbreak of war he initially offered his services to the Canadian military but was refused (he believed there was an anti-Semitic element to this decision). Markowitz remained resolute in his desire to fight Hitler and the Nazis, so joined the RAMC in April 1941, hoping to serve in the European war. Instead, he was sent to the Far East.

Lieutenant Jacob Markowitz

Markowitz was posted to 5CCS in north-west Malaya at Bedong, a small town in the state of Kedah. Despite having just one row of shops, Bedong was strategically important, lying on the main road passing north to south, and within easy reach of the RAF airfields at Alor Star and Sungai Petani. 5CCS was supporting troops of 11 (Indian) Division and was equipped to treat battle casualties requiring major surgery. Its commanding officer was Lieutenant Colonel L.G. Pearson IMS, described as 'old-fashioned, a strict disciplinarian and politically incorrect.'[89] Nearly all members of the unit were Indian, although his second in command was Major Nardell. Markowitz joined 5CCS on 8 December 1941, after hostilities had started and he, along with another new arrival, Captain J. Gibbs RAMC, were soon busy treating battle casualties. With the rapid advance of Japanese troops, 5CCS was ordered to move south. Over the following month they established themselves at a number of sites but never for more than 10 days, before finally reaching a rubber plantation at Rengam in the middle of January 1942. It was here that Markowitz commented that 'I hope we are not going to have to learn Japanese?' This thought had never occurred to anyone, and Nardell replied, 'Don't be afraid, how such a thing can happen? Singapore is a real fortress.' Markowitz, along with the rest of 5CCS, was evacuated to Singapore where they were billeted in the Chinese High School only 2 miles or so from Tanglin Military Hospital, and where they attempted to establish a 200-bed facility.

Bill remembered Markowitz as a 'great teacher' who told people that he was 'first and foremost an experimental physiologist, but one who most enjoyed working with human patients.' They first met at Alexandra Military Hospital where Markowitz, despite having little recent experience of human surgery, repaired an inguinal hernia in a soldier. Bill recalled that Markowitz, being keen to teach, had a number of nurses watching him operate. He carefully explained the surgical procedure, highlighting the need to avoid certain anatomical structures, including blood vessels. He proceeded to operate only to damage one of the arteries that he had assiduously told his audience

---

89 Bill would encounter Pearson at Changi, and remembered him as 'not my cup of tea'.

to avoid. He deftly repaired the damage and completed the operation without any apparent setbacks.[90]

Further Education

Not long after their arrival at Changi men started to find ways to alleviate the boredom of imprisonment. Amongst the men, especially the other ranks, there was a real thirst for knowledge, and before long Changi University was established. Many of the teachers were from Raffles College, and were assisted by a number of academics from Britain who had been taken prisoner. Before long the university was in full swing, offering a range of courses including mathematics, engineering, law, and accountancy, languages (both European and Asian) as well as music.

Other groups also met; Charles Wells described how in June 1942 'Masonic history was made' with the first meeting of a lodge held in a prisoner of war camp, the Negeri Sembilan Lodge presided over the first meeting, at which over 60 Freemasons were present, although he noted that 'no regalia or lodge furniture was present'. Interestingly, the 100th anniversary of the founding of Rossall School was celebrated by a number of old boys in Changi, but took place in 1944, by which time Bill had moved to another camp.

The medical community established their own forum, the Changi Medical Society, and Bill served as its secretary for nearly 18 months. This was a gathering of medical staff, held every Wednesday at

---

90 Markowitz was later one of the surgical team at Chungkai Hospital on the Burma Railway where he, along with Lieutenant Colonel E.E. 'Weary' Dunlop AAMC, undertook surgery in the most austere conditions, and yet managed to save hundreds of lives. Markowitz was to describe the Japanese code of Bushido as 'remorseless villainy portrayed as chivalry'. Markowitz also made significant contributions by developing a blood transfusion service using the most primitive and improvised apparatus, a process which contributed to saving many lives. Defibrinated blood was produced by stirring fresh blood with a wooden spatula, causing a clot to form. The blood was then filtered through 16 layers of gauze before being administered to the patient. He was awarded the MBE in 1945, and described his own experiences as those of a 'knife, fork and spoon surgeon'.

Roberts Hospital, and started on 18 April 1942. The first lecture was by Colonel Taylor, President of the Society, his subject was 'Wilfred Totter.'[91] The second meeting was a discussion of a case of 'pus under the diaphragm' led by Major de Soldenhoff and Captain Cruickshank. In his role as secretary, Bill was responsible for organising the meetings and co-ordinating the speakers. Many officers stood out for their ability to cover a range of subjects: for example, Lieutenant Colonel Middleton gave lectures on both medical topics, such as 'An update of anaesthetics', as well as non-medical topics including 'The history of English literature.' One of the first to deliver a lecture was Lieutenant Markowitz, who spoke on physiology; he later spoke on Canada, and Jack Ennis concluded that the country was 'lovely place' and felt it would be the place for him and his wife Elizabeth to visit, for their 'first good holiday.' There were some non-medical speakers, including Major G.T. Denaro DSO, who talked on 'The Siege of Malta'.[92] The lecturer who stood out for Bill was Colonel Julian Taylor. Not only was he able to speak, often at short notice, on a range of medical topics, both surgical[93] and non-surgical, but he could just as easily speak knowledgeably on subjects including 'Sailing round the UK', 'Underground Rivers of London' and 'French History.' Captain Marshall wrote that Taylor's lectures were *'tres amusant et tres illuminant!'* De Wardener was also very impressed by Taylor describing him as 'very precise and erudite', and noted how he had given ten lectures, each of one hour's duration on the French Revolution, without a single note. Julian Taylor's skills were not confined to the Changi Medical Society, and he made a lasting impression on both his colleagues and his patients. He was able to produce results in weak and emaciated patients with very limited resources, described as 'a tribute to his skill and courage and

---

91 Wilfred Trotter (1872-1939) was a surgeon at University College Hospital, who pioneered many developments in neurosurgery, as well as mental health. He had treated King George V for chronic empyema, and had corresponded with Sigmund Freud, as well as giving his advice in respect of the latter's colon cancer.

92 Many years later, Bill met Major Denaro's son, Major General Arthur Denaro, when he was visiting the National Arboretum at Alrewas, Staffordshire.

93 In April 1942 he gave lectures on 'peptic ulcer' and 'surgery of the stomach'.

indomitable will.'[94]

Throughout his time as secretary Bill found colleagues exceptionally helpful in contributing to the Society, with one exception, a man whom Bill did not find at all friendly. Major P.M. Bloom RAMC was a gynaecologist and when Bill approached him to give a lecture he offered only one topic, the menstrual cycle of women. Bill felt this was totally inappropriate considering the audience, and asked Bloom to reconsider. Bloom would not; he had only one subject that he could or would speak about, and so the invitation was withdrawn.

Bill also gave lectures, with his audience being men confined to their wards due to the severity of their illness. Many were suffering from deficiency scrotal dermatitis. Bill spoke on hypnosis, a topic which he had seen practically demonstrated when he was a medical student. He had seen group hypnosis, and took a keen interest in this. By 1942, when Bill was lecturing to men in Roberts Hospital he considered hypnosis somewhat dangerous, and, although he knew he could do it, decided not to give a practical demonstration. Amongst his audience Bill spotted a sergeant serving with the RAMC, who he thought would be a potential subject. At the end of the lecture, the sergeant approached Bill and asked if he would hypnotise him; 'No,' was the reply. However, against Bill's better judgement, he agreed to do so.

There were also opportunities to learn more about medicine beyond attending the Changi Medical Society. Bill helped an Australian medical student from Melbourne who had interrupted his studies in order to serve in the war. Bill had with him a large medical textbook, and gave it to the student, who read it avidly. He also received tutorials from several other medical officers, and by the end Bill was of the opinion that he 'knew enough to be a doctor.' The young man qualified soon after returning home at the end of the war.

---

94 Julian Taylor survived the war, but the years of imprisonment took their toll on him. On arriving home in Britain, he fell and broke both his arms as a result of them being so thin. He returned to clinical practice, was a member of Council of the Royal College of Surgeons of England from 1946, becoming Vice President in 1955, and died in April 1961, aged 72.

Captain 'Dickie' Dawson

Several officers who wished to pursue a career in surgery advanced their knowledge of anatomy by spending time in the mortuary. In February 1943, Jack Ennis described how Captain R.L.G. 'Dickie' Dawson RAMC came to the mortuary every afternoon to dissect bodies. Bill came across Dawson on several occasions and remembered that he was a good-looking man, who described how, as a medical student, he had undertaken modelling assignments to earn extra money. On several occasions he had modelled alongside his friend the actress, Dinah Sheridan. He was a handsome and extrovert young man who had qualified from University College Hospital in 1939. After a number of hospital jobs he was commissioned in the RAMC in April 1941. Described as 'debonair and of easy manner', he did not fit into military life easily, refusing to take part in saluting drills. He volunteered for a posting abroad and sailed for the Far East in September 1941. Just a few days before departure he met a young lady in The Red Lion pub in Colchester, a lady who he would later marry at the end of the war. He took with him to Singapore a number of textbooks covering the basic sciences of surgery. Before long, he was joined in the mortuary at Changi by Captain Tom Smiley, also keen to learn his anatomy in preparation for a surgical career. Smiley, who had stared death in the face at the Alexandra Military Hospital in February 1942 and been saved by his cigarette case, encountered a further problem at Changi. The Japanese had provided the prisoners with cigarettes and cheroots, some of which appeared to be very powerful. Jack Ennis recorded how 'Tom Smiley required resuscitation after 20 puffs at one cigarette and a man was admitted to hospital after smoking another.'[95]

Sporting Success

A range of sports were played at Changi, with matches arranged between messes, units and even some internationals. Bill contributed to a number, both as a player and as a spectator. Bill had played hockey at both Oxford and St Mary's and also played at Changi. In May 1943 he completed in an inter-mess match at Roberts Hospital, which was described as 'fast and enjoyable, but neither team scored.' Captain Marshall recorded in his diary that 'Frankland plays a very good game.' Later that year, Bill and Marshall watched an international cricket match, 'Australia vs. The Rest.' The Rest won by eight wickets in what was described as an 'unexciting match.'

Whilst at school at St Bees Bill had been intrigued by the game of

---

95 Dawson would be sent in one of the last working parties (K-Force) to the Burma Railway in 1943. Both Smiley and Dawson had successful careers in surgery on their return to Britain. Smiley obtained FRCS in 1948, and later was appointed as Consultant Thoracic Surgeon in Belfast; Dawson obtained FRCS in 1947 and was appointed Consultant Plastic Surgeon at Mount Vernon and Royal Free Hospitals. He died in 1992, and a ward at the Royal Free Hospital was named after him. Bill was invited to the official opening, and on arriving at the hospital met the local MP, Glenda Jackson, who opened the ward after giving a faultless speech, delivered without notes, a speech which left a lasting impression on Bill.

rugby and, although he had played at school, had never made the first team. At Changi, Bill took up rugby again, and found himself playing alongside men of considerable talent; all the other members of his team had played for county sides at home. Bill, being relatively small and fast, played on the right wing. Inside him was a dentist who had had a trial for Scotland before the war. In attack, the dentist would draw men towards him, pass the ball out to Bill on the wing, who was free to run and score a try. In January 1943, Bill heard that a party of Australian prisoners was coming to Changi from Java. They arrived on 7 January 1943 and spent barely two weeks on the island. The party of 878 men was commanded by Lieutenant Colonel E.E. 'Weary' Dunlop, AAMC, a surgeon and an outstanding international rugby player who had been capped for Australia between 1932 and 1934. A tall man, 6ft 4in, he was described as:

... a huge, slow, affable, shambling bear of a man who spoke slowly, courteously and calmly. He seemed the very personification of his undergraduate nickname but, in the true Australian tradition, the label 'Weary' was no more accurate than 'Tiny' would have been. His apparent slowness concealed a mind like a steel trap.

Having qualified as a doctor from Melbourne in 1934, he undertook a number of positions in Australia, before travelling to London in May 1938. He worked his passage, serving as assistant physician *en route* and on arrival in London undertook a number of locums, in Woolwich and Sidcup. At the same time he studied for his FRCS at St Bartholomew's Hospital. He sat the examination in November 1938 and much to his surprise passed. One of his most important advisors was Gordon Gordon-Taylor, senior consultant surgeon at the Middlesex Hospital, and a man who had made significant contributions to the surgery of abdominal wounds in World War 1. He advised Dunlop to seek a position at Hammersmith Hospital, but in the meantime Dunlop worked at the Brompton Chest Hospital for the surgeon Tudor Edwards. At the same time Jack Lovelock, a contemporary of Bill's at both Oxford and St Mary's, was the house surgeon on the firm. Dunlop was finally offered a post at Hammersmith Hospital, initially working in orthopaedics before transferring to work with Professor Grey Turner. In April 1939

Dunlop was conscripted into the Emergency Medical Service (EMS) at St Mary's. He may not have been aware at the time, but Sir Charles Wilson, Dean of St Mary's Medical School, was responsible for running the West London sector of EMS. Wilson was the man responsible for recruiting so many talented rugby players to the hospital, making it the force that it had become, and obviously saw Dunlop as both a medical and sporting asset. Dunlop played for St Mary's during 1939, in a team captained by Tom Kemp, a future England captain. With the outbreak of war, Dunlop volunteered to serve with the Australian forces, and in the summer of 1940 was posted to the Middle East. He served in Palestine, Greece, Crete and Tobruk before being sent to Java where he was the Commanding Officer of No 1 Allied General Hospital, at Bandoeng. His unit arrived at Java on 19 February 1942, having been unable to land on either Sumatra or Batavia as had been planned, due to the Japanese occupation. They had barely established the hospital on Java, when his unit was forced to surrender, on 5 March 1942.

Lieutenant Colonel 'Weary' Dunlop (on the right) with Lieutenant Colonel A.E. Coates. September 1945

When news spread around Changi that a party of Australian rugby players would be arriving, rumours soon emerged that the Australians considered themselves invincible. Bill recalled that he had heard vaguely about Dunlop at St Mary's in 1939, but had never met him. Dunlop's team played their first match on 13 January 1943, on a grassy pitch near the sea. The match was limited to 20 minutes each half, due to the poor health of many of the players. Dunlop himself had to dash off the field every now and then due to diarrhoea. Five days later, Dunlop's team played a team from Roberts Hospital, captained by Bill. Just prior to the match Dunlop pulled on his St Mary's rugby shirt. As the two captains met for the tossing of the coin, Bill found himself facing a large man who, he noted, was wearing a St Mary's rugby shirt, with the very distinctive *fleur de lys* crest. Bill immediately asked Dunlop why he was 'wearing my hospital's rugby shirt'; Dunlop gave a brief answer before they commenced the game. Again each half was limited to 20 minutes, and despite the Australian's reputation, Bill's team won, 12-5. Bill scored all 4 tries, again being able to run almost unimpeded on the wing whilst the opposition focussed their attention on his Scottish dentist colleague. On the other side Weary Dunlop scored one try which was converted. After the match Dunlop recalled that the match was 'enjoyable, despite the ragged play.'

Just two days after the international rugby match, Dunlop left Singapore, leading a force of nearly 900 Australians who travelled by train to the Burma Railway. Over the coming months Dunlop would work in makeshift field hospitals along the railway, treating the sick and injured. He worked in extremely challenging conditions, often alongside Jacob Markowitz, and was cruelly treated by his captors, being beaten up on more than one occasion, usually for standing up to the Japanese in order to protect his men. In July 1944, having been found playing bridge after lights out, he was summoned to the parade ground the next morning. Here he was forced to stand in the sun and was beaten mercilessly by guards armed with sticks, chair legs and rifle butts. Having suffered several broken ribs, Dunlop was worried that he may have also suffered a ruptured spleen, knowing that his spleen was enlarged as a result of malaria. His captors next tied him up kneeling backwards over a log, causing the circulation to his legs to be impaired. He wondered how long it would take for gangrene to develop. After the sun had set he was finally released, and having slowly and painfully regained the feeling in his feet, got up and stood to attention. His response to the Japanese was clear and unambiguous when he said, 'And now if you will excuse me, I shall amputate the Dutchman's arm who has been waiting all day.' His actions and leadership during imprisonment endeared Dunlop to his men, and after the war he worked hard to reconcile relationships with the Japanese. Continuing his career in surgery, he travelled widely, and would often visit London. Each time in the city, he would have tea with Bill Frankland, along with another St Mary's doctor, Henry 'Cocky' Cockburn, who had played rugby for St Mary's and the Barbarians. Cockburn, who had applied for the same position as Bill at St Mary's, as houseman to Sir Charles Wilson, served with distinction in the war. He commanded a field ambulance in North-East India in early 1944 just prior to the Battle of Kohima, and was awarded the Military Cross. He later became the last medical superintendent of St Mary's Hospital, retiring in 1979.

Moving On

The first work parties destined for the Burma Railway left Singapore on 14 May 1942. Comprising 3000 men, 'A-Force' travelled by ship to Burma and represented the first of many thousands of men who would be sent to work on the infamous Burma Railway. One month later, 3000 British prisoners left Changi and travelled north by train to Bam Pong, about 40 miles south-west of Bangkok. Herded into cattle trucks, they spent five days on-board in the most atrocious conditions, and on their arrival were used as slave labour on the eastern end of the Burma Railway. Each party had with it a contingent of medical officers and a number of medical other ranks, who would do their best to care for men being used as slave labour. Often the medical officers sent were some of the older doctors, being told that 'it was an easy job that they were to do.' Nothing could be further from the truth, as most of the men were already suffering from malnutrition, along with infectious diseases as well as deficiency diseases resulting from the poor diet.

Not all working parties headed north, some went overseas by ship, men having to endure atrocious sailing conditions, with destinations including Taiwan, Japan, French Indochina and the Dutch East Indies. One of the most infamous, but little known, left Singapore in October 1942, a party of 600 men from the Royal Artillery, under the command of Lieutenant Colonel J. Bassett. Named the '600 Gunner party', there were two medical officers attached. Captain B.H.M. Aldridge RAMC had qualified from Edinburgh University in 1938, and was serving with 1 Malay Field Ambulance at the Fall of Singapore. Alongside was Captain J.W. Lillico IMS, a graduate of St Catherine's College, Cambridge (1934) and St Thomas' Hospital (1938), who had served with 12 Indian General Hospital in Singapore. Jack Ennis recorded meeting up with Lillico in Changi in May 1942, describing how he 'looked well' and had been 'drawing up plans to go as a medical officer with British troops abroad', but those plans had been cancelled.

On 18 October the 600 men boarded the *Kenkon Maru*, a cargo ship, at Singapore Harbour. They were loaded into the ship's hold where conditions were atrocious; 200 men in one hold and 400 in the other. There was no water, and only five men at a time were allowed on deck to relieve themselves. They believed they were heading for Japan, but soon noted they were sailing south. On 5 November they disembarked at Rabaul on New Britain, to the east of Papua New Guinea. Here they were forced to work in appalling conditions, with no shelter from the elements. Many became ill and at the end of November 1942 just 517 were deemed fit. These men were taken by another ship to Ballale Island, one of the Solomon Islands where, under atrocious conditions, they were forced to build an airstrip for the Japanese. In January 1943 the island came under attack from American aircraft and it is believed some prisoners were killed in the raids. The Japanese believed that Ballale would be retaken by the Americans, and on 5 March 1943 they ordered that all remaining prisoners be executed. The bodies of over 400 men were found on the island at the end of the war. Of the original members of the '600 Gunner' party only 18 men, who had been left behind at Rabaul, survived. Both Captains Aldridge and Lillico, along with at least 5 RAMC orderlies, were murdered on Ballale. They are commemorated at Kranji War Memorial.

By the end of 1942 nearly 40,000 men had left Changi as members of working parties. At the beginning of November 1942, there were 3000 patients in Roberts Hospital, being cared for by 100 British medical officers and 900 NCOs. Barely two weeks after the '600 Gunner' party had left Singapore, plans emerged for nearly 10,000 men to travel to the Burma Railway. Jack Ennis noted on 1 November 1942 that '20 Medical officers and 400 men from Roberts Hospital' were to be travelling north, and as plans evolved, the names became known. Those selected to travel were Lieutenant Colonel MacFarlane, Major Malcolm (who had swapped duty with Bill at Cape Town in October 1941), Major E.C. 'Cyril' Vardy RAMC, and Bill. Bill never knew that he had been detailed for this party to go north, and only became aware many years later. Plans soon changed and Major R.D. 'Soldy' De Soldenhoff IMS, a surgeon, was to be attached to the group. Noting this, Ennis wrote: 'it may become more peaceful in the Mess now.' Soldy had qualified from Edinburgh University in 1929, and then worked in Sierra Leone before joining the Indian Army where he saw service in the North West Frontier. Leaving the Army, he worked as a gynaecologist, and was appointed Professor in Bombay. He rejoined the Army at the outbreak of war and was sent to Singapore. The party was seen off on 6 November 1942, but Bill was not amongst its numbers; he would spend another year at Changi.

More working parties left for the Burma Railway in March and April 1943, including the infamous F- and H-Forces, composed of some 10,000 men. On Japanese orders, F-Force contained many described as 'lightly sick.' As figures would later show, the death toll amongst F-Force was over 45% during their time on the railway. In May 1943, the Japanese ordered that Roberts Hospital was to change its name to 'Changi Hospital.' The last party to move to the Burma Railway was L-Force, a party of about 200 men, all from the RAMC, who left Singapore on 24 August 1943. They were sent to help treat the vast numbers of sick men on the railway and were commanded by Lieutenant Colonel H.C.B. Benson RAMC. As they left there were further changes at Changi as the Japanese ordered all men, along with the hospital, to move from Roberts Barracks to Selarang Barracks. This involved about 5500 men and was to be completed by the end of August. Over the coming days all those who could helped to move equipment, patients and a variety of stores over to the new hospital, a task that was completed by 26 August. The result was significant overcrowding at Selarang, leading to a recurrence of several infectious conditions including diphtheria and scabies. At the same time local working parties were deployed at Changi as the Japanese commenced construction of a new aerodrome. After the war this became RAF Changi and part of the site was later used for the development of Changi International Airport.

In October 1943, news was received that Bill was to move from Changi to join an established working party on the island of Blakang Mati, just to the south of Singapore Island. He left Changi on Friday 5 November 1943, and an Australian doctor, Captain Charles Huxtable AAMC, wrote:

Fifty British and 50 Australians left today for Blakang Mati; also Captain Frankland of BGH and Major Harold Park, dentist from our side. The men went cheerfully enough, poor fellows...... there is uncertainty as to their length of stay.

CHAPTER 7

BLAKANG MATI: HELL ISLAND

Arrival

When Bill arrived on the island of Blakang Mati on 5 November 1943, little did he know that this would be his home for the next two years. Forced to travel light, he had managed to bring two chickens and a cockerel from his farming enterprise at Changi. His colleague Jack Ennis was left to look after the others and wrote about his new responsibilities, stating, 'there is not an awful lot to do. The chickens are coming along magnificently.' Bill was fortunate to get the birds to the island, since the Japanese stole a number of his personal belongings, including his watch, although they did allow him to keep his ophthalmoscope. They also stole his patella hammer, but he acquired a new one on the island, made for him by an Australian soldier from a chair leg with a rubber end, the latter fashioned from a rubber tyre taken from an old Ford car on the island.[96]

Blakang Mati

---

96 The new hammer would survive the war and Bill brought it home with him (along with his ophthalmoscope). He donated it to the museum at the National Hospital for Nervous Diseases, Queen Square, London, although on visiting many years later, was disappointed to find it had been lost.

Pulau Blakang Mati is a small island lying approximately three-quarters of a mile south-west of Singapore Island and marks the southern boundary of the strategically important Keppel Harbour. Its importance was recognised early during the British influence in Singapore. Gun emplacements were built on the island in the 1860s and further reinforcements were constructed in 1878. In 1904, barracks were established to house soldiers manning the guns. In 1924 Major General Sir Webb Gillman's review of Singapore's defences advised that modern fortifications should be established, both on Singapore Island, as well as on Blakang Mati.

Bill, and many others, would refer to Blakang Mati as 'Hell Island', and there is more than a hint of irony that this name has a medical derivation from the 19th century. Corporal Joey Arnold of 6th Battalion, Royal Artillery arrived on the island in 1885 and soon after wrote to his mother describing how Blakang Mati was a Malay name, translated as either 'Island of death' or 'Island beyond death.' It is believed the name was given by settlers on the island when, in 1840, many died from malaria; the few who were barely alive fled to the safety of the mainland from this 'island of death.'[97] A military hospital, the first in Singapore, was opened on Blakang Mati in 1909. It had a very short life, closing in 1912 when a new military hospital was opened at Tanglin. Although no longer a medical facility, Blakang Mati had more recently served as an animal quarantine facility, for goats imported to provide food for men of 3 (Indian) Corps. During 1941, several thousand goats had been imported to the island, but as some displayed signs of rinderpest,[98] all had been slaughtered by government veterinary officers.

---

97 In 1972, the island was renamed Sentosa, which means 'peace and tranquillity', a name which was ironic in the extreme for Bill and others imprisoned there.

98 Also called 'cattle plague', this is a highly contagious disease of ruminants, and other ungulates, such as deer and antelope. It is caused by a Morbillivirus, and causes pyrexia, mucosal lesions and severe diarrhoea. Mortality amongst infected animals may reach 100%. Although not a zoonosis, it has been responsible for thousands of human deaths, due to the loss of livestock.

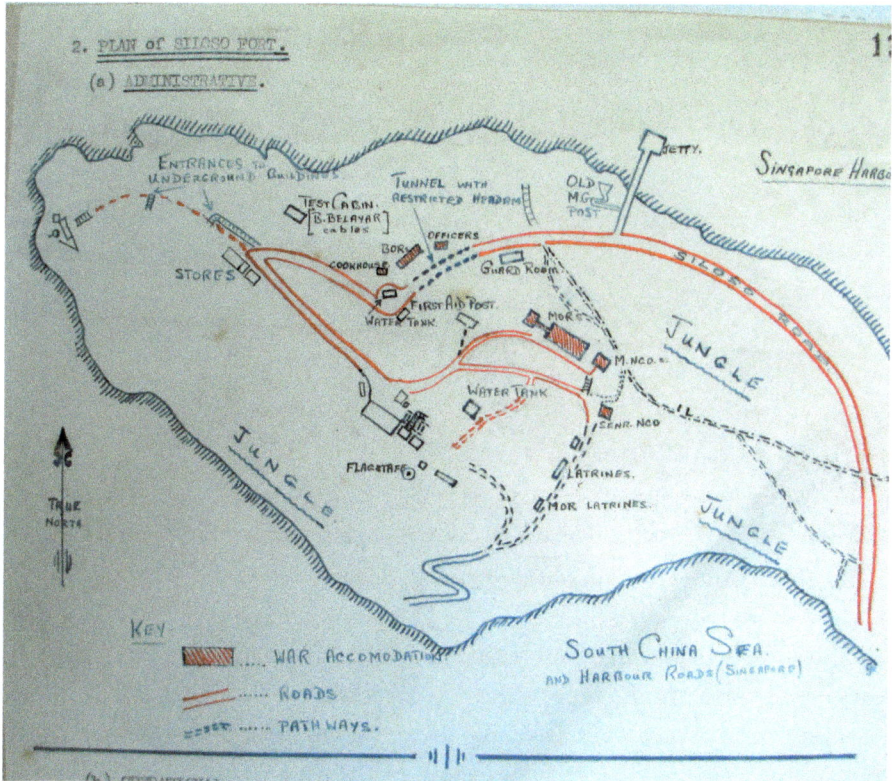

Map of Blakang Mati, 1941

During the defence of Singapore the batteries on Blakang Mati were manned by members of the Royal Artillery as well as men of the FMSVF; all were involved in heavy fighting. The long-held view that the guns on the island were of no use since they 'only pointed out to sea' is now clearly disproven. Guns at Fort Siloso, on the west of Blakang Mati, were turned to fire inland, aiming at Johor. Bill remembered being at Victoria Theatre in February 1942 and hearing shells, fired from Blakang Mati, passing overhead towards Johor Bahru Railway Station. The sound of the guns was deafening, and was followed 3 to 4 seconds later by the noise of the shells hitting a target. The guns were also fired out to sea, and were responsible for destroying at least one Japanese troopship. They were also used to set fire to a number of oil refineries, just off the coast of Singapore, depriving the Japanese of valuable fuel.

6-inch gun at Fort Siloso, Blakang Mati.

The Japanese first raised working parties of prisoners at Changi in April 1942, and many were detailed to sites on Singapore Island. At the same time a party of Australians was dispatched to Blakang Mati. Their commanding officer was Major D.T. Okey 2/18th Battalion, AIF. Born in 1903 in New South Wales, he had been a housemaster at Knox College before the war. Having joined the Australian Army, he arrived in Singapore in February 1941, and spent six months in Malaya in what appears to have been quite a relaxed period. In August 1941 his battalion was sent to the eastern district of Mersing, to prepare against Japanese attacks. Having encountered the enemy in December 1941, the battalion was soon ordered to retreat and before long found themselves back on Singapore Island.

On 22 April 1942, an advance party of 30 Australians left Changi for Blakang Mati and a week later they were joined by Major Okey, leading the main party of 170 men. They were informed that their stay would last 'about six weeks.' A week later 300 more arrived, followed by a further 100 the next month. Many of the first to arrive were Australians from 2/30th Battalion, AIF. Like Major Okey, they came from New South Wales, most from the Sydney area. Bill remembered one in particular who came from a rural area outside Sydney, a man who spent one day a week sharpening the kitchen knives in the camp. The battalion had previously been under the command of Lieutenant Colonel F.G. 'Black Jack' Galleghan,[99] a strict disciplinarian and a veteran of World War 1, who had been injured twice whilst serving in the trenches of France. On 14 January 1942, 2/30th Battalion had the distinction of being the first Australian troops to engage Japanese forces in the Malayan Campaign. They established an ambush at the Gemencheh River Bridge, some 100 miles south of Kuala Lumpur. Having mined the bridge, they entrenched and concealed themselves on its southern side. Just after 4.00pm the first Japanese troops crossed the bridge on bicycles, followed by the main column of infantry and tanks. As to plan, the mines were detonated, causing devastation as the bridge collapsed. The Australians opened up with accurate gunfire. Although there was substantial loss of Japanese life, they were able to call in artillery support against the Australian troops, forcing them to retreat. Although showing great courage, planning and determination, the ambush caused only a minor delay to the Japanese advance.

The next party to arrive at Blakang Mati was made up of 250 men of the FMSVF, and by the end of May 1942 there were over 500 prisoners on the island. For some, including Okey, a prediction of six weeks on the island would soon change into three and a half years. Amongst the FMSVF contingent was Corporal H.F.C. 'Peter' Lucy. Ironically, Lucy was 'extremely lucky' to be in a position to be selected for this or any working party. A tin miner, he had joined the volunteers in 1929, and described how most of their number were 'either tin miners or rubber planters, who met twice a month to hold parades.' Lucy, a member of the Armoured Car Battalion, had been wounded at Kuantan (in eastern Malaya) on 4 January 1942 and was hospitalised for 3 weeks. Discharged from hospital he returned to his unit and, along with his driver, was wounded on 13 February 1942 in Singapore. Taken to Alexandra Military Hospital, he was placed in a first-floor room. The following day he heard firing followed by patients screaming as the Japanese entered

---

99 Later promoted to brigadier.

the hospital. All the men in his room kept quiet, until one man stood up and declared he had been a parson in Norfolk before the war. He said a few words, telling the men that 'all knew what to expect in the next few minutes' and that they should 'have faith, knowing that God is present.' For some reason, Japanese troops did not enter Lucy's room and all the men survived. Such could not be said of his driver, Corporal Veitch, who was killed on the operating table in the same hospital.

There were two barrack blocks on the island which, before long, would be identified as Australia House and English (or Victory) House, the latter initially occupied by men of FMSVF.[100] Lucy described how the 'barracks had roofs and even running water, far better than the conditions facing many other prisoners.' The Japanese forces based on Blakang Mati included members of a supply unit for the Imperial Japanese Air Force, responsible for handling ammunition, oil and petrol at the docks on the main island. The newly arrived prisoners were immediately put to work, loading and unloading boxes of ammunition weighing 45 kg, and petrol drums holding 65 gallons. They were also tasked to move bombs, and the rule was straightforward: one man for one bomb, regardless of the size of the former or latter. Working on the docks, however, did have one advantage: prisoners were able to pick up food that had fallen out of sacks, giving them an essential, but erratic, source of extra food. As the Japanese forces continued their advances in South-East Asia, they became increasingly dependent on ammunition being shipped through Singapore Docks. The result was increasingly arduous demands on the prisoners.

One of the first medical officers to arrive on Blakang Mati, in 1942, was Captain J.F. Mitchell FMSVF, a medical practitioner from Banting, Selangor, who had qualified from Aberdeen Medical School, Scotland in 1931. By mid-1943 there were two medical officers on the island, both Australians. Captain R.D. 'Bob' Puflett AAMC hailed from Sydney. Described as 'an outstanding all-round sportsman' he also had a fine singing voice. He qualified in medicine from Sydney Medical School in

---

100 Many of the volunteer men became ill early on, and were sent back to Singapore, being replaced by a number of prisoners, both Australian and British.

1939 and developed an interest in clinical pathology. With mobilisation he was appointed as pathologist to 2/10 AGH,[101] and on arrival in Malaya served in Malacca, before the unit withdrew to Singapore. The other was Captain H.F. 'Horace' Tucker AAMC. He attended Melbourne Grammar School, described by Bill Frankland as a 'very superior school', and qualified from Melbourne Medical School in 1938. After joining the Army he served as medical officer to an Australian anti-tank regiment. On 1 October 1943, Puflett travelled from Blakang Mati to Changi with 20 men in need of hospital care. He left just one case requiring medical attention, the removal of sutures. This left Tucker on his own, but on 5 November 1943 he was joined by Bill Frankland.

The situation on Blakang Mati over the few months prior to Bill's arrival was noted to be 'increasingly difficult' by the Medical Command at Changi. In August 1943 they made a request to the IJA that the working party on Blakang Mati, which had recently been joined by a working party from Woodlands Camp (to the north of Singapore), should return to Changi. This was refused. Just a few days later reports were received that deficiency diseases were very common on Blakang Mati, and in early November personnel destined for the island were advised 'to take mosquito nets if possible'. This piece of advice did not reach Bill, but fortunately on arrival he found a net ready for him.

Once on the island, Bill soon encountered the strict demarcation between prisoners of different nationalities. Although he was billeted just a quarter of a mile from Captain Tucker, he would only see him once every 2 to 3 months, but remembered him as a man who 'smoked all the time.'[102] When Tucker was ill for several weeks with dysentery, Bill became responsible for all the prisoners on the island. The other 'medical' officer on the island was Captain H. 'Harold' Park, an Australian dentist, a

---

101 Australian General Hospital.

102 Bill later became great friends with Horace Tucker and after the war he, and his wife, stayed with Tucker and his wife, Noel, at their home in Melbourne. Both were very accomplished golf players. Bill and Horace attended a Test match, and on Australia Day they attended a formal parade at the Royal Melbourne Golf Club. Horace Tucker died in 2005.

man whom Bill came across as, and when, his dental skills were required, although Bill recalled that Park could 'only do extractions.' Since his arrival on the island in August 1942, Park's skills had been effectively requisitioned by the Japanese and he spent all his time, and used all his dental material, on treating Japanese soldiers on the island.

Bill was responsible for men in English House. His accommodation was in the former barrack blocks, and he was later to remark that although facing extremely tough conditions, 'at least I had a bed and a solid roof over me.' He was fortunate that he was not living in an atap hut, a fate that befell those who were sent to the Burma Railway. The barrack blocks were surrounded by jungle on all sides, and as Bill was later to tell his wife, Pauline (when visiting the island many years after the war), he only saw the sea twice during his whole time on the island.[103] His commanding officer was one of the few Englishmen on the island, Captain D.R. Mathews FMSVF. Born in London in 1911, he had followed his father's footsteps and became a rubber planter in Malaya, firstly in Perak, later moving to Negeri Sembilan. Like so many of the expatriate community, he had served with the local volunteer forces. He married in 1937, and in late 1941 ensured that his wife, along with their young daughter and son, were evacuated to Australia. Captain Mathews was in the first party to arrive on Blakang Mati in April 1942, and in early 1943 had taken command of English House. He was a man who was noted to be 'tireless in his devotion to duty and always stood up to Japanese coming into the camp who were either looking for trouble or had the objective of going through personal belongings.'

---

103 Nearly 75 years later, the barrack block, having been converted into the luxurious Capella Hotel, would serve as the site for the historic meeting between the President of the USA and the President of the Democratic People's Republic of Korea (North Korea).

Routine

The daily routine on Blakang Mati commenced at first light, at 7.00am, with reveille. Here, 'other ranks' saluted the officers and from then on all men were equal. Bill later likened this to 'a form of communism'. It contrasted with life in many other camps, especially those holding Dutch prisoners, where strict demarcation remained, often extending to the amount and type of food enjoyed by officers and other ranks. For Bill, a meal of weak green tea along with some rice, 'passing as breakfast', was eaten before the work parade assembled. Captain Mathews would have received prior notification of the number and size of parties required for that day. Up to 12 parties were formed and each would comprise between 1 and 14 men. They were dispatched to wherever they were required, often at the docks on Singapore, and would return around 6.30pm, although this time was far from fixed. After eating their evening meal there was a further parade. On some occasions night parties were required and men would depart after dinner to be forced to work all night. When the first men arrived on the island in 1942, officers had been assigned to working parties, but there were several incidents involving their guards, with some receiving a bashing from the Japanese. Changes followed and officers remained in the camp, where their duties included chopping wood and gardening.

Evening parade was the time when the Japanese punished the officers for the misdemeanours of their men, ensuring this took place in front of the men, in order to ensure maximum humiliation. The Japanese rarely missed an opportunity to humiliate a prisoner, especially an officer. Bill and his colleagues routinely witnessed the workings of the IJA where it was accepted, if not encouraged, that a man of inferior rank could be ill-treated by one of superior rank. Prisoners were viewed as 'the lowest of any rank.' The level of violence was severe, broken jaws were reported (although Bill never came across a case himself) and as Bill was later to remark, 'these were real bashings. Not just a slap across the face.' One Japanese sergeant stood out, one whom Bill described as a 'most nasty man' who thoroughly enjoyed bashing prisoners. If a prisoner collapsed unconscious from the assault, and the sergeant felt the man had collapsed 'too easily', he would order another prisoner to throw water on him to revive him, before hitting him again. On one occasion, Bill was hit across the face so hard that it knocked out a molar tooth, and rendered him unconscious. When he finally came to he said to his commanding officer, 'that was the best bashing I have ever had, I did not feel a thing'. The reply from Captain Mathews was far less upbeat, saying, 'We thought we had lost you, Doctor.' Mathews then went on to explain that after falling to the ground Bill had tried to stand up, dazed and incoordinate. As he rose, his hands were clenched in front of him, and he appeared to be making a threat against the Japanese officer. A Japanese private immediately stepped in front, with his bayonet ready to dispatch Bill. Fortunately the officer ordered the private to stand back; he said that they 'needed all the doctors that they could get.' Bill fell back to the ground and later recovered consciousness. For Bill it was yet another occasion when he had come very close to death; it would not be his last.

Blakang Mati had been heavily bombed in 1942, causing disruption to much of the island's water supply. Before long there was a shortage of water and at one evening parade the commanding officer asked if any of the men could divine for water. Bill volunteered, found two pieces of copper wire, bent each into the correct 'L-shape' and set to work. He found he was able to find water easily and located a number of underground streams which were then opened up, allowing enough water for the men to have showers every day after they returned from work. On returning to Britain, Bill attempted to divine for water in London, but found that the number of underground pipes and conduits prevented him from doing so; however, he was more successful in the countryside of Sussex.

After evening parade men had the rest of the evening with little to do. To pass away some of the time, the Australians made a Monopoly board. Unlike the original game, the places were streets and roads in and around Sydney and other Australian cities. Bill soon not only learnt the geography of Australia, but also became an expert at the game. Playing alongside Australians he developed an Australian accent as well as many Australian expressions, both of which would remain with him on his journey home to Britain.[104] During the earliest days on the island prisoners were allowed one day per week as rest but as the pressure of work increased, days off became increasingly irregular, often six weeks passing before any time off was granted. Later in the war, in 1944 and '45, men were lucky to receive half a day of rest per fortnight.

Disease

As part of his daily routine Bill would hold a sick parade to examine prisoners and assess their ailments. Bill's professional opinion was critical in determining which prisoners were fit to work. Major Okey wrote in his report after the war that 'the opinion of the medical officer was final in deciding who would work', and even noted that 'no one who was really sick was compelled to work.' This was not Bill's experience at all. On several occasions, having identified men too sick to work, Bill was told that there were not enough fit men, and more had to be found. Bill soon found his medical decisions were rapidly overturned, not by a medical officer, but by a Japanese NCO, with neither medical training nor qualification. This man ordered sick prisoners to report for work, his criterion apparently being that if 'a man could stand and not faint', then he was fit.

Bill came to know all his men individually, and was equally proud that, of the nearly 300 men for whom he was responsible, all lived until the end of the war. On several occasions his patients were suffering from conditions which required more specialist treatment than he could offer. Perhaps with more than a little irony, he found himself having to inform sick men that a 'consulting surgeon[105] would visit, but perhaps not for 3 or 4 months.' During two years on Blakang Mati, Bill was allowed to leave the island on just two occasions, but only to accompany men

---

104 In fact, the Australian influence would last even longer. Bill recalled how, in the early 1950s, his two eldest daughters, aged about 5 and 6, were at school in Wimbledon and would be teased for using Australian slang, such as 'Good on you' picked up from their father.
105 Captain Horace Tucker.

whom he had predicted would not survive without hospital treatment. He first returned to Singapore on 5 December 1943 taking with him half a dozen very sick men, and met Captain Marshall who wrote:

Frankland was in this morning with sick. I thought he was looking thinner, but he is feeling fit. He was saying that the Nips were stacking up plenty of bombs and petrol there. One bomb dropped in that area and he was saying that they wouldn't know much about it. They have no news but are able to smuggle in a Syman Times about once a week, but have to be very careful. When they went across today they were all very thoroughly searched and they would be searched again on return.

Barely six weeks later, on 14 January 1944, Bill visited Changi again. After this, there was a change in Japanese policy, and only men in immediate need of an operation or who were dangerously ill or dying were allowed to go to Changi for treatment. In mid-1944 Bill was caring for several very sick men suffering from a combination of malaria, dengue and malnutrition, and who he felt were unlikely to survive on the island. He persuaded the Japanese authorities that the men needed hospital treatment and the Japanese organised an ambulance to take them to Singapore, but Bill never found out what happened to these patients.

On Blakang Mati, Bill encountered many diseases which he had seen in the previous 18 months at Roberts Hospital. Malaria was rife, although the Japanese had denied its existence until August 1943 when it had spread to some of their own men. One of those affected was the sergeant who enjoyed savagely beating prisoners; he died on the parade ground as a result of a ruptured spleen. Bill and the other prisoners were pleased that the man had died from a disease which the Japanese claimed they did not have. As a consequence, the Japanese allowed preventative actions, including oiling of ponds to disrupt mosquito breeding sites. 95% of men on the island suffered from malaria, although Bill was one of the few who did not. Exactly why is unclear and some 75 years later, Bill wondered if he had developed immunity to infection. The other major insect-borne infectious disease was dengue fever and for Bill it was vital to differentiate between the two, which often had similar presenting symptoms, as treatment was only available for malaria. Dengue, caused by a virus, is spread by mosquitoes of the *Aedes* family (which bite in the afternoon, as opposed to the *Anopheles* mosquito responsible for the transmission of malaria, which bite at night). Infection is followed by fever, with muscle and joint pains as well as headache. Men described being 'unable to look at food' but the infection always resolved within two to three days. All men on the island, including Bill, suffered from dengue at some point. As men recovered from dengue or malaria, then as soon as they could walk, Bill detailed them to return to work.

For a definitive diagnosis, a microscopic examination of a blood smear was required to identify the presence or absence of the *Plasmodium* parasite responsible for malaria. Captain Puflett had brought a microscope to the island in 1942 which was used by medical officers. However, in December 1943, not long after Bill's arrival, the Japanese removed the microscope, placing it in the Japanese hospital, which was half a mile's walk from English House. When Bill wished to use the microscope he had to be escorted there. His escort was the only Japanese Christian on the island, a man who Bill described as being 'very unpopular with the other Japanese, due to his religious beliefs'. This was probably why he was given the escort role. The man did not see the end of the war, dying from malaria in the last few days of hostilities. There was one Japanese medical officer who worked in the Japanese hospital and Bill recalled one occasion when, using the microscope, he saw the medical officer looking very sick indeed lying in a ground-floor bed in the hospital. Bill was asked to review a blood film and diagnosed that the patient had a dual infection with malaria. Although not being told so, it was apparent to Bill that the blood film was that of the Japanese medical officer who, it appears, did survive until the end of the war.

Using the microscope was not without risk as demonstrated by an incident on 28 July 1945. That day, Bill had gone to the Japanese hospital and, having completed his work, was waiting for an escort for the return journey. At this point, a private, whom Bill had never seen before, arrived and for no reason started to attack him, hitting Bill in the face and then smashing a chair over his head. Bill managed to break free and ran down the stairs, but was kicked and struck again. At the bottom of the stairs he found the Japanese medical officer and complained to him about the attack. He gave an order for the beating to stop, and it did. To protect himself Bill had raised his forearm above his head in the attack, and the arm subsequently became very painful and swollen; later Bill suspected that he had sustained a fracture. An official complaint was made, to which the Japanese replied that Bill's punishment was fully authorised since he had not asked the correct permission to use the microscope. It appeared, however, that the Japanese were in fact lying in wait, looking for an opportunity to punish him.

By the time Bill arrived on Blakang Mati, all the medical supplies had been virtually exhausted, except for a small supply of anti-malarial tablets and some sulphonamides. Fortunately one of Bill's last acts at Tanglin in February 1942 was to secure a large supply of the anti-malarial drug, mepacrine. Most were deposited in the pharmacy at Roberts Hospital, but Bill was able to take 3000 tablets to Blakang Mati in November 1943. This was just enough to treat men suffering from malaria until the end of hostilities. Ensuring that mepacrine was only dispensed to those suffering from malaria was important to optimise the valuable stock: one tablet of mepacrine was worth one month's pay. Just once Bill was persuaded to give mepacrine to a man who was, in fact, suffering from dengue. For this particular patient, Private Cole, an Irishman, time was against Bill, and he was unable to make a microscopic diagnosis for 2 to 3 days. He did not believe that Cole was suffering from malaria, but could not be sure, and so against his better judgement, prescribed mepacrine.

Many working parties were sent to unload ships in Keppel Harbour whilst others were involved in removing munitions dropped in and around the harbour. Men were also detailed to build slit trenches and repair bomb-damaged roads. Accidents were common amongst members of working parties, at least one occurring every day. They ranged in severity; at least two men were drowned whilst going by boat to Singapore. Bill heard the story of an Australian who had fallen overboard, his colleagues alerted the Japanese guards to the situation, and pleaded that they might turn the boat around and rescue him. The reply was typical of their callous captors who said that 'the sharks will take him.'

Corporal Lucy was one of many who were wounded whilst in a

working party, and wrote of his experiences. He described that they had 'a prisoner doctor who helped tremendously but had no medicines', and how 'salt water was standard treatment for all wounds.' This was his description of Bill Frankland, and Lucy described how he had sustained a gash to his arm which turned septic; he was about to have the arm amputated when it was saved by Bill's treatment, again using just salt water. He was left with a huge scar, but at least his arm was still functioning.[106]

Bill also treated men suffering from tropical ulcers, a condition he had first encountered at Tanglin Military Hospital in December 1941. Although it was reported that a large number of bacteria could be found in these ulcers, no specific organism was isolated. However, one thing was certain; they were very difficult to treat. On Blakang Mati their treatment was compounded by a lack of medicines and dressings. For Bill, it was a case of returning to the 'ways of his teachers' and he used sea water. This had been advocated and used by Sir Almroth Wright during World War 1. He had recognised the harmful effects of antiseptics applied to wounds, causing destruction of neutrophils and macrophages, cells whose purpose is to provide protection to wounds.[107] From this Wright advocated the use of saline solution and Bill realised that on Blakang Mati they had a ready supply of salt water. For Sir Almroth Wright the most important feature of treatment was to use a wet dressing, kept moist at all times. His success was replicated by Bill so that all of his patients on Blakang Mati with tropical ulcers treated in this way recovered, although many took a long time; the only exception being a certain Corporal Coleman, who Bill recalled was a good friend of Corporal Lucy.

Bill also had to treat a number of cases of allergic disease, a branch of clinical medicine that would later become his area of expertise. One

---

106 Bill would meet Peter Lucy again, several years later at St Mary's Hospital, in the special summer hay fever clinic.
107 Alexander Fleming, when working with Almroth Wright, reported how the antiseptic carbolic acid, when placed on a wound, inhibited the natural antiseptic function of blood, thereby making it a 'first class culture medium'.

evening a soldier presented with severe nettle-rash, which was causing much suffering and misery. Bill had a small amount of adrenaline, which had been stored in a jam jar for over two years. Exposed to the sun, it had turned brown. Bill injected the man with adrenaline and was amazed to see that it had retained some of its activity; the patient improved but only for about 30 minutes before relapsing. At this stage, Bill felt it was better not to give a further dose.

Food

Alternative supplies of food were always being considered by the prisoners to supplement the meagre and totally inadequate rations provided by the Japanese. Men became emaciated, and Bill banned them from weighing themselves, in an attempt to prevent them knowing exactly how much weight they had lost. Bill was one of the few prisoners who had time to garden and grow food, mostly pawpaws and tapioca, crops which saved many lives. Gardening was not easy, hindered by the poor quality of soil, intermittent drought and a lack of tools. On one memorable occasion a local Chinese man walked past the edge of English House. Unable to stop, he threw six beans to Bill and his colleague and said, 'Plant them under a tree.' Bill thought this seemed rather strange, if not silly, advice but decided to follow it. He dug a hole next to a tree, planted the beans and kept them well watered (using a solution with a high nitrogen content, namely his and other men's urine). The beans sprouted and grew rapidly, so much so that within 3-4 weeks they were quite tall and displaying purple flowers. Beans soon formed and these were knocked off the lower branches with a stick. Bill was with his colleague, Lieutenant A.J. 'Benny' Goodman, Irish Guards, the interpreter on the island.[108] With the beans safely harvested, they set about boiling them in water. Bill started to drink the bean water; one mouthful was enough and he spat out the terrible-tasting fluid. He gave

---

108 Along with a good command of Japanese, Goodman also possessed great tact in handling the Japanese, 'being fearless in the way he approached the most irate of Japanese soldiers'.

the rest to Goodman who drank it all. Barely 5 minutes later, Goodman collapsed and Bill thought he was dead. He was not, although he was barely alive with a very weak pulse. Fortunately after about 10 minutes, Goodman vomited and then made a slow recovery. Bill later learnt that eating the beans was perfectly safe, but that on boiling a cardiotoxic substance was released into the water, and he heard of two men who had died as a result.

Bill realised that apart from vegetables, wild animals would be a good source of protein. Seeing monkeys on the island, they attempted to catch one. This was totally unsuccessful. It was made worse for Bill and others as they watched bananas grow and then ripen around the camp. They hoped to harvest them, but their hopes were completely dashed when they saw monkeys move in and take all the ripening fruit for themselves.

Six deer lived in and around the barrack block and offered another potential source of sustenance. In late 1944 the prisoners obtained permission from the Japanese to try to capture them. Men formed a cordon on the parade ground around the animals and gradually encircled them. Four deer escaped, leaving just two; the cordon of men moved in closer, believing that they would capture at least one. Suddenly the two deer made their escape, jumping up over the men's heads. Two men suffered fractured ribs and a third, a serious head wound, and it was left to Bill to treat the injured.

Despite being so close to the sea, Bill never saw any fish, and meat was also a rarity; when provided to the prisoners, it was barely enough to form a gravy, eaten with rice. In Changi, cats had been eaten by prisoners, often being purchased on the black market. On Blakang Mati, Bill came across just one cat, which lived in Australia House, and was looked after by prisoners. It was just a kitten and the men were closely attached to the animal. However, the Japanese tried to be cruel towards the kitten, a move that enraged the prisoners, who told the Japanese to stop; quite remarkably they did.

Law and Order

Amongst the earliest groups sent from Changi to Blakang Mati, were several men of 'bad character' dispatched to the island as a form of punishment, and a way of ensuring that they were no longer potential sources of trouble at Changi. Bill came across three of these men, who were stealing food in the camp. Their actions got everyone into trouble with the Japanese and led to the officers receiving a bashing from their captors. The culprits were two Australians and one British soldier, the latter being Private Skate, a member of the 1St Bn Leicestershire Regiment.[109] Skate had a record of dishonesty. On one occasion he asked to be relieved from parade suffering from dysentery. Bill recalled that when the parade was finally dismissed, about 30 minutes later, men found that their tobacco had been stolen. The culprit was Skate and in their anger the men attacked him, kicking and beating him until he was almost senseless. Bill was forced to intervene to stop the assault. Skate then spent three weeks recovering, but then started his criminal activities again. In order to prevent further incidents Bill allocated him to a working party the following day. The very next day Skate thanked Bill for saving his life, twice.

Following a further spate of thefts, Captain Mathews pondered what to do on the next occasion. He decided that if those responsible were caught they would be handed over to the Japanese. However, events overtook him and the Japanese apprehended the three men stealing. They were immediately punished and sent to a small island near Blakang Mati for 6 months, a sentence which was effectively certain death. Skate, trying to seek a release from the island, deliberately wounded himself with an axe. The three men were moved by their captors to Singapore Island and Bill was sent across to treat them. Here he found the men locked inside a structure resembling a pigsty; all three were very weak, covered in their own faeces and blood, and Skate had an axe wound in his foot. Bill decided to take all the men back to Blakang Mati. As they

---

109 Although Skate had been a member of this regiment, his name did not appear on any official lists; Bill believed that he may well have been a deserter.

made their way back, Bill spotted a number of non-Asians; they were sailors from a German submarine docked in Keppel Harbour. Seeing Bill, and recognising him as the enemy, they started to throw stones at him, but missed; as Bill was later to observe, 'none of the Germans were cricketers'.

Man Overboard

The Japanese recognised that many of their prisoners were highly skilled and were put to work building a boat for the Japanese commandant on the island, who went by the nickname of 'Shuffleboots.' He was an unhappy and angry man, who wanted to be fighting rather than being put in charge of prisoners, men whom he despised and considered to be 'the lowest of the low.' Men spent almost two years building what was acknowledged to be a 'fine yacht.' They asked if they could be allowed to go on-board, when it was launched, believing this not to be unreasonable in light of the effort that they had put in. The Japanese were not swayed by this in the slightest: the answer was no. To seek revenge the prisoners sabotaged the yacht and just prior to its launch they cross-wired the engine and the electrical systems. As she glided down the slipway into the water, the Japanese crew started the engine, only to find the boat starting to smoulder. Soon she was ablaze and Bill was told of the rather hilarious sight of the Japanese jumping off the boat into the water, to avoid the flames.

News

News from outside of the island was strictly limited. Early on, prisoners were allowed to read the Japanese-controlled *Syman Times* newspaper, but as the Japanese came under increasing pressure from Allied forces, and started to suffer real setbacks in their military conquests, this source of news was banned. Fortunately there was a secret radio, maintained and operated by Sergeant Dinoen FMSVF. Having arrived on the island he constructed a radio set, which became vital in helping to maintain the morale of the men. The radio was hidden in a workshop where Dinoen, a telephone mechanic, worked every day and, ironically, where he was responsible for maintaining Japanese radio sets and other electrical devices. Dinoen was well aware of the risks he ran, knowing that if caught he would be executed. It appears that the Japanese were never suspicious of his activities, although the secret was almost given away by Private Skate. On one occasion Captain Mathews had threatened Skate that if there was any further misbehaviour on his part, he would be handed over to the Japanese. Skate replied, saying if that were to happen he would 'immediately inform them about the radio.'

It was over a year before Bill's wife, Pauline, learnt that he was alive and a prisoner in Singapore, information that had reached her through the Red Cross. Bill did not receive a letter for over 1 year following the fall of Singapore, and some letters took over 18 months. They were marvellous to receive and to learn of news from back home. His first letter from Pauline arrived exactly one year after she had written it. At the outbreak of war Pauline had been employed as a VAD cook at Queen Alexandra's Military Hospital, but later decided to join the WRNS. She had written to Bill asking his permission to join up. He had also received a letter from his brother, Jack, telling him that this father had moved from High Hesket to Newton Arlosh in Cumberland.[110] Prisoners were allowed to send postcards home, with a maximum of 15 words. Bill wrote home to his wife, addressing her as 'First Officer' to his father's new address in Newton Arlosh. In this way it was clear to them that he had received their letters and their news. In all Bill sent three postcards to his wife during the three and a half years of his imprisonment.

Paper was in short supply on Blakang Mati, and by late 1944 all supplies were exhausted. Prisoners had three uses for paper, as cigarette papers, for writing and for using as lavatory paper. When the paper ran out, men asked for permission to use the former officers' library, and each man was allowed one book, Bill acquired a large tome, a treatise on 'The Book of Job' which he read. Job is viewed by many theological opinions as exploring the nature of faith of a just man in an unjust world. More recently, in 2000, it has been suggested in an article in the *British*

---

110 Henry Frankland moved just before Christmas 1943.

Medical Journal that, if read by a clinician, it is 'a treatise on illness and loss as well as the doctor-patient relationship.' This might explain why, on reading Job, Bill became quite depressed, and was unclear if his own suffering as a prisoner was the result of him leading a good life or a bad life? Some 55 years after his release from captivity, Bill annotated one part of that *British Medical Journal* article:

My flesh is clothed with maggots, my skin is a clod of earth; it curdles and decays. My days are swifter than a weaver's shuttle, and are spent without hope.

Job 7:5-6

There were few opportunities for religious services on the island, but in early 1945, the Japanese allowed prisoners half a day every fortnight to attend a church service. This was led by an Australian padre, a man described by Bill as 'a good padre, but not particularly intelligent.' His commanding officer refused to go to any services, and Bill challenged him on this, pointing out that there was more to the service than just listening to a sermon. His commanding officer replied that he had real issues with reciting the Lord's Prayer, especially the line 'give us our daily bread', especially as the men had not seen bread for nearly three years. The Communion bread was in fact made from rice, and the wine from fermented pineapples.

Meeting an Old Friend

Among the Englishmen on the island, Bill soon encountered one of his former patients, Sapper G.C. 'Geoffrey' Munton, 560 Field Company, Royal Engineers, who arrived on Blakang Mati in May 1943. A year earlier, in June 1942, Bill had treated Sapper Munton at Roberts Hospital suffering from dysentery, associated arthritis, optic neuritis and beriberi, with the latter leading to heart failure. Bill was most surprised that Munton had recovered from that first episode.

Munton had landed in Singapore on 29 January 1942, part of 55 Brigade, one of three brigades that made up 18 Division. He was born in 1918, in Stamford, Lincolnshire, and had left school at the age of 14. Some three years later he was working in the building profession, overseeing a number of projects in Yorkshire, and had developed his drawing skills, which would be of great value in both civilian and military life. With the outbreak of war, he was conscripted into the Army, and soon met three other conscripts, Sappers Douglas Lawrence, Gerald Peters and Jack Hazard, and all were posted to 560 Coy. The four men would be together, through trial and tribulation, for the next six years.

After two years of training in Britain, men of 560 Coy sailed from Liverpool on 28 October 1941. For Munton and many others, it was the first time they had been on a ship. Their destination was unknown, although many on-board felt they would be heading to North Africa. Sailing in convoy, they travelled north to Greenock, onto Reykjavík in Iceland, before reaching Halifax, Nova Scotia. Here they transferred to an American vessel, USS *West Point*. Launched on 1 August 1939 as SS *America*, she was the flagship of the United States Lines, and was that country's latest luxury liner. As part of American aid to the Allies, under the 'Lend-Lease' agreement signed in March 1941, she was converted to a troopship in June 1941. Although she had changed her name, she had not given up her luxury. Troops recalled enjoying the state cabins 'with all their finery', and despite serving as a troopship, the shops and swimming pool remained open for business. Munton was one of 5500 troops who transferred to *West Point* on 9 November 1941. The following day they sailed as Convoy HS124 with five other American troopships, USS *Wakefield, Mount Vernon, Orizaba, Leonard Wood* and *Joseph T. Dickman*, with an escort of numerous warships, including the aircraft carrier USS *Ranger*. Travelling south, past Trinidad and South America, they headed across the Atlantic Ocean towards South Africa. On-board, Munton and his friends were rather shocked to find that many of the American crew appeared to have less experience of sailing than they did. Be that as it may, coming from war-torn Britain, with stringent rationing, they were pleased to be offered chocolate and eggs, foods many had not seen for several months.

On 7 December 1941, as they were sailing east, they received news of the attack by Japanese aircraft on the US Pacific Fleet at Pearl Harbor; the Americans were now at war alongside British and Empire forces. The convoy arrived at Cape Town on 9 December, a day marked by more bad news, with the sinking of HMS *Prince of Wales* and *Repulse,* and the loss of 800 men. Five days later *West Point* departed in a convoy supported by HMS *Dorsetshire*. Sailing north, most on-board thought they were being sent to the Middle East, but after celebrating Christmas at sea, they landed in Bombay on 27 December. Following disembarkation they travelled by train to Delhi, only to return some 10 days later, re-embarking on 9 January 1942. They were now informed of their final destination: Singapore. *West Point* sailed with *Wakefield, Empress of Japan* and *Duchess of Bedford* supported by a number of Royal Navy escorts.

Sailing to the west of Sumatra they passed east through the Sunda Strait to avoid Japanese submarines. The Strait, which separates Sumatra from Java, is a challenge to navigation at the best of times, with a real risk of running aground. Here they came under attack from Japanese aircraft. The ships all increased their speed and made a dash for Singapore's Keppel Harbour, arriving early on Thursday 29 January 1942. Here Munton and the other members of the brigade disembarked around the time of a Japanese air attack, during which all the native workers fled, leaving the crew and troops to unload the ship. Like all other ships arriving in Singapore, they were met by Bill, whose port duties now had to be carried out at Keppel Harbour following the effective abandonment of the Royal Naval base at Sembawang.

560 Coy arrived on an island which was coming under ever-increasing attack from the Japanese forces, and Bill, whose medical responsibilities had included meeting the arriving ships, was, by now, resigned to the likely fall of Singapore. The arrival of large numbers of reinforcements was only likely to increase the number of men who would be taken prisoner. Over the ensuing two weeks Munton was posted to a number of sites on Singapore, and during the last days of fighting was based at the Chinese High School, near the Cathay Building.

Following the fall of Singapore, Munton was imprisoned in Changi. Nearby, to the south, was the Changi Camp Burial Site, very close to the Johore Battery. The death toll at Changi rose, initially men dying from wounds sustained during the fighting, but before long, poor conditions, dietary deprivation, and the ravages of infectious diseases led to the deaths of many prisoners. Amongst the first to be buried at Changi were Sappers K.F. Cooke and T. Bateman, both from Munton's own unit.

Graves at Changi Cemetery.

Changi Cemetery, Sketch by Geoffrey Munton.

It was just before Christmas of 1942 that Captain C.D. Pickersgill, 287 Field Coy, Royal Engineers, felt that there should be something for the dead servicemen to pass through on the way to their burial, as a sign of Christian faith. He approached the Japanese commandant who gave permission for the erection of lych-gates at the entrance to the burial site. Chengai wood was obtained by a number of local working parties, and barbed wire was fashioned to make fastenings, in place of nails. The design was to be based upon the lych-gates at Holy Trinity Church, Startforth, Co. Durham. Sappers Munton and Lawrence acted as draughtsmen for the project, responsible for drawing of the lych-gate design, and the artwork involving British national emblems, engraved in the timbers. Munton himself was responsible for the words inscribed just inside the gates and below the eaves, which read:

To the glory of God and in memory of those who laid down their lives for King and Country

Erected by 18th Division, Dec 1942

Almost 600 bodies passed through the lych-gates to be buried in the cemetery at Changi during the war.[111]

The lych-gates from Changi, at National Memorial Arboretum, Alrewas

111 The bodies were later exhumed and buried in the CWGC Cemetery, Kranji, Singapore, where they are remembered to this day. In 1952 the lych-gates were moved and erected in front of St George's Church, Tanglin Barracks. In 1971, with the withdrawal of British forces from Singapore, the lych-gates were moved to Bassingbourn Barracks, Cambridgeshire, and Munton, Lawrence and Peters all attended the ceremony of rededication in December 1972. The lych-gates were moved to their final home at the National Memorial Arboretum, Arlewas, England, in 2003.

On Blakang Mati, Geoffrey Munton made a huge impression on Bill since he was the only man under his care who did not have a day off sick for a whole year. In recognition of this Bill arranged that Munton should have a day 'off sick' on his birthday. On the day in question Bill was told, by a non-medical Japanese private, that there were 'too many on his sick parade' and that Munton would have to work. Thinking rapidly, Bill managed to convince the soldier that Munton was ill, still recovering from malaria. This was a dangerous course of action, and as Bill pointed out many years later, if his true motives had become apparent, there would have been 'hell to pay, all round.' Fortunately this did not happen and Munton had a day of rest. Bill also recognised Munton's quiet inner strength and his ability to have a beneficial influence on other men, and would ask him to sleep near to those who were sick and at real risk of giving up the will to live.

The Start of Peace

By the middle of 1945, men on Blakang Mati were aware that victory had been achieved in Europe, with the surrender of Germany in May. However, fighting was continuing in the Far East, with advances being made to the west, in Burma, and to the east, with the Americans retaking the Philippines. For men on Blakang Mati, life was increasingly difficult with further reductions in their rations. It was in late-July 1945 that, faced with the Allied advances, Emperor Hirohito issued a deathly order. If any troops landed on Japan, all prisoners held by the Japanese, regardless of where, were to be killed; a figure of some 120,000 men. On Blakang Mati, just as in many other prison camps in the region, plans were put in place. Bill heard guards working at night around the parade ground. At morning parade he saw that three machine gun emplacements had been erected ready to be used if landings took place in Japan. Fortunately the Emperor's orders were never enacted since on 6 and 9 August 1945, American aircraft dropped atomic bombs on Hiroshima and Nagasaki, respectively. This ended Japanese hostilities, and soon after when Bill spotted Allied fighter aircraft overhead, he knew that the war was over. As Bill would later reflect, he had been very close to death, yet again, but had survived, and this time his survival was due solely to the dropping of the atomic bombs.

Although none of the prisoners were murdered at this time, the same was not the case for the occupants of the 'comfort house' on the island where eight prostitutes lived. Bill learnt that during the last week of hostilities all the prostitutes had been shot by the Japanese. Amongst the Japanese soldiers on the island several contracted venereal diseases, and one, suffering from syphilis approached Bill. The man had his own supply of medicines, arsenical compounds, which needed to be given by injection. He asked Bill to administer the medicine but Bill, seeing that the man was already unwell, and suffering with jaundice, refused to administer the medicine.

On 20 August 1945, the prisoners asked to see the commandant, 'Shuffleboots', and complained that, despite the war having ended, they were still on Hell Island. He agreed for men to move back to Singapore Island. Bill, along with about 200 men, left on 23 August 1945 and were taken by road to a camp next to the hospital facility at Kranji, in the north of Singapore Island. Kranji Hospital had been established in 1944, when all hospital facilities were moved from Changi. There were 30 doctors at the hospital, many of whom Bill remembered from his time at Changi. Bill asked if one of them would look after his men. He was given three days off work and then started back, working alongside Captain Marshall, again looking after his men. Despite being next to a hospital, Bill found that it now took longer for a blood film to be examined for malaria than had been the case at Blakang Mati. Having been at Kranji for about three days, Bill saw the men assembling at the perimeter fence and then witnessed a yellow Rolls-Royce drive past. It was carrying the Sultan of Johor, who had spent the war in an increasingly uncomfortable relationship with the Japanese. He got out of the car and started to pass 50- and 100-dollar bills through the fence to men in the camp. Bill acquired two 50-dollar and one 100-dollar bills, it was the first time he had seen paper money for over a year. Thinking that the notes were probably next to useless as currency, he used them as lavatory paper the next morning, an experience he described as a 'great luxury.' When Bill arrived home to Britain he learnt that his assumption about the currency was wrong, and that he could have easily exchanged the notes. In fact he had spent about £75 wiping his bottom at Kranji.

Bill and other men at Kranji were literally dressed in rags, many were almost naked, wearing just the remains of the clothes that had survived over three years of imprisonment. Suddenly they all received a great shock when women walked past the perimeter of the camp. Firstly, they had not seen women for many years, and secondly, many men were in a state of undress, so they rushed away from the fence in order to hide their, and the ladies', embarrassment.

The Japanese government, on behalf of the Emperor, formally surrendered to General MacArthur on 2 September 1945, on-board the USS *Missouri*, in Tokyo Bay. Two days later a flotilla of Allied vessels, led by HMS *Rotherham* and *Sussex,* sailed into Keppel Harbour, to start the reoccupation of Singapore, an operation codenamed 'Operation Tiderace'.[112] The flotilla included a British hospital ship sent to assist in the care and evacuation of sick prisoners. The second in command of the medical team on-board was Captain J.B. 'John' Mitchell RAMC, who had qualified in 1938 from St Mary's Hospital, and was Bill's greatest friend; they had shared accommodation just off the Gloucester Road.[113] Bill decided to make his way down to the harbour and located a Jeep. This was the first time he had seen, let alone ridden in, a Jeep, since these were new vehicles, only being distributed after 1942. Arriving at the harbour he met Mitchell who quickly obtained some food for Bill and another medical officer travelling with him, both of whom were still starving. The initial offering was a number of 'rather small' sandwiches,

---

112 On 12 September, Lord Mountbatten, Supreme Allied Commander, South-East Asia, recently arrived from his headquarters in Kandy, Ceylon, took the surrender of some half a million Japanese forces in the South-East Asia area from General Itagaki. The signing took pace in the City Hall, Singapore and Mountbatten insisted that the senior Japanese officers offer up their swords to the Allied forces. The surrender was signed at 03.41 (GMT) on 12 September, and although Bill had left the island by then, he received a copy of the document.

113 Bill described their accommodation as 'very cheap', but it was within walking distance of St Mary's; it was destroyed in a bombing raid in the war. Bill would later be godfather to John Mitchell's daughter.

and, although welcomed by Bill, John Mitchell realised that they were not sufficient. Quickly a number of 'proper-sized' sandwiches arrived. This was the first bread that Bill had eaten in over three and a half years. Bill's mission to the hospital ship had not been solely for food, since he was seeking help for an urgent medical case. He had not been able to believe his eyes when he arrived at Kranji Hospital and found Sapper Munton lying on a pallet, weighing less than 5 stones and desperately ill. As he was later to write:

He was almost unrecognisable, looking like a skeleton, running a fever, extremely anaemic following starvation, relapsing dysentery and malaria. This was also complicated by beriberi. He was moribund and in desperate need of a blood transfusion.

Mitchell arranged for a blood transfusion for Munton, who then made a slow but steady recovery. He spent several months in Singapore, before returning home, recuperating in Bombay before finally arriving at his home in Lincolnshire one week before Christmas 1945. He was discharged from the Army the following year, when he found that deductions were made from his final pay for the loss of a rifle! Bill was never sure of Geoffrey Munton's fate, and did not know if he had survived the war or not. The answer came about 15 years after the war, when Bill was walking down Piccadilly and bumped into Sapper Munton and his daughter, Sally. Many years later, Sally Munton painted a portrait of Bill, which was presented to the Frankland Allergy Clinic at St Mary's Hospital. Munton lived in Lincolnshire and died in 1993. The funeral was held in the village of Digby. Sally Munton clearly remembers that day when a 'man in a pin-stripe suit' was seen walking from Sleaford to Digby. This was Bill who had travelled by train to Sleaford. A motorist stopped and gave him a lift to Digby, where he told Sally that his reason for travelling was quite straightforward: 'I couldn't not be here.'

At the liberation of Singapore, Bill remembers that it was Gurkhas who were so critical to the stability of the island, ensuring that looting did not occur. Bill believed that without them there would have been a disaster, since there was little, if any, food available. By contrast, Sikh troops were also deployed to the island, and led a victory parade where instead of being cheered, they were openly booed by the prisoners of war and civilians alike. All were acutely mindful of the number of Sikhs who had sided with Japanese, and how many had been responsible for dishing out inhumane behaviour.

The commanding officer at Blakang Mati had maintained a diary of his time on the island: after liberation he returned to the island to retrieve the diary, which he had buried. There he found the body of 'Shuffleboots', who had committed suicide by exploding a grenade next to his abdomen. His body was in a storm drain and, as was described to Bill, the ants appeared to 'have a very good meal on his body.' It was suggested that this was quite a fitting end for the man.

Bill was rightly proud of his service of nearly two years on Blakang Mati, during which not a single man under his care died. This was recognised by the Captain Mathews[114] who, in Bill's words:

Congratulated me on my work as the doctor on the island and kindly said that he really would like my compassion, care and professionalism to be formally recognised. He probably felt that I had saved a number of lives. I said that I was merely doing my job.

Later Captain Mathews, I understood, recommended the Wireless Operator for his wonderful work in passing valuable information around the camp. Since there could only be one award made, it went to the right man in my opinion; nevertheless it was thoughtful of Captain Mathews to feel the way he did about my work.

Homeward-Bound

On VJ Day[115] plus 11, Bill along with other prisoners started their journey home. He received what he called 'VIP treatment', being flown first to Penang. Here they were looked after by a young RAF officer, who said, 'I know what you want,' and disappeared, returning with a bottle of whisky. As Bill pointed out to him, they were still incredibly hungry,

---

114 Captain Mathews returned to Malaya after the war, as a tin miner. He later retired to Devon and wrote on a number of occasions to Bill, who kept the letters for several years, but they were later discarded.

115 Victory over Japan Day, 15 August 1945.

and wanted food, not alcohol.

The next leg of the journey was to fly from Penang to Rangoon. Sitting down in an aircraft was very painful because of the emaciation; Bill described the experience as 'just bones on a hard seat.' By now the monsoons had arrived, bringing torrential rain. Three Dakota aircraft were to fly the men north, although, as Bill later admitted, they really should not have been flying at all in the dreadful conditions. Bill boarded one aircraft and soon after take-off became very frightened. Amongst his group was a naval chief petty officer, who was anaemic, so much so that, as the aircraft flew higher, the man collapsed and became unconscious, due to lack of oxygen. Bill persuaded the pilot to fly lower, and the man recovered. Bill asked the pilot 'what height they were flying at', and was told, 'about 8000 feet.' 'But,' Bill commented, 'many of the mountains are higher than 8000 feet, how did he avoid them?' The reply was quite straightforward: the pilot was hoping to 'fly between the higher peaks.' In fact the pilot had no oxygen himself, so could not fly above 12,000 feet. On arriving at Rangoon, Bill learnt that one of the three aircraft had crashed into a mountain *en route* and all on-board were killed.

Once on the ground at Rangoon, Bill was offered bread and jam, food that he had not seen for over three years. After that he was examined by a medical officer who, on palpating Bill's abdomen, advised him that he had a large spleen, suggesting this was the result of malaria. Bill was able to correct him straightaway, the doctor was actually palpating about a loaf of bread lying in Bill's stomach. Despite that, Bill was admitted to hospital for observation and had to wait to join a ship destined for Britain.

Bill travelled home from Rangoon on-board SS *Orduña*, which sailed on 21 September 1945. *Orduña*, displacement 15,500 tons, was built by Harland and Wolff in 1914 as a passenger liner, but during World War 1 had served as a troopship, primarily on the transatlantic route. Reverting to a civilian role after the cessation of hostilities, she was again requisitioned following the outbreak of World War 2. Under the command of Captain J. Williams, *Orduña* had been sent to the Far East to act as the commodore ship for the planned invasion force destined to reoccupy Malaya. With the surrender of Japanese forces, the ship was reconfigured as a passenger transport. Leaving Rangoon, the ship carried over 1700 prisoners of war, along with 20 civilians. Amongst those on-board was Captain Chilton,[116] who had served with Bill at Tanglin nearly four years earlier. At Tanglin they had played bridge together and on the journey home they partnered each other in more rubbers of bridge.

The ship docked briefly at Colombo, Ceylon, and then carried on heading west. They sailed through the Suez Canal and at Ismailia all men received new uniforms and clothing; up until this time they were wearing shirts and shorts, remnants of clothing from their time as prisoners. With Bill now back in RAMC uniform, a Red Cross nurse approached him and, realising that he was a doctor, asked where he had qualified. 'St Mary's,' he replied. 'Oh, they have been in the news recently.' Bill immediately thought this would be related to the rugby team and asked how they had done. She knew nothing about rugby scores, but told Bill that a doctor from St Mary's, Alexander Fleming, had recently been awarded the Nobel Prize for his discovery of penicillin.[117] Leaving Port Said, the ship stopped briefly at Gibraltar, but no one was allowed to disembark and they sailed on across the Bay of Biscay.

Bill arrived in Liverpool on 13 October 1945; it was over four years since he had left the same port on-board *Dominion Monarch* to serve his King and Country overseas. His country had changed, not least politically, with Prime Minister Clement Attlee forming a socialist government in the summer of 1945, a change which Bill described as 'dreadful.' Having been away so long, he wanted to speak to Pauline but, with nearly 2000 new arrivals in Liverpool, the chances of finding an available public telephone were very slim. Having disembarked, the men were sent to a camp in Huyton from where Bill, along with a colleague, walked nearly 5 miles to a nearby village where the vicar was allowing returning prisoners to use his telephone. Bill managed to ring

---

116 After demobilisation, Captain Chilton became a general practitioner in Lewisham, South London.

117 Sir Alexander Fleming (knighted in 1944) had been awarded the 1945 Nobel Prize in Physiology or Medicine, jointly with Sir Howard Florey and Ernst Chain from Oxford.

Pauline at their home in Dolphin Square in London. The next morning he travelled by train to London, and was met at Euston by his wife, along with a new addition to the family, a dog.

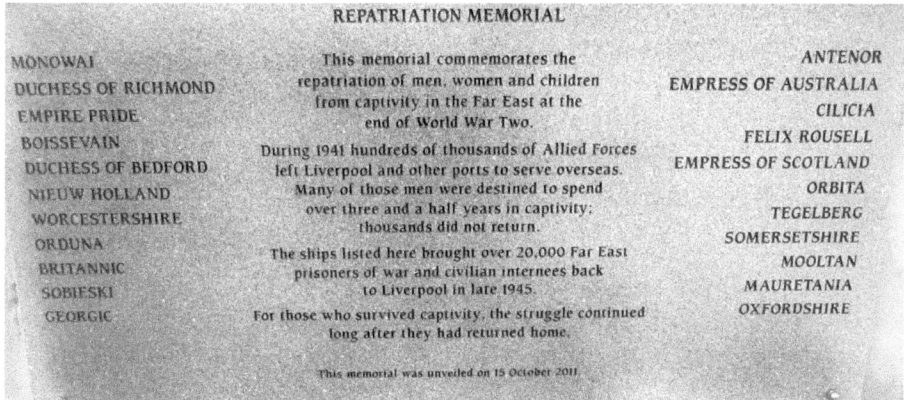

REPATRIATION MEMORIAL

MONOWAI	This memorial commemorates the repatriation of men, women and children from captivity in the Far East at the end of World War Two.	ANTENOR
DUCHESS OF RICHMOND		EMPRESS OF AUSTRALIA
EMPIRE PRIDE		CILICIA
BOISSEVAIN	During 1941 hundreds of thousands of Allied Forces left Liverpool and other ports to serve overseas. Many of those men were destined to spend over three and a half years in captivity; thousands did not return.	FELIX ROUSELL
DUCHESS OF BEDFORD		EMPRESS OF SCOTLAND
NIEUW HOLLAND		ORBITA
WORCESTERSHIRE		TEGELBERG
ORDUNA	The ships listed here brought over 20,000 Far East prisoners of war and civilian internees back to Liverpool in late 1945.	SOMERSETSHIRE
BRITANNIC		MOOLTAN
SOBIESKI		MAURETANIA
GEORGIC	For those who survived captivity, the struggle continued long after they had returned home.	OXFORDSHIRE

This memorial was unveiled on 15 October 2011.

Plaque at Liverpool recognising the Orduña and other ships which repatriated Far Eastern Prisoners of War

CHAPTER 8

RETURNING HOME

Forgetting the Past

In 1945 Bill returned to a country where most people knew little of the horrors of imprisonment and forced labour which had been endured by so many in the Far East. Many at home believed that the war had ended with the surrender of Germany in May 1945, and overlooked hostilities which continued for a further four months in Asia. Those returning home received little, if any, help. Far too many received a cursory medical examination followed by the issue of civilian clothes (a so-called 'demob suit') before being sent on their way with a railway permit to their home. Bill was an exception: he received his civilian clothes whilst passing through the Suez Canal. There was little attempt to confront, let alone address, the many health issues, physical and mental, which affected many of these men over the coming years. Long-term psychiatric problems were not uncommon, which in some cases led to suicide. Some of those arriving home were explicitly told not to talk about their experiences of imprisonment; others were informed that if they talked, they risked losing their entitlement to a war pension. Men were also told that if they recounted their stories of imprisonment, they would not be listened to, or believed. Over the ensuing 70 years, stories of the mental turmoil endured by these men have emerged. Perhaps one of the best known is that of Captain Eric Lomax, who described his battles with Post-Traumatic Stress Disorder in his book *The Railway Man*, published in 1995. In this he detailed his harrowing attempts to confront the issues faced following his release from imprisonment, culminating in reconciliation with the Japanese guard who had tortured him. Others faced years of psychological disturbance as they were wracked by frustration, anger and hatred for the suffering endured by them and their colleagues. For many there was also a sense of guilt that they had survived, while their friends and colleagues had died.

Interestingly, Bill was one of the few to be offered any help. On the morning after disembarkation at Liverpool he was asked if he wished to see a psychiatrist; his reply was an emphatic 'No. I want to see my wife!' Having made his way to London, and been reunited with Pauline, Bill was summoned for a medical examination at Queen Alexandra's Military Hospital, Millbank, London, on 23 December 1945. Radiographs were taken, and there was immediate concern over areas of calcification in his chest. Bill was not fazed since he knew these were the result of infection with bovine tuberculosis acquired in childhood. Bill quickly realised that the doctor undertaking the examination knew little, if any, medicine, and even less about prisoners of war. Perhaps this was not surprising when Bill learnt that the man had qualified just two days earlier. Bill had no intention of remaining in the Army, having found during his six years of service that the medical services were very inefficient in many areas. Bill was placed on the 'sick list' until the end of March 1946, but was deemed 'fit to be released' from the Army. Keen to resume his career, Bill started back at St Mary's Hospital on 1 January 1946 and for the first three months received two salaries, one from the Army and one from St Mary's.

On returning to civilian life, Bill decided not to talk about his wartime experiences, not even to his wife or, later, his children. This decision was based upon his own assessment that, despite the dreadful suffering that he had endured and witnessed, he was alive. He felt he should not dwell on the past and become depressed, but instead adopt a positive attitude to his life ahead. He would later say, 'I've made it home, let's forget about it.' Moreover, he continued to act upon his father's memorable advice given nearly 30 years earlier regarding the issue of 'hate', and Bill refused to hate his captors. Over 70 years later, Bill summarised his approach:

You must not go on hating people; it does you harm but it does not do them any harm. I am a Christian who was taught to love, not hate. That's how I live my life...... you feared the Japanese....I feared them. I would not use the word hate.

It was not until Bill was 98 years old that he finally talked openly about the events of World War 2, and it is those that now form the basis of this book.

In London, two events convinced Bill that his decision was correct. Firstly, he heard that a fellow medical officer from Changi, Hugh de Wardener, had been repatriated to Britain, but was suffering from tuberculosis and malaria. De Wardener had left Changi in 1943, being sent to the notorious Burma Railway. Following the Japanese surrender he returned home and was reunited with his wife, who had previously been informed that he was 'missing, presumed dead', and also met his son for the first time. Bill visited de Wardener in hospital at Millbank. He was taken aback and shocked when de Wardener (who had spent many hours talking with Bill at Roberts Hospital, on a range of subjects, including de Wardener's many girlfriends) was either unable, or perhaps unwilling, to recognise Bill. This alone made a significant impact which was compounded a few weeks later by an incident with a pharmacist. At home in Howard House, Dolphin Square, London, Bill developed urticaria and decided to write a prescription for an antihistamine tablet, 'Phenergan', to alleviate the symptoms. He presented the prescription to a local pharmacist but was upset when the man pointed out that it had been completed incorrectly. He then proceeded to make a real 'song and dance' about how requirements relating to prescriptions had changed in recent years during the war. As a final insult he asked if Bill 'even knew that there had been a war on?' Rather shocked, Bill did not answer, but saw this incident as another reason not to talk about his wartime experiences.

There was, however, one exception, namely for his brother, Jack. Having been ordained in 1937, Jack had served several curacies in North-West England, before being appointed to St Ann's Warrington in 1944. Jack asked Bill to speak on his wartime experiences at St Michael's Church, Burgh-by-Sands, their home village from the age of 11. Bill explained that, unlike his brother, he was not used to speaking to non-medical audiences and was worried that he would 'freeze.' Jack gave him some sound advice, namely to focus on one person in the audience throughout the talk. Bill duly settled his gaze on a lady of 'more advanced years', seated in the front row. All went to plan, until after about five minutes Bill noticed the lady had fallen asleep, and remained so throughout the talk.

A Return to Work

Arthur Porritt, Consultant Surgeon at St Mary's, was responsible for ensuring that doctors returning from the war were able to apply for a job of their choice, for a period of 6 months, at their teaching hospital. These positions were termed 'ex-service registrars.' Porritt had served with the RAMC throughout the war, both in Europe and in the Middle East. In 1944 he was appointed as Consultant Surgeon to 21 Army Group, in the rank of brigadier. Amongst his many responsibilities, he acted as personal surgeon to Field Marshal Montgomery. Bill applied to St Mary's to work in dermatology and 'special clinics' (venereal diseases), the two specialities he had pursued at Tanglin Military Hospital, Singapore. Dermatology clinics were held on Monday and Thursday mornings, and the VD clinic was held in the evening. The consultant in charge of the dermatology department was Dr G.B. Mitchell-Heggs OBE (also Dean of the Medical School) and the Director of the VD department was Dr G.L.M. McElligott. It was a busy practice and the two consultants were assisted by two doctors. One, a South African, Dr J. 'Jack' Suchet,[118] who was also a gynaecologist, and Dr M. 'Mike' Feiwel. The latter had qualified from St Mary's a year before Bill, had served in the RAMC during the war and had married Penny Phelps in 1938. His wife, a nurse, had travelled to Spain in early 1937 and fought for the International Brigade in the civil war. Having been injured, she was evacuated by the Royal Navy in 1938, on-board HMS *Sussex*.[119] Once back at St Mary's, Bill found that neither he nor other doctors who had served during the war talked of their experiences. Even those who had received awards for gallantry – for example, Henry Cockburn, who was awarded the MC

118 Jack Suchet's sons were the actor David Suchet, and broadcaster John Suchet.
119 She died in 2011, aged 101, the last survivor of a group of some 75 women who had fought in Spain.

– did not talk of their wartime service. Interestingly, older members of staff, who themselves had served during World War 1, never asked Bill about his military service.

After less than a month in post, Bill saw an advertisement in the hospital asking for a doctor to assist in the Allergy Department for two mornings and one afternoon a week. He was free at these times, and thought this would give him a chance to acquire some experience in an area of medicine about which he knew nothing. Although he knew little about the area, Bill had suffered from seasonal hay fever since he was about nine years old. Bill applied to the physician in charge of the department, Dr John Freeman,[120] (invariably referred to as 'JF') and was duly appointed. By February 1946, Bill was enjoying the job so much that, despite having to do all the work, he approached Freeman and asked if he could work full-time in the department. The answer was an immediate 'Yes', and thus commenced over 70 years' interest in allergy and aerobiology.

Bill had known his new boss for some time, having been taught by him before the war. Freeman had lent Bill his car on several occasions whilst he was a medical student, enabling him to compete in shooting matches at Bisley. Bill also used the car to complete his community-based medical training in North London. Freeman was described as 'a fine type of man, active and vigorous and remarkably handsome, full of charm with a kind and generous nature.' Although appointed to St Mary's as a bacteriologist, some 30 years earlier, Freeman had become a leading light in the field of allergy.

An Introduction to Allergy

The Allergy Department at St Mary's Hospital was established in 1906 with support and guidance from Sir Almroth Wright of the Department of Inoculation. By 1946, John Freeman was leading a very busy department, which had been his professional home for nearly 25 years.

---

120 His full title at the time was Director of the Department of Clinical Bacteriology and Director of the Asthma and Hayfever Clinic.

He had acquired considerable experience and expertise, and by this time the department was running eight or more 'clinics for the allergic disorders' each week. Freeman was a recognised leader in the field of allergy, and his clinical and research activities were dominated by the study of summer hay fever also called seasonal allergy. Although there are references to this condition dating as far back as the 10th century (or even further, according to some sources), it is accepted that the first clear description of the condition was made by John Bostock, a British physician working at Guy's Hospital, London. In 1819 he described a 'case of periodical affection of the eyes and chest' a condition he later called *'catarrhus aestivus'* or summer catarrh, the condition which was later known as hay fever. Like many of those who have worked in this field of medicine, Bostock suffered from the condition himself. However, it was not until 40 years later that the role of grass pollen was clearly proven. Research was undertaken by Dr Charles Blackley, a Manchester-based medical practitioner and homeopath, who suffered from what he described as 'that curious malady, hayfever'. In the 1860s he performed a number of experiments on himself. Having grown grass and isolated its pollen in the spring and summer, he stored this until the winter. He subsequently challenged himself, administering pollen into his nasal cavity, onto his soft palate and onto scarified skin, and noted the development of symptoms of hay fever. He published his results in 1873 in his book entitled *Experimental Researches on the Causes and Nature of Catarrhus Aestivus*. Thirty years later, Dunbar working in Germany, claimed to have extracted an active 'toxic substance' from grass pollen.

Further studies of hay fever led to the belief that the disease involved an immune response to the pollen, and one of the earliest treatments involved the administration of immune serum, raised by inoculating horses with grass pollen. Called Pollantin, this had to be administered topically, since if given by injection could cause serious adverse effects. Dunbar, who had developed Pollantin, received one dose by injection, and was recorded as 'falling unconscious on the floor.'

The work of Blackley inspired Leonard Noon to study hay fever, and it was John Freeman who persuaded Noon to join St Mary's in 1909, where he was appointed as 'Assistant in the Inoculation Department'.

He entered a department where, under Sir Almroth Wright 'ideas for research on immunisation were as thick as blackberries in Wright's laboratory at that time', and it was here that he developed his ideas on immunotherapy. Noon believed that hay fever was the result of repeated absorption of a soluble toxin in grass pollen, leading to hypersensitivity. He was aware of Dunbar's work involving Pollantin, but described its use as 'difficult, laborious and not giving a permanent cure'.

In the autumn of 1910 Noon embarked on a programme of active immunisation in patients suffering from hay fever, continuing through the winter until the spring of 1911. He used pollen extracted from Timothy grass (*Phleum pratense*) which had been grown by his sister, Dorothy Noon. Pollen extract was injected subcutaneously every 3-4 days. In June 1911 Noon published his results, and concluded that 'the sensibility of hay fever patients may be decreased at least 100 fold, while excessive or too frequent inoculations only serve to increase sensibility.' He was cautious as to the long-term effects, and wrote: 'it remains to be seen if immunity is sufficient to carry patients through a season when hay fever occurs.' Although Bill regarded Noon's work very highly, he later pointed out that, since the paper was published in June, it was unclear as to the exact period of observation of patients who had been desensitised. Most importantly, Noon appeared not to have studied patients during a whole hay fever season (normally accepted as May to July). In fact, he could not have done so, being forced to retire from work in February 1911 suffering from tuberculosis. In his paper, Noon wrote that 'the work is now in the hands of my colleague, John Freeman, who kindly came to my assistance and carried on the observations during my enforced absence of some months.' Freeman continued Noon's studies and in September 1911 published further observations on Noon's 20 patients who had received desensitisation treatment for hay fever. Assessing the clinical responses of patients objectively he concluded that 'there seems little doubt there has been a distinct amelioration of symptoms', although he went on to recognise that 'there were some cases of failure.'

Noon, having been forced to retire through ill health, was advised by Sir Almroth Wright that he should undertake physical exercise 'in order to stimulate the immune system.' Noon took this advice and went rock climbing. It was whilst climbing in the Peak District that he suffered a massive pulmonary haemorrhage. Severely weakened, he returned to London and died in January 1913, aged 35. His name is remembered in the field of allergy, by the award of the Noon Award from the European Academy of Allergy and Clinical Immunology; in 2011 the recipient was Dr Bill Frankland.

Bill Frankland receiving the Noon Award 2011 from the European Academy of Allergy and Clinical Immunology, exactly 100 years after Noon's paper was published.

Although Noon is credited with undertaking the first studies in immunotherapy, Bill's own research has questioned whether this really was the case. In March 1898 Charles Blackley wrote in the *British Medical Journal* that:

I have been for the last fifteen years engaged on a set of experiments on the subcutaneous injection of the active portion of the pollen grain. These have given much the same result in the matter of dose and the matter of symptoms as my other experiments. These have not yet been published, but I hope soon to do so.

Blackley died in September 1900, and unfortunately never published the results of his studies.

Bill's studies of the literature also clarified that the first published report on desensitisation appeared three years before Noon's. Dr Alfred Schofield, a physician in London, published a report in *The Lancet* in 1908. He described his treatment, in 1906, of a 13-year-old boy who had a severe allergy to eggs. He successfully desensitised the boy by feeding him very small, but increasing, quantities of egg each day. Over six months the boy consumed the equivalent of one egg. Eight months after commencing therapy the boy was able to eat eggs without any harm.[121]

After the death of Leonard Noon, John Freeman continued to pursue techniques and regimen for desensitising patients suffering from hay fever. In doing so, he described a number of regimen, including 'intensive desensitisation' where patients received daily injections and 'rush desensitisation' in which patients received several injections on one day. Freeman also encouraged most patients to self-inject for desensitisation, although it had been argued that there was little scientific rationale for this, and that the decision to pursue this course of therapy was usually guided by a patient's hectic lifestyle preventing them attending a clinic regularly. Through his links with the Inoculation Department, Freeman was involved with the development of commercially available pollen preparations, Pollaccine, manufactured by the American pharmaceutical company Parke-Davis, who built a factory in Hounslow for this purpose. This formed the basis for current desensitisation protocols, in which patients, over the age of 15, are supplied with a box of aqueous extract grass pollen dilutions from 100 to 100,000 Noon units. They also receive a bottle of adrenaline, being told to give an immediate injection of adrenaline if injection of pollen extract is followed by either generalised urticaria or anaphylaxis. It is estimated that Bill oversaw the desensitisation treatment of some 30,000 patients with seasonal hay fever at St Mary's, with no deaths recorded.

---

121 In about 1960 John Freeman was asked whether oral desensitisation might be attempted in adults who had not grown out of their food allergic reactions. His answer was a definitive no. The reason being that Sir Almroth Wright had once tried oral immunotherapy to see if it might replace injection therapy with typhoid vaccine. It failed to protect. Wright and Freeman might have both been very interested in developments in the late 1950s with the development of oral vaccines, both against viral and parasitic diseases.

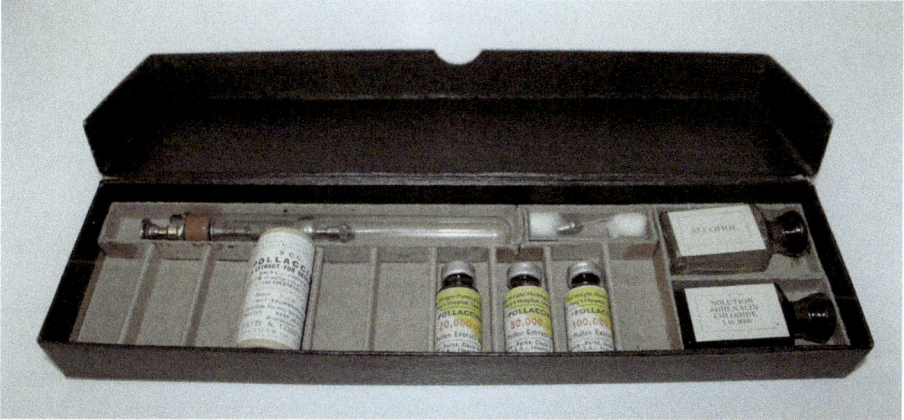

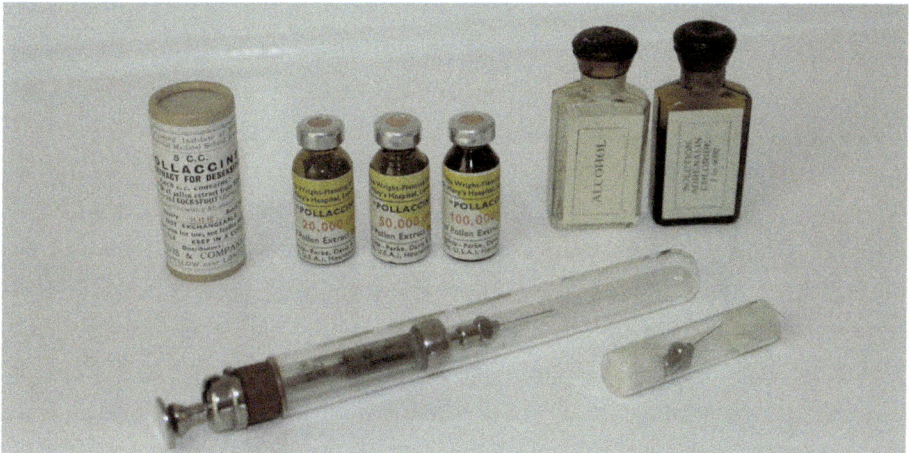

Pollaccine kit issued by Bill Frankland to provide immunotherapy to Roland Evans. He was a very atopic individual and received therapy between 1946 and 1948, 1950 and 1952, and 1955 and 1958.

When Bill joined the Allergy Department, he saw very little of his boss, Freeman, who spent considerable periods away from the clinic. His time was spent pursuing a number of social interests, running his private practice, and trying to complete a book entitled 'Hayfever: A Key to the Allergic Disorders.' This was very much a labour of love, which Freeman had started over 20 years earlier. The drive to write the book came from his mentor, Sir Almroth Wright, who advised him that 'before your ship of life flounders be sure to get all the goods up out of the hold and onto the quayside.' By 1946 Freeman was finding the manuscript a constant bind and would come to describe it as 'The Bloody Book', usually shortened to the 'BB.' Finally published in 1950, the book failed to reflect the international esteem in which Freeman was held, and certainly did not make for easy reading. The book had few references and evidence from Freeman's own clinical data was lacking in many areas. Throughout the book he used new terms which he had introduced, and in doing so caused confusion to many a reader. He described a range of conditions, referring, for example, to 'classical hayfever', 'cryptic hayfever' and 'para-hayfever', the latter being those cases which were not due to grass pollens. But perhaps most disconcerting to many interested in the field was Freeman's admission of his dislike for the word 'allergy', describing it as 'a linguistic mess', believing that the term allergy 'obscures more than it illuminates in medicine.' At a meeting in Oxford in 1949 Freeman stated that the word allergy had so many meanings that 'we might particularise as Allergy I, Allergy II, etc.' Instead, from 1919, he had used the term 'idiopathies', and described the 'toxic idiopathies' due to grass pollen, a term which he admitted was the same as 'allergic disorders.' Freeman described how a normally harmless protein substance becomes a specific poison, which he called an 'idiotoxin', for example, grass pollen in a case of hay fever. He would never use the term immunotherapy, and if a patient were to receive desensitising immunotherapy, Freeman always wrote 'PTD.' After working for Freeman for two years, Bill asked him what 'PTD' stood for. Freeman replied, 'Too long to write it, but it is Prophylactic Thoroughgoing Desensitisation.' Bill never asked what 'Thoroughgoing' meant. Another feature of Freeman's work was his view of the superiority of 'experiential' over 'statistical' methods of assessing the results of treatment. Bill was shown the proofs of the book before publication and advised Freeman that he should use modern nomenclature, and that use of his own terms merely clouded the important issues that he was attempting to address. Bill's advice was met with Freeman's reply, 'I invented the words with advice from Almroth Wright and I am not going to change them, the book has taken 25 years to write and rewrite.' Bill was thanked for his help in the book, and received a signed copy, in which Freeman had written 'Thank you for all your help for this B.B.', although as Bill was to later point out, the help had not been accepted.

Freeman's book was not a success; of 1000 copies printed only 500 sold, although Bill was to later learn that, ironically, the copy in the library of the Royal Society of Medicine had actually been stolen. Several years later the publishers, Heinemann Medical, had 100 copies remaining and were unwilling to store them any longer. These were sent to Bill who initially housed them at St Mary's. However, with increasing demands on space he was forced to move them to his home. Here they were stored in his garage, but finally after many years, and no interest in the publication, he was forced to dispose of them himself.

Early Research

Bill's interest and commitment to the field of allergy soon led him to commence clinical research in patients attending the clinic. Interestingly his position was, at that time, funded by monies which John Freeman acquired from a tobacco company, J. Wix and Sons Ltd, the manufacturers of Kensitas cigarettes. There is more than a little irony in this, especially since one of the advertising slogans of the brand was that they 'protect the throat.' Bill had no difficulty in gaining funds for research, and was helped by the Inoculation Department which had significant income from the sale of vaccines to a number of pharmaceutical companies. Later, Bill attended Wix's funeral, held at a synagogue. He had consulted a colleague about the dress code for a Jewish funeral, never having been to one before, and was told 'there is no need to wear a hat, it is a liberal synagogue.' Bill found the service very interesting, being greatly impressed by the women's choir singing from the gallery, and by the rabbi who gave an excellent address on Wix's activities, especially the range of charitable causes which had benefited from his financial support.

In 1913 Henry Dale demonstrated the role of histamine in allergic reactions, especially anaphylaxis, and this was followed by attempts to identify antihistamine drugs. The first was discovered in 1937, and in the 1940s this class of drug started to enter clinical practice, with the belief that they may be of benefit in both hay fever and asthma. In 1948 Bill was closely involved in the trial of a new antihistamine drug chlorcyclizine (histatin). His results suggested that this class of drug could help mild cases of asthma, but may precipitate the onset of asthma in more severe cases, a view that came to be accepted by most authorities in 1952. Next Bill studied another new antihistamine, assessing its effect in both hay fever and asthma. The trial stands out for its rigorous design and implementation. Bill recruited Dr R.H. Gorrill, a bacteriologist and statistician, to ensure there was statistical input in the design, enactment and analysis of the trial. Three treatments were assessed, the antihistamine, mepyramine, a new antihistamine, named 405-c-49, and an inert (or control) treatment, the sugar, lactose. All tablets were to be white, in order that neither the patients, nor Bill, knew which treatment they were receiving. For this to occur Bill had to ask May & Baker to manufacture mepyramine as a white tablet, rather than its normal green.

A total of 174 patients were recruited to the study, each meeting the entry criteria of irritation of the eye, rhinorrhoea (runny nose) and sneezing during the month of June, indicating that they suffered from hay fever. Patients were randomly assigned to one of the three treatments. In another first for a clinical trial, Bill issued all patients with a diary in which they made a daily record of their symptoms. They also graded their response to treatment as 'Good, Moderate or Poor.' Results from the trial demonstrated that mepyramine was significantly better at controlling symptoms than the inert treatment, and that the new drug compared favourably with mepyramine. It was also found that the antihistamines did not increase the incidence of asthma, nor did they help the symptoms of asthma when it occurred.

In 1951 Bill asked Freeman's permission to undertake a study which would mark the first double-blind controlled trial in immunotherapy, a trial of pollen extracts used in desensitising patients with hay fever. Freeman told Bill that such a trial was not necessary because of the large numbers of patients who had attended the hay fever clinics over many years to receive injections, and who described the results of the treatment as 'heavenly' or 'simply perfect.' At this time desensitisation was undertaken by injecting grass pollen extract, as Pollaccine, but Bill was concerned that this contained a lot of clinically useless material which could be responsible for some of the untoward side effects seen. He wanted to identify which part of the pollen extract was biologically effective. Bill worked with Rosa Augustin, a chemist who had experience in identifying and isolating proteins from pollen. When working with Bill she was married to her third husband, and Bill remembered how her prime aim in life was to become a mother. In the summer of 1953, Bill recruited 200 patients to the trial: all suffered from hay fever, and none had received any previous injection therapy. They were randomised to one of four treatment groups, and all were asked to keep a daily record of their symptoms. The treatments were:

Standard grass-pollen extract (Pollaccine), used for many years for desensitisation in the Allergy Clinic;

Ultrafiltrate of grass pollen extract, non-proteinaceous material which was known to be practically inactive when administered in skin tests;

Purified pollen protein, effectively the material remaining following ultrafiltration of grass pollen extract;

Physiological saline, with 0.4% phenol, to act as the inert control.

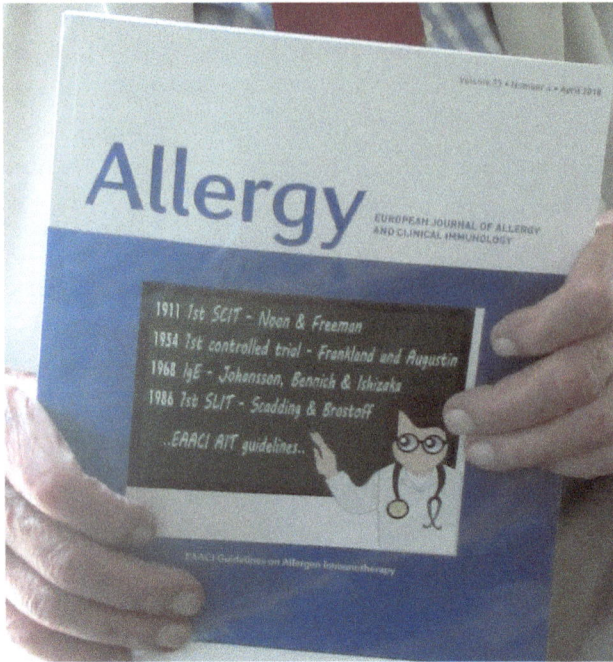

Bill holding the April 2018 edition of Allergy, on the front cover of which his 1954 paper is cited as one of four seminal papers in the field of allergy. Spring 2018.

The results demonstrated that there was no difference in the efficacy of either grass pollen extract or purified pollen protein in desensitising patients, both providing significant benefit. Interestingly, 32% of patients receiving either ultrafiltrate or phenol saline reported either good or excellent results, compared with 72% receiving pollen. The paper was submitted and there were no corrections. It was published just three weeks later, in May 1954, and acknowledged as a milestone in clinical allergy, being the first double-blind controlled clinical trial in immunotherapy, although Bill doubted if John Freeman ever read it. Nearly 65 years later, Bill was able to see his work highlighted on the front cover of the journal *Allergy*.

At this time Bill also became interested in a condition which appeared to affect many local residents in the Paddington area. Working with Professor Philip Gregory from Rothamsted he became interested in the medical problems associated with dry rot. Gregory was an aerobiologist and was also interested in fungal diseases of plants. Bill was later to describe how he was responsible for teaching Bill all he knew about aerobiology. In the Paddington region over 95% of houses were affected by dry rot, caused by the mould *Merulius lacrymans*. This was the result of bomb damage during the war, with the properties being thoroughly soaked by the fire service to limit the spread of fires. On entering the properties Bill was able to smell the dry rot. With Gregory, he described the first case of an inhalation sensitivity to the basidiospores produced by the mould.

Bill examining specimens for dry rot.

A Tale of Two Chiefs

In 1953, as well as working full-time in the Allergy Department, Bill also found himself working as 'Clinical Assistant' to Sir Alexander Fleming, a man Bill later described as 'fascinating in so many ways, and extremely clever.' Fleming was the Director of the Inoculation Department[122] and

---

122 This was renamed the Wright-Fleming Institute in 1946.

a Nobel Laureate, who had discovered the antibacterial[123] penicillin in 1928. Bill was placed in charge of the experimental ward, where there was an array of patients suffering from a range of rare conditions. It was his duty to see Fleming every morning at 10.00 in his office, which Bill did without fail. Fleming was not interested in clinical patients since he was, after all, a bacteriologist. He and Bill talked about a range of issues, other than clinical medicine, conversations which Bill loved. Later in life Bill wished that he had written down details of their meetings, as he thought it could have made a quite interesting book. However, working for Fleming, Bill heard much about the discovery of penicillin, its later purification and production for therapeutic use, as well as many stories relating to Fleming himself.

At this time, Bill effectively had two 'chiefs' but there was, unfortunately, long-standing animosity between the two men, despite earlier good relations. Sir Alexander Fleming was a Scot, born in Darvel, Ayrshire in 1881, the youngest son of Hugh Fleming, a farmer. After leaving the local school at the age of 14, Fleming moved to London in 1895 to live with his elder brother, Thomas, a doctor who practised in the Marylebone Road. Alexander continued his studies at the Regent Street Polytechnic but, after two years, economic pressures forced him to leave and find a job. He worked for a shipping company based in Leadenhall Street, London and in 1900 he, along with two other brothers, John and Robert (both of whom were opticians) joined the London Scottish, a volunteer infantry regiment. Here Alexander excelled at shooting, and helped his regiment win a number of trophies. Fleming retained an enthusiasm for shooting and years later, Bill often shot alongside him in competitions. Bill recalled how Fleming's lip would invariably bleed, having been struck by the bolt on recoil, the result of his close holding of the stock.

---

123 Although the term 'antibiotic' is now used to describe such a substance, at this time Fleming used the term 'antibacterial'. As he pointed out, the term 'antibiotic', describing a class of antibacterial substances produced by living organisms, was first used in 1889 but fell into disuse. Use of the term 'antibiotic' was revived in the 1950s.

Alexander Fleming represented his regiment in a number of other sports, including swimming and water polo. On at least one occasion he played water polo against St Mary's Hospital, a fixture which would influence a decision in his later life. In 1901 Fleming received a small legacy and decided it was time to pursue an alternative career to shipping. His elder brother suggested he consider medicine, which he did. He then had to choose a medical school and he later admitted that he knew nothing about any medical school, except for St Mary's, against whom he had played water polo. His mind was made up; he applied to St Mary's and, having won an entrance scholarship, commenced his medical studies in 1902. He shared rooms with Leonard Colebrook, and was taught by the newly appointed Professor of Pathology, Almroth Wright.

From an early stage, Fleming made it clear that he wished to pursue a career in surgery and, on qualifying in 1906, faced having to leave St Mary's to achieve his goal. John Freeman heard that Fleming was an accomplished shot and persuaded him to remain at St Mary's, suggesting that 'it was the best place to be as he awaited a surgical position.' Freeman's main motive was, in fact, to bolster the St Mary's shooting team, hopefully allowing it to win the Armitage Cup. Freeman was a close colleague of Sir Almroth Wright, being described as one of Wright's 'favourite disciples', and had lived in his home until leaving to marry. Freeman persuaded Wright to offer Fleming a position in the Inoculation Department, which Fleming accepted, believing it would only be a short-term position, before he could pursue his surgical aspirations. He commenced his new job on his 25th birthday.

Fleming found his new position rewarding and before long was publishing the results of his studies. His first paper, with Leonard Noon, was published in *The Lancet* in 1908. Three years later, with co-author Leonard Colebrook, he reported the successful treatment of syphilis, by Salvarsan, an arsenical compound, describing 'the first truly effective chemotherapeutic agent.' Many of those treated in this study were members of the London Scottish. At the same time Fleming still held out for a position in surgery and found himself embroiled in an argument with another aspiring surgeon at St Mary's, Zachary Cope. Cope was pursuing a surgical career, and would later be recognised as an authority on surgery of the abdomen, as well having unique experience in treating actinomycosis. Fleming suggested that the Fellowship examination, FRCS, required by all surgeons, was easy to pass; Cope suggested otherwise, believing it to be very difficult. Moreover, he suggested that if Fleming believed it was easy, he should sit it himself. This he did in June 1909, and passed.

In 1914, Fleming was appointed Lecturer in Bacteriology at St Mary's, jointly with John Freeman. With the outbreak of World War 1, Fleming followed Almroth Wright to serve with the Royal Army Medical Corps in France. At the end of war, Fleming returned to St Mary's and in 1921 Wright appointed him as 'Assistant Director of the Department of Inoculation', an appointment that affronted Freeman. He had always looked up to, and been loyal to, Wright who had called him his 'son in science.' Freeman believed that he should have succeeded Wright in leading the department. Moreover, Freeman was four years older than Fleming, and was convinced that Fleming had engineered the decision. This appears unlikely as Fleming was also upset by Wright's actions. As a consequence Freeman decided to move to the Allergy Department at St Mary's where he worked full-time and where he made a number of important contributions to the field. Although Freeman had effectively moved out of the Inoculation Department, he had not gone far; his new base was just one floor below Fleming's laboratory. As Bill Frankland has pointed out, despite the two men having little to do with each other, their physical locations would have a huge impact on probably the most important medical discovery of the 20th century.

A Chance Observation

Fleming's research was influenced by many of his observations made during the war, especially the high mortality amongst wounded men who contracted infection. He later described how they encountered 'thousands of septic wounds which we could do very little for.' His investigations focussed on the control of wound infection, seeking what he described as 'natural protective agencies of the body', a term he first used in his Hunterian Lecture to the Royal College of Surgeons in 1919. During his wartime research he studied the use of antiseptics in wounds, especially the Carrel-Dakin method, involving irrigation of a wound with hypochlorite solution. Fleming clearly demonstrated that the antiseptic action of the fluid was lost within 10 minutes of infusion. In 1922 he read a paper at the Royal Society describing 'a substance present in tissue and secretions of the body which is capable of rapidly dissolving certain bacteria. I have called this substance lysozyme.' With an element of serendipity, this discovery had followed studies of his own nasal secretions obtained whilst suffering from a heavy cold in November 1921. He later defined the properties of lysozyme, a substance found in a range of human secretions and in high concentrations in the white of bird eggs. Fleming was struck by the antibacterial activity of lysozyme, later writing that 'he had never seen such rapid killing of bacteria.' When lecturing to medical students, Fleming made them clip their nails in order to demonstrate the presence of lysozyme activity in the nails. As a student, Bill also took part in experiments involving dropping lemon juice onto the front of the eye, in order to stimulate tears, another rich source of lysozyme. However, the potential for using lysozyme in clinical medicine was short-lived since before long Fleming reported that it was most active against bacteria which were not pathogens in man.

In the summer of 1928 Fleming was studying the bacterium *Staphylococcus aureus* at the request of the Medical Research Council. His laboratory was a small room in the Inoculation Department, situated in the turret of the Clarence Memorial Wing, overlooking Praed Street. The room was barely 10 feet by 12 feet, and would later serve as an 'on-call' room for junior doctors including, in 1938, Bill Frankland. As part of his study Fleming was observing bacterial colonies under a dissecting microscope. To do this required him to temporarily remove the lid of the Petri dish, place the dish under the microscope and then replace the lid, a process which exposed the plate to possible contamination. On Monday 3 September 1928 Fleming made a 'flying visit' to St Mary's in order to assist a surgical colleague in the treatment of an abscess. He had been on holiday with his family at their country home, The Dhoon, in Barton Mills, Suffolk, a property that he purchased shortly after the end of World War 1, and where he spent weekends and holidays, enjoying the open air of the countryside. It was his first day at work since being promoted to Professor of Bacteriology in the University of London. He examined a number of Petri dishes which he had studied some weeks earlier, but had not discarded. Many bacteriologists discarded these dishes soon after use, but Fleming often had 40-50 samples accumulated in his laboratory for possible further inspection. On one plate he observed a mould growing on the agar, and around it an area with no bacterial growth. Just at that time a former research scholar, Merlin Pryce, called on Fleming. Pryce was later described as 'an unconventional but somewhat gifted son of the Welsh mining valleys' and 'a dedicated St Mary's man.' Having initially studied medicine in Cardiff, he moved to St Mary's and qualified in 1926. In 1927 he was awarded a Junior Research Scholarship, under Alexander Fleming, with whom he studied Staphylococci. Pryce's position ended in April 1928 when he was appointed as Second Assistant Pathologist to Professor Newcomb, a post he held for two years.

Pryce's exact role in the discovery of penicillin remains, to this date, unclear. It has been suggested that it was Pryce who first noted a culture plate on which there was an area of no bacterial growth near to a mould, having been tasked to clear plates from Fleming's laboratory since technical staff, who normally carried out the job, had 'withdrawn their labour.' Fleming remarked to Pryce, 'That's funny,' referring to the failure of bacterial growth, to which Pryce replied, 'That's just how you discovered lysozyme.' Realising the potential significance of the observation, Fleming immediately made a subculture of the mould into a tube of broth. In 1965, Pryce wrote that 'Had I not walked into (the laboratory) at that time and talked to him, he would never have picked up the plate and there might be no such thing as penicillin'.[124]

---

124 In 1954 Pryce succeeded Newcomb as Professor of Pathology at St Mary's, and was noted to be an 'excellent teacher'. He retired in 1967, and died in 1976. He had been both a great friend and strong supporter of Fleming's. In March 1941, Fleming's house, 20 Danvers Street, Chelsea, had been badly damaged by bombs and he, with his wife Sareen, immediately moved to live with Pryce for several months.

Fleming returned to complete his holiday in Suffolk, not starting work again until the end of September, but by this time had already asked Stuart Craddock (who had replaced Merlin Pryce) to undertake some experiments with the newly discovered substance.

Professor Sir Alexander Fleming

The identification of the mould was not straightforward and, as Fleming was to later write, 'we had a little trouble with the identification of the mould.' Fleming approached Charles La Touche, an 'academic botanist' working in Freeman's laboratory. La Touche was an Irishman of Huguenot descent, who was born in Kowloon, China, in 1904. After studying botany at university in Dublin he was appointed by John Freeman in 1927 to work on the potential role of fungi in allergy. La Touche identified the fungus isolated by Fleming as *Penicillium rubrum*, and from this Fleming named the substance responsible for killing bacteria as Penicillin. Fleming wrote up his findings and in May 1929 submitted a paper entitled 'The Antibacterial Action of Cultures of a Penicillium with Special Reference to their use in the isolation of B. influenzae'. It has been suggested by some that Fleming had wanted the paper to be co-authored with Pryce, but for whatever reason, this did not occur. The paper was published in the *British Journal of Experimental Pathology*, later that year. In it, Fleming acknowledged 'Mr la Touche for his suggestions as to the identity of the Penicillium.' He also concluded that 'It may be an efficient antiseptic for application to, or injection into, areas affected by penicillin-sensitive microbes.' Several years later, in 1936, Bill attended lectures by Fleming. He recalled how Fleming was far keener to talk about lysozyme than penicillin, and more hopeful that the former would, one day, be used therapeutically. It was apparent to Bill that he was in constant search for the 'magic substance' which would cure wound infections. When referring to the substance from the mould Penicillium, Fleming proudly stated: 'I have named this substance Penicillin, and it will make huge changes to the practice of medicine.' During the lectures Fleming admitted that he had encountered problems in trying to concentrate the substance, but told his students that when penicillin was freely available it would 'be overused and resistance will soon develop.' In the same year, Bill attended a lecture by La Touche at St Mary's. La Touche was now employed by the Dermatology Department, and was responsible for the laboratory techniques used for the diagnosis of ringworm infection. Bill recalled that La Touche was a very good lecturer, who spent considerable time demonstrating the use of ultraviolet light, emitted from a Wood's Lamp, in the diagnosis of the condition. His prop for this was, as Bill clearly remembered, 'a very dead, and stuffed cat, which was riddled with ringworm, which La Touche moved around the medical school.'

Not long after Fleming's paper was published he became aware of a significant error: the fungus was not *Penicillium rubrum*, but in fact *Penicillium notatum*.[125] Again, perhaps with hindsight, Fleming later wrote that 'our mycologist who put it through its paces called

---

125 *Penicillium notatum* is now named *Penicillium chrysogenum*.

it *Penicillium rubrum.*' However, Fleming had noted it made a bright yellow colour and 'even with my small knowledge of Latin, I thought "rubrum" did not mean "yellow."' The definitive identification was made by Dr Harold Raistrick of the London School of Hygiene and Tropical Medicine, and was confirmed by an American mycologist, Dr Thom. Fleming had to make corrections to the batch of 500 reprints, since there was heavy demand for copies of his publication. Hence, in the original paper the fungus is described, incorrectly, as P. rubrum, but in later reprints, correctly, as P. notatum. Fleming was, by all accounts, furious over the misidentification of the fungus, and directed his anger, not at La Touche, who had in effect made the error, but at his boss, John Freeman. This only fuelled their already long-standing animosity.

The source of the fungus which had contaminated Fleming's cultures, and in his words 'found a congenial home and grew and multiplied' in the summer of 1928 has remained a matter of much speculation. It was suggested that it had come from the air of nearby Praed Street, some people even proposing that it came from houses damaged in the Blitz, a totally implausible suggestion since the discovery took place at least 12 years before German bombing raids on London. The public house opposite Fleming's laboratory, The Fountain's Abbey, proudly states to this day that 'Fleming was a loyal and regular visitor, and it was mould spores from this ale house which blew through Fleming's window.' This source appears unlikely since the windows in Fleming's laboratory were never opened, the sashes were broken, and to reach them involved leaning across a host of material stored on the cills. A more likely source of the mould appears to have been much closer to home, and as Bill has often stated, it was the study of allergy which led to the discovery of penicillin. John Freeman had been researching 'whether inhalation of fungal spores could cause rhinitis and asthma'. This was not his first encounter with fungi, since in 1905 he, along with Leonard Noon, had spent time in Professor Borrel's laboratory at the Pasteur Institute in Paris studying pathogenic moulds. Subsequently, Freeman had attended a lecture at the Royal Society of Medicine in London in 1924 delivered by Professor Storm van Leeuwen from Leyden in Holland. An authority on fungi, he had proposed that asthma may be the result of inhalation of fungal spores, citing his studies with *Penicillium glaucoma* and *Aspergillus fumigatus*. Freeman approached Dr Harold Raistrick,[126] a biochemist and recognised authority on fungal metabolism, who was working at the London School of Hygiene and Tropical Medicine. He supplied two seasonal and three non-seasonal fungal spore cultures to Freeman. It is unclear if Freeman knew Raistrick, and it is Bill's belief that he came across him during the 'question time' which followed van Leeuwen's talk. At the same time Freeman recruited La Touche. The Allergy Department was situated immediately below Fleming's laboratory and it appears most likely that the mould which contaminated Fleming's bacterial cultures was actually one of the non-seasonal cultures being studied in Freeman's laboratory. Merlin Pryce was to note how, although the windows in Fleming's laboratory never opened, the door to the laboratory was never closed. In a similar vein, it was noted that the door of La Touche's laboratory was never closed. In retrospect, Fleming should not have been quite so angry with John Freeman for the incorrect sample identification, but perhaps should have thanked him for, indirectly, providing the sample of Penicillium. In 1995 Bill wrote about the discovery of penicillin and remarked how '...it was the interest of allergists in moulds that was responsible for starting the beginning of the antibiotic era.' As he has also pointed out, Fleming was very lucky, since P. notatum is one of the very few species of Penicillium which is not toxic to man.

Divided Loyalties

The story of the discovery and subsequent large-scale production of penicillin was one which involved two institutions with which Bill was closely associated, namely Oxford University and St Mary's Hospital. Bill was party to many stories and anecdotes about the discovery and early use of the drug, especially in his position as Clinical Assistant to Sir Alexander Fleming. As the story of penicillin unfolded during World War 2, there was (and to some extent still is) rivalry between

---

126 Later Professor Harold Raistrick.

the two institutions as to who was responsible for penicillin becoming an accepted part of medicine. Bill has always felt, 'somewhat in the middle', having allegiances to both establishments.

Although penicillin had been discovered at St Mary's by Alexander Fleming in 1928, it was the work of a team led by Howard Florey in Oxford, a decade later, which allowed penicillin to enter clinical practice, and contribute to a monumental change in medical practice. Many authorities have written that Fleming failed to isolate penicillin, let alone investigate the drug. This is far from true. He admitted that there had been difficulties in concentrating the drug, noting 'he was a bacteriologist, not a chemist.'[127] Along with Stuart Craddock there was another young doctor working in Fleming's laboratory, one who had a biochemical background. This was Frederick Ridley, a young ophthalmologist who had been studying the effect of lysozyme in treating eye infections. Working with Penicillium broth cultures, Ridley used a technique of vacuum distillation at low temperature (4°C), and subsequent evaporation to successfully produce a crude extract of penicillin. The drug was tested on cells in the presence of bacteria, and Fleming reported that it was the first substance that he had encountered which had a more powerful effect on bacteria than cells. Despite the drug being very unstable, they managed to treat a few clinical cases. One was Craddock himself, who was suffering from sinusitis, and the crude penicillin extract was instilled into his nasal antrum on 9 January 1929, but with no effect. However, a second patient, a medical student, Keith 'Beaky' Rogers, who was an Olympic standard shot, and captain of the London University shooting team, had a more successful outcome. He was due to represent St Mary's in a rifle competition when he developed pneumococcal conjunctivitis, preventing him from shooting. He mentioned this to Fleming who set about treating it. Rogers described how 'he put in some yellow fluid which he assured me was safe and which I imagine was penicillin, that was made in the lab.' The local instillation of penicillin extract was effective, and Bill was later told that

---

127 It is reported that Sir Almroth Wright despised chemists, and refused to entertain their employment in the department.

it 'worked marvellously.' Rogers made a swift recovery and was able to compete at Bisley two days later. Fleming recorded how he had been unable to evaluate penicillin in patients with severe infections, noting that either there were no septic patients when penicillin was available or that, due to its instability, there was no penicillin when septic patients were presented for possible treatment.[128] Fleming also performed experiments with penicillin in animals, initially demonstrating that it was non-toxic in both mice and rabbits. He then proceeded to study 12 mice, all having been infected with staphylococci: 6 received penicillin, and 6 placebo. Those receiving penicillin survived, all those in the placebo group died.

Howard Florey was an Australian doctor, who was awarded a Rhodes Scholarship to Oxford in 1921. He studied physiology under Sir Charles Sherrington and later obtained a position in the Department of Pathology, Cambridge. Here in 1929, perhaps by sheer coincidence, he was studying the actions of lysozyme, when Fleming's paper on penicillin was published. In 1931 he was appointed to the Chair of Pathology at Sheffield. Following the death of Professor Georges Dreyer, Florey was appointed to the Chair of Pathology in Oxford in December 1934. His appointment was not without question, many asking why a man who was first and foremost a physiologist had been appointed to a pathology department. Bill remembered the Sir William Dunn School of Pathology from his days as a student, and felt its name was somewhat inappropriate, since in his mind it was the school where 'no pathology was ever done!'

In the spring of 1935 Florey moved to the Dunn School of Pathology. On his arrival in Oxford, he wished to pursue his studies of lysozyme, aiming to understand its mechanism of actions. He recognised that this needed a biochemist dedicated to the programme, so he approached Sir Gowland Hopkins, Professor of Biochemistry at Cambridge, asking if he could recruit Norman Pirie. This was not deemed acceptable. Instead Hopkins suggested he approach a German refugee, E.B. 'Ernst' Chain,

---

128 Ridley became an eminent ophthalmic surgeon at Moorfields Eye Hospital in London, and Craddock became a general practitioner in Holsworthy, North Devon.

who was just completing his second PhD thesis. Chain had been forced to leave Germany in 1933 as the result of Hitler's anti-Semitic policies. Fleeing the country with less than £10 he arrived in England in April 1933 and initially worked at University College London under J.B.S. Haldane. He appeared unsatisfied with the facilities in London, and approached Hopkins in pursuit of a position at Cambridge. He moved to Cambridge in October 1933, and was one of six German refugees hosted by the Department of Biochemistry.[129] Chain subsequently moved to Oxford in September 1935, full of enthusiasm for his new appointment, and through Florey took an interest in lysozyme. At around this time Florey secured funding to allow further studies of lysozyme, leading to its purification two years later. During this period, Chain read Fleming's paper from 1929 and recognised that the instability of penicillin presented a challenge to a biochemist such as himself. In the winter of 1938/39 Florey and Chain commenced studies of Penicillium, using a culture of mould which had been given by Fleming to Dreyer, Florey's predecessor. At this time they both believed it to be 'an interesting scientific project' and neither was driven by the potential therapeutic implications of success. In August 1940 they reported in *The Lancet* on 'the chemical, pharmacological and chemotherapeutic properties' of penicillin having developed a method for obtaining increased yields from the culture and extracting penicillin such that it was now available as powder, which was both stable and soluble in water. The work had been funded by both the Medical Research Council and the Rockefeller Foundation. One of Florey's many attributes was his ability to convince institutions to fund his work, but in fact it was Chain's suggestion that Florey approach the Rockefeller Foundation. The paper in *The Lancet* represented a culmination of work from many people, not least that by N.G. Heatley, who devised methods to increase production from the Penicillium cultures as well as developing a rapid assay for penicillin activity. Chain himself introduced the technique of freeze-

---

129 Others included Hans Krebs, who was awarded the Nobel Prize in Physiology or Medicine in 1953.

drying to increase extraction of the drug. The authors described the effect of penicillin in mice infected with Staphylococci, Streptococci, or Clostridium, in which treatment provided almost 100% protection against death. When Fleming read the paper it was the first time he was aware of Florey and Chain's work. Soon after, he visited Florey and was provided with some of the purified penicillin. Whether he visited Chain's laboratory is unclear, but if he had, he would have seen prominently displayed a Gestapo 'hit list' which included Chain's name; as Chain was to recount, if the Germans had invaded Britain he certainly would have been killed.[130]

The Oxford Group published a much more detailed paper on penicillin in *The Lancet* in August 1941, building on their earlier paper. It described their method for large-scale production and also reported further animal studies as well as the intravenous administration of penicillin in man. The paper described in great detail the treatment of a number of patients. The clinical trials were undertaken at the Radcliffe Infirmary under the guidance of Dr C.M. 'Charles' Fletcher. The first patient was 43-year-old Albert Alexander, a police constable from Abingdon who was suffering from widespread sepsis of the face, scalp and orbits. He had not responded to sulphonamides or surgical drainage and on 12 February 1941 received penicillin which was repeated over the following 4 days. Although there was some improvement, there was insufficient penicillin available, and Fletcher, in desperation, took the patient's urine over to the Dunn School in order that penicillin could be retrieved from it. The patient unfortunately relapsed and died a month later as a result of multiple abscesses. In the same month a 15-year-old boy who had acquired a surgical infection was successfully treated with penicillin. For Fleming it would be another year before he was able to use the newly produced penicillin in a patient. In August 1942 he was faced with a 52-year-old patient, a friend of his, suffering from meningitis. On 1 August Fleming cultured Streptococci from the man's cerebrospinal fluid and demonstrated that it was sensitive to penicillin, but not to

---

130 Both Chain's mother and sister were killed in late 1942 in a Nazi concentration camp.

sulphonamides. He contacted Florey and explained the situation, and on 6 August took the train to Oxford. Fleming noted how Florey had been 'good enough to supply me with his whole stock of penicillin', and on returning to London, the drug was administered intrathecally into the patient. Within a week he had made an almost full recovery.

The importance and impact of penicillin soon became recognised, both in Britain and abroad. At Oxford, Florey sought advice from Sir Henry Dale at the Royal Society on issuing a patent on the technique for producing penicillin. However, it was proposed that this was not appropriate, since the development was 'for the good of all.' Interestingly, Chain was keen to seek a patent, but his views appeared to be overruled.[131] The pharmaceutical company, Glaxo, received cultures of Penicillium in 1941 and set about commercial production. By the autumn of 1943 there were sufficient quantities of penicillin to allow the Medical Research Council to supply the drug to four centres for clinical trials. One of these was Birmingham Accident Hospital, where trials were overseen by Dr Ethel Florey, wife of Howard Florey. However, production failed to keep up with demand, and in the summer of 1943 the use of penicillin was limited to servicemen. Later that year Howard Florey travelled to North Africa and treated wounded soldiers with penicillin. At this time the production of penicillin was given the highest priority by the British government; it was now a 'designated' project, of similar importance to aircraft production. With the prospect of the invasion of Western Europe in 1944 production of penicillin was increased again, helped by techniques of deep fermentation, developed in America. In May 1945, Field Marshal Montgomery was to write:

The healing of war wounds has been revolutionized by the use of penicillin. Many men who in the last war would have been permanent invalids were fit and ready to go back to the line within a month of being wounded.

A chance discovery by Fleming in 1928, followed by input from workers in Oxford, had a monumental impact, not only during World

---

131 American companies who were involved in the production of penicillin did issue a patent, so that the use of penicillin in Britain led to a royalty having to be paid to these companies.

War 2, but also in the years that have followed. Today, we take for granted the use of antibiotics in medicine. However, the developments and advances which have allowed the development of antibiotic therapy also led to friction between the two institutions, and were due entirely to the actions of those who were not directly involved with the programmes. So, when in 1941 and 1942 the results of investigations from the Oxford Group appeared in the medical literature, a number of senior figures at St Mary's wrote openly in support of Fleming, perhaps fearing his contribution would be overlooked. Amongst these was the man Fleming would later describe as 'probably the greatest man associated with St Mary's Hospital in its 100-year history.' This was Sir Almroth Wright who, in the autumn of 1942, sent a letter to *The Times* claiming for Fleming both the discovery of penicillin and the original suggestion of its therapeutic potential. Added to this was a clever publicity campaign directed by Lord Moran (who was great friends with Lord Beaverbrook, Minister of Aircraft Production as well as owner of the *Daily Express*) which further supported Fleming's role in the discovery. At Oxford, Florey was unwilling to talk about penicillin to the press, and this inevitably led to Fleming being seen as the 'hero of penicillin'. This led to considerable friction between St Mary's and Oxford, although, it was stressed, not between the actual parties involved. Fleming found the situation rather embarrassing and wrote how:

The resuscitation of penicillin as a chemotherapeutic remedy is due to the brilliant work of Florey and his colleagues at Oxford. The success of the Oxford workers is a great argument for team-work in a detailed investigation of this sort. Whether team-work is an advantage for the initiation of something new is quite a different matter.

Recognition of those involved in the discovery and production of penicillin was forthcoming both at home and abroad. The Nobel Prize in Physiology or Medicine for 1945 was awarded to Fleming, Florey and Chain, each receiving one-third of the prize 'for the discovery of penicillin and its curative effect in various infectious diseases'. The announcement of the award was made in October that year, and Bill had learnt about it whilst returning from the Far East on-board *SS Orduna*. In Britain, Florey was elected to a Fellowship of the Royal Society in 1941; two years later, Fleming was also elected. It was not until 1948 that Chain was elected to the Fellowship. Fleming and Florey were both knighted in July 1944, whereas Chain (despite having become a British citizen in 1939) did not receive a knighthood until 1969.

Fleming, always keen to talk about penicillin, was approached by the BBC in the summer of 1945 to talk about the impact of penicillin. By this time, the drug had been widely used, especially amongst servicemen injured on battlefields around the world. It was clear that this was literally life-saving. In 1943, the decision was made by the Army to allow some penicillin, destined for treating septic wounds in battlefield casualties, to be trialled in the treatment of gonorrhoea. Here, it was found to be highly effective, so much so that men with infection could return to military duty within 4 hours of receiving treatment; previously they would have been relieved of duties for at least 7 days. In considering the impact of penicillin, Fleming wished to include its use in treating venereal disease. There was a problem: the BBC were not keen for Fleming to mention gonorrhoea in a broadcast to the nation. An impasse was reached and it was agreed that they should approach the Prime Minister, Winston Churchill. Churchill was well aware of the impact of penicillin, since his personal physician was Lord Moran, who had spoken strongly in support of Fleming's achievement.[132] He was quite clear: Yes, of course Fleming could use the word, and should. He did.

Penicillin and Allergy

In 1946 Fleming had published his book *Penicillin: Its Practical Application*. A multi-author book, it contained a number of chapters ranging from the history and discovery of penicillin through to its use in a range of infectious diseases. In a chapter covering the pharmacology of penicillin, Dr L.P. Garrod described how sensitisation to penicillin had been reported, often manifesting as urticaria. He concluded that '…these

---

132 Reports that Churchill had been treated with penicillin by Moran in 1943 appear incorrect. In February 1943 Churchill developed pneumonia and was prescribed the sulphonamide, M&B 693.

findings are perplexing, but fortunately of no grave moment. It is rarely necessary to interrupt treatment by reason of such reactions.' The book was deemed the 'medical bible' of its time and sold over 175,000 copies; every doctor felt he should own a copy in order to use the 'miracle drug' in his own specialty. In 1948 the publishers, Butterworths, decided that there should be a second edition. They wanted two more chapters: one on the new drug streptomycin, which had recently been discovered by Waksman, and one on allergic reactions. Fleming was highly suspicious of the issue of allergic reactions to the drug. He insisted that such reactions were due to impurities in the preparations, which were invariably given by injection at the time. His opposition was such that he refused to use the word 'allergy' in the context of penicillin. Bill subsequently learnt that early preparations of penicillin were markedly impure, with the active material making up just 3% of the preparation, the rest being effectively 'rubbish.' Fleming came under increasing pressure to deliver a second edition of the book. One morning at 10.00am Bill, as usual, went to see Fleming and was told 'Frankland, you're going to write this chapter on the side effects of penicillin. I'll give you a week to do it; 3,000 words – not more; and not more than 30 references.'

Bill wrote the chapter that week, adhering to the guidelines he had received. The chapter was entitled 'Penicillin Sensitivity' in which Bill referred to 350 papers having been published since 1943 on the subject of penicillin sensitivity. He also included details of one of his own patients with penicillin sensitivity. The man, who had been badly wounded in May 1940 at Dunkirk, was successfully desensitised by Bill using an oral regimen. Bill went back to see Fleming the following Monday morning at 10am and presented the manuscript. 'I will read it tonight and I'll tell you tomorrow morning what I think about it,' was Fleming's response. Come the following morning Bill was quite dreading what he might say. Fortunately Fleming was, as always, his charming self and said, 'I'm not saying that I agree with everything that you have written, but I'm not going to change it, except your very last sentence on the last page.' Bill had written: 'With the increasing use of penicillin, it is to be expected that allergic reactions will become more common.' Writing in Indian ink and 'beautiful handwriting'

Fleming crossed out the last sentence out and wrote, 'With increasing use of penicillin, reactions due to impurities will become less common.' Bill felt in no place to argue with a Nobel Prize-winner, and it was Fleming's words that were published in the second edition in 1950. However, in later years Bill felt that, although Fleming was, to some extent, correct, his own opinion was also correct.[133]

On Her Majesty's Service

One day Sir Alexander Fleming asked to see Bill, and informed him that he had received a request from the Foreign Office. Unbeknown to Bill, the request related to a case of possible penicillin allergy, and Fleming had shown no hesitation in recommending Bill's expertise. He was to go to Benghazi in Libya in a week's time. Although Fleming did not reveal the reason for the visit, Bill was assured that he would receive 'VIP treatment.' Unsure as to why he was being sent, Bill thought it might be an issue involving allergy, perhaps to penicillin. He had just read a paper describing a patient in New York who had received a skin challenge test with penicillin to assess any allergic response, but had died from anaphylaxis. Fortuitously as it turned out, Bill made a copy of the paper and packed it in his case. Bill left from Heathrow Airport where he was seen off by his wife and two daughters, Penelope and Jenifer. The piston-engined aircraft was *en route* to Nairobi but was due to refuel at Benghazi. Bill travelled in first-class where he had his own air hostess and received 'marvellous hospitality.' The aircraft arrived in Benghazi at midnight and in the pitch darkness just three passengers disembarked: Bill along with two men from the economy cabin.

Entering the airport buildings Bill had his passport checked by an 'illiterate man' and was disappointed to find there was no one to meet him. At 2am the airport shut and still Bill was on his own. Fortunately

---

133 Nearly 70 years later, Bill's initial suggestion regarding the incidence of allergy has clearly been demonstrated to be correct. In a report issued in 2018 the Royal College of Anaesthetists reported that the most frequent cause of anaphylaxis in patients undergoing surgery was the administration of antibiotics.

he came across another Englishman, who was 'slightly drunk.' Bill asked how far it was to the town to which the man replied, 'I'll give you a lift.' Bill was taken to his car, a Volkswagen Beetle. This had travelled 175,000 miles, its brakes barely worked and the clutch was well past its best. They set off from the airport, with Bill unsure if they were to drive on the left or right side of the road. They passed a convoy of lorries and arrived in the centre of Benghazi where they located Bill's hotel, conveniently opposite the British Embassy. Looking back, Bill felt the journey would have taken at least 5 hours to walk. The entrance to the hotel was up a slope and, since the car did not have a first gear, Bill had to walk the last part of the journey. Arriving at 3am, Bill was met by the night porter, who spoke very good English, and asked Bill to complete the registration form. One of the questions was 'purpose of visit' to which Bill wrote 'to visit.' With these formalities complete Bill was shown to his room, and was informed that the hotel offered 'dancing downstairs', an offer which Bill politely refused.

After finally getting to bed, Bill awoke later that morning and made his way to the British Embassy arriving at about 10am. His reception was far from friendly, and he was asked, 'What do you want?' to which he replied, 'To know why I have been asked to come here.' The embassy staff then realised that their visitor had arrived a day earlier than they expected; they had failed to read the flight times correctly and this explained why there had been no reception for Bill on arrival. With this matter now clarified, Bill was informed that he had been asked out to Benghazi in order to visit the hospital. He duly made his way there and was introduced to an Italian doctor who was in charge. Before long, Bill was horrified to find that most of the patients were being treated for leprosy, a disease which he knew nothing about and so asked how the condition was treated. He was informed that patients were sent to a special isolation hospital for treatment. However, most returned to be close to their family, usually arriving back in the original hospital within three days. Bill visited the hospital again the following day when the reason for his visit became apparent. It transpired that the Italian doctor was in trouble with the Libyan authorities over a patient he had treated. This patient was the Prime Minister's secretary, a man acknowledged to be the 'brains behind' the Prime Minister. He had developed eczema following administration of penicillin, and the Italian doctor had attempted to determine the cause of the eczema. In taking a history he found that the patient had not been tested for penicillin allergy, so he performed a skin prick test with dilute penicillin. Within 15 minutes of administration the patient developed anaphylactic shock, and despite the doctor administering adrenaline at the correct dose, he died. Immediately following this, the doctor was assaulted by the dead man's brother and badly injured. Next he was imprisoned, but was released after two days as he was needed desperately in the hospital.

Bill now found himself in the midst of an international political problem. The doctor was in serious trouble with the Libyan authorities, but was also a great friend of the Prime Minister of Italy. Heated arguments ensued between the prime ministers of Italy and Libya over the case, which escalated to involve the price of Libyan oil being sold to Italy. Now, some six weeks after the death, a court of law was to be constituted at which the Italian doctor was to be tried for murder; Bill was to be both judge and expert witness. The court duly sat and all evidence was given in Arabic, which had to be translated for Bill. The prosecution deemed the Italian doctor to be 'a murderer and a liar', the latter because the patient had died at 9.30am, whereas the doctor had written in the notes that he died at 10.30am. As lunchtime approached the prosecutor finished presenting his evidence and, addressing the court, said that Bill had only one decision to make, namely 'should they shoot the doctor or hang him?' Unaccustomed to such suggestions, Bill informed the court that under international law there was a need to hear evidence from both sides, and that they would hear from the defence that afternoon. After lunch the case resumed, and Bill picked up on the issue of the timing of death; the doctor admitted he had made a mistake, and that his patient had died at 9.30am (not at 10.30am, as stated in the notes). At about 4pm, with the case nearing completion, Bill pulled out the copy of the paper he had brought with from London describing anaphylaxis to penicillin. He told the court that this showed how side effects could occur and went on to say that the Italian doctor had, in his opinion, acted very carefully in treating the patient and that death was a very rare side effect of the investigation. All in the court appeared happy with Bill's judgement and the next day the doctor flew home to Italy. Over the coming weeks and months Bill received many thank-you letters from the man's wife in which she explained that Bill had 'saved her husband's life.' As a follow-up to this, Bill later heard that the doctor had published the case of anaphylaxis to penicillin, but without reference or acknowledgement to Bill.

Following his time in Benghazi Bill planned to travel to Cairo in order to meet a number of colleagues. However, he found that despite being a VIP, flights to Cairo were 'full', so the British Embassy suggested he travel by road. It later transpired that the flights did have space, but a significant bribe had to be paid in order to secure a first-class seat. Bill located a 'much squashed vehicle', a Bedford minibus, which could accommodate ten passengers. The minibus set off towards the easterly city of Tobruk along a route which involved numerous hill passes, with hairpin bends. Bill looked down from the side of the road and saw a long drop, at the bottom of which were numerous rusting vehicles. These had all failed to make the journey, having tried, unsuccessfully, to cut the corners. Bill described the whole journey as 'very scary', but finally they arrived safely in Tobruk, where they were to rest before continuing their journey. Bill found Tobruk at night to be 'awful' with the accommodation being one dormitory in which people were sleeping on the floor. He was determined that he would at least find a bed and located the best, and only, hotel where he paid 5 dollars for a room. Although he had a bed for the night, it was far from peaceful, having to endure the sounds of nearby donkeys braying all night.

The next morning he made his way back to the minibus and observed that on two of the four wheels the inner tubes were clearly visible through the outer tyre. The party set off and made their way to the Egyptian border. Here there was a long queue and Bill found himself standing in line, becoming very tired. Unexpectedly, he was moved up the queue and was soon through the border. The reason for his accelerated treatment was that, 'I spoke English and told people I would be staying in the Hilton in Cairo.' Soon after crossing the border one of the minibus's inner tubes exploded with a loud bang, causing the vehicle almost to tip over; this was yet another unpleasant shock in the journey. The driver stopped, changed the wheel and the journey continued. However, barely an hour later, there was another explosion, another inner tube had disintegrated and this time there was no spare wheel. The party was now stranded in the desert with the driver having, somehow, to find a lift to the nearest town, Sidi Barrani, in order to buy two new wheels. Two Egyptians in the party approached Bill and asked if he would like something to eat? 'Yes,' was his reply and so they set off on a five-mile walk through the desert, in the middle of summer, to a nearby village. As they approached the village there were a number of guards, but they were all asleep. On arrival they found a building that appeared to Bill to be a pigsty, but in fact was a café where they were able to purchase Coca-Cola, eggs and some rye bread. Bill felt the meal was a 'nice interlude' to the journey but was soon followed by a further five-mile walk back to the minibus. Whilst at the café a local man approached Bill and told him that he had been 'Monty's batman' during the war and produced a bullet, a memento of his time with the great general, which Bill found to be most impressive. However, Bill's Egyptian colleagues pointed out that he would hear the same story from many other men in Egypt.

With the minibus again roadworthy they drove to Sidi Barrani where they spent the night. Bill made his way, with his two colleagues, along the main street, home to numerous cows, to the hotel where they checked in for the night. They found their accommodation was sheer luxury, although all three beds were in the same room. All were exhausted as they entered the room, and Bill was somewhat perturbed to see the first Egyptian lie down on a bed, still with his boots and clothes on. His other colleague did at least take off his boots before falling into bed. Bill, feeling that despite the hardships of the journey certain standards had to be maintained, changed into his pyjamas before settling down to sleep.

The next morning, the party continued travelling east, stopping at El Alamein for breakfast where Bill was served exceptionally tough camel meat which he found quite inedible. They continued across Egypt, finally reaching Alexandria where they transferred to a taxi for the journey to Cairo. Amongst the passengers Bill remembered a policeman who got a free trip to his home, about halfway to Cairo. As they approached Cairo, passengers were dropped off at different points on the periphery of the city, such that by the time they reached the centre of Cairo, Bill was the only passenger. He arrived at the Hilton in a somewhat dishevelled state, having travelled for three days across North Africa. He was asked if he wished to have a cheap or an expensive room. Opting for the latter, he made his way to the room on the fifth floor, which was refreshingly cool, courtesy of the air conditioning, so much so that he opened the window to allow some warm air in. Nearby were huge clouds of the Nimitti fly, a small, chironomid midge found along the banks of the River Nile. Typically these swarm around dusk, 'filling the air as snow in a storm.' This was the first time he had seen these insects, but he was very interested in them, since in 1949 he had treated a commercial airline pilot who had flown to Khartoum in Sudan and had developed severe asthma in June and July, believing the Nimitti fly to be responsible. This was the first, and would be the only, time that Bill observed the clouds of flies, despite returning to Cairo on a further eleven occasions.

Once settled in his room, Bill realised that he was both very hungry and very dirty, and was unsure whether to eat or wash first, he opted for a wash before heading down for a 'marvellous dinner' after which he slept extremely well. Whilst in Cairo he tried, unsuccessfully, to make contact with two professional colleagues, both of whom he had met in London. One was the Professor of Medicine at Ain Shams University, the other, Professor of Paediatrics at Cairo University. Despite his best efforts he was unable to make contact with them by telephone from the Hilton. He mentioned this to the chambermaid who cleaned his room, a lady who spoke perfect English. Responding to his predicament, she gave Bill instructions how to reach another of Bill's acquaintances, a patient whom lived near to the British Embassy. Making his way there on foot, he found he was able to make telephone calls to his colleagues without any difficulty. It later transpired the difficulty in communications from the hotel was the result of a block placed on his telephone, as the authorities believed him to be a spy. After the trials and tribulations of the journey across the desert, Bill was pleased to be able to fly home, first-class, and on his return wrote a five-page report for the Foreign

Office. He soon received a reply; the Foreign Office were exceptionally grateful for his work in Benghazi, and that his actions had 'prevented a war.' However, two days later a second letter came, requesting that he send his report in triplicate. Bill was extremely cross at this, and sent a postcard which read: 'I am sure you have a photocopier as I do not!'

Encounters with a Nobel Laureate

During the two years that Bill worked for Sir Alexander Fleming, he continued to undertake all the clinical work in the Allergy Department. He rarely saw Freeman, and never in the very busy outpatients' department. Bill discussed this with Fleming, who felt that the issue should be addressed. Bill and John Freeman were invited to Fleming's office. After knocking they were invited in and, as always, Fleming continued to look down his microscope, apparently oblivious to his visitors. Finally the meeting started. Freeman explained that Bill, who now had a wife and two young children, was working very hard but was earning only £550 per year, barely enough. Fleming asked if Freeman was suggesting that Bill should have either more money or fewer children. Despite this rather uncomfortable meeting, Bill received a pay rise which, it transpired, was very much at the behest of Freeman.

Fleming's concern for staff went beyond the medical cadre, and extended to the care on the ward, although he rarely, if ever, actually set foot there himself. The ward sister for Almroth Wright Ward between 1947 and 1955 was to be married, and was friendly with Bill. He asked Fleming if she could hold the marriage reception in the library of the Wright-Fleming Institute. Reluctantly Fleming agreed, but on one condition, that this was a 'one-off' event. He then said to Bill, 'What a pity she is getting married, we will lose her.' Bill reassured him that she would not be leaving the ward after her marriage, to which Fleming replied, 'Now I do not mind that she is getting married.' Bill was struck by Fleming's ability to sum up the character and capabilities of a nurse whom he hardly ever saw, and regret that she might leave a job which she filled so well.

Despite having worked for Sir Alexander Fleming for two years, having been taught by him as a student, and having spent time shooting with him at Bisley, only one photograph exists of the two men together. This was taken on 30 November 1954 at St Mary's on the occasion of a visit by Queen Elizabeth, The Queen Mother. She had a long connection with St Mary's, first visiting in 1931 as The Duchess of York, laying the foundation stone for the new medical school. She had served as President of the Medical School since 1934, and once Queen, had spent time at first aid posts in the hospital during the war. Her Majesty's visit in 1954 followed a 3-week trip to the United States and Canada, her first trip abroad without another member of the Royal Family since her husband's death in February 1952. She had sailed west on-board RMS *Queen Elizabeth*, which she had launched in 1938, and returned on-board her sister ship RMS *Queen Mary*.

Bill with Pauline and daughters

At St Mary's she was to lay a foundation stone for the extension to the medical school library. Into the stone she placed a copy of Sir Zachary Cope's *History of St Mary's Hospital*, a stopwatch marking 3 minutes 59.4 seconds (the time recorded by Roger Bannister,[134] a final-year medical student at St Mary's when he ran the first sub-four-minute mile on 6 May 1954 at the Iffley Road Track, Oxford) and a culture of Penicillium. On that occasion, Bill was presented to The Queen Mother by Sir Alexander Fleming.

Queen Elizabeth, The Queen Mother, Sir Alexander Fleming and Bill Frankland.

This was not the first time Bill had been in an audience with members of the Royal Family. In June 1954, The Duke of Edinburgh visited St Mary's, to mark the centenary of the hospital and 25 years since the publication of Fleming's paper on penicillin. At an official ceremony, the Chancellor of the University of Edinburgh (the Duke), presented

---

134 Bill would remember Roger Bannister as 'the most intelligent student I ever taught'. Just like Bill, Bannister had undertaken his pre-clinical education at Oxford, before moving to St Mary's for clinical studies.

the Rector of that same university (Sir Alexander Fleming) with two tureens, or as the Duke called them 'broth boats.' Fleming in his reply presented the Duke with a vial of Penicillium, having previously given one to The Queen Mother. Bill overheard the Duke say, 'It's the same vial as last time!'

Fleming was recognised around the world for his discovery of penicillin. Bill would often see his secretary, Pauline Hunter, work her way through up to 40 letters a day addressed to Sir Alexander, thanking him for the 'miracle drug' which had saved either their own life, or that of a loved one, and asking for a reprint of his now famous paper. He was happy to oblige, signing reprints before they were sent off to all parts of the world. Bill remembers how Pauline Hunter commented that 'the Post Office is doing well out of this.' Although many of those wishing to thank Fleming were unknown to him, there were several well-known celebrities who wished to recognise his work. One of these was Marlene Dietrich. She was on her way to Germany and wished to meet Sir Alexander Fleming, since she had been treated with penicillin for pneumonia during the war and her daughter had also been treated with the 'miracle drug.' She considered Fleming to be one of her greatest heroes, and wrote to him on several occasions. She flew to London, where she stayed at Claridge's. She invited Fleming to lunch at the hotel, which he readily accepted. He gave his host a sample of the original Penicillium culture. Bill remembers very clearly how he was late back from lunch: it was the only time he noted Fleming arriving late for a lecture. The following day a signed picture of Miss Dietrich arrived in Fleming's office, and was opened by his secretary. It sat on her desk for a week; every time Bill went into her office he admired it, hoping it might be offered to him. After a week, Pauline Hunter had obviously tired of the photograph, tore it up and threw it in the bin.

Florey and Fleming each took a very different view regarding speaking about the isolation, evaluation and commercial production of penicillin. Florey never spoke about it, except to scientific audiences, whereas Fleming was keen to engage with the media about the subject. However, Fleming was not the most engaging of speakers, talking in his rather soft Scottish accent, with a noticeable softening of his 'r's, those in the audience often found it difficult to hear him, many complaining that he was inaudible. In fact, Fleming recognised his own failings, and said, 'It's a pity I have not the gift of tongues, it's worth more than anything else to be able to talk.' Bill remembers some of these issues when Fleming gave a lecture on penicillin at St Mary's. Notice of the lecture had been circulated widely, and the lecture theatre was packed. At the end of the lecture, Bill was approached by a Scottish doctor who had travelled all the way from Aberdeen to hear the Nobel Laureate. He told Bill in no uncertain terms that it had been a 'complete waste of time', since he had not heard a single word spoken by Fleming. There was, however, one positive outcome, Bill remembered that a microphone and speaker system was installed in the theatre soon after.

There was a stream of visiting dignitaries to St Mary's coming to meet Sir Alexander Fleming and it often fell to Bill to entertain them for some time before meeting his boss. There were several memorable times, including one American visitor who arrived with the preconceived idea that, since penicillin had been such a success, Fleming must be an exceptionally rich man. Bill took great delight in showing him Fleming's car, pointing out it was 12 years old. Another American visitor also left quite a memory with Bill. Dr Leung was an authority on asthma, having written a textbook before the war, which Bill had read. Fleming had invited Leung to speak at St Mary's. On the day of the lecture he arrived early, and Bill was told to entertain him for about an hour, with the directions 'we have sherry but not whisky'. Bill duly entertained the guest, having three glasses of sherry himself. At the start of the lecture, Bill was tasked by Fleming to introduce the speaker. He suddenly found that the sherry was having too much effect, his lips would not do as he wanted them to! He learnt a moral from this incident: 'never have alcohol before a lecture.' The lecture was not of outstanding quality, which Bill found to be a pity, since he had encouraged a lot of staff from St Mary's to attend. Several years later, Bill was invited to Chicago to give the Leung Memorial Lecture. This went well, and after the lecture his hosts asked what he was going to do. 'Walk back to my hotel,' was the answer. 'No, you cannot,' was the reply. 'Why?' Bill asked. 'Because it is too dangerous to walk through the city.' One doctor offered Bill a lift in his car, and Bill asked why that was safer. 'Because I have one of these,' replied the doctor, pointing to the revolver on his gun belt.

Whilst at St Mary's Bill was to come into contact with Sir Alexander Fleming's wife, or more correctly, his second wife. Fleming had first married in December 1915, two days before Christmas. His bride was an Irish nurse, Sarah McElroy from County Mayo in Ireland, who was working in London, running a nursing home in Baker Street. Described as 'blonde with pink cheeks and grey-blue eyes' she was noted to be 'gay and very volatile' in marked comparison to her husband, who was both reserved and quiet. The contrast was noted by Fleming who later said of his marriage that his wife 'does all the work and provides all the conversation.' Sarah (whose twin sister Elizabeth was married to Alexander Fleming's brother, John) changed her name to Sareen but was invariably known as Sally. Sareen's health started to fail after the end of the war, and she was taken ill on a trip with her husband to Spain in 1948. The exact nature of the affliction was unclear, although Bill was led to believe it was a form of neurological disorder, possibly psychiatric. Sareen was admitted to the Lindo Wing of St Mary's Hospital and died in October 1949. The next morning Sir Alexander Fleming came to work as normal, and to Bill it appeared he was unaffected by her death, although he did notice there was even more cigarette ash than normal caught up on his shirt and tie, perhaps indicating that his smoking had been heavier than usual.[135]

In April 1953, Fleming married again, his bride being Dr Amalia Koutsouri-Vourekas, a Greek doctor who specialised in microbiology. Born in 1912 in Constantinople, then part of the Ottoman Empire, at a young age she moved to Greece with her family. Here during World War 2 she fought for the Resistance movements, was captured and sentenced to death by the occupying German forces. Fortunately, before sentence could be carried out, she was released by Allied forces. Although married to a Greek architect, she divorced and in 1947 was

---

135 Sir Alexander Fleming officially retired as Professor of Bacteriology in 1948, having reached the statutory age of 67, but was appointed Emeritus Professor. He continued as Director of the Wright-Fleming Institute until his death.

appointed to the Wright-Fleming Institute where she worked on the newly discovered antibiotic streptomycin. After about four years she returned to work in a hospital in Athens.

Exactly when the relationship between Fleming and Amalia started is unclear; some have suggested it may have commenced during her time working at the Wright-Fleming Institute. It is clear that it was kept very much a private matter, although one of the first to be aware of it was Bill. In October 1952, Fleming had spent just over one month travelling in Greece, where he had been entertained by a host of dignitaries, including a lunch hosted by the King and Queen, and received a Gold Medal. On 9 November Fleming had been entertained to supper by Amalia in her flat. As he was leaving he proposed marriage to her; she barely heard his words but accepted. A few weeks later, at St Mary's, Bill informed his boss that he had to travel to Paris in order to present a paper, and explained, therefore, that he might be late for their normal morning meeting. Fleming quizzed him as to the time of his return flight from Paris, something Bill found somewhat strange. Bill duly travelled to the conference but on arriving back at the airport was informed that his flight had been cancelled, and he would be on a later flight. As he waited, he found himself face to face with his boss, who was somewhat embarrassed at being found in Paris. It appeared that the he had been spending the weekend with his fiancée.

Sir Alexander Fleming married Amalia on 9 April 1953, and she returned to work at St Mary's. She was given a room in the Allergy Department, without any consultation with Bill, and where she set about developing further microbiological techniques, especially micromanipulation. Bill never spoke to her during this time, and was pleased when she moved out, freeing up his space. She accompanied her husband on his trips abroad, of which one stood out for Bill. Fleming was awarded a Gold Medal by the Indian Medical Association, and invited him to India to give a lecture and receive the medal. Fleming wanted to say no, but Bill persuaded him otherwise, saying that he had to go, and besides, Bill knew that Lady Fleming loved travelling. On their return, Fleming thanked Bill, saying, 'You always give me such good advice.'

Sir Alexander Fleming died on 11 March 1955, the result of a coronary thrombosis. His funeral was held on 18 March at St Paul's Cathedral, and Bill was amongst the congregation paying respects to a most remarkable man. The cathedral was full, and in the country flags flew at half-mast as a sign of respect to a man who had laid the foundations for changing the practice of medicine throughout the world. After the service, Fleming's ashes were interred in the crypt of St Paul's, close to the final resting places of Nelson and Wellington.

Bill lost contact with Amalia after the death of her husband. She returned to Greece in 1963 where she was outspoken in her socialist views. In 1967 a military *coup d'état* led to the exiling of King Constantine and the imposition of martial rule. Amalia was arrested, accused of plotting to aid the escape of Alexandros Panagoulis, who had, in 1968, been convicted for his attempt to assassinate the Greek Prime Minister. She was suffering with diabetes and her health deteriorated whilst in prison. On 7 September 1971 a number of those who knew Amalia wrote a letter to *The Times* 'appealing for all necessary care and medical attention, so her health is not further imperilled by imprisonment'. The letter had been instigated by Sir Ernst Chain,[136] and the second signature was Bill Frankland. Others who signed included Sir Peter Medawar and Merlin Pryce. Amalia was released later that year and exiled. After the fall of the junta in 1974, she returned to Greece and served as a Member of Parliament for several years. Bill met her once more, many years later, after he had retired from St Mary's, when he visited former colleagues at the hospital. Amalia noticed Bill and came up and introduced herself, saying that 'he was the only person she recognised.' She had put on a lot of weight (the result of myxoedema) and Bill barely recognised her; if she had not introduced herself he would not have known who she was. Lady Fleming died in 1986.

---

136 Unlike Fleming and Florey, Bill never met Sir Ernst Chain.

Exploding the Myth

It was whilst working for Sir Alexander Fleming that Bill undertook a further clinical trial, into the effectiveness of autogenous bacterial vaccines in 'infective non-allergic asthma.' His other boss, John Freeman, was a great advocate of the use of autogenous vaccines for the control of this condition, effectively cases of hay fever or asthma that were not apparently allergic in nature. Throat swabs taken from the patients would demonstrate growth of bacteria and Freeman would tell his colleagues, such as Bill, that the patients 'are reacting to this, they haven't got an immunity.' Treatment would involve vaccination. The bacteria isolated were grown in the patient's own blood and from this a vaccine created. Bill developed the view, based upon clinical observations, that these autogenous vaccines, which were time-consuming to make and expensive to produce, gave little, if any, specific help to patients. To try to elucidate the effectiveness of the vaccines, Bill undertook a double-blind controlled trial, aided both by Dr Gorrill and Dr W.H. 'Howard' Hughes, a bacteriologist. Nearly 200 patients with bronchial (or infective) asthma were entered into the trial. Hughes, who believed that the vaccines were effective, prepared an autogenous bacterial vaccine from each patient. These were then randomised by Gorrill into one of two groups, to receive either the autogenous vaccine or a control, namely carbol-saline. Patients received their allocated treatment by means of weekly injections, increasing in dose over time, and were then assessed according to a number of clinical criteria every fourth month, for a year. Bill, on reviewing the patients, was unaware of which treatment they had received. Some 192 patients were studied, and it was demonstrated that 58% of those receiving autogenous vaccine showed signs of clinical improvement, for the control group the figure was 52%. As Bill was later to comment, there was no real need for statistical analysis since there was obviously no difference between the two groups.

Despite some sources stating that the trial had been done with Freeman's support and approval, it had not. In presenting the results Bill was surprised that he kept his job, since they flew in the face of Freeman's long-held views. Undoubtedly Bill was helped by Sir

Alexander Fleming, who brought together the members of the Wright-Fleming Institute at teatime to hear a summary of Bill's findings. Fleming asked the audience if they thought Bill should be allowed to publish this work, and a vote was taken. The result was 100% in favour. It was published in October 1955, six months after Fleming's death. Fleming said that he would support Bill in his results and before long his findings were recognised internationally. Bill was soon invited to talk at a number of high-profile international meetings on his findings despite, as he pointed out, not yet being a consultant. His first invitation was to a meeting in Madrid three months after the paper was published, and then two months later he was invited to speak in Los Angeles in 1955. The latter was most memorable, as Bill was given a lift in his host's secretary's car, a two-seater Rolls-Royce, a gift she had received from her boss as a token of gratitude for her efficiency. He provoked considerable interest in the press, and whilst in Beverly Hills was asked for his views on the hereditary basis of allergy. Bill stated that 'I am sure no one is born with allergies. My identical twin brother hasn't a single allergy while I have lots of them.' John Freeman never talked to Bill about the findings from this paper: Bill believed he never read it and perhaps that was why Bill kept his job. Interestingly, Mrs Freeman rang Bill following the paper's publication: it was the only time she had contacted him. She told Bill that 'he must not stop her husband in his work on autogenous vaccines, since it was the only thing that kept him alive.'

Bill attending the 3rd European Congress of Allergy, Madrid, March 1956.

This work, and that before it, formed the basis for Bill's submission for the degree of Doctor of Medicine from the University of Oxford. His examiners included Professor Sir Howard Florey.[137] Bill was not summoned for a *viva voce* examination, and the degree was awarded in 1956. Bill attended the degree ceremony at Oxford, with his wife and two daughters, who watched with interest. He was one of two graduands receiving a Doctorate of Medicine, the other being Dr Margaret Turner-Warwick, who had entered Lady Margaret Hall in 1943. Bill was the first to be presented for his degree, a decision based upon the precedent of his college, being significantly older than Lady Margaret Hall. After the ceremony, Bill's daughters informed him that he was 'very rude' in not allowing the lady to go first in the ceremony.[138]

---

137 In 1962 Florey was appointed as Provost of The Queen's College, Oxford and in 1965 he was ennobled.

138 In 1989, Margaret Turner-Warwick became the first female president of the Royal College of Physicians, in 1991 was appointed Dame Commander of the Order of the British Empire.

Bill at International Meeting of Physicians. Madrid 1964.
On the reverse of the print, it states, 'My subject: Autogenous bacterial vaccines in infected
asthma give no specific help.' This was a double-blind controlled trial which went against all
the teachings of his chief, Dr John Freeman.

The Problems with Pollen

Amongst the responsibilities that passed to Bill was that of the pollen farm, also called the Pollenarium, located at Pyrford near Woking. It was the world's largest pollen farm and had been built on 3 acres of an experimental dairy farm, gifted to the Inoculation Department of St Mary's Hospital by Lord Iveagh, a friend of Sir Almroth Wright. Its origins lay with Leonard Noon who, nearly 50 years earlier, had required significant quantities of pollen for his studies of treating seasonal hay fever. He was assisted by his sister, Dorothy, who went on to manage the newly established pollen farm, providing grass pollen for both the diagnosis and treatment of hay fever. Initially the principal species grown were *Phleum pratense* (Timothy grass) and *Dactylis glomerata* (Cock's foot grass), *Phleum* being the grass used by Noon in his pioneering desensitisation trials. Pollen extracts were processed in a laboratory at St Mary's, before either being used there, or being sold abroad, the major customers being in Spain and USA.

Grasses were cut just prior to pollination, and the farm employed a number of young ladies for this task, undertaken by hand, using scissors. They were managed by Dorothy Noon who had rather strict and, what appeared to Bill, antiquated views. In 1955 Bill took over the running of the farm, and continued to do so for the next 15 years until its closure in 1970. To keep pace with developments and demands, it was decided that a botanist should be employed to undertake the daily pollen counts. Twelve ladies applied for the post; none seemed to have a great understanding or knowledge about pollen, and there seemed to be no obvious perfect candidate. Reaching an impasse, and having read all the letters of application, Bill informed John Freeman that the answer was very clear, one candidate was obviously destined for the position... her name was Miss Muriel Hay! She was duly appointed. Not long after her appointment grass had to be harvested on a Sunday. Muriel Hay was happy to do this, and gathered a small group of girls to help her. When Dorothy Noon heard of the plans, she was far from happy, believing that on a Sunday, 'ladies should not be in work, but in church.' Muriel Hay was more than a little taken aback, and stated,

'No one tells me if I am to go to church.' Bill was not impressed and not long after this he gave full support to Dorothy Noon's retirement from the farm.

Bill at Pollenarium, preparing to take samples back to St Mary's, 1949

For Bill, one of the delights of visiting the pollen farm was to be invited to lunch at Pyrford Court by Lord Iveagh. This had the most wonderful gardens (believed in part to have been designed by Gertrude Jekyll) which Bill enjoyed exploring in the company of Lady Iveagh, herself a most knowledgeable gardener. Many of Bill's colleagues assumed that he would be offered champagne in such grand surroundings but he enjoyed pointing out that lunch was always served with the family drink, Guinness. The Pollenarium was closed a year after Bill retired from St Mary's.

At the same time as running the pollen farm, Bill became very aware through running the seasonal allergy clinic at St Mary's that there was no guidance for patients as to the onset or ending of the pollen seasons, and no information on the daily levels of pollen. He set about addressing this. He was aware that Hyde and Williams had made daily pollen measurements in Cardiff in the early 1940s, and was determined to provide a similar service in London.[139] He convinced Freeman that an automatic volumetric spore trap (capable of sampling 8 litres of air per minute) should be purchased. This was the 'Hirst Spore Trap' which had been developed in the 1950s by Professor John Hirst, an agricultural botanist, working at the Agricultural Research Council's Rothamsted establishment in Hertfordshire. It was placed on the roof of the nurses' home at St Mary's and daily measurements were made. Initially the results, first obtained in 1953, were given to those members of the British Association of Allergists who had shown an interest. In 1963, the information was given to the media. Bill, or one of his staff, would telephone *The Times* and *The Daily Telegraph* by 10.30am and provide them with the pollen count, speaking 'on behalf of the Asthma Research Council'; at no time was it mentioned that the source of the information was St Mary's Hospital. Thus started what became the longest continuous recording of pollen levels, stretching over 30 years. Today, the pollen count is an accepted part of the daily weather forecast during the spring and summer months, and data is obtained by the Meteorological Office in conjunction with the National Pollen and Aerobiology Research Unit.

Bill's investigations into the quantity and distribution of pollen led him to explore other sites, apart from the standard one at roof level of St Mary's. In the early 1960s, in collaboration with Professor Gregory he obtained a piece of specialist equipment, a Rotorod sampler, which allowed him to take air samples at street level and also on the underground, all part of his goal to gain a fuller picture of the potential exposure to airborne allergens. He found no pollen either at street level or in the underground, but instead captured a lot of 'black material' which appeared to be atmospheric pollutant. Bill also ventured out onto golf

---

139 Dr D.A. Williams was a chest physician in Cardiff and was responsible for the volumetric air analysis and worked with Hyde, a botanist. Williams later died from pulmonary aspergillosis.

courses with the equipment and demonstrated very high levels of pollen in the spring, especially in the 'rough' of the course. Having undertaken these sampling studies, he was ready to publish when he was informed by members of the Security Services that he could not. Somewhat taken aback, he was unclear as to why his work was suddenly so secret. It was explained that the Rotorod was very new, and that Russian authorities did not know that British scientists possessed it. Moreover, the same equipment was currently being used, undercover, by British agents working in Russia. They were sampling air in a number of sites in and around Moscow to determine the level and extent of radioactive fallout following Soviet nuclear tests in the east of the country. Bill's studies never did reach their way into print.

Hirst Spore Trap at St Mary's Hospital

Bill recognised at an early stage that if advances were to be made in the field of allergy, he would have to seek expertise and input from a range of specialities, both medical and non-medical. The first to work with him was Rosa Augustin. Others soon became involved and one was a botanist, called Davies, recruited from St Thomas' Hospital. A very intelligent man, who was awarded a D.Sc., he was a difficult man to work with. However, there was one advantage of employing him: he lived in Twickenham and Bill was able to park his car at Davies' house when attending international rugby matches.

Although Bill has often been referred to, incorrectly, as an immunologist, and has always been at pains to point out that he is not, he recognised the importance of immunology in understanding and treating allergy. He was instrumental in recruiting the first immunologist to St Mary's, Professor R.R 'Rodney' Porter. A biochemist, he had studied for his PhD at Cambridge University under Frederick Sanger (who was awarded the Nobel Prize in Chemistry, twice) before working at the National Institute for Medical Research, Mill Hill. In 1960 he was appointed Professor of Immunology at St Mary's, and in 1964 was elected a Fellow of the Royal Society. In 1967 he was appointed as Professor of Biochemistry at the University of Oxford. His research had focussed on elucidating the structure of antibodies, and in 1982 he was awarded, jointly, the Nobel Prize in Physiology or Medicine with Gerald Edelman. In the months leading up to the award, Bill received a number of representatives from the Karolinska Institute, the body responsible for awarding the Nobel Prize, seeking his opinion on the Porter's work. Amongst the issues raised was that Porter was not a medical doctor. Bill soon realised the nature of the discussions and was fully supportive of Porter's work, regardless of him not holding a medical qualification. However, since the discussions related to a possible Nobel Prize, Bill was sworn to the strictest of secrecy about the meetings, an undertaking which, as might have been expected, he adhered to fully.

Close to Death: Again

Like many of the pioneers of allergy, Bill also experimented on himself. Having developed seasonal hay fever when a child, he later developed allergy to a number of biting insects. He wished to explore further the effect and impact of anaphylaxis, but since this was a potentially lethal study he could not perform it on volunteers. Instead he proceeded to expose himself to an insect, one that he had never encountered before. He identified the South American conenose or 'kissing bug', *Rhodnius prolixus*, and approached the London School of Hygiene and Tropical Medicine who provided the insect. For the purposes of the study, he kept it in his car. When feeding on a subject the insect first introduces a small amount of saliva before sucking blood. Bill exposed himself to the insect at weekly intervals, on a Monday morning before making his way to work. On the first occasion there was no reaction but on the second there was a slight swelling at the feeding site after 48 hours. The fifth exposure caused his arm to be swollen and remained so for about three days. On the eighth exposure, however, Bill developed severe anaphylaxis. This took place in a side ward at St Mary's and fortunately Sister found him, saying, 'Oh you've done silly experiments on yourself, I will give you some adrenaline.' Fortunately this happened about 1 minute after Bill developed anaphylaxis, but by this time he had a sense 'of impending doom', feeling he was going to die. He was pulseless, unable to breathe and speak, his face was swollen, and he had generalised urticaria. Within 90 seconds of receiving the adrenaline, Bill had changed his outlook on the future, and felt he would live. The action of the adrenaline was somewhat short-lived, and he needed a second dose about 10 minutes later. Following such an event most people would have gone home, but Bill carried on working. About 3 hours later he was seeing patients in the clinic. It was a February evening and a nurse was struggling to drive her car up a ramp. Bill offered to help and went outside on a cold and snowy evening. The strenuous exercise of pushing the car caused the symptoms to recur and he required a third dose of adrenaline.

Bill's encounter with the kissing bug did not stop in London, and about 6 years later he was visiting Rio de Janeiro, with his wife, to attend a scientific conference. On the third day they went on a tour of the city, and stopped to take some photographs of the panorama. Bill looked down, and there next to his toe was a kissing bug. Bill was not carrying any adrenaline and swiftly realised there was real danger here. He thought to himself, 'I must get out of here quickly,' which he did, and moved away from the potentially lethal insect.

The Allergy Clinic

The Allergy Clinic at St Mary's became the busiest clinic in the country, attracting patients from all over the country. In 1952 nearly 7500 consultations (including 1140 new patients) took place in the seasonal hay fever clinic and almost 5000 consultations (including 3000 new patients) in the 'clinic for allergic diseases.' Since Freeman was barely to be seen, it was a busy time for Bill. In 1965 over 6000 patients with seasonal hay fever were seen in the clinic, and Bill was asked by the hospital administrators to cut the number to 3000 or less for the following year.

Bill in the Allergy Clinic, St Mary's Hospital

Running the Allergy Clinic at St Mary's, Bill came across both a large number and wide range of patients. On one occasion at the very busy hay fever clinic, a patient arrived suffering from seasonal hay fever, who Bill recognised. It was Peter Lucy, a former prisoner at Blakang Mati, whom Bill had treated for a serious wound on the island, and who was now a stockbroker. 'Oh gracious,' was Lucy's initial comment on seeing Bill, who clearly remembered his patient as being 'rather superior' in the clinic; Bill described him as 'not the best cup of tea.' Bill remembers another occasion, in the early 1960s, when at one clinic all those attending, which included several prominent politicians, had a title of one form or another, except for one gentleman. The latter was later to receive a title, after he had served as Prime Minister in the following decade. Amongst those already titled was a well-known politician, who invariably attended Cabinet meetings on his bicycle, and whose only relief from seasonal hay fever was obtained from swimming in the sea at Eastbourne, allowing him to clear his eyes and nose.

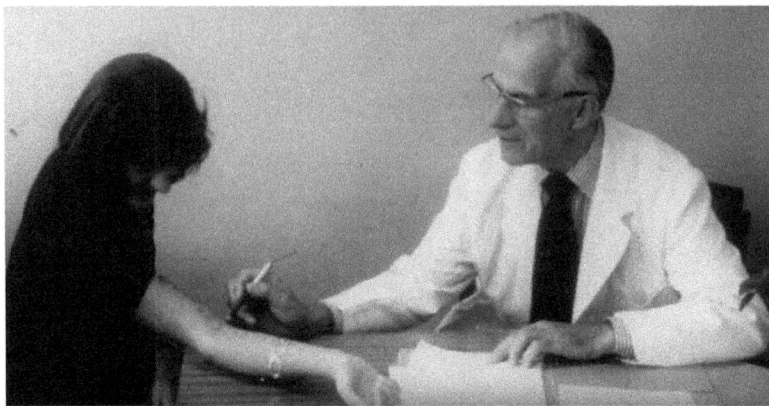

Bill assessing the cutaneous response to allergen testing

When Bill had started back at St Mary's in 1946, John Freeman was aged 68. The National Health Service had yet to be inaugurated (this occurred in the summer of 1948) and, although technically Freeman continued to work and direct the Allergy Clinic, the work fell increasingly to Bill. Over the following 10 years Bill made significant advances in the field of allergy, effectively ran the Allergy Clinic and worked for Sir Alexander Fleming. During all this time his salary came from both private sources and from the Wright-Fleming Institute. In doing so, he was not employed by the NHS, which would provide a problem later. In 1958 the post of Director of the Allergy Clinic was advertised, Freeman, now aged 80, having effectively retired from the role.[140] This is the job that Bill had always envisaged as being his and he was not alone, since Sir Alexander Fleming was of the same opinion. However, by the time

---

140 John Freeman died in 1962.

that the appointment took place, Fleming was dead. Three candidates were selected for interview, Jack Pepys, David Harley and Bill.

Jack Pepys was a South African doctor, who had qualified at Witwatersrand Medical School in 1935 and spent the next 12 years in general practice. Here he developed an interest in allergy, himself suffering quite seriously from atopy. In 1948 he, with his wife and three-year-old son, left the country in response to the racial discrimination of apartheid. They initially settled in Edinburgh from where he gained membership of the Royal College of Physicians, both in London and Edinburgh, in 1949. Keen to pursue a career in allergy, Pepys's first appointment was working part-time with Bill at St Mary's; as Bill was later to point out, following Pepys's illustrious career, 'I gave him his first job in the UK'.[141] Pepys's first area of research interest focussed on the allergic mechanisms involved in eclampsia in patients with tuberculosis. The other applicant was David Harley. Qualifying from Edinburgh in 1929, he had worked as 'First Assistant' to John Freeman in the Allergy Clinic before the war, carrying out research into hay fever. His more recent involvement in this field was, however, more limited. He was appointed as allergist to Moorfields and the Western Eye Hospitals in London, and spent just one day a week in the clinic at St Mary's. The rest of his time was taken up either in his private consulting rooms in London, or at his farm in Wiltshire.

The interview panel was chaired by Professor Albert Neuberger, Professor of Chemical Pathology. Neuberger was born in Germany where he later studied medicine. On graduation he undertook research in Berlin at the same time as Ernst Chain; they both became lifelong friends. Forced to leave Germany in 1933 he settled in Britain, working in the Department of Biochemistry at Cambridge, where his first PhD student was Frederick Sanger. He then moved to the National Institute

---

141 In 1967, Jack Pepys was appointed Professor of Clinical Immunology at the Brompton Hospital, and made significant contributions to the field of allergy, especially in the area of allergic lung diseases. His son, Sir Mark Pepys, became Professor of Medicine at University College, London, and was elected a Fellow of the Royal Society in 1998.

for Medical Research, Mill Hill, before joining St Mary's in 1955. Bill was the last of the three to be interviewed, and it went well; he was appointed to the position. He was later to learn that the other candidates had been asked about the history of allergy, and were asked to whom the line 'Allergy is immunity gone wrong' was attributed.[142] This had been proposed by von Pirquet in 1903, but neither Pepys nor Harley knew the answer. Bill did, but for some reason was not asked that question. Bill's appointment to a consultancy position was his first job in the NHS, and there were two immediate problems. The first related to the fact that neither he, nor his previous employers, had contributed to a pension, so this had to be remedied. The second was the nature of Bill's title; there was a move by the University of London to have the post titled as a bacteriologist or failing that, an immunologist. Bill refused, he was an allergy specialist, and his position was Physician in Allergic Disorders.

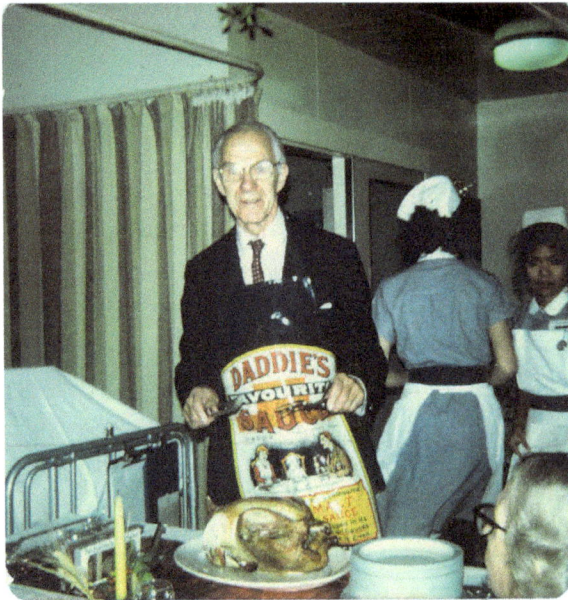

Bill carving turkey on the ward. Christmas 1974, St Mary's Hospital.

---

142 In 1972, Bill gave the Presidential address to the Section of Clinical Immunology and Allergy of the Royal Society of Medicine. It was entitled 'Allergy: Immunity gone wrong'.

Now a consultant Bill was in a position to establish a private practice. As was the accepted practice he rented consulting rooms close to Harley Street. He shared rooms at 38 Devonshire Street with three other doctors, including Neville Southwell. Bill practised from Devonshire Street until the winter of 1962/63 when he moved to 139 Harley Street. The timing of the move was most fortuitous, since just a few weeks later, the spotlight of the world's press fell on 38 Devonshire Street, courtesy of another resident, Dr Stephen Ward, an osteopath. Ward had become embroiled and entwined in the relationship between the Secretary of State for War, John Profumo, and Miss Christine Keeler, a young lady who was living with Ward. At the same time, Miss Keeler was involved in a relationship with a Soviet diplomat (a relationship which, allegedly, had been engineered by the British Security Services). The resignation of John Profumo, for having lied to the House of Commons, was followed by the arrest of Ward who was charged with 'living off immoral earnings.' The trial took place at the Old Bailey in the summer of 1963 under the full glare of the press and was overshadowed by Ward committing suicide towards the end of the trial.

CHAPTER 9

NOT THE RETIRING SORT

A New Home

In 1977 Bill retired from St Mary's Hospital after almost 45 years' association with the institution. He had reached the statutory retirement age, but was far from ready to stop working as a doctor. His association with St Mary's did not end on his retirement and a few years later, the hospital renamed the Allergy Clinic as the Frankland Allergy Clinic, which was to specialise in treating patients with allergies whom their own doctors found it difficult to manage. The clinic was officially opened by Professor Margaret Turner-Warwick, with Bill in attendance.

Having retired from St Mary's, Bill moved to Guy's Hospital, where he was offered an honorary contract by Professor Maurice Lessof, Professor of Medicine. Bill always recognised this gesture as being exceptionally kind and one he would remember throughout his life. It allowed him to continue practising in the field of allergy within the NHS, and train younger doctors, for a further 20 years. At the same time, he was offered an honorary contract at the Middlesex Hospital by Dr Jonathan Brostoff, who had been Bill's registrar. This appointment lasted for just over three years, during which time Bill attended each Monday afternoon, having earlier taken a clinic at Guy's. It did not take long before Bill found that Brostoff was away from the clinic on days he was due to see certain 'demanding' patients. They were expecting to see Brostoff at the start of the clinic, but in his absence, Bill saw them as and when his schedule permitted. As such he encountered a number of irate patients, who appreciated neither waiting, nor seeing Bill. Moreover, Bill found Brostoff's relationship with other doctors was not to the standard that Bill had come to expect, and so made the decision to end his association with the Middlesex.

At Guy's Bill extended his areas of academic interest in allergy. He had a long-standing interest in allergies to insects, dating back as far as 1949 when he treated an airline pilot who developed an allergy to the Nimitti fly during trips to Khartoum. Bill had encountered numerous examples of insect allergies closer to home, and had been responsible for desensitising many patients with allergic symptoms, either to venoms or to other parts of an insect. Amongst his many patients was a man who was the keeper of locusts at the Anti-Locust Research Centre, housed on the top floor of the Natural History Museum. He developed a severe allergic rhinitis and asthma in response to locust faeces, so much so that it prevented him from carrying out his duties. Bill successfully desensitised the man, who not only returned to work, but later became Director of the Research Centre. Bill also encountered more than 30 patients suffering from an allergy to maggots. All were fishermen who, on returning home from a day's fishing, developed rhinitis, local urticaria and asthma. In seven patients a contact allergy developed to the insects. The cause here was the men having maggots on their fingers during the day, and then not washing their hands before urinating (usually having drunk a lot of beer during the day). The result was development of marked penile swelling.

When Bill arrived at Guy's insect venom immunotherapy was commencing, Purified bee and wasp venoms had recently been shown to be effective, unlike the 'whole-body' insect extracts previously used for skin testing and immunotherapy. The department at Guy's was active in trying to find out how immunotherapy worked and how to evaluate its efficacy. Most patients were evaluated at Guy's and started on venom immunotherapy, which was then continued by their own general practitioners. However, in 1986 this approach was stopped because of safety concerns. The Committee on Safety of Medicines (CSM) recommended restricting immunotherapy to hospital clinics with resuscitation facilities and making patients wait for two hours under supervision after each injection. This was a big problem for patients, and a deputation, including Bill, was sent to the CSM, to persuade them to relax the conditions, specifically the 'two-hour wait' rule. Bill, who had significant experience in this field, made no secret of his opinion that the CSM had overreacted. He followed his oral evidence with a detailed letter to the *British Medical Journal*, in which, drawing on his vast experience, he rejected much of the evidence that had been used by the CSM in coming to their decision. He highlighted how they had failed to identify variations in the incidence of adverse reactions to different products, and pointed out that most patients were unwilling to wait for two hours following a desensitising injection, regardless of whether full resuscitation facilities were available.

Whilst at Guy's Bill also started to identify and treat patients with the condition of peanut allergy and saw over 100 children suffering from this condition. He noted how in other parts of the world, for example, in Israel, where children were exposed to peanuts very early in life, the incidence of this condition was virtually nil. He has suggested that early exposure of children (before the age of 1) to peanut butter should be encouraged in order to prevent development of the allergic condition.

Reporting Rare Cases

In 1908, the first recorded case of egg desensitisation was published by Dr Alfred Schofield, the subject was a young boy acutely sensitive to eggs. Bill saw many patients during his career suffering from this type of allergy and one in particular stood out. The patient was a man whom, by the age of 21, was unable to eat any food outside of his own home because of the fear of his egg allergy. He was so sensitive that an anaphylactic response could be stimulated by just coming into contact with an apparently clean utensil which had previously had egg on it. Bill hospitalised the man, and undertook a course of rapid desensitisation involving 52 injections, as always, ensuring that adrenaline was available for the man at his bedside. The treatment was a success: the man proceeded to monthly injections, and wrote to Bill, telling him that he had 'changed his life.' Many years later, the patient, now in his eighties, contacted Bill seeking advice regarding his own 6-month-old granddaughter who had developed an allergic disorder.

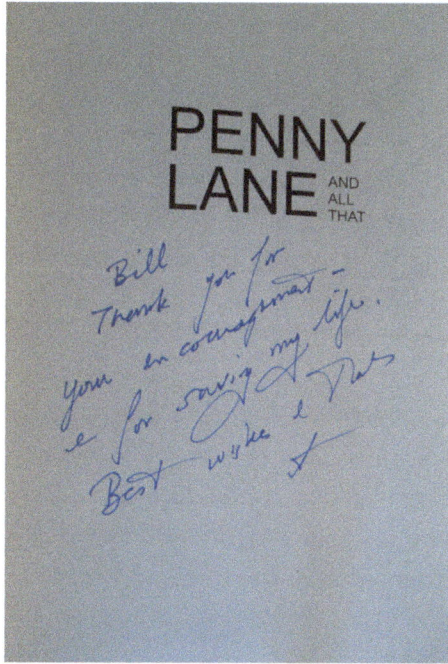

A message from one of many grateful patients.
(From Penny Lane and All That by Ann Carlton)

During this period of 'retirement' Bill was able to write up a number of unusual cases which he had encountered in his career, many representing small series. One involved a 33-year-old lady who had been married, and had three children. Following a divorce she remarried, but living with her second husband she developed significant health problems and remained sterile. She described how, about five minutes after intercourse, she developed acute vaginal irritation along with abdominal pain, and urticaria of the face, head and neck. If her husband used a condom, symptoms were absent. Bill investigated and found no evidence of any skin response by the patient to material from her husband. However, placing a small volume of her husband's semen onto her vaginal mucosa led rapidly to oedema developing. Further studies identified that she had a rapid onset immune response to glycoprotein present in the semen. In all Bill treated ten women with semen sensitivity. One lady, aged almost 50 years, was completely desensitised and as Bill commented, 'she was a devout Roman Catholic.' Although affecting only a small number of patients, the condition of semen sensitivity was one that has profound effects on those affected, and as Bill was to later comment, 'Lovemaking is not a common indication for having adrenaline available at the bedside!'

In 2014 Bill described the first case in the world of an allergy to human saliva. The patient was a 25-year-old lady who reacted with immediate local urticaria of the face and swelling of the eyes when kissed by her partner. She had developed asthma five years previously, following a traumatic divorce, a condition which was exacerbated by her and her partner's heavy smoking. The patient also suffered from manic depression, made worse at times by steroid treatment for her asthma. Bill demonstrated a positive skin test to her partner's saliva. He also evaluated the same saliva in both normal and atopic patients, and interestingly observed that none responded to the challenge. Bill's patient was very willing to try immunotherapy using her partner's saliva. Unfortunately this case did not end well, as the patient failed to keep a follow-up appointment and it was later learnt that she had taken a fatal overdose.

Recognition and Awards

Throughout his career Bill has received numerous awards in recognition for his work and contributions. In April 2018, aged 106, he was presented with a Lifetime Achievement Award from Allergy UK. The event was held at Haberdashers' Hall, London, and following the presentation Bill stood and gave the organisers and their guests a short history of his involvement in allergy and anaphylaxis. Amongst the other recipients of awards that night was 6-year-old Arlo Gillard-Moss, recipient of the Child Allergy Hero Award, who on meeting Bill said, 'Meeting Doctor Frankland was awesome!'

Bill meeting HRH The Duchess of Gloucester, Patron of Asthma UK

Bill with Arlo Gillard-Moss, April 2018

Bill is personally closely associated with an award given by the British Society for Allergy and Clinical Immunology (BSACI), 'for outstanding services in the field of clinical allergy in the UK.' This is the William Frankland Award which was first awarded in 1999. On that occasion the recipient was Bill's friend, Dr Harry Morrow-Brown, a Consultant Chest Physician from Derby whom Bill first met in 1959. Born in Scotland, Morrow-Brown had made major advances in the treatment of asthma. He had been the first to identify which asthmatic patients would, or would not, respond to oral steroid therapy. He developed and hosted 'The Charles

Blackley International Symposia on Clinical Aspects of Allergic Diseases' in the 1970s and early 1980s, and was responsible for the introduction of aerosol steroid therapy (beclomethasone) for the treatment of asthma. Like Bill, Morrow-Brown had a major interest in aerobiology.

Bill has regularly attended BSACI's annual meeting, now held in October each year, and presented the William Frankland Award. He continues to contribute to the academic programme and learn of advances in the fields of allergy and clinical immunology. He has been involved with the organisation from its very earliest days, and seen it grow from a very small group to a current membership of over 800.

Bill presenting the William Frankland Award 2015 to Dr Adam Fox

The origins of BSACI can be traced back to a meeting held at St Mary's Hospital, on 24 January 1948. In 1947, Dr Vera Walker an eye specialist from Oxford with an interest in allergy, wrote to John Freeman suggesting the formation of an allergy society. A meeting was planned and advertised widely. At the meeting in January 1948, there were two speakers. John Freeman spoke on hay fever, and Sir Henry Dale[143] spoke on more general aspects of allergy. The meeting was well attended and attracted about 50 people from both clinical and scientific specialities. Dale effectively

---

143 Dale was awarded the Nobel Prize in Physiology or Medicine in 1936. He was President of the Royal Society 1940-45, and President of the Royal Society of Medicine 1948-50.

ran the meeting and, after he had spoken, said that if they were to form a society, they must first agree a definition of allergy. He told those present that they should write down their own definitions and send these to Bill, whom Dale had just unilaterally made the Secretary of the society, a post he held for many years. Despite his *modus operandi*, Bill found Dale's support a great stimulus for the society. Bill received about a dozen responses to Dale's request; most were completely useless, but one, from a doctor in Scotland, stood out. He defined allergy as a 'grossly overused word by the lay public.' Although not a definition, Bill felt that this observation was still valid some 70 years later. Although the British Association of Allergists was formed in 1948, it did not have a written constitution until 1951. Others have commented that in those early days, that it was 'the tremendous enthusiasm' of Bill which pushed the society forwards. Members of the society at this time included Dr D.A. Williams, from Cardiff, Bruce Pearson from King's College Hospital and Blair Macaulay from Liverpool. In 1962 the society changed its name to the British Allergy Society and Bill was President from 1963 to 1966, being succeeded by Jack Pepys. In 1973 the society changed its name once more, to become the British Society for Allergy and Clinical Immunology.

Bill at preliminary meeting of the British Association of Allergists November 1947

Following their initial meeting in 1948, Bill had several dealings with Sir Henry Dale, whom he described as a 'delightful man, but one who could be very definite in his opinions.' On one occasion Bill challenged Dale's research, asking if there was any evidence that Dale's findings from experimental animals were directly applicable to man. Dale was furious on being challenged on this issue. Bill met Dale at the 3rd International Meeting of Allergology held in Paris in 1958 and they started talking. Bill mentioned that he had supplied some human tissues to a research worker, Dr W.E. Brocklehurst in Aberdeen who was interested in anaphylaxis. Brocklehurst was the first to describe SRS-A (slow-reacting-substances of anaphylaxis) a highly potent bronchoconstrictor (over 600 times more potent than histamine). Brocklehurst had studied SRS-A in animals, and wished to confirm his findings in human tissue. He had approached Bill, and asked if he could supply any human lung tissue. At the time, Bill was treating a patient, a lady, who had a sensitivity to grass pollen and was also suffering from 'open' tuberculosis, the latter being resistant to antibiotics. Bill persuaded her that she should have a lobectomy to remove the infected lung, an operation which was performed by Mr Lance Bromley, Consultant Cardiothoracic Surgeon. On the day of surgery, Bill waited for the lung to be removed, then immediately placed it on ice before securely packing it. He took it to Euston Station and having identified the train to Aberdeen, placed it in the guard's van. The guard asked if the package was urine, to which Bill replied, 'No, lung.' The sample arrived safely and Brocklehurst demonstrated that SRS-A was just as active in human tissue as in animal tissue. From this, Brocklehurst reported in 1963, 'we can understand why antihistamines do not help in allergic asthma and that SRS-A are major factors in asthma.'

Having informed Dale of Brocklehurst's preliminary results at the meeting in Paris, Bill was surprised to find Dale speaking the following day about SRS-A, and going way over time in the presentation. Despite this, Dale failed to acknowledge the input of either Bill or Brocklehurst in the discovery. Bills' disappointment was partly assuaged later that day at the conference dinner. This was held at the Louvre, and marked by 'much champagne and good food.' Dale again made an impression, when he starting telling, at times, risqué stories about a number of acquaintances and colleagues.

Bill and Sir Henry Dale, the Louvre Paris, 1958.

Sailing and Inhaling

In 2002, on his 90th birthday, Bill was the focus of the BSACI newsletter, in which he gave a 'potted' autobiography. He drew special attention to two colleagues in the field of allergy, namely Jack Pepys and Roger Altounyan. Bill had come to know the latter well, and it transpired that they both had strong connections not only to allergy, but also to the Lake District. Roger was born in 1922 into an Anglo-Armenian family in Aleppo, Syria, where his father, Dr E.H.R. 'Ernest' Altounyan, ran the family-owned hospital, established by his own father. Ernest was married to an English lady, Dora Collingwood, whose family home was at Lanehead, Coniston, in the Lake District. In 1928 Ernest and Dora took their children, Taqui, Susan, Mavis (always known as 'Titty'), Roger and Brigit, on holiday to Coniston. Here they stayed at Bank Ground Farm, near to Dora's family.

The Collingwoods knew a journalist, Arthur Ransome, who had, many years earlier, actually proposed marriage to Dora, and now lived nearby with his wife. Some 10 years earlier, Ransome had reported on the Russian Revolution and whilst in Russia met his wife, Evgenia Shelepina, Trotsky's personal secretary. By coincidence, Ernest and Arthur Ransome had learnt to sail together in 1904, and in the summer of 1928 they bought two dinghies, named *Swallow* and *Mavis*, and taught the Altounyan children to sail on Coniston Water. At the end of the holiday, the children gave Ransome a pair of red slippers for his 45th birthday, before returning to Aleppo. Ransome reflected on the summer's activities and used this as the basis for his book, *Swallows and Amazons*, in which the Altounyan family are portrayed as the Walker family, and Roger Altounyan as Roger Walker. The book was published in 1930, and became an international bestseller, remaining so to this day. Bill only read the book many years later.

In 1932 Ransome visited the Altounyans in Aleppo, taking with him a gift of a small dinghy. The same year Roger returned to Britain for schooling. In 1939 he returned to Aleppo but with the outbreak of war, joined the Royal Air Force. Posted to Rhodesia (now Zimbabwe), he learnt to fly. Having gained his 'wings' he initially served with Bomber Command before serving as an instructor in fighter aircraft, becoming a highly qualified pilot and instructor. After the war he followed his father's footsteps and undertook medical training, entering Emmanuel College Cambridge in 1946, then moving to the Middlesex Hospital, qualifying in 1952. It was whilst at the Middlesex that Roger suffered his first severe asthma attack. In 1951, as a final-year medical student, he married and he and his wife spent the first two nights of their honeymoon camping on an island in Coniston Water. On qualifying he moved back to Aleppo to work in the family hospital. The political situation in Syria changed for the Altounyans after the Suez Crisis of 1956 and he, and his family, were forced to leave and move to Britain. Here he was appointed as medical liaison officer for Bengers Pharmaceutical Company, at Holmes Chapel, Cheshire. His duties involved a combination of research and clinical work and he ran three outpatient clinics for patients with asthma at Monsall Hospital, Manchester. His research was initially targeted at development of injectable iron formulations used in the prevention of neonatal anaemia in piglets. Before long his attention focussed on the control of asthma, and he researched the properties of khellin. This is derived from the plant *Ammi visnaga* and has been used in a soup for over 5000 years by the Egyptians to relieve spasm. Central to his studies, Roger Altounyan used himself as a 'guinea pig' for evaluating the efficacy of compounds extracted from khellin. He would simulate an asthmatic attack in himself (using dander from guinea pigs) and then administer the test compound. Although initially supported by Bengers, after two years he was told that work was to stop. Convinced that there was an active compound to be identified, the work continued in secret, much being undertaken at Monsall Hospital. In 1965, after eight years' work, during which time over 600 compounds had been evaluated and Roger Altounyan had subjected himself to some 600 allergic challenges, an active compound was finally identified. This was disodium cromoglycate, which was shown to prevent asthmatic attacks if given before the allergic challenge, acting to stabilise mast cells responsible for the release of histamine. It was given the name *Intal* since it 'interfered with allergy'. Writing about his discovery 10 years later, Roger noted the changing landscape of drug development and considered that if such a discovery had been made 'with present-day regulations it would have taken generations of chemists, pharmacologists and physicians to have achieved the same objective, and the amount of paper and red-tape would have been incalculable.'

Bengers was acquired by Fisons and regulatory approval was granted for *Intal* in 1968. As a powder there was, however, a major problem for delivering it into the lungs. Again it was Roger Altounyan who found a solution, developing the Spinhaler. This small piece of equipment aided aerosol delivery of the powder, with its design being based upon his observations of propeller action during his time with the RAF. In 1969, a symposium on Disodium Cromoglycate in Allergic Airways Disease was held at the Royal Society of Medicine, and the proceedings, edited by Jack Pepys and Bill Frankland, were published the following year. Not only did Bill meet Roger in the field of allergy, but would often meet him socially. When Bill was returning from the Lake District, having visited his family, including Aunt Ella and his brother Jack, he would often stop at the Altounyan's home to break the journey. Bill remained in contact with Roger Altounyan for many years, during which time Roger's health progressively deteriorated. He would spend the winters in Australia, in warmer climes, to help his asthmatic condition, itself not helped by his smoking. In his later years he required ambulatory oxygen. He died in 1987.

The Most Grateful Patient

Over his career Bill has treated thousands of patients, and many have been extremely grateful for his professional help. Writing to him, one lady described how the treatment he had prescribed, a course of desensitisation for seasonal hay fever, had prevented her from committing suicide. However, in his own words, one patient stands out as being the most grateful of all, one who was not treated in this country, but abroad.

One Thursday morning Bill was in the outpatients department at St Mary's Hospital when he was told that there was a telephone call for him. He never answered the telephone during outpatients, but was told it was 'very important as it was an embassy calling.' Bill took the call; it was the Iraqi Embassy asking him to go to Baghdad that weekend. His immediate response was that it was not possible as he was busy, but he could go the following weekend. They agreed to his timetable. He asked about a visa, and was told that this would be arranged. An official from the Iraqi Embassy collected his passport and arranged for the relevant authorisations. At this stage he was still none the wiser about the reason for his trip.

On arrival at Baghdad Airport he was directed to the diplomatic channel, thereby avoiding any queues, and subsequently taken to the Presidential Palace. Here it took over 20 minutes to gain access to the building and Bill asked why it was taking so long. He was told that 'they had to be very careful with security.' Once over this hurdle he met his patient, the President, Saddam Hussein, who had recently come to power, and a man who Bill had never heard of before. Bill asked why he had been summoned to Baghdad, and was told that it was because 'he was the best allergist in Europe.' The president did not speak English, so Bill had to take a history through an interpreter, the president's niece, who spoke with a slight American accent. He learnt that the president has been diagnosed with asthma and fungal spore sensitivity, and had been receiving desensitisation injections, but his condition was getting worse. Bill examined the president and soon concluded that his patient was not suffering from asthma, nor from any allergic condition, according to 'any of the accepted definitions.' He proved the latter by performing a skin challenge test which was negative, and lung function tests. Bill's diagnosis was quite straightforward as to the cause of his patient's condition; if he was not eating, praying or sleeping he was smoking – about 40 cigarettes a day. Bill's advice was clear and to the point, he told the president that if he carried on smoking 'he would not be head of state in two years' time.' In retrospect this was quite a stupid thing to say, since Bill later learnt that, about five years later, a health minister disagreed with Saddam Hussein in Cabinet. They both left the room and Saddam Hussein personally shot the man dead.

Bill was not convinced that the president would follow his advice, but the next morning returned to the airport as planned. As Bill was sitting in the VIP lounge – he was probably the first person to use the new facility – a little man came up and talked to him. He asked when Bill would be returning to see his patient. (Saddam Hussein's name was never mentioned.) Believing the advice given the previous day would have fallen on deaf ears, Bill replied that he would not see his patient again. In fact, Bill was wrong, and Saddam Hussein had given up smoking straight after their meeting.

Some three months later, Bill was invited to lunch by one very grateful patient. The invitation from President Hussein was to Bill, his wife and up to 5 children, although first-class travel would only be offered for all the party if just one child came. Bill, Pauline and their youngest daughter, Hilary (aged 19), set off to Baghdad. Here they were entertained by the president. Bill commented on the fine grand piano and the president asked if he played. 'No,' was the reply, and the president asked Bill if Pauline played. Again the answer was no but, Bill said,

Hilary did. Hilary said she was too embarrassed to play without sheet music, at which point palace staff produced a range of music, including some by the president's favourite composer, Mozart. Hilary gave an impromptu recital after which Bill asked the president if he played. 'No, but I am learning,' was the response. They sat down for lunch at the end of which Saddam Hussein said, 'All women like shopping' and told Pauline and Hilary that they would be taken shopping by his entourage. 'Go anywhere you, like and buy what you wish, I will pay for it.' Bill accompanied them on the trip, and chose a set of engraved silver napkin rings. These were to replace others recently lost from their home in London, when it had been burgled. Bill asked the president if he could visit the Hanging Gardens of Babylon. This was initially met with resistance, but the president relented. The following day all three guests travelled in the presidential car to the historic site. They passed a number of high-security airbases, as well as significant amounts of military equipment being transported around the country, as well as seeing camels all along the route. Finally reaching their destination, Bill was very disappointed to find no evidence of the ancient historical site, merely 'modern tarmac.'

This was Bill's last contact with Saddam Hussein, although to this day, Bill still uses the napkin rings acquired on the trip. Saddam Hussein's portrayal on the world stage changed markedly in the years after Bill treated him, earning a reputation as a ruthless dictator. In many subsequent interviews Bill has been asked about treating Saddam Hussein. Speaking on BBC1 in 2012 he pointed out that, regardless of who his patient was 'be they a beggar or a head of state', it made no difference to him who, as a doctor, wanted to help them. However, treating Saddam Hussein, and talking about it, led to a complaint to the General Medical Council. A doctor in Ireland wrote and complained that Bill had broken patient confidentiality by naming his patient (even though the patient had died in 2006). Bill wrote a somewhat humble apology.

Bill visited Baghdad on a number of occasions to support and review an allergy clinic that he had helped to set up, but did not meet the president again. In the autumn of 1980 Bill was asked if he would visit for 4-5 weeks. Both he and Pauline felt this was too long a period and he wrote back suggesting a trip of 4-5 days. Two days after sending the letter news was received that war had broken out between Iran and Iraq; Bill never visited Iraq again.

Travels Abroad

Throughout his career Bill has travelled widely, and certainly following the publication of his seminal papers in the 1950s he was a sought-after speaker at conferences. Bill thoroughly enjoyed visiting numerous parts of the world and forming, and renewing, acquaintances with others working in the field of allergy, and has continued to do so as a centenarian. Amongst Bill's many trips to scientific conferences, several stood out and were remembered with great affection. Not least was a meeting of the European Academy of Allergy and Clinical Immunology, held in Rome in May 1975. At this time Bill was President-elect of the society, and the local organiser was Professor Serafini, whose father was the personal doctor to Pope Paul VI. Before the conference Bill was informed that attendees may receive an invitation to visit the Vatican. They were advised that, if this happened, the Pope may come and talk to them, and that accompanying ladies needed to be suitably dressed to meet the pontiff. An invitation was indeed forthcoming and Bill, along with others from the conference, made their way to the Vatican. Having been admitted by the Swiss Guards, they entered the drawing room, as the Pope was just finishing a speech delivered from the balcony overlooking St Peter's Square. He entered the drawing room and came over to talk to the delegates. He then gave a short sermon, twice; first in Italian and then again in French. After the sermon the Pope came and shook hands with all the delegates in the front row, which included Bill. The Pope only spoke to one person, Bill. The Pope spoke in Italian and Bill replied that he did not know any Italian, to which the Pope said, in perfect English, 'No matter, I always like to talk to people in their own language.'

Bill at the Vatican, 1975

A colleague of Bill's, a Jewish doctor from Dublin, was also at the conference. He had with him a rosary, given to him by his housekeeper, a lady from Dublin, who had asked for it to be blessed by the Pope. Certainly the rosary made its way to the Vatican, although whether it had actually been blessed by the pontiff is uncertain. However, Bill's colleague returned to Dublin and proudly gave it back to the owner. After the conference Bill sent a copy of the photograph of him shaking hands with the Pope to his colleague in Dublin. He had this framed and displayed it prominently in his consulting rooms where it was readily seen by all his private patients. Bill was intrigued why a Jew would do this, and was told that, as well as displaying the photograph, the doctor had doubled his consultation fees.

At the close of the conference the president of the society would normally give a farewell speech. However, the President, Professor Charpin, was unable to attend and Bill stepped in, at Professor Charpin's request, to give a final address of thanks. He stressed that the scientific side of the conference was very memorable but suggested that most delegates would have forgotten most of it in 10 years' time. But, he suggested, the visit to the Vatican and meeting the Pope would stay with everyone involved for the rest of their lives. Over 40 years later, Bill still recalled the occasion very clearly. His speech that day was not without controversy, since he received a rather rude letter from the chairman of the scientific committee of the conference, stating that Bill's speech 'did not include enough about the congress, and too much about the Pope.'

Other trips also stood out, and one in particular was a trip to Georgia in the Soviet Union, where Bill learnt the true meaning of being a 'VIP.' He received an invitation to attend a scientific meeting held in the city of Sukhumi. The invitation was worded in Russian throughout, and it was only after Bill finally found someone to translate it that he realised the true nature of the invitation. The conference was on the subject of asthma. Having visited the Russian Embassy in London to clarify visa requirements, Bill flew to Georgia. He was one of just two foreign speakers, the other being an Italian doctor whom he met on his arrival at the airport. They were conveyed to their hotel which was shrouded in scaffolding. After being shown to their rooms, his colleague went out for a walk. On returning barely one hour later he found his room had been raided, and his money and passport had been stolen, the thieves having gained access via the scaffolding. Bill meanwhile had stayed in his room, and after half an hour the telephone rang; a man introduced himself, 'I am your interpreter.' Bill met the man, who had previously studied for a PhD on the works of Shakespeare at St Petersburg, and spoke excellent English, as well as seemingly knowing Shakespeare 'backwards.' Bill was to be lecturing on the subject of pulmonary aspergillosis, and speaking in English; his lecture would be translated for the audience. He soon found that his translator could cope with all the words except one, aspergillosis. A prominent feature of the conference was numerous lectures by a number of 'fat Russian women', lectures that were, in Bill's view, simply awful. He was not alone in this view, as even the interpreter agreed, saying that the women were giving outdated information.

After the conference had finished there was an official dinner, to which Bill's interpreter was invited. The dinner was memorable for two reasons: lots of speeches and lots of vodka, so much so that the interpreter became very drunk. Fortunately this happened after he had completed his role of interpreting for Bill. Bill later learnt the reason for the man's behaviour was that vodka was very expensive in the town, but was free at the dinner.

Following the conference Bill had to fly back to Moscow. Time was moving on and he was worried that he would miss his flight. He need not have worried since he later learnt that flight timetables in Russia were all based on Moscow time, and not local time. Arriving in Moscow he waited for half an hour for a taxi which took him to his hotel, and, on registering, was informed that 'food had to be paid for in US dollars'. Assigned a 'minder', Bill was to remember Moscow as a city where he learnt what being a VIP really meant. He was taken to the ballet and was slightly taken aback when his minder ejected a man from his seat, making space for Bill. Although an apparently kind act, Bill found himself very close to the percussion section, and found the performance, overall, very noisy. The following day, Bill was to fly home. On arriving at the airport he was informed that the flight was full. He need not have worried, since his minder arranged for a passenger to be removed, so making way for Bill; being a VIP had its advantages.

On another occasion, Bill was invited to Turku in Finland in order to act as an advisor on pollen counts, and act as an external examiner for a PhD thesis. He remembered very well how the candidate, a young lady, who was quite nervous, was asked a question by the chairman of the panel, an academic from Prague. The candidate admitted that she did not know the answer; she was in good company, since neither did Bill. However, it came as a surprise that chairman was also ignorant of the answer. Despite this uncomfortable start, the candidate had presented a very interesting thesis which she defended well.

Bill has visited Cairo on 12 occasions over the years and visited many friends and colleagues. Two stood out. Professor El-Hefney was the Professor of Paediatrics at Cairo University and she published papers with Bill on allergy to dust mites. Professor El-Mehary worked at Ain Shams University. In the early 1950s, when visiting Cairo, Bill was asked by Professor El-Mehary if he would examine President Gamal Nasser who was suffering from hypertension and diabetes. Since Bill did not consider himself an expert in either of these conditions, he declined the invitation. El-Mehary's brother was head of the Cairo Police and when Bill went on holiday with his family to Cairo, they arrived to a VIP welcome at the airport, where they passed through immigration in just a few minutes.

Bill with friends at Shepheard's Hotel, Cairo.
On the reverse it reads: '30 March 1966, Midnight. To Whom It May Concern. This is to certify that Dr Frankland has never seen this girl before, and probably will not see her again.'

Trips to Egypt have allowed Bill to explore numerous historical sites. In the early 1960s he described a trip he had made on the River Nile to Aswan, to see the recently completed Aswan Dam:

It was very hot -95 degrees. There were no mad dogs, only me ashore to visit the Aga Khan's Mausoleum on top of the nearby hill. He had been asked to be buried here as he considered it the most beautiful spot that he knew. I skirted round and then above the Begum's villa and finally reached the top of the

341

hill. The long drawn out wailing of someone reciting the Koran came from inside what seemed to be a deserted building. I took off my shoes and went in. Not more than ten people are allowed inside at a time, so a notice said, in amongst other languages, English. But it was so hot no one else was there, so I sat crossed legged in front of the pure white tomb. The pinkish purple stonework gives an overall shade of brown to a building of bare simplicity. The carving in the wall by the tomb is of intricate Arabic lacework and very beautiful, but to me the building did not seem quite an adequate memorial compared with a very simple one that is renewed at sunrise every day by the Begum when she is staying at the villa. This is one large red rose placed in a small glass vase on the tomb.

The begum had left a rose on the morning of Bill's visit, and she had then departed to Paris on a shopping expedition.

On visits to Kuwait Bill helped establish a national pollen count. Although mostly desert, with little, if any, grass, many trees are to be found which produce pollen in spring and autumn, causing allergic conditions. There has been continuous recording of the pollen count since Bill helped establish the service, the only break being in 1990 and 1991. This, ironically, followed the decision by Bill's former patient, Saddam Hussein, to invade Kuwait. Iraqi forces stole the air sampling machine, but after the liberation of the country a new machine was installed. This was placed on the top of the hospital buildings and on a subsequent visit Bill found it somewhat hazardous to reach the roof and collect samples from the apparatus. The Kuwaitis established good links with Bill and would regularly send slides for him to comment on.

The King Faisal International Prize is an award made by the King Faisal Foundation, and was established in 1979. There are five categories for an award, including medicine. In the annual nomination cycle, the Foundation initially identifies a topic area within the category and seeks nominations therein. In 1999 the topic in medicine was allergic diseases, and Bill was asked to be one of the judges. Travelling to Riyadh he, along with the other judges, was entertained royally but had to work hard to evaluate the submissions. Over 40 applications had been received and an initial scrutiny reduced this to 8 which were assessed by Bill and his co-judges. After two days of discussion and deliberation it was decided that the prize be awarded to Professor Patrick Holt from Australia.

However, it was realised that he was not a clinician, and so not eligible for the prize. The judging panel reconvened for a further half-day and it was decided that the King Faisal Prize for Medicine would be awarded to Professor Stephen Holgate from Southampton, England. Although not viewed as being as prestigious as the Nobel Prize (and not being of quite the same monetary value) many of those who have been awarded the prize have later been awarded the Nobel Prize.

Bill's work was not quite finished and he was asked by the Chairman of the panel, a former Professor of Anatomy in Riyadh who 'spoke perfect English', if Bill would please draft a short summary about the winner which would be read out at a ceremony later that day. Bill was limited to 250 words, and reached his target. Handing it to the Chairman, before it was to be translated into Arabic, the man congratulated Bill on the statement. He went on: 'But… there is just one issue….do you mind if I correct your English?' He proceeded to tell Bill that there was an issue with his use of English in one sentence, which he wished to correct.

On this visit, Bill was also asked to examine a royal patient. This was the sister of the King, who was dying from pulmonary aspergillosis. Bill found himself somewhat constrained in undertaking his clinical examination, being only allowed to examine her chest from the back, and not from the front.

Judging the King Faisal Prize, Riyadh 1999

343

Bill's travels have also taken him to the Far East, having visited Singapore on a number of occasions, most recently in 2014 when invited to Singapore by an academic colleague. This gave him the opportunity not only to share his vast clinical knowledge, but also to revisit many of the sites on the island which he had visited whilst serving with the RAMC. Along with a visit to Kranji War Memorial and the Changi Museum, Bill was entertained to lunch at the Singapore Cricket Club (later described by Bill as the 'snobbiest club' in Singapore) where he was able to tell current-day members about his time there 72 years earlier. Then he, along with two other doctors, was given the task of destroying all the stores of alcohol in the days immediately prior to the Fall of Singapore.

Bill at Changi Museum, Singapore

On another occasion when visiting the Far East Bill went to the Bangkok Allergy Clinic in Thailand, a clinic which had been established by an ENT specialist. A former student, she had spent 6 months working with Bill at St Mary's and then returned to establish the first allergy clinic in Bangkok. Here he was most impressed to see 12 doctors in the clinic, seeing over 100 new patients in one morning, despite water leaking into the clinic as a result of local flooding. Following this, he travelled by train to Kanchanaburi, the site of the infamous Bridge over the River Kwai (or more correctly the River Kwai Yai). This was Bill's first visit to the Burma Railway, although if fate had been different in November 1942 he may well have been sent there as a prisoner, part of one of many working parties sent by the Japanese to construct the railway. Kanchanaburi was a major southern base during the construction of the railway, and hosts two Commonwealth War Graves cemeteries, one at Kanchanaburi and the other nearby at Chungkai. Nearly 9000 Allied servicemen, who died whilst constructing the railway, are buried there. This includes 35 members of the RAMC. In all, some 15,000 prisoners and nearly 100,000 civilians (also used as slave labour) died as a result of disease, malnutrition, exhaustion and mistreatment during the railway's construction. As many have pointed out subsequently, one man was lost for very sleeper laid on 'Death Railway'.

Bill on the bridge over the River Kwai. Kanchanaburi.

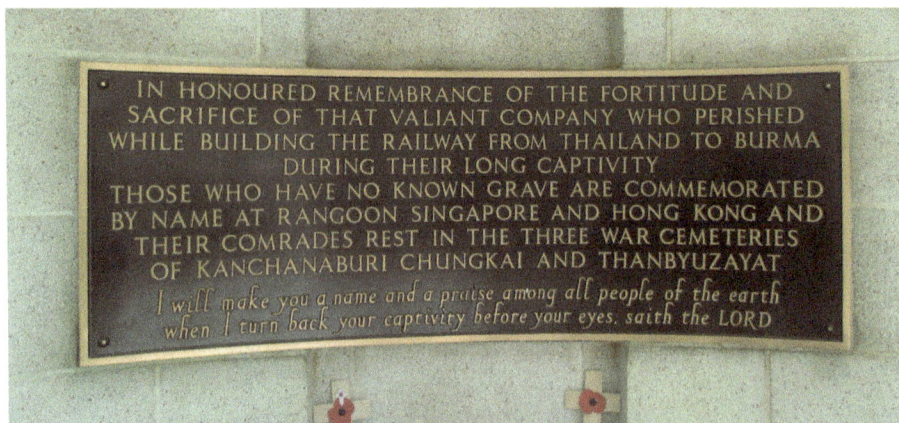

IN HONOURED REMEMBRANCE OF THE FORTITUDE AND
SACRIFICE OF THAT VALIANT COMPANY WHO PERISHED
WHILE BUILDING THE RAILWAY FROM THAILAND TO BURMA
DURING THEIR LONG CAPTIVITY
THOSE WHO HAVE NO KNOWN GRAVE ARE COMMEMORATED
BY NAME AT RANGOON SINGAPORE AND HONG KONG AND
THEIR COMRADES REST IN THE THREE WAR CEMETERIES
OF KANCHANABURI CHUNGKAI AND THANBYUZAYAT
I will make you a name and a praise among all people of the earth
when I turn back your captivity before your eyes. saith the LORD

Memorial at Kanchanaburi CWGC

Chungkai CWGC

Reconciliation

For many who were prisoners of war in the Far East, the prospect of
just meeting Japanese people after the war has filled them with fear
and dread. Some have sought reconciliation, perhaps most notably
Eric Lomax, author of *The Railway Man*. He had been severely affected

by his imprisonment, and was mentally tortured for many years after repatriation. On his retirement in 1982 he attempted to seek out the Japanese guard who had tortured him. In 1998, some 50 years after his imprisonment, Eric Lomax met that man, Ngase Takashi, at an unprecedented meeting at Kanchanaburi. As Lomax was to write:

After our meeting I felt I'd come to some kind of peace and resolution. Forgiveness is possible when someone is ready to accept forgiveness. Some time the hating has to stop.

For Bill there has never been hate in his life, ever since the time his father told him off 'for hating his brother.' As Bill has explained on several occasions, using his father's words: 'You must not go on hating people; it does you harm but it does not do them any harm.' Bill visited Tokyo in 1973 to attend an International Conference on Allergy. In fact, in his role as the General Secretary of the European Allergy Association, Bill was instrumental in the decision to choose Tokyo as the venue. Bill had no fear in visiting the country of his former captors, and, although it was a successful and interesting meeting, he did not like Japan. However, one feature of the country impressed him, namely the high-speed Bullet Train. At that meeting in 1973 very few, if any, of those attending would have known of Bill's time as a prisoner of war.

Bill's association with the Japanese has continued in recent years and Bill has been a frequent visitor to the Japanese Embassy in London, invited on the occasion of the annual Reunion of Peace and Friendship, held each summer. He has also been invited as a guest to the Ambassador's residence. Bill has always been struck by the 'perfect English' spoken by his hosts. On Sunday 16 August 2015 Bill attended evensong at Canterbury Cathedral, a service organised annually by the International Friendship and Reconciliation Trust and the Burma Campaign Society. At the start of the service Bill read the fourth stanza of Laurence Binyon's poem, *For the Fallen:*

> *They shall grow not old, as we that are left grow old:*
> *Age shall not weary them, nor the years condemn.*
> *At the going down of the sun and in the morning*
> *We will remember them.*

Afterwards, he met the Japanese Ambassador, HE Keiichi Hayashi, who later wrote to Bill and recorded how 'it was a moving occasion to renew our determination to further promote reconciliation between Japan and the UK'.

Bill at the Japanese Embassy. London

An Apology

In 2016 at the behest of the *British Medical Journal*, Bill was asked to complete a short questionnaire, the answers to which would form a publication in the journal. The questions ranged from 'Who has been your biggest inspiration?' to which Bill answered, 'Professor Sir Alexander Fleming,' through to 'To whom would you most like to apologise?' The answer to this question was: 'My late wife. I spent too much time away from home travelling the world lecturing.'

Having been married in 1941, Bill and Pauline did not see each other for over 4 years during the war. After the Fall of Singapore Pauline did not know for over a year if her husband was alive or dead, and throughout his captivity she received just three postcards from him. Pauline had initially served with the VAD but later joined the WRNS, rising to the rank of first officer. Her service was recognised by the award of the MBE (Military Division) in 1946. Returning to civilian life, Bill summarised his wife's achievements as 'whatever she did, she did well.' Pauline became closely involved with the St Mary's Hospital Ladies' Association, becoming its Chairman. Although there was already a small shop run by the association at the hospital, Pauline established a café in the outpatients' department to raise funds. She was very successful and the café was soon recognised as offering good, wholesome and cheap food. Before long, it was serving not just people at the hospital, but members of the general public who frequented in large numbers. The association made a profit of over £70,000, but this was not without some controversy. A number of local restaurant owners complained about the café. They found their turnover had fallen, with regular customers now deciding to go to the hospital, and complained that the hospital was undercutting their prices.

Pauline was also closely involved with numerous organisations outside of the hospital. A keen member of the Sea Rangers, Pauline had founded the Frobisher Battersea Crew and was skipper when she and Bill married. She continued to be heavily involved and as Bill noted, if the telephone rang in the early hours of the morning it would never be for the 'doctor in the house.' Invariably the caller would report that the Sea Rangers' boat, moored opposite Chelsea Church, had broken free from its mooring and had been spotted drifting downstream of Greenwich.

Amongst the many unofficial positions that Bill filled was chauffeur to senior members of the Girl Guide movement. Pauline served as Deputy Chief Commissioner of Girl Guides in London and South-East England and was often visited by the Chief Guide, Lady Baden-Powell. It fell to Bill to act as chauffeur for official visits to numerous Girl Guide units. There was, however, recognition as he and Pauline would be invited by Lady Baden-Powell to tea at her 'grace and favour' apartment at Hampton Court Palace. Lady Baden-Powell had been widowed in 1941 when her husband, Lord Baden-Powell, died in Kenya. On a visit to Kenya, Pauline and Bill stayed at Treetops Lodge. During their very enjoyable holiday, Bill signed the visitors' book. He turned back the pages and there was an entry on 5 February 1952 by Princess Elizabeth who, the following day, acceded to the throne following the death of her father King George VI. On their way back to Nairobi Airport Bill persuaded their driver to make a detour to nearby Nyeri where he and Pauline were able to visit the grave of Lord Baden-Powell. Pauline's contribution to guiding was recognised in 1979 by the award of an OBE (Civil Division). Unfortunately, Pauline died in 2002.

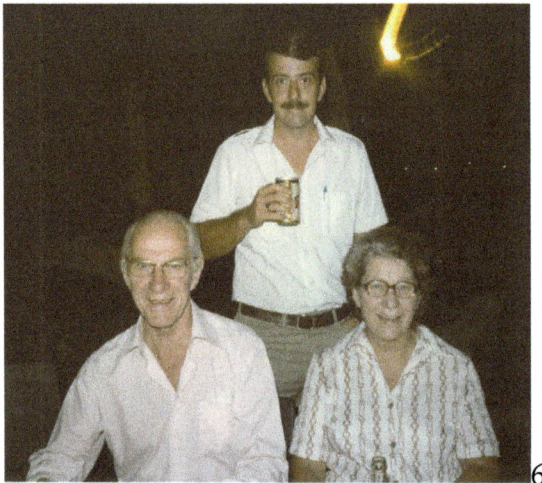

Bill and Pauline on a trip abroad.

One Hundred, Not Out

In March 2012 Bill celebrated his 100th birthday, receiving congratulations from friends and family and, of course, receiving a birthday card from Her Majesty The Queen, it would not be the only card he would receive from his monarch. Since turning 100, Bill has spoken more widely about his life, and his time both as a prisoner of war and as a doctor. Media appearances have been numerous, involving newspaper, radio and television appearances, for both national and international audiences. The summer of 2015 was a busy period for Bill, appearing on Radio 4's long-running programme, 'Desert Island Discs'. Introduced by Kirsty Young, Bill was able to share with listeners around the world more details of his life, starting with his childhood in the Lake District, through to his 'retirement', and ongoing contributions to the field of allergy. His choice of book to take with him to the desert island was a copy of *The Story of San Michele* by Axel Munthe, the book that had made such an impact at St Bees and stimulated him to pursue a career in medicine.[144] Of his eight pieces of music, he considered the one he would rescue in a fire was Robert Schumann's *Fantasie* in C major. His one luxury on the island was a pair of binoculars, as this would allow him to watch birds and 'see the ship that was going to rescue me.' And when asked what lesson he had learnt from life, Bill replied that 'I have been very lucky I have never been depressed and always when I was a prisoner I was hopeful that I would live.'

Just a few weeks later Bill was again interviewed by Kirsty Young, this time on television as the BBC covered the national service for remembrance recognising the 70th anniversary of VJ Day. Bill again explained more about his time serving as a doctor at the Fall of Singapore and his years of captivity. Having attended the service at St Martin-in-the-Fields, Trafalgar Square, Bill made his way to Horse Guards Parade where a drumhead service took place later that afternoon. Following this, the veterans were invited to make their way along Whitehall to

---

144 Castaways on the programme are all given the *Complete Works of Shakespeare* and the *Bible*, and have to choose one other title.

Westminster School where The Prince of Wales and The Duchess of Cornwall hosted tea. Bill, aged 103, walked the whole length of Whitehall on a warm August afternoon, helped only by his walking stick and ably supported by his wonderful secretary, Suzanne Browne. Such a remarkable display of fortitude and strength was seen throughout the country as the proceedings were broadcast.

Bill celebrating his 100th birthday with his family, March 2012

Bill at a party marking his 100th birthday

Bill walking in Whitehall. August 2015.

In The Queen's Birthday Honours for 2015 Bill was appointed a Member of the Most Excellent Order of the British Empire (MBE) for 'Services to allergy research'. Aged 103, he was the oldest recipient of this award, from an order of chivalry which was inaugurated when Bill was aged five. Bill attended an investiture at Buckingham Palace in October of that year, where he was presented with the medal by The Duke of Cambridge. The duke engaged in conversation with Bill on the issue of allergy, which Bill found most enjoyable. After the investiture Bill was invited to a special reception at the Palace for some of the more distinguished guests attending that day.

Bill at Investiture at Buckingham Palace. 2015

Although on his return home in 1945 Bill decided not to talk about his wartime experiences, his attitude has changed in more recent years. Not only has he talked about his experiences, but he has also met with other former prisoners of war who were imprisoned in the Far East. The Java Far Eastern Prisoners of War Club 1942 was formed in the 1980s by a small number of former Far Eastern Prisoners, and over the years has acted to support its members, many of whom suffered terribly during captivity and after. With the march of time the number of members has declined, but still members meet for an annual reunion weekend at Stratford-upon-Avon in late summer. Bill has attended a number of these reunions, which he has found most interesting; he is without doubt their oldest member. The club has two patrons, The Countess of Wessex and Dame Vera Lynn. The Countess has taken a keen interest in the members and wrote to Bill in March 2018 to congratulate him on reaching the age of 106.

Bill's dedication to medicine and academic endeavour has not wavered since becoming a centenarian. He has had four scientific papers published since 2012, the most recent in 2017, something that he was to describe as 'a little unusual.' These have been on a range of subjects, including the issue of rosewater, published in the *Drapers Journal* in 2017. Bill was elected a Liveryman of the Worshipful Company of Drapers in the 1950s, his father-in-law having at one time been the Master. Apart from The Queen, who was made a Freeman of the Company in 1947, Bill is its longest-serving as well as its oldest member, and continues to attend functions at Drapers' Hall.

Bill's latest paper is one of joint authorship entitled 'Flight Lieutenant Peach's Observations on Burning Feet Syndrome in Far Eastern Prisoners of War 1942-45.' Published in January 2017, the authors reassessed the contemporaneous medical records made by Noel Peach, an RAF medical officer, who had been taken prisoner in Java in 1942. The records relate to patients in Tandjong Priok Camp, examined during the period November 1942 to March 1943. The condition of Burning Feet Syndrome was seen by Bill at Changi during the war, where it was called Painful Feet Syndrome or 'electric feet'. There he learnt of Captain Cruickshank's approach to the condition (Chapter 6) and treated six patients himself, four with success. In this paper, the authors reassessed the clinical findings made by Peach, using modern neurological criteria. They concluded that the condition had a nutritional origin, caused by a multiple deficiency of B vitamins and that there was also possible neuropathic pain. Although a fascinating study to read, it is very apparent that, over 70 years earlier, the doctors in prison camps in the Far East, had undertaken very thorough and astute observations about both the condition, as well as its possible causes and treatments.

Bill, still working aged 105.

Bill has also continued to act as an expert medical witness in court, despite some consternation from the General Medical Council. Undoubtedly he is the oldest medical expert witness in the country. Several cases have remained firmly in his mind. One involved a defendant accused of murdering a man whom, from all accounts, was a most unpleasant individual (many associated with the case would have liked to kill him themselves). The defendant was allergic to dogs, and yet the van used by the murderer to go to and from the scene of the crime had dogs in it. The expert witness for the prosecution was called and gave a very thorough and complete résumé of the issues relating to allergy to cats, including some very recent findings from the published literature. Bill was called, and was asked to give his expert opinion. He informed the court, and pointedly the prosecution barrister, that the defence rested around an issue of allergy to dogs, and that the prosecution had offered an opinion relating to allergy to cats. At this point there was obvious chuckling in the court from the jury and the judge, at which point the prosecution offered 'no more questions'. The defendant was acquitted. In another case, a careless driver argued that his actions whilst driving were the result of a wasp sting. Acting as expert witness for the prosecution, Bill's evidence secured the conviction, having convinced the court that the driver could not have been suffering an allergic reaction.

In 2012, at the age of 100, Bill was elected to an Honorary Fellowship of his college, Queen's, at Oxford, giving him immense satisfaction. In doing so he joined a select group of honorary fellows including the constitutional expert, Vernon Bogdanor, cell biologist, Ron Laskey, actor Rowan Atkinson (who also attended St Bees School) and the founder of the worldwide web, Sir Tim Berners-Lee. As such Bill is invited to numerous functions at the college, and most especially for him, the Boar's Head Gaudy, a dinner held just before Christmas.[145] A rich musical event, the occasion is marked by the procession of a boar's head into the dining hall accompanied by the choir singing carols, the first always in English, the next in Latin, as the head is presented to the Provost. Members of college make their way to high table where the Provost gives each one a small piece of mistletoe from the table decoration. Bill remembered clearly the first time he attended the Boar's Head Gaudy, some 25 years after his matriculation, when the Provost was Sir Howard Florey. As Bill approached high table Florey appeared to have given out the last piece of mistletoe so Bill received a sprig of holly instead. In 2017 Bill, now aged 105, and having matriculated 87 years earlier, attended the Boar's Head Gaudy and was able to distribute mistletoe himself, on behalf of the Provost. Halfway through the meal, diners normally retire for a short period whilst the tables are cleared and reset. Bill, being slightly restricted in his physical activity, chose to stay at his

---

145 Gaudy means a 'happy gathering'.

place on high table during the break. He was very pleased that another honorary fellow came and spoke to him. Bill soon found out that this man knew a lot about computers, and quite a lot about Bill. He had introduced himself to Bill as 'Tim', but Bill later admitted that, pleasant and charming as the man was, he did not know who he was. It was later that Bill learnt that 'Tim' was Sir Tim Berners-Lee. However, Bill could easily be forgiven since he has never used a computer in his life. In fact, when interviewed by Jon Snow for Channel 4 earlier that year, Bill had answered his questions of 'Do you have a computer?' and 'Do you have a mobile phone?' with an emphatic 'No' to both.

Bill's remarkable stamina is clearly shown by his activities in just two months towards the end of 2017. In early October he was invited to the 'Who Cares Wins' awards ceremony, organised by *The Sun* newspaper, and held at the paper's headquarters at London Bridge. The ceremony recognised a range of people who had made special or outstanding contributions to the NHS, and was presented by a range of well-known media personalities. Bill received a 'Special Recognition Award.' Despite fine hospitality, Bill had to keep an eye on the clock, since he was due at St Mary's Hospital later that afternoon. He gave a lecture to about 30 students studying on a Master of Science course in allergy at St Mary's, talking to them about the history of allergy and his involvement in the field. Despite his long day at London Bridge, he spoke for an hour, and then answered questions from the audience, at the same time enjoying a glass of wine.[146] This lecture has been an annual event for Bill, and he had been particularly pleased to give the lecture in 2016. On that occasion, he followed Professor Thomas Platts-Mills FRS, from the University of Virginia. Platts-Mills had been employed by the Medical Research Council at Northwick Park Hospital in the 1970s and during that period had undertaken clinical studies in allergy with Bill. For Bill, it was particularly enjoyable to talk at the same meeting as the only allergist who had been elected to a Fellowship of the Royal Society.

Barely a week after receiving an award from *The Sun*, Bill was attending the Paediatric Allergy and Asthma Meeting organised by the

---

146 The lecture in October 2017 was to be Bill's last public lecture.

European Academy of Allergy and Clinical Immunology, in London. As a special guest Bill received a standing ovation from the delegates as he was presented with an Allergy Legend Award. In between award ceremonies Bill contributed to a number of radio and television programmes, both for the British media, as well as for programmes produced by German, Brazilian, Iranian and Greek companies.

The following month, Bill was invited to the Royal British Legion Service of Remembrance held at the Royal Albert Hall on 11 November. For Bill remembering the fallen has always been an important part of his life, perhaps more so in recent years when he has started to talk about his own wartime experiences. He has attended the Service of Remembrance at the Cenotaph on several occasions and, at the invitation of the Not Forgotten Association, has attended the Service of Remembrance held on 11 November at Lloyd's of London. He has also laid a remembrance cross in the Field of Remembrance at Westminster Abbey. However, he had never attended the Royal British Legion Service of Remembrance at the Royal Albert Hall. Treated as a VIP, the BBC laid on transport to take him to the venue. It took nearly 1 hour to cross Hyde Park and he arrived barely 15 minutes before the start of the service. There was, however, just time to be offered a glass of champagne, which he found most acceptable. In the presence of The Queen, the service featured many members of the armed forces, either past or present. At one stage in the service the presenter, Huw Edwards, focussed on decisive actions which happened 75 years earlier during World War 2. One of these was the Battle of El Alamein, a turning point in the North African campaign, and in the audience was 99-year-old Sergeant Major Len Burritt who had fought at El Alamein. Next the focus shifted to the tragic loss of Singapore on 15 February 1942 and Huw Edwards praised the work of Dr Bill Frankland, aged 105. As the cameras and spotlights turned on Bill and Len, seated directly opposite the Royal Box, those in the hall applauded two remarkable men. Close observation revealed that Bill, wearing his RAMC tie, also displayed two sets of medals. One, on his left, were his own, but he also wore Pauline's medals, on the right. This may have been overlooked by many, but was especially poignant as throughout the service reference was made to 2017 representing the centenary of women being allowed to serve in the armed forces. Later in the service, the cameras focussed on Bill who, with a little assistance, stood to show his respects to the fallen during the two-minute silence when thousands of poppies floated down from the roof of the hall. A few minutes later, Bill was again on his feet, to show his respect to The Queen during the singing of the National Anthem.

Bill at Royal British Legion Service of Remembrance, Royal Albert Hall, November 2017

A Life Well Lived

As midsummer day of 2018 fast approaches, Bill is looking forward to another Royal Garden Party at Buckingham Palace, hosted by the Not Forgotten Association. In the presence of their Patron, The Princess Royal, over 2500 guests are expected to enjoy royal hospitality, and undoubtedly Bill will be the oldest amongst them. He has become a regular attendee, to an occasion which he thoroughly enjoys. At the same event in 2017 he was introduced to Prince Harry who spoke with Bill for quite some time. Having been briefed, Prince Harry knew that Bill was 105, and that he 'retired', and that Bill was not keen on golf and was no longer able to garden. Keen that Bill should perhaps find another leisure pursuit, Prince Harry asked, 'Have you thought about going up in a plane and jumping out of it?'

HRH Prince Harry speaking with Bill, Royal Garden Party, June 2017

Bill remains busy, ensuring that he keeps abreast of the literature in his field, a task that involves reading numerous journals and papers each week. He continues to research, and is keen to write a paper on the history of the discovery of penicillin. Although this was undoubtedly the result of an 'unplanned' interaction between bacteriologists and allergists, Bill's research has identified the possibility that the earliest descriptions of Penicillium are actually to be found in the Bible. When completed it will be his fifth paper as a centenarian. Now in his 107th year, he continues to take an interest in a range of subjects, most recently having found the World Snooker Championship an enthralling competition. At the same time, his opinion is sought from a range of people, most recently by several sources researching the foundations of the NHS, which this summer celebrates its 70th birthday. Bill qualified 10 years before the NHS was founded and thus has a unique and unrivalled view on the changes in medicine which have occurred over its lifetime. In the coming months he will appear in a BBC Television programme, the Great British Menu banquet, which has as its theme the 70th anniversary of the NHS. This was filmed in the Great Hall of St Bartholomew's Hospital, where

Bill greatly enjoyed not only the food, but also the opportunity to walk on the red carpet to enter St Bartholomew's Hospital.

Bill celebrating his 106th birthday. March 2018

But what of this life well-lived? Repeatedly when asked why he has lived so to such a great age Bill has replied, 'Because I have been lucky.' He has pointed out that he has been close to death so many times and yet has been lucky and survived. Throughout his long life he has been supported by his steadfast Christian faith, which provided hope and guidance during what must have been the most dreadful and darkest hours of his life, enduring conditions in captivity which few of us now could even imagine. On his repatriation in 1945 Bill put the suffering that he had endured, and seen, behind him. He has continued to follow the words of his father, Henry Frankland: 'You must not go on hating people; it does you harm but it does not do them any harm.' During Bill's life he has upheld the Hippocratic Oath and helped countless patients, both at home and abroad. He has treated all who have sought his help, regardless of their nationality, creed or political persuasion. Details of his service in World War 2 have, until recently, remained a very private memory, but hopefully this book will help inform many readers as to his, and others', experiences in that most dreadful of conflicts. As 11 November 2018, the centenary of the end of World War 1, approaches to be followed next year by the 80th anniversary of the start of World War 2 (3 September 2019) the lives of the multitudes lost in conflict must never be forgotten. Bill counts himself as one of the 'lucky ones', surviving the war and able to forge an outstanding career in the years after. He continues to attend the annual Reunion of Peace and Friendship at the Japanese Embassy, and has every intention of attending this year's event on 18 June 2018. It is hoped that this book, in its own small way, will give support to the views of the Japanese Ambassador when, in 2005, he wrote:

The dreadful events of the Second World War gave solemn lessons to us all. We should not forget the past, and we must pass on the lessons learnt from the war to future generations.

The final words in this biography of Bill Frankland, the 'Grandfather of Allergy', are those of 'a blonde girl with beautiful blue eyes' whom he first met in 1937 at St Mary's Hospital. She was the future Mrs Pauline Frankland. The words were handwritten on the back of a small card, which Bill has treasured for over half a century, and kindly gave to the author in April 2018. They were prepared as the closing verse of the Annual General Meeting of the St Mary's Hospital Ladies' Association in May 1963, and read:

May God bless us and keep us.
May He give us light to guide us,
courage to support us, and
love to unite us, for evermore.

****

BIBLIOGRAPHY

Books

Allan S., *Diary of a Girl in Changi* Kangaroo Press, Australia 1994
Bennett P., *A Very Desolate Position* Rossall Archives 1992
Blackley C.H., *Experimental Researches on the Causes and Nature of Catarrhus Aestivus*, London 1873
Brooke G., *Singapore's Dunkirk* Leo Cooper, Barnsley 1989
Bruton P., *The Matter of a Massacre. Alexandra Hospital Singapore 14/15 February 1942* Privately published
Chalker J., *Burma Railway Artist* Leo Cooper, London 1994
Churchill W.S., *The Second World War* Cassell, London 1954
Clarke B.L.W., *Behind the Wire* Royal Children's Hospital, Brisbane 1989
Collison C., *Ye Boke of Ye Busie Bee* P.C. Dickinson & Son, Millom, Cumbria 1940
Cope Z., *The History of St Mary's Hospital Medical School or A Century of Medical Education.* William Heinemann, London 1954
Craig O. & Fraser A., *Doctors at War* The Memoir Club, Weardale, Co. Durham, 2007
Dalemain, the Home of the Hasell-McCosh Family. Private Publication
Dawson R.L.G., *Light and Shade from Japanese Prison Camps* Privately published
Dunlop E.E., *The War Diaries of Weary Dunlop* Penguin, Australia 1986
Ebury S., *Weary: The Life of Sir Edward Dunlop* Penguin, Australia 1994
Elliott S. & Humphries S., *Britain's Greatest Generation* Penguin Random House, London 2015
Elphick P., *Singapore: The Pregnable Fortress* Hodder & Stoughton, London 1995
Elphick P. & Smith M., *Odd Man Out* Hodder & Stoughton, London

1993

Fleming A., *Penicillin: Its Practical Applications.* Butterworth, London 1946

Frankland A.W., *Penicillin Sensitivity*, p425-434 in: *Penicillin: Its Practical Applications*, 2nd Edition. Ed. Fleming A., Butterworth, London 1950.

Freeman J., *Hay-Fever: A Key to the Allergic Diseases.* Heinemann, London, 1950.

Fyans P., *Captivity, Slavery and Survival as a Far East POW: The Conjuror on the Kwai* Pen & Sword, Barnsley 2011

Gill G. & Parkes M., *Burma Railway Medicine* Palatine Books, Lancaster 2017

Gough R., *The Escape from Singapore* William Kimber & Co, London 1987

Heagney B., *The Longs Days of Slavery* Royal Australasian College of Physicians 1996

Heaman E.A., *St Mary's: The History of a London Teaching Hospital.* Liverpool University Press 2003

Huxtable C., *From the Somme to Singapore* Kangaroo Press Australia 1987

Jackson M., *Allergy: The History of a Modern Malady* Reaktion Books, London, 2007

Kinvig C., *Scapegoat: General Percival of Singapore* Brassey's, London 1996

Lomax E., *The Railway Man* Vintage, London 1995

Ludovici L.J., *Fleming: Discoverer of Penicillin* Burleigh Press, Bristol 1952

MacArthur B., *Surviving the Sword: Prisoners of the Japanese 1942-45.* Time Warner, London 2005

Marshall G.K., *The Changi Diaries* Privately published 1988

McBryde B., *Quiet Heroines: Nurses of the Second World War.* Chatto & Windus, London 1985

Middlebrook M. & Mahoney P., *The Sinking of the Prince of Wales & Repulse* Pen & Sword, Barnsley 2004

Munthe A. *The Story of San Michele* John Murray Publishers 1929

Nardell S.G., *Jungle Medicine and Surgery* Book Guild Publishing 1999

Nielson D., *The Story of Changi Singapore* Changi Publication Singapore 1974

Noble W.C., *Coli: Great Healer of Men. The Biography of Dr. Leonard Colebrook FRS* William Heinemann Medical Books, London 1974

Owen F., *The Fall of Singapore* Michael Joseph, London 1960

Parkes M. & Gill G., *Captive Memories* Palatine Books, Lancaster 2015

Sherrington C.S., *Mammalian Physiology: A Course of Practical Exercises.* Oxford Clarendon 1919.

Smith C., *Singapore Burning* Penguin Books 2005

Smyth J. *Percival and the Tragedy of Singapore* Macdonald & Co, London 1971

Somerville C., *Our War* Weidenfeld & Nicolson, London 1998

St Bees School Cumberland, Prospectus, Oxford University Press 1932

Taylor J., *Surgery in Japanese Prisoner Camp in Singapore Island 1942-45.* Chapter 25 in *History of Second World War*, United Kingdom Medical Services Editor Cope Z.

The Rossall Register, Seventh Edition 1871-1939. Cambridge University Press 1940.

The Story of St Bees 1583-1939. Issued by the Special Committee of the Old St Beghians' Club, Buck & Wootton, London 1939

Tyquin M., *Little by Little: A Centenary History of the Royal Australian Army Medical Corps.* Army History Unit, Department of Defence, Canberra 2003

Walker A.S., *Australia in the War of 1939-45.* Series Five, Medical Volume II Middle East and Far East Canberra Australian War Memorial

Wilson C., (Lord Moran) *The Anatomy of Courage*, Constable London 1966

Wilson C., (Lord Moran) *Winston Churchill: The Struggle for Survival 1940-65* Constable & Company London 1966

Published Papers

Abraham E.P, Gardner A.D., Chain E., Heatley N.G., Fletcher C.M., Jennings M.A. & Florey H.W. *Further Observations on Penicillin.* Lancet

August 16 p177-189. 1941

Abraham E.P., *Howard Walter Florey, Baron Florey of Adelaide and Marston 1898-1968*. Biographical Memoirs of the Royal Society Vol 17, 253-302. 1971

Abraham E.P., *Ernst Boris Chain 1906-1979*. Biographical Memoirs of the Royal Society Vol 29, 42-91. 1983

de Wardener H.E, & Lennox B., *Cerebral beriberi (Wernicke's encephalopathy); review of 52 cases in a Singapore prisoner-of-war hospital*. Lancet Jan 4, 11-17. 1947

Fleming A., *On a remarkable bacteriolytic element found in tissues and secretions*. Proceedings of the Royal Society Series B. May 1. 93. 1922

Fleming A., *On the antibacterial action of cultures of a Penicillium, with special reference to their use in the isolation of B. influenzae*. British Journal of Experimental Pathology. 10 (3) 226-236. 1929

Fleming A., *Antiseptics Old and New*. Proceedings of the Staff Meeting at the Mayo Clinic February 20, 1946

Frankland A.W., *Dangers of Sulphapyridine*. British Medical Journal, January p33. 1941

Frankland A.W., *Mumps Meningo-encephalitis*. British Medical Journal July 12, p 48. 1941

Frankland A.W., *Deficiency Scrotal Dermatitis* in P.O.W.s in the Far East. British Medical Journal May 29 p1023-1026. 1948

Frankland A.W., *Hayfever* Medical Illustrated 3 193-7. 1949

Frankland A.W. & Gorrill R.H., *Summer hayfever and asthma treated with antihistamine drugs*. British Medical Journal April 4 p761-4. 1953

Frankland A.W. & Augustin R., *Prophylaxis of summer hayfever and asthma; controlled trial comparing crude grass pollen extracts with isolated main protein component*. Lancet May 22 1055-7. 1954

Frankland A.W., Hughes W.H. & Gorrill R.H., *Autogenous bacterial vaccines in the treatment of asthma*. British Medical Journal October 15 p941-4. 1955

Frankland A.W., *Aerobiology and allergy-an autobiography* Aerobiologia 12 55-61. 1996

Frankland A.W., *Tropical ulcers and diphtheria*. Journal of the Royal Society of Medicine 91: 174. 1998

Frankland A.W., *BMJ Confidential*. British Medical Journal September 17 p394-5 2016

Freeman J., *Further observations on the treatment of hayfever by the hypodermic inoculations of pollen vaccine*. Lancet II: 814-817. 1911

Freeman J., *Leonard Noon* International Archives of Allergy and Applied Immunology, 4:282-284. 1953

Henriques C.V.A., *Experimental treatment of Scabies with Derris Root Powder* Journal of the Royal Army Medical Corps 81: 186-8. 1943

Irwin W.J., *The Alexandra Outrage* Journal of the Royal Army Medical Corps 118:221. 1972

Obituary, *Craven J.W.*, British Medical Journal October 14, p1030. 1961

Obituary; *Jacklin I.*, Journal of the Royal Naval Medical Service Vol XXIX, 1943

Obituary, *Middleton D.S.*, British Medical Journal 283 p1065. 1981

Obituary, *Taylor J.*, British Medical Journal, April 29, p 1225. 1961

Noon L., *Prophylactic inoculation against hay fever*. Lancet I: 1572-3. 1911

Oakley C.L., *Leonard Colebrook. 1883-1967*. Biographical Memoirs of the Royal Society Vol 17, 90-138. 1971

Partridge J., *Alexandra Hospital from British Military to Civilian Institution, 1936-1996*. Alexandra Hospital and Singapore Polytechnic, Singapore

Roocroft N.T., Mayhew E., Parkes M., Frankland W.A., Gill G.V., Bouhassira D. & Rice A.S.C. *Flight Lieutenant Peach's observation on Burning Feet Syndrome in Far Eastern Prisoners of War* Quarterly Journal of Medicine 110, 131-9. 2017

Saunders L., *The Derris Root Treatment of Scabies* British Medical Journal April 26, p624-6. 1941

Archival Sources

(TNA = The National Archives, Kew, England)
Admission and Discharge Register, Roberts Hospital Changi 1942 TNA WO 347/43
Alexandra Military Hospital, Capture by the Japanese TNA WO 222/119

Board of Education, Inspection of St Bees School 1924, TNA ED 109/628
Board of Education, State of Finances of St Bees School 1929, TNA ED 35/3778

Board of Education, Inspection of St Bees School 1931, TNA ED 109/629
Cruickshank E.K. Review of 500 Cases of 'Painful Feet Syndrome'. Wellcome Library, Reference PP/EK6/A/2/15
Cumbria Archive Centre, Carlisle England
1)   St Michaels' Church, Burgh-by-Sands (Catalogue Reference PR44)
         A History
         Parochial Church Council minutes Book 1921-1966
         Preacher's Book
         Register of Services
         Record of Parochial Church Meeting and Vestry Meeting
2)   St Andrew's, Dacre (Catalogue Reference PR167)
         Dacre Parochial Church Council, Minute Book
         Licences of Curates
         Preacher's Book
         Record of Vestry Meetings
Escape from Singapore by Major L.E.C. Davies RAMC TNA WO 222/255
Frankland H., Matriculation details 1897. Wadham College Oxford Archive
Information on sinking of ssTanjong Penang and ss Kuala carrying evacuees from Singapore TNA CO 980/237
Middleton D.S., Papers from No 1 Malaya General Hospital. Wellcome Library, Reference PP/MID/A/1/3
Middleton D.S., Lectures given at Changi Camp. Wellcome Library, Reference PP/MID/A/2/1; PP/MID/A/2/2
Operational Records Book RAF Station Alor Star (Kedah) 1941 TNA AIR 28/1
P.O.W. Camp Changi 1942-43 TNA WO 222/1383

P.O.W. Camp Changi 1943-44 TNA WO 222/1384
Second World War Prisoners of war Camps: Medical Reports on
Conditions at Changi Singapore TNA PIN 15/2891
Service Record for H. Frankland TNA WO 339/132513
Taylor J., List of medical Officers at the Fall of Singapore Wellcome
Library, Reference RAMC 1319
Taylor J., Private Papers Wellcome Library, Reference RAMC 439/1
The Campaign in Malaya P.O.W. Camps TNA WO 222/1387
War Diary Military Hospital, Tanglin. July 1940 to February 1942. TNA
WO 177/1090
War Diaries SMO Changi, December 1941 TNA 177/225

Other Sources

Census of the United Kingdom 1881,1891,1901,1911
Crockford's Clerical Directory
de Wardener H.E., Oral History: Imperial War Museum Catalogue No
23228
Ennis J., Personal Diary kept during Imprisonment 1942-45
Fast V.F., *Missionary on Wheels: Frances Hatton Eva Hasell and the Sunday
School Caravans.* University of Manitoba, Canada. Thesis submitted
in partial fulfilment for the degree of Master of Arts, Department of
History, September 1978
Frankland A.W., Oral History: Imperial War Museum, Catalogue No 32250
Frankland A.W., Desert Island Discs. August 2015 Accessed at http://
www.bbc.co.uk/programmes/p02z0bpl
Hartley R., Account of Lieutenant Robert Hartley 137 (Army) Field
Regiment, Royal Artillery Accessed at http://www.far-eastern-heroes.
org.uk/2nd_Lt_Robert_Hartley/html/orders_to_sail.htm
Lancaster W.E., Private Diary 1941-45
Lucy D., Private Papers: Imperial War Museum Catalogue Doc 23364
Lucy P., Oral History: Imperial War Museum Catalogue No 8404
Markowitz J, *Some Experiences as a Medical Officer with the Royal Army
Medical Corps*, Address given at The Empire Club of Canada 17
October 1946

Natten P.I.S., Oral History: Imperial War Museum Catalogue No 10691

Oxford University Gazette 1930, 1931

Parkinson S., (née Kershaw) Obituary *The Times* 2002

Parkinson S.Y., (née Kershaw) Oral History: Imperial War Museum Catalogue No 18739

St Bees School Magazine, Vol 1 No 1, November 1928

St Mary's Hospital Gazette 1934, 1935, 1936, 1937, 1938

St Mary's Hospital Medical School, Annual Reports for Sessions 1935-36, 1936-37, 1937-38, 1938-39

Webster F.L., Private Papers: Imperial War Museum Catalogue Doc 16723

Wells C.W., *For Most Men* Personal Diary 1941-45. Imperial War Museum

SOURCE OF ILLUSTRATIONS

Chapter 1

Figures on pages 36 and 38 are used with kind permission of Rossall School.

Figures on pages 44 to 49 are used with kind permission of Dr Reeves Archivist of St Bees School.

Chapter 2

Figure on page 60. Portrait of Sir Charles Sherrington. Source Wellcome Collection, https://wellcomecollection.org/works/maqm4ded?query=charles%20sherrington&page=1

License by https://creativecommons.org/licenses/by/4.0/

Figures on pages 61 and 62 are used with kind permission of The Queen's College, Oxford

Figure on page 67. Portrait Baron Charles Wilson McMoran Moran. Source Wellcome Collection,

https://wellcomecollection.org/works/qv56mk97?query=lord%20moran&page=1

License by https://creativecommons.org/licenses/by/4.0/

Figure on page 69. Portrait of Sir Almroth Wright, Sir Gerald Kelly, 1934. Source Wellcome Collection, https://wellcomecollection.org/works/kabvdhe3?query=sir%20a%20wright&page=1,

License by https://creativecommons.org/licenses/by/4.0/

Figure on page 73. Leonard Noon, Photograph after Freeman. Source Wellcome Collection, https://wellcomecollection.org/works/mqy6mx48?query=leonard%20noon&page=1

License by https://creativecommons.org/licenses/by/4.0/

Figure on page 78. Portrait of Leonard Colebrook by Walter Stoneman. Source Wellcome Collection, https://wellcomecollection.org/works/jhfr3c3s?query=leonard%20colebrooke&page=1

License by https://creativecommons.org/licenses/by/4.0/

Chapter 5
Figure on page 139. Source The Australian War Memorial, Ref 012468.
Figure on page 143 used with kind permission of Fiona Wright.
Chapter 6
The Australian War Memorial is the source of figures on page 167 (Ref, 127906), page 174 (Ref, PO4485.040), page 174 (Ref, PO4485.019), page 210 (Ref, PO132935) and page 221 (Ref, 17362).
Figure on page 180, Jack Ennis by F.J. White. By kind permission of Jackie Sutherland.
Figure on page 196 is reproduced with permission of the Wellcome Collection.
Chapter 7
Figure on page 227. Singapore: a view across part of Blakang Mati Island. Watercolour by J Taylor 1880. Source Wellcome Collection https://wellcomecollection.org/works/wtcc669k?query=blakang%20 mati&page=1
License by https://creativecommons.org/licenses/by/4.0/
Figures on page 250. By kind permission of Sally Munton, from her late father's collection.
Chapter 8
Figures on page 269. By kind permission of Dr Sian Ludman and Claire Evans.
Figure on page 281. Sir Alexander Fleming. Source Wellcome Collection https://wellcomecollection.org/works/ k4ezny6h?query=alexander%20fleming&page=1
License by https://creativecommons.org/licenses/by/4.0/

INDEX